SHAKUGAN NO SHANA™

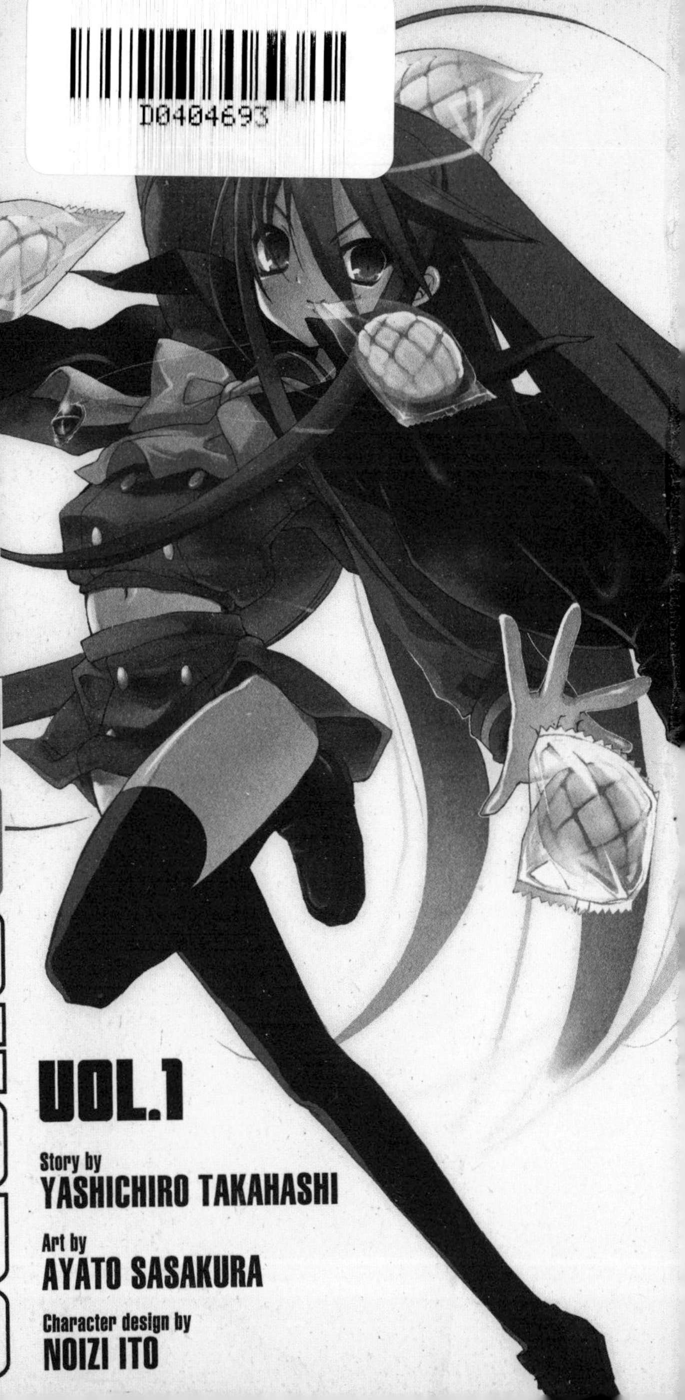

VOL.1

Story by
YASHICHIRO TAKAHASHI

Art by
AYATO SASAKURA

Character design by
NOIZI ITO

SHAKUGAN NO SHANA™

VOL.1

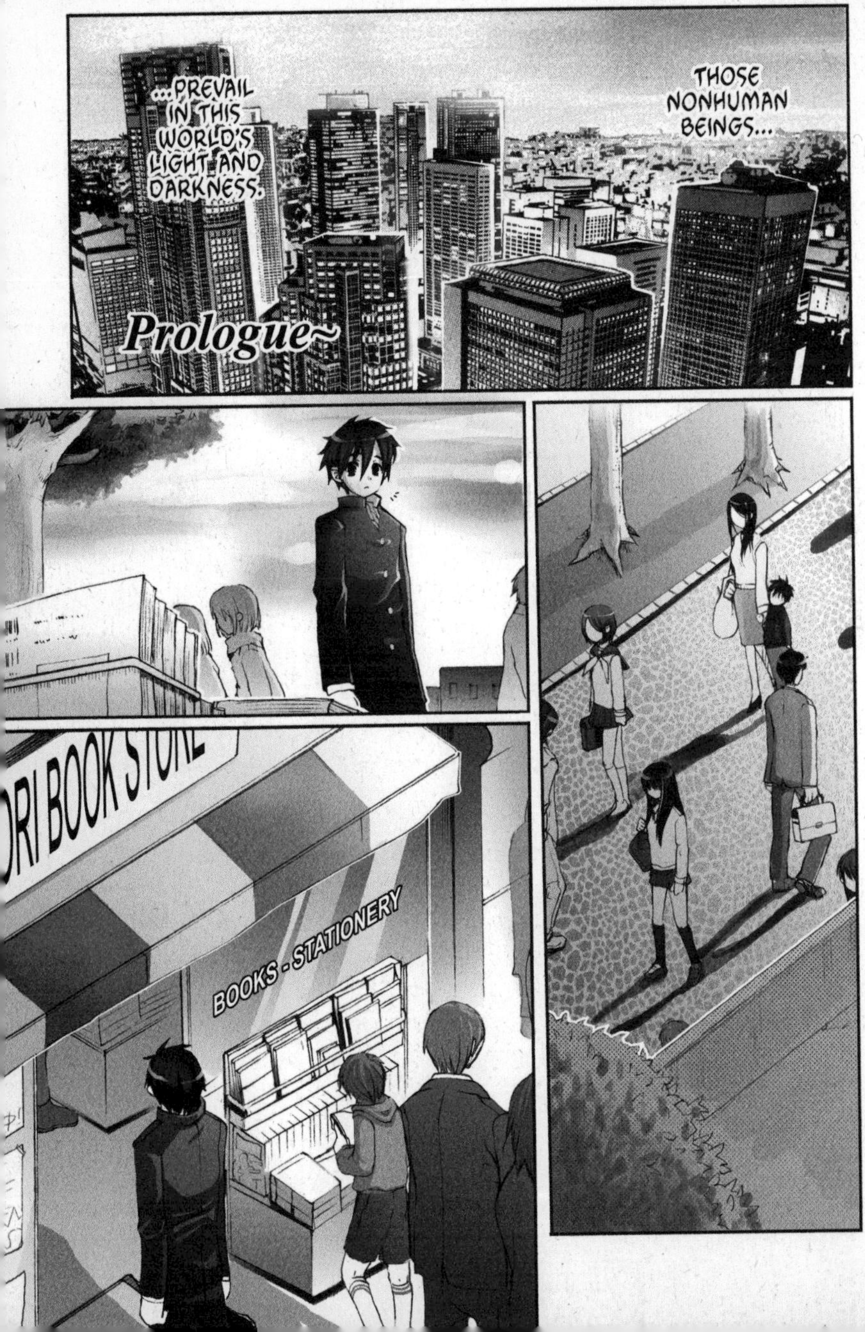
THOSE NONHUMAN BEINGS...
...PREVAIL IN THIS WORLD'S LIGHT AND DARKNESS.
Prologue~
ORI BOOK STORE
BOOKS - STATIONERY

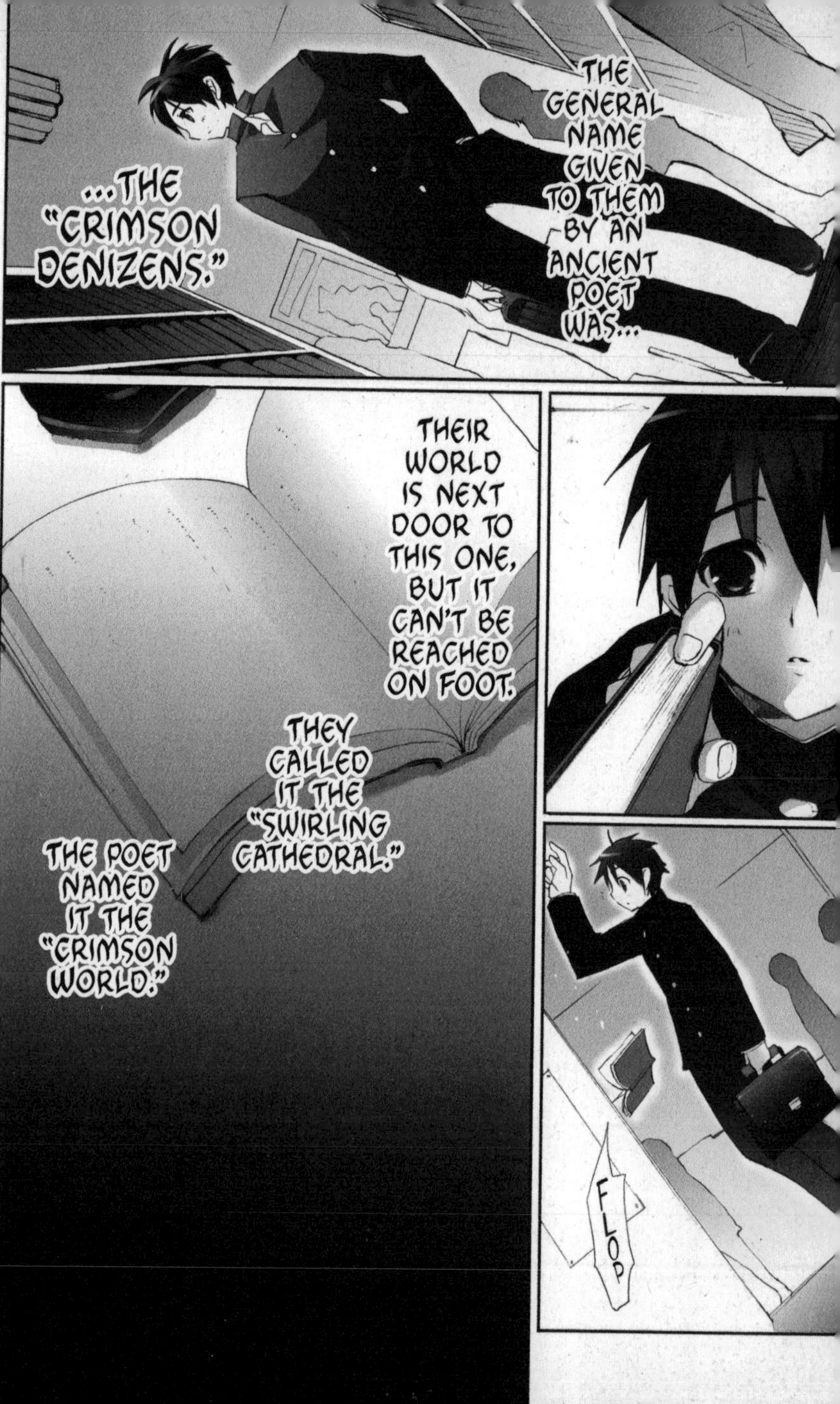
THE GENERAL NAME GIVEN TO THEM BY AN ANCIENT POET WAS...
...THE "CRIMSON DENIZENS."
FLOP
THEIR WORLD IS NEXT DOOR TO THIS ONE, BUT IT CAN'T BE REACHED ON FOOT.
THEY CALLED IT THE "SWIRLING CATHEDRAL."
THE POET NAMED IT THE "CRIMSON WORLD."

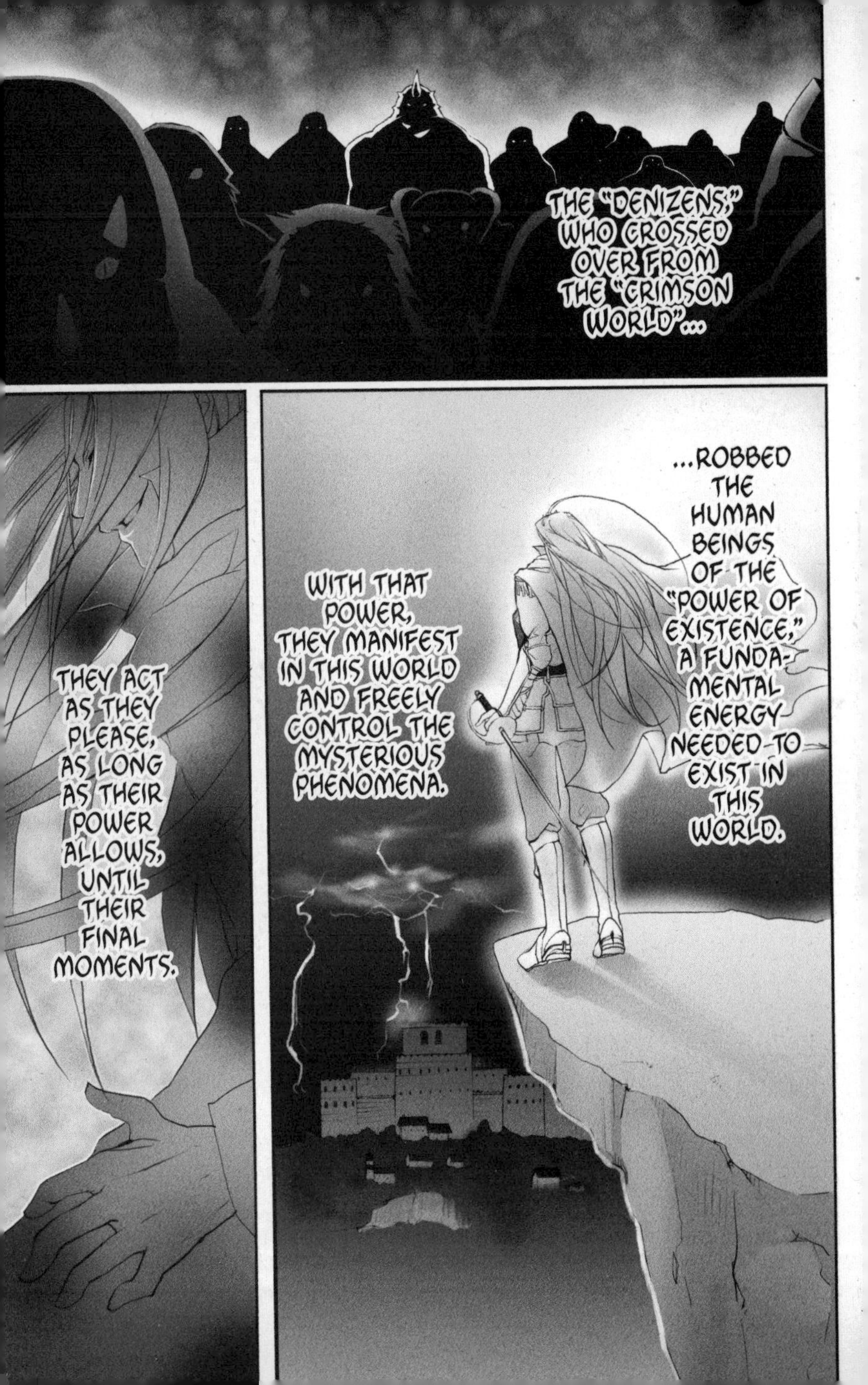
THE "DENIZENS" WHO CROSSED OVER FROM THE "CRIMSON WORLD"...
...ROBBED THE HUMAN BEINGS OF THE "POWER OF EXISTENCE," A FUNDA-MENTAL ENERGY NEEDED TO EXIST IN THIS WORLD.
WITH THAT POWER, THEY MANIFEST IN THIS WORLD AND FREELY CONTROL THE MYSTERIOUS PHENOMENA.
THEY ACT AS THEY PLEASE, AS LONG AS THEIR POWER ALLOWS, UNTIL THEIR FINAL MOMENTS.

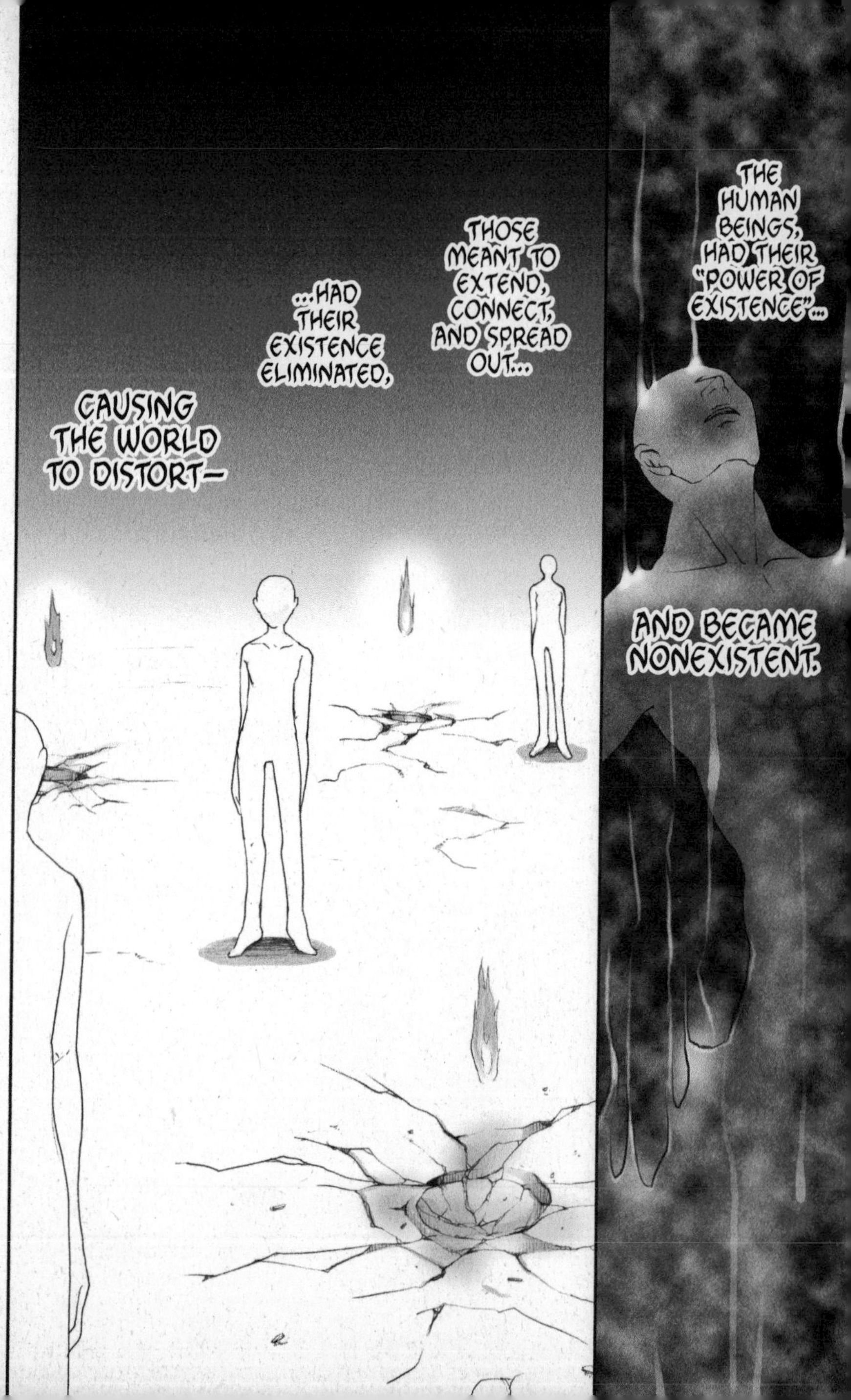
THE HUMAN BEINGS, HAD THEIR "POWER OF EXISTENCE"...
AND BECAME NONEXISTENT.
THOSE MEANT TO EXTEND, CONNECT, AND SPREAD OUT...
...HAD THEIR EXISTENCE ELIMINATED,
CAUSING THE WORLD TO DISTORT—

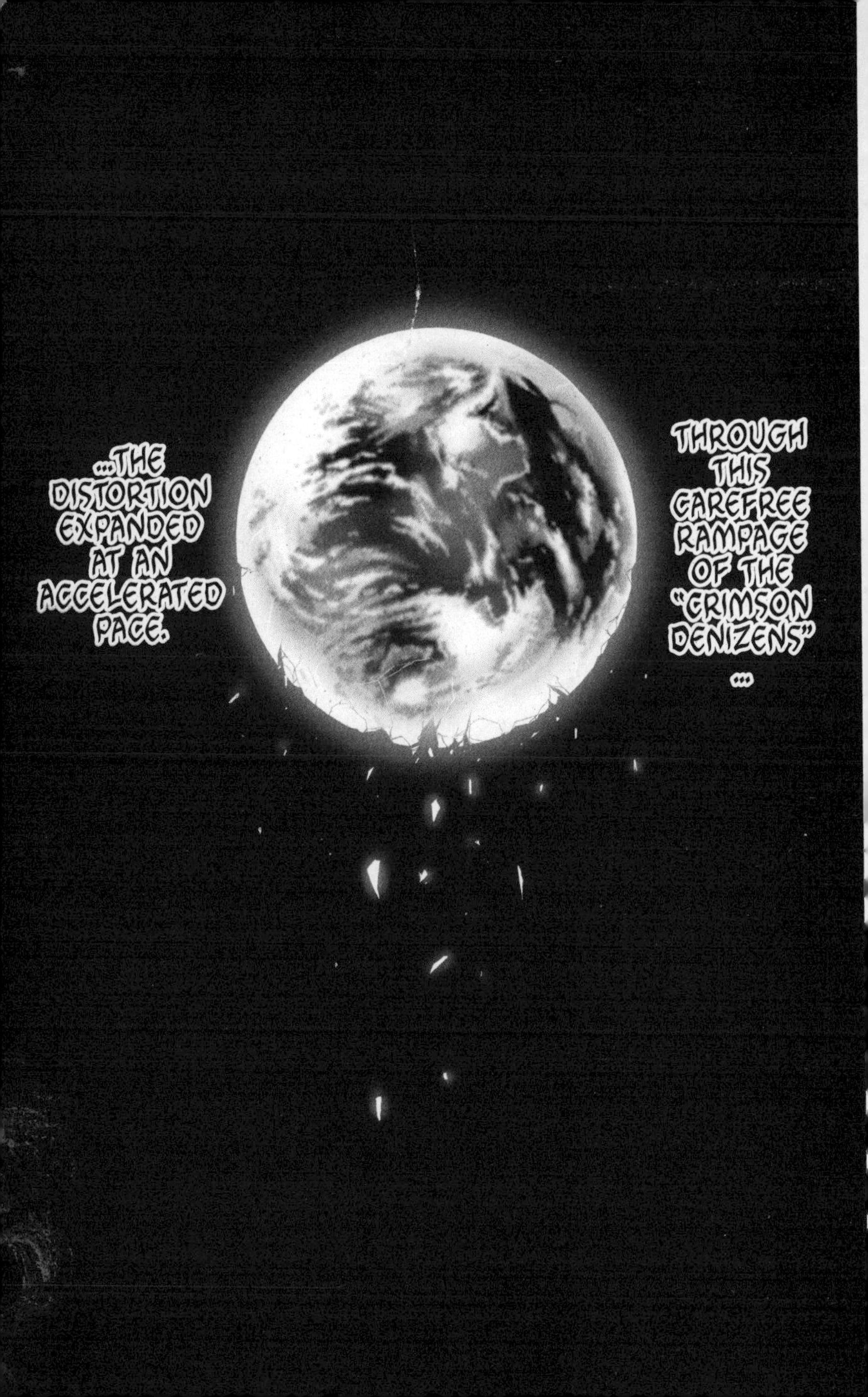
THROUGH THIS CAREFREE RAMPAGE OF THE "CRIMSON DENIZENS"...
...THE DISTORTION EXPANDED AT AN ACCELERATED PACE.

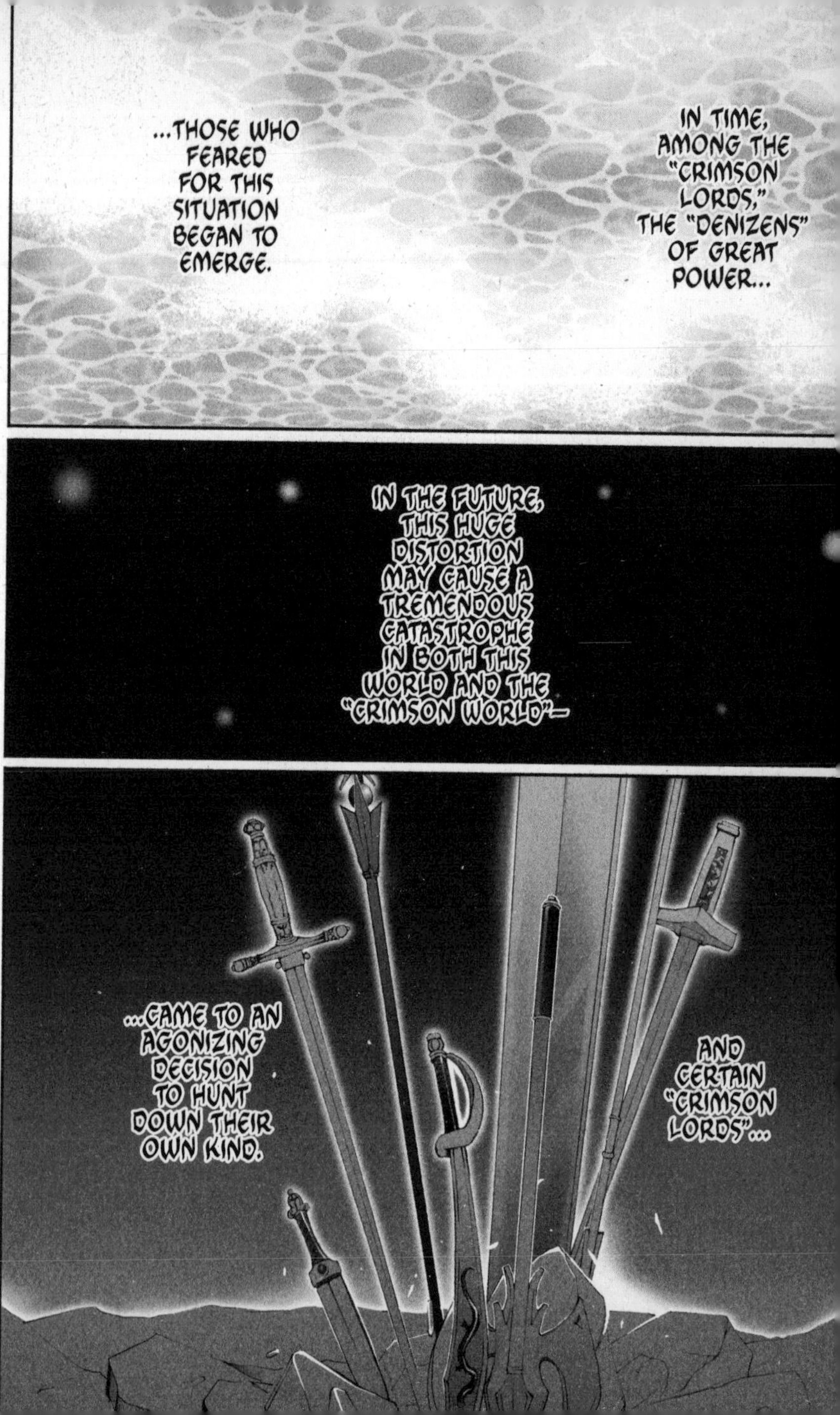
IN TIME, AMONG THE "CRIMSON LORDS," THE "DENIZENS" OF GREAT POWER...
...THOSE WHO FEARED FOR THIS SITUATION BEGAN TO EMERGE.
IN THE FUTURE, THIS HUGE DISTORTION MAY CAUSE A TREMENDOUS CATASTROPHE IN BOTH THIS WORLD AND THE "CRIMSON WORLD"—
AND CERTAIN "CRIMSON LORDS"...
...CAME TO AN AGONIZING DECISION TO HUNT DOWN THEIR OWN KIND.

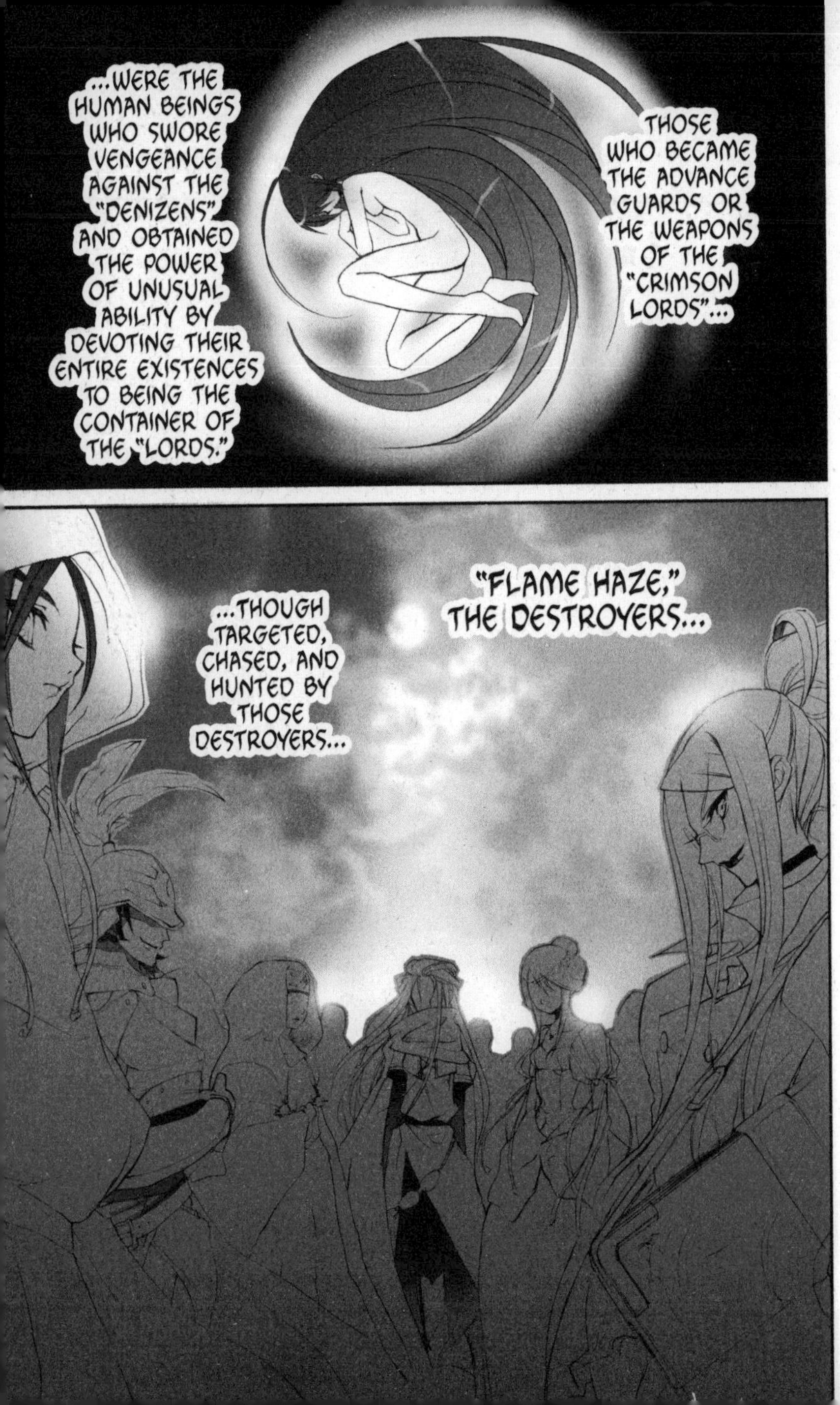
THOSE WHO BECAME THE ADVANCE GUARDS OR THE WEAPONS OF THE "CRIMSON LORDS"...
...WERE THE HUMAN BEINGS WHO SWORE VENGEANCE AGAINST THE "DENIZENS" AND OBTAINED THE POWER OF UNUSUAL ABILITY BY DEVOTING THEIR ENTIRE EXISTENCES TO BEING THE CONTAINER OF THE "LORDS."
"FLAME HAZE," THE DESTROYERS...
...THOUGH TARGETED, CHASED, AND HUNTED BY THOSE DESTROYERS...

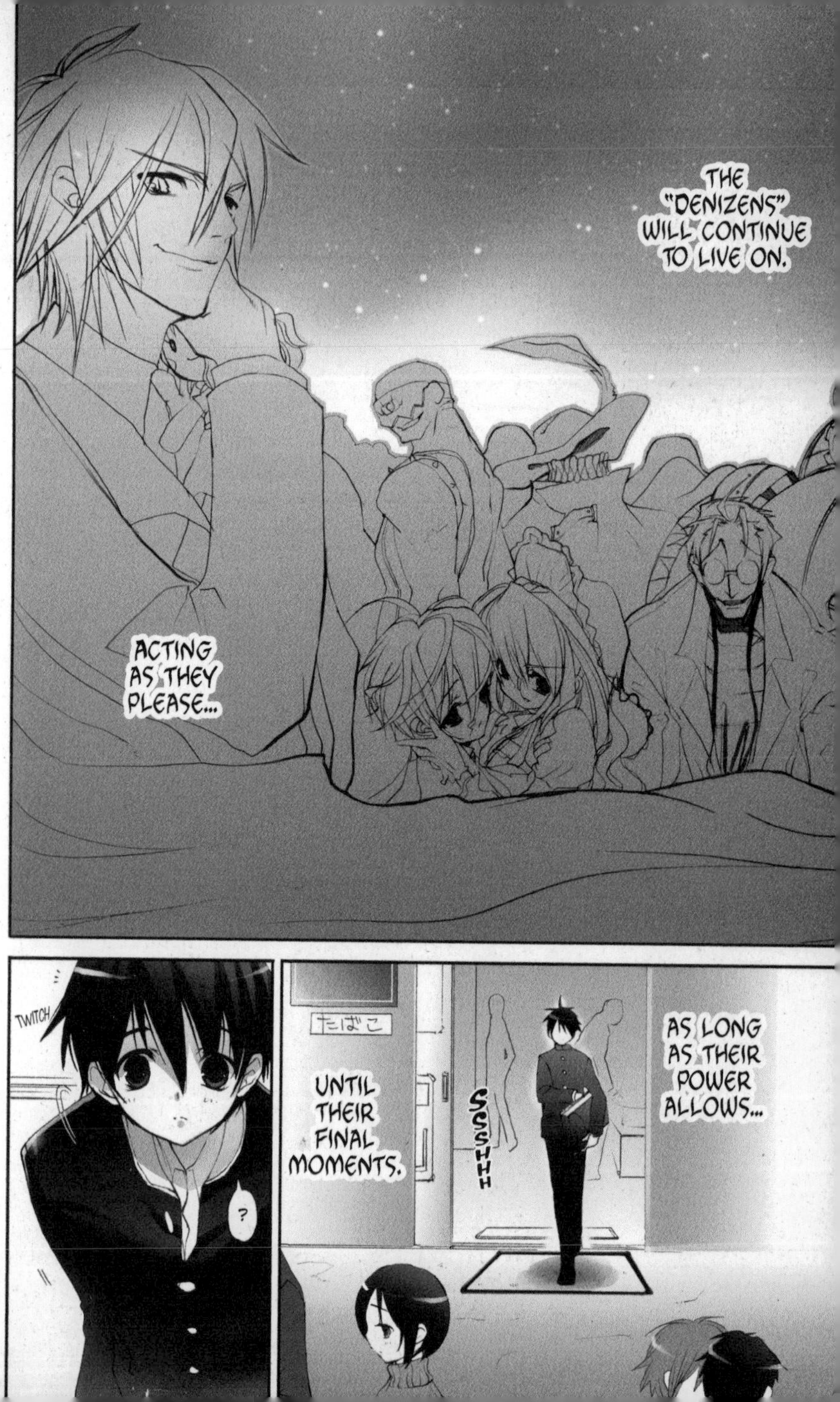
THE "DENIZENS" WILL CONTINUE TO LIVE ON.
ACTING AS THEY PLEASE...
AS LONG AS THEIR POWER ALLOWS...
たばこ
SSSHHH
UNTIL THEIR FINAL MOMENTS.
TWITCH
?

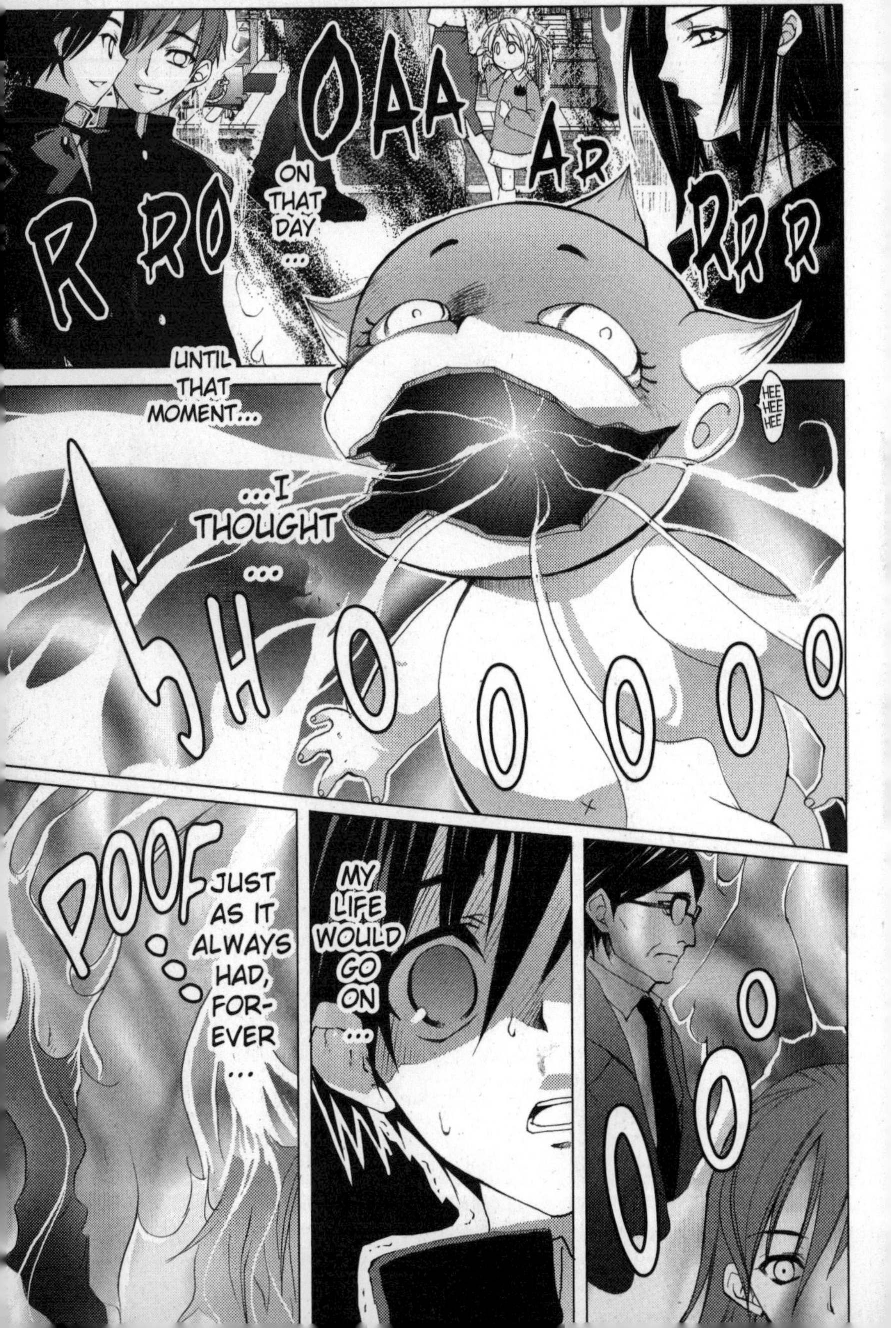
R RO OAA AR RRR
ON THAT DAY...
UNTIL THAT MOMENT...
HEE HEE HEE
...I THOUGHT...
SHOOOOOOO
OOO
MY LIFE WOULD GO ON...
JUST AS IT ALWAYS HAD, FOR-EVER...
POOF OOO

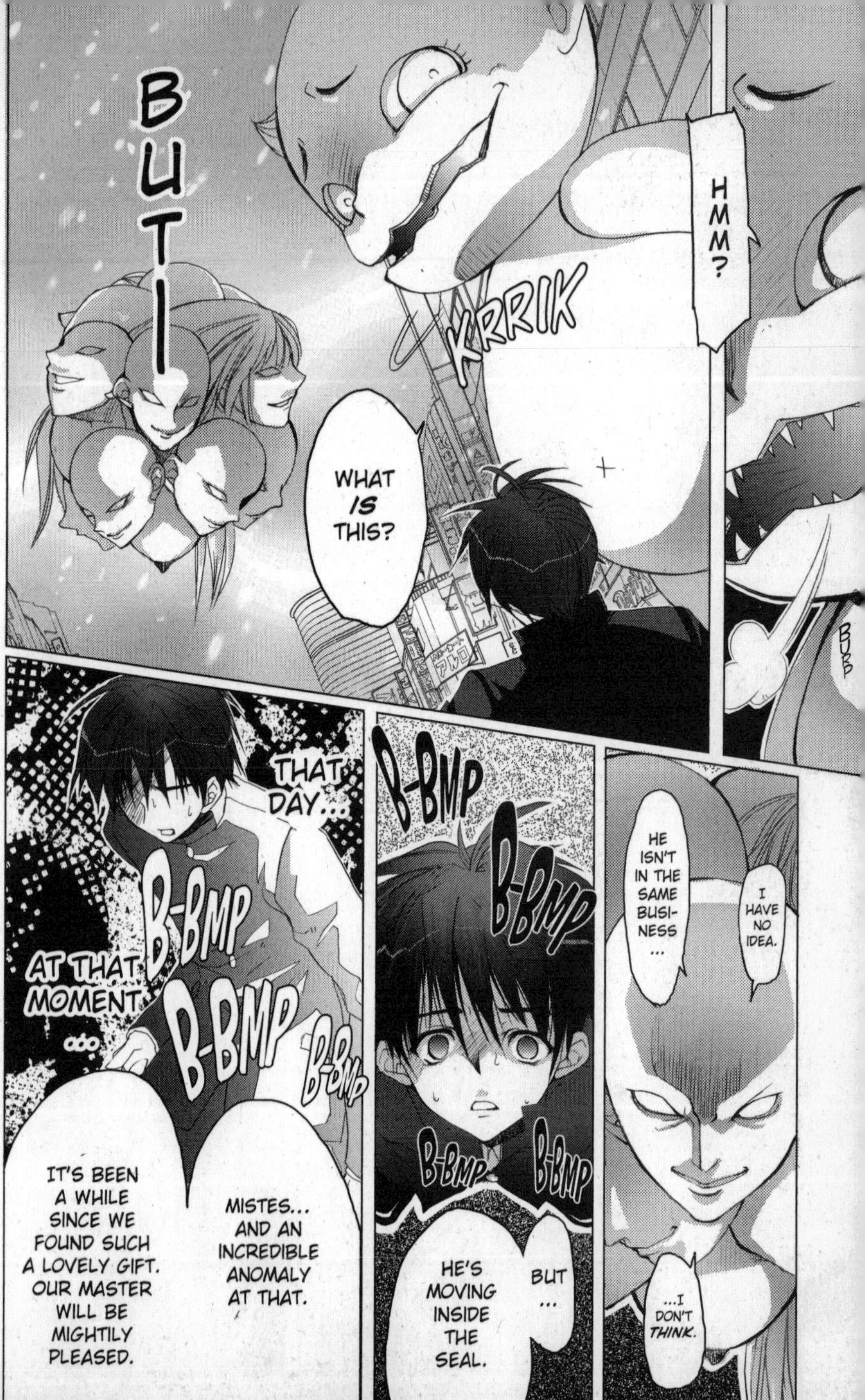
HMM?
BURP
KRRIK
WHAT *IS* THIS?
BUT—
I HAVE NO IDEA.
HE ISN'T IN THE SAME BUSINESS...
...I DON'T *THINK*.
B-BMP
B-BMP
B-BMP
B-BMP
BUT...
HE'S MOVING INSIDE THE SEAL.
THAT DAY...
B-BMP
AT THAT MOMENT...
B-BMP
B-BMP
MISTES... AND AN INCREDIBLE ANOMALY AT THAT.
IT'S BEEN A WHILE SINCE WE FOUND SUCH A LOVELY GIFT. OUR MASTER WILL BE MIGHTILY PLEASED.

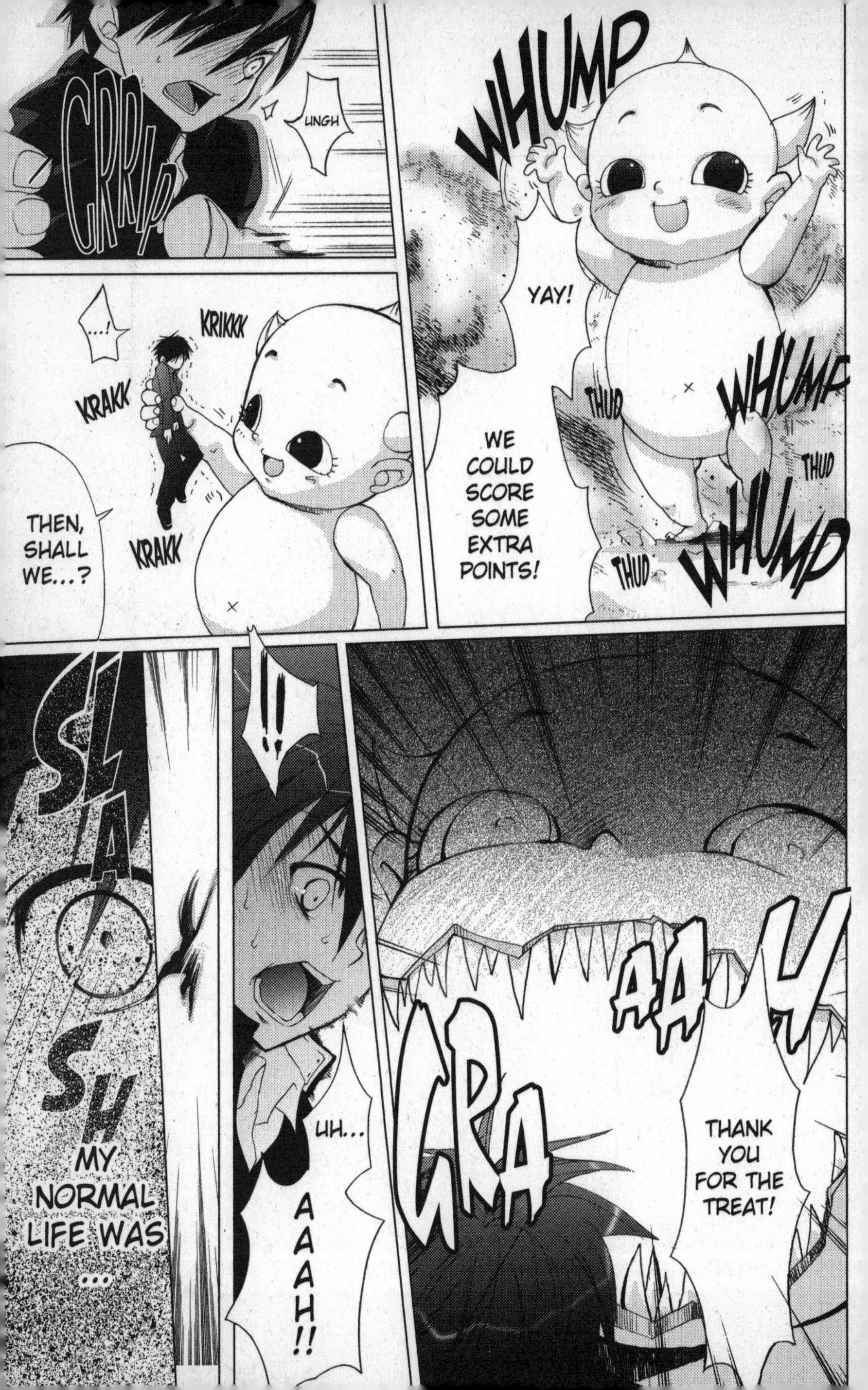
WHUMP
YAY!
WE COULD SCORE SOME EXTRA POINTS!
THUD
WHUMP
THUD
WHUMP
THUD
CRRIP
UNGH
...!
KRIKKK
KRAKK
KRAKK
THEN, SHALL WE...?
THANK YOU FOR THE TREAT!
!!
UH...
AAAAH!!
SLASH
MY NORMAL LIFE WAS...

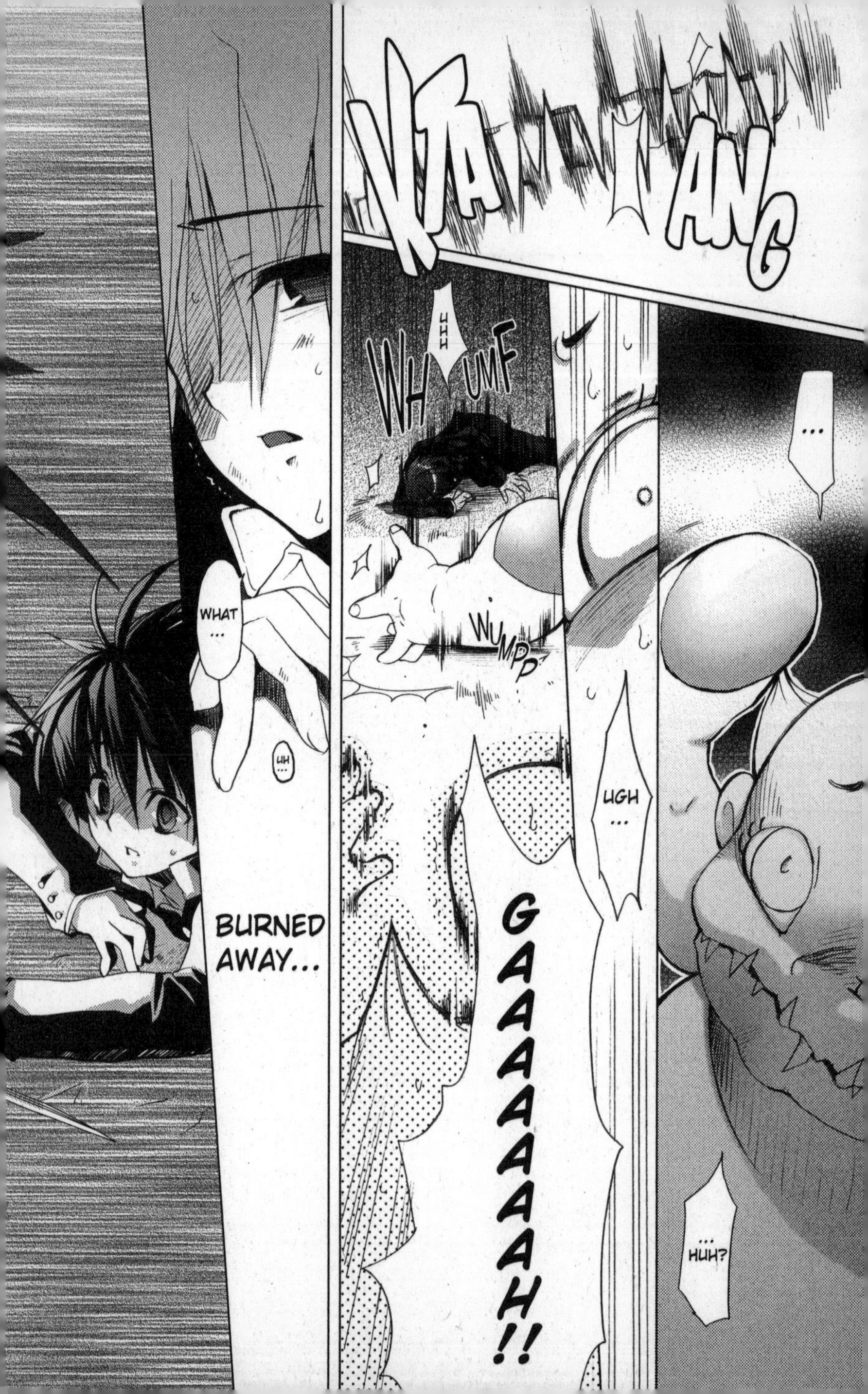
...
... HUH?
UGH ...
UHH
WHUMF
WUMPP
GAAAAAAAH!!
WHAT ...
UH ...
BURNED AWAY...

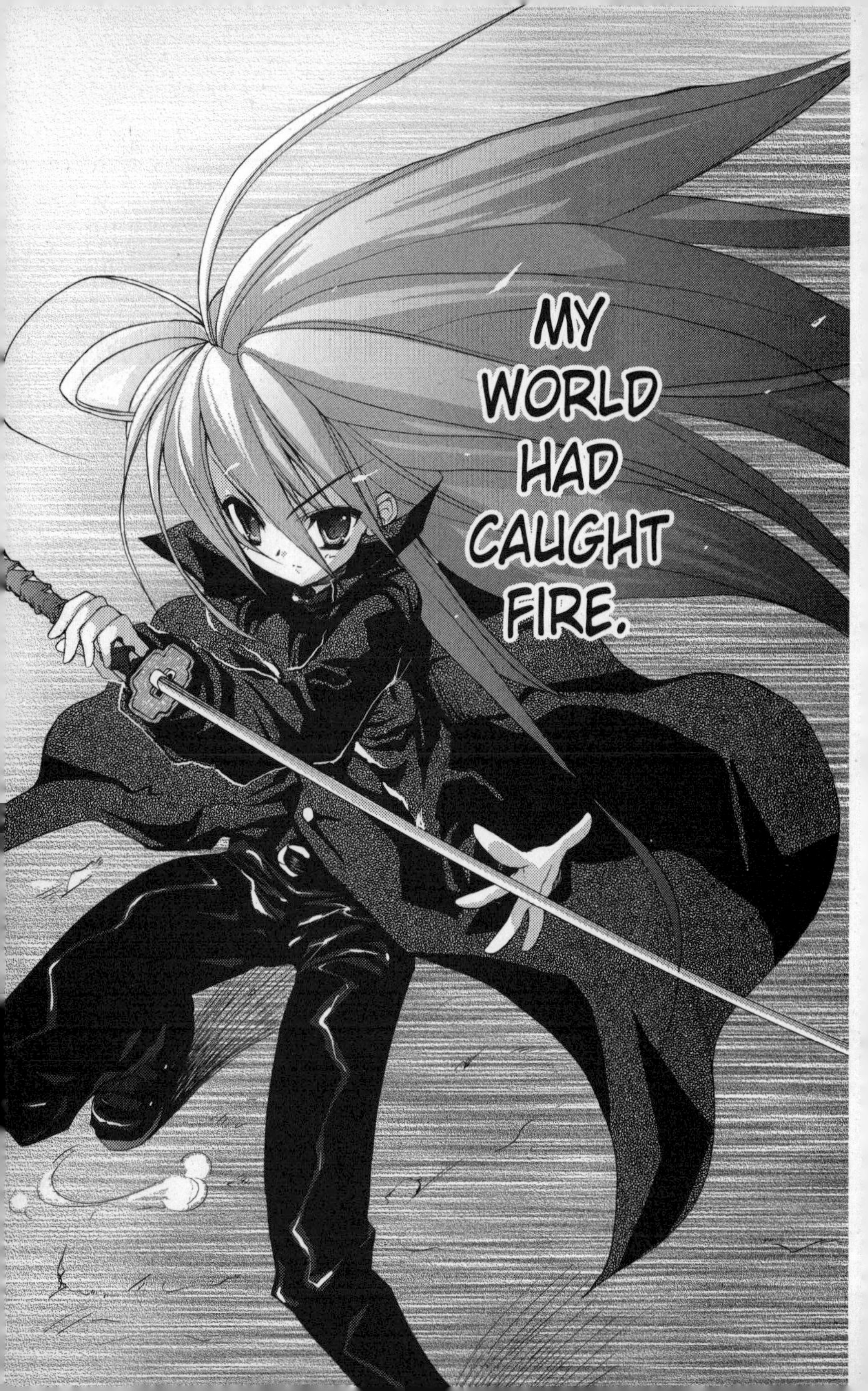
MY WORLD HAD CAUGHT FIRE.

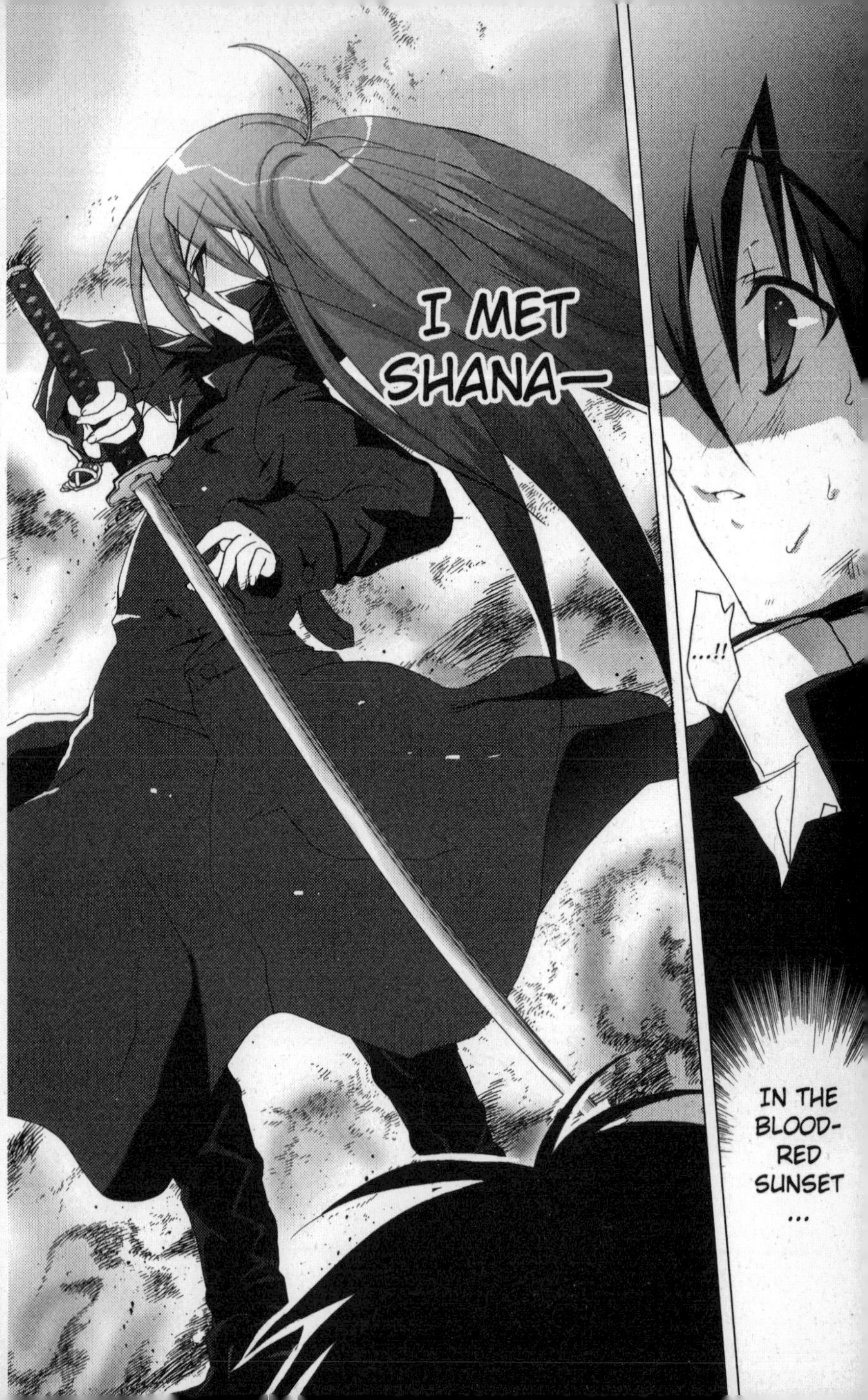
...!!
IN THE BLOOD-RED SUNSET ...
I MET SHANA—

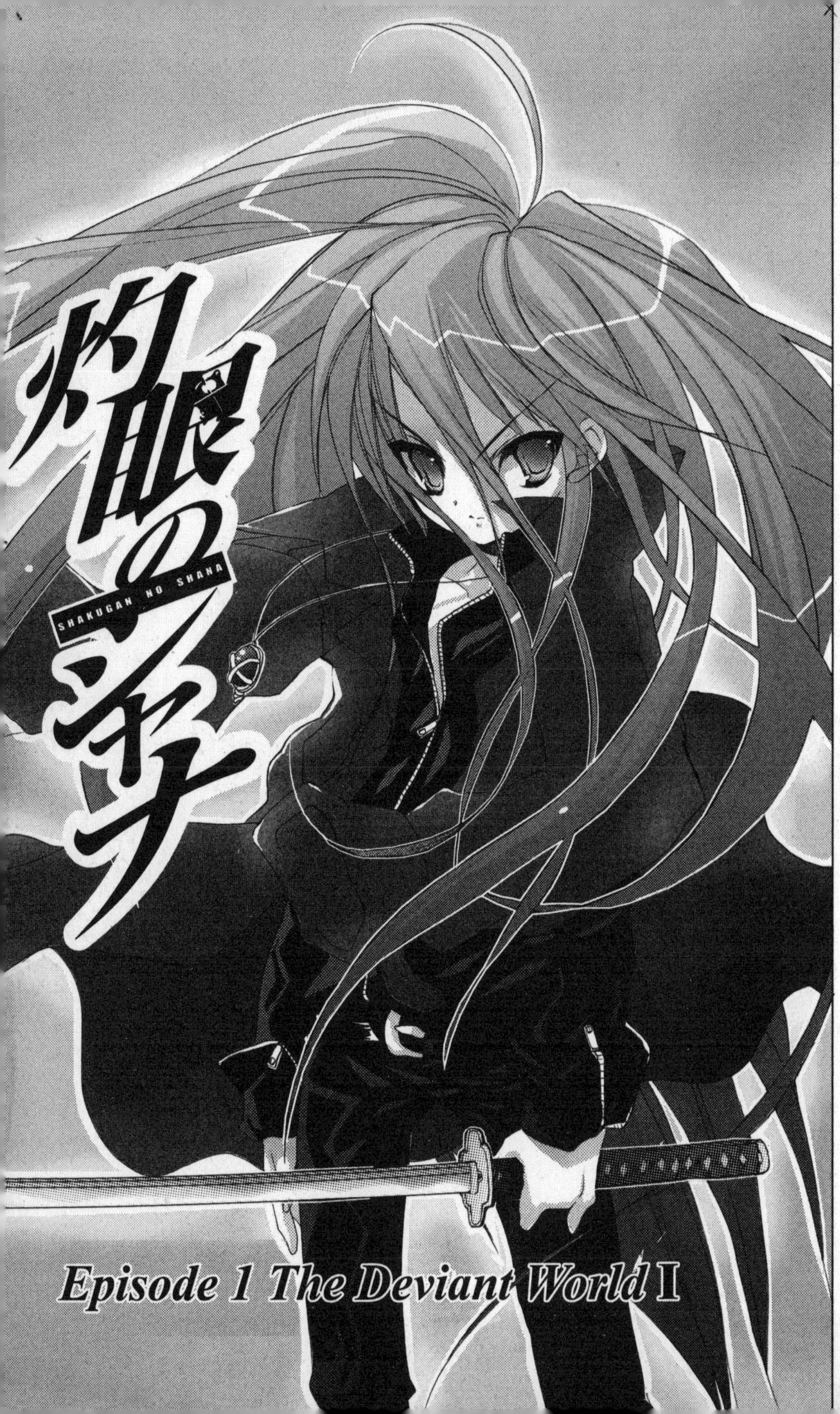
灼眼のシャナ
SHAKUGAN NO SHANA
Episode 1 The Deviant World I

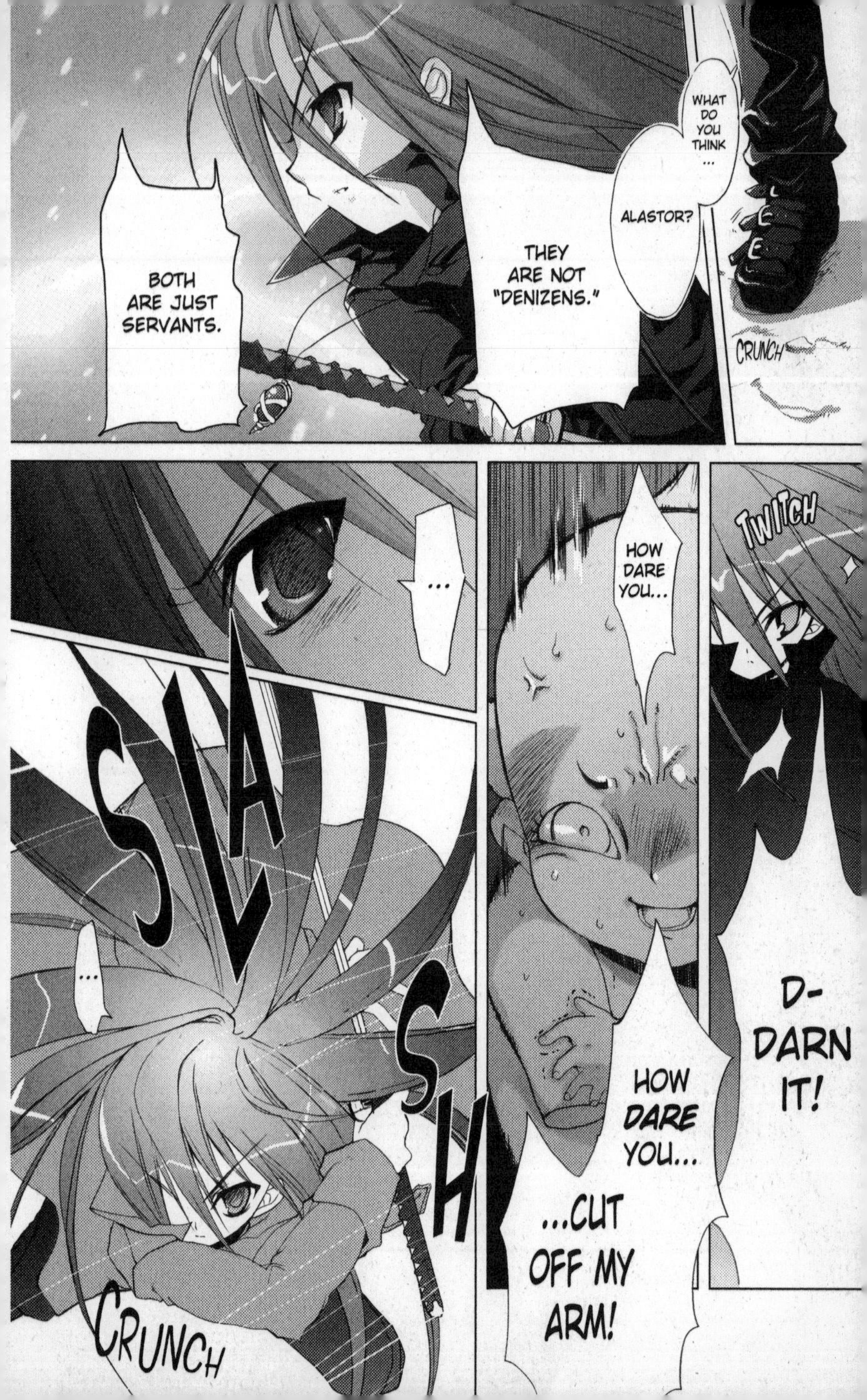
WHAT DO YOU THINK ... ALASTOR?
CRUNCH
THEY ARE NOT "DENIZENS."
BOTH ARE JUST SERVANTS.
TWITCH
D- DARN IT!
HOW DARE YOU...
HOW DARE YOU...
...CUT OFF MY ARM!
...
SLASH
...
CRUNCH

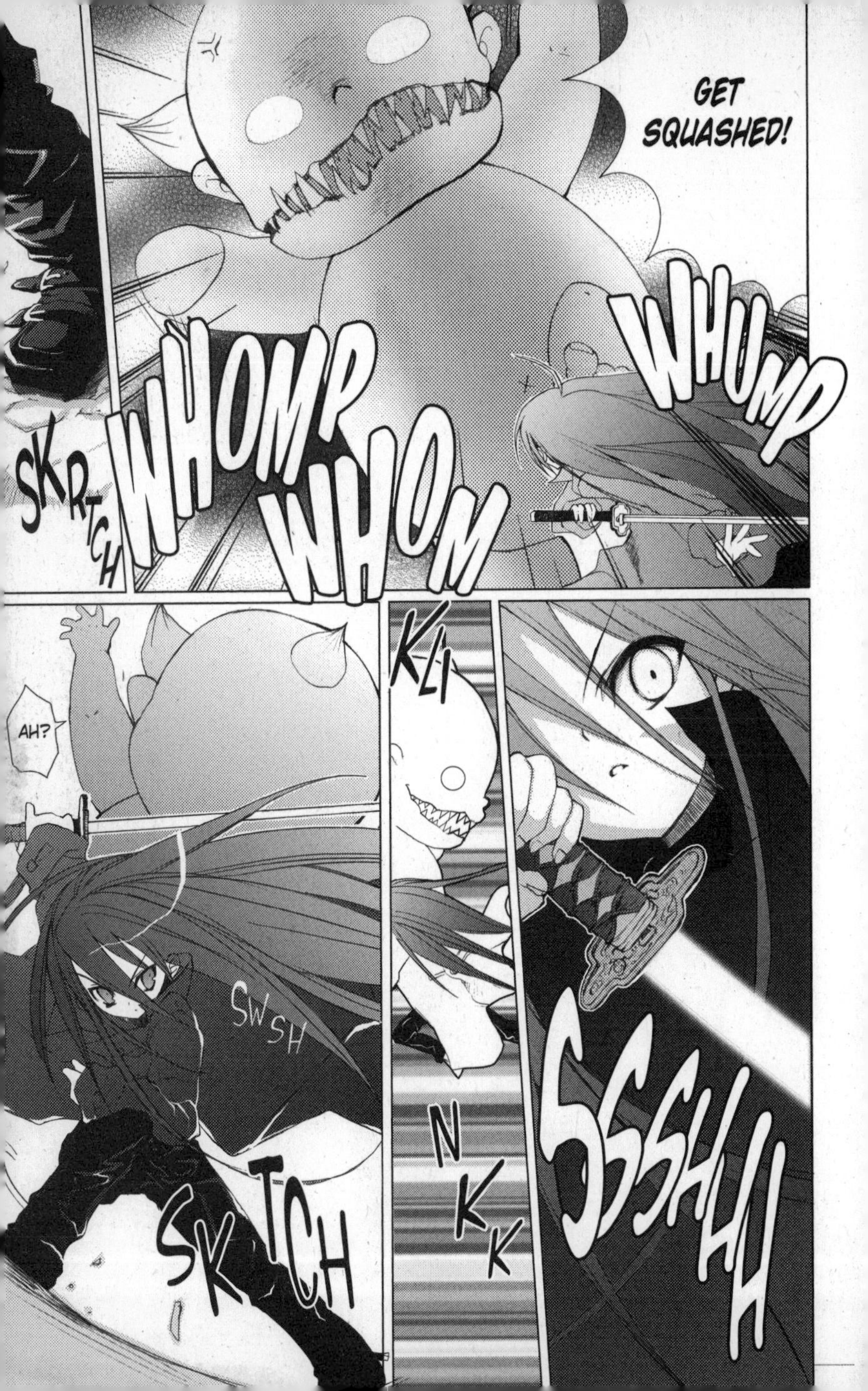
GET SQUASHED!
WHUMP
WHOM
WHOMP
SKRTCH
SSSHHH
KLI
NKK
AH?
SWSH
SKTCH

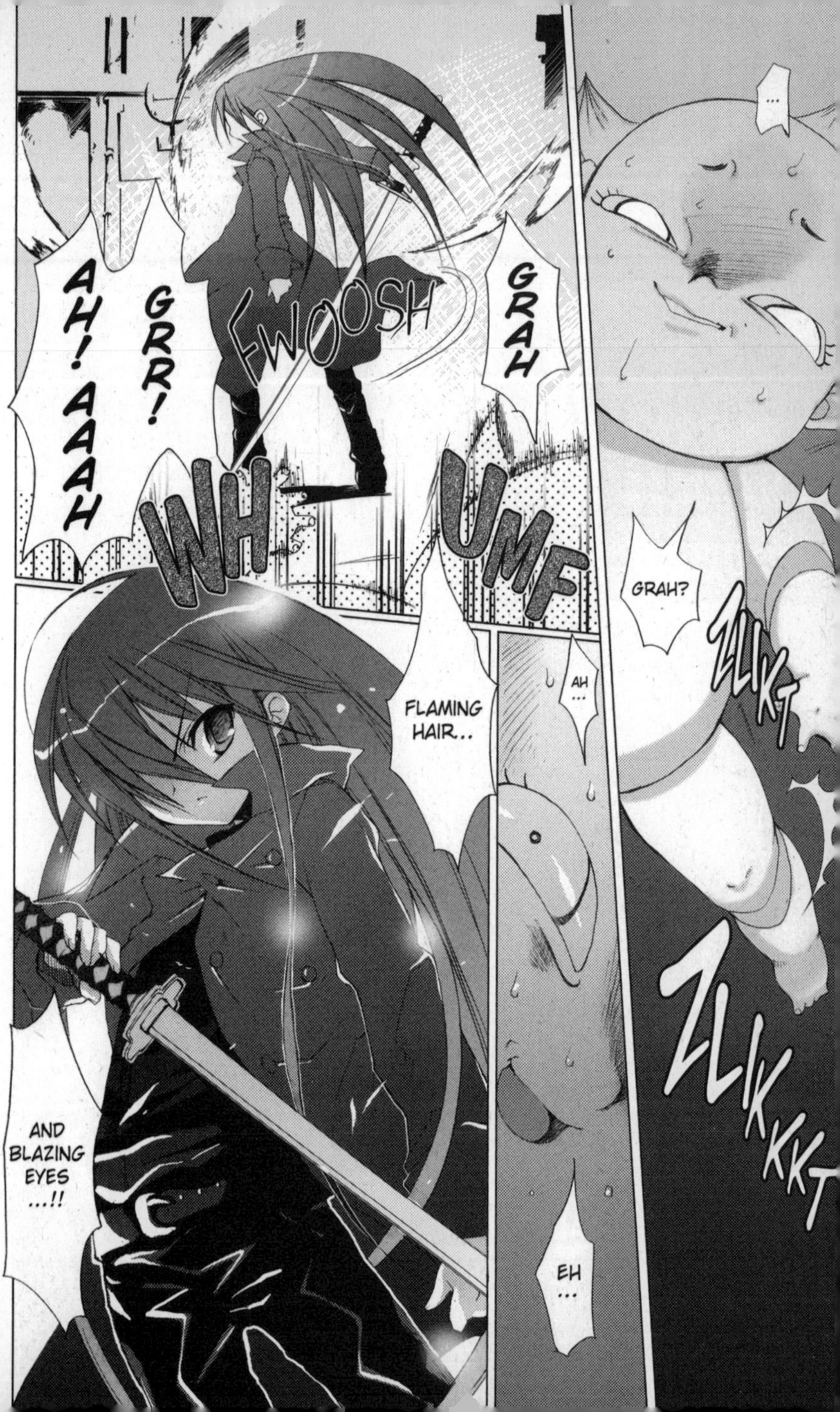
...
GRAH?
ZZIKT
ZZIKKKT
GRAH
FWOOSH
GRR!
AH! AAAAH
WHUMF
AH ...
EH ...
FLAMING HAIR..
AND BLAZING EYES ...!!

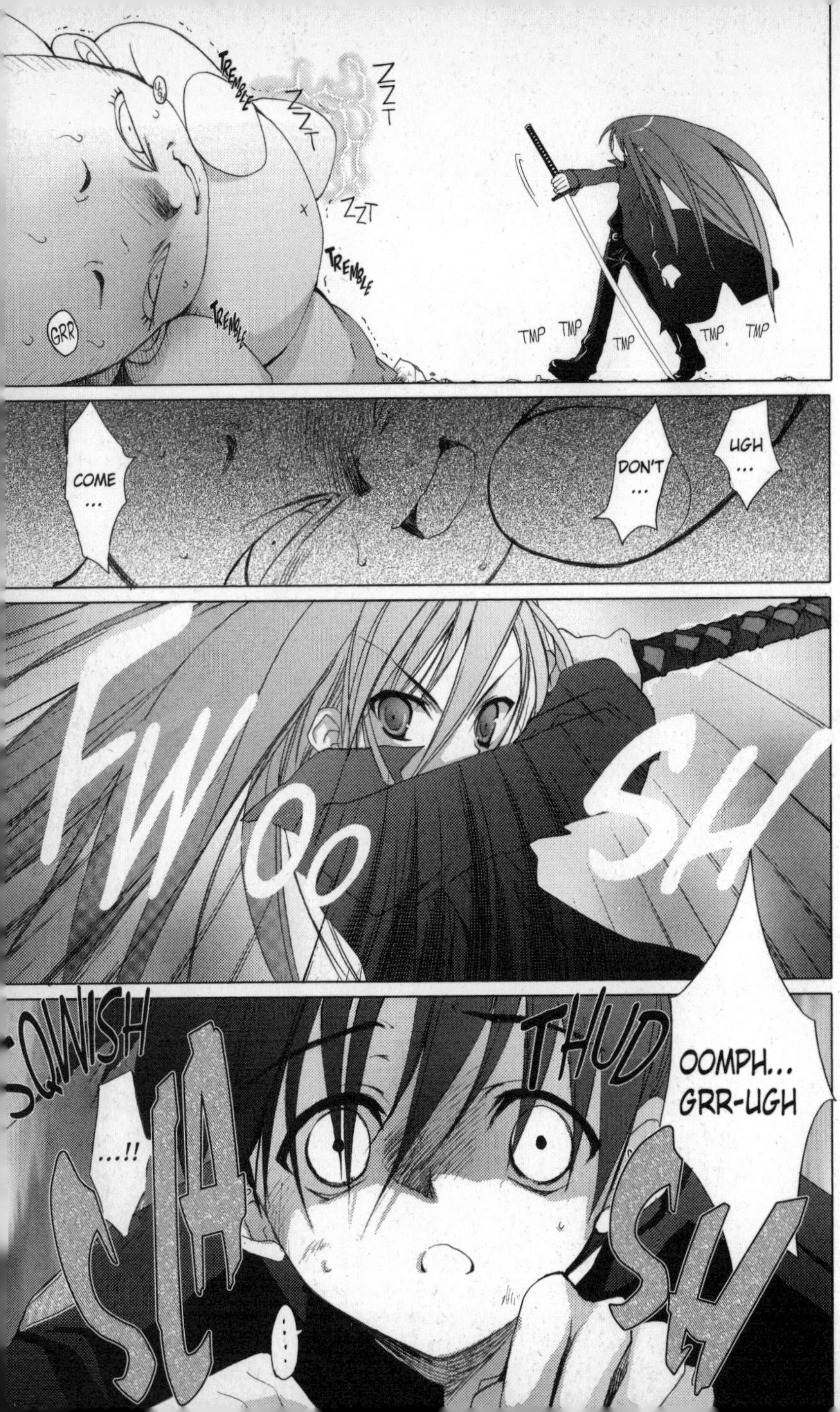

TMP TMP TMP TMP TMP
ZZZT
ZZZT
ZZT
TREMBLE
TREMBLE
TREMBLE
GRR
UGH ...
DON'T ...
COME ...
FWOOSH
OOMPH... GRR-UGH
THUD
SLASH
SQUISH
...!!
...

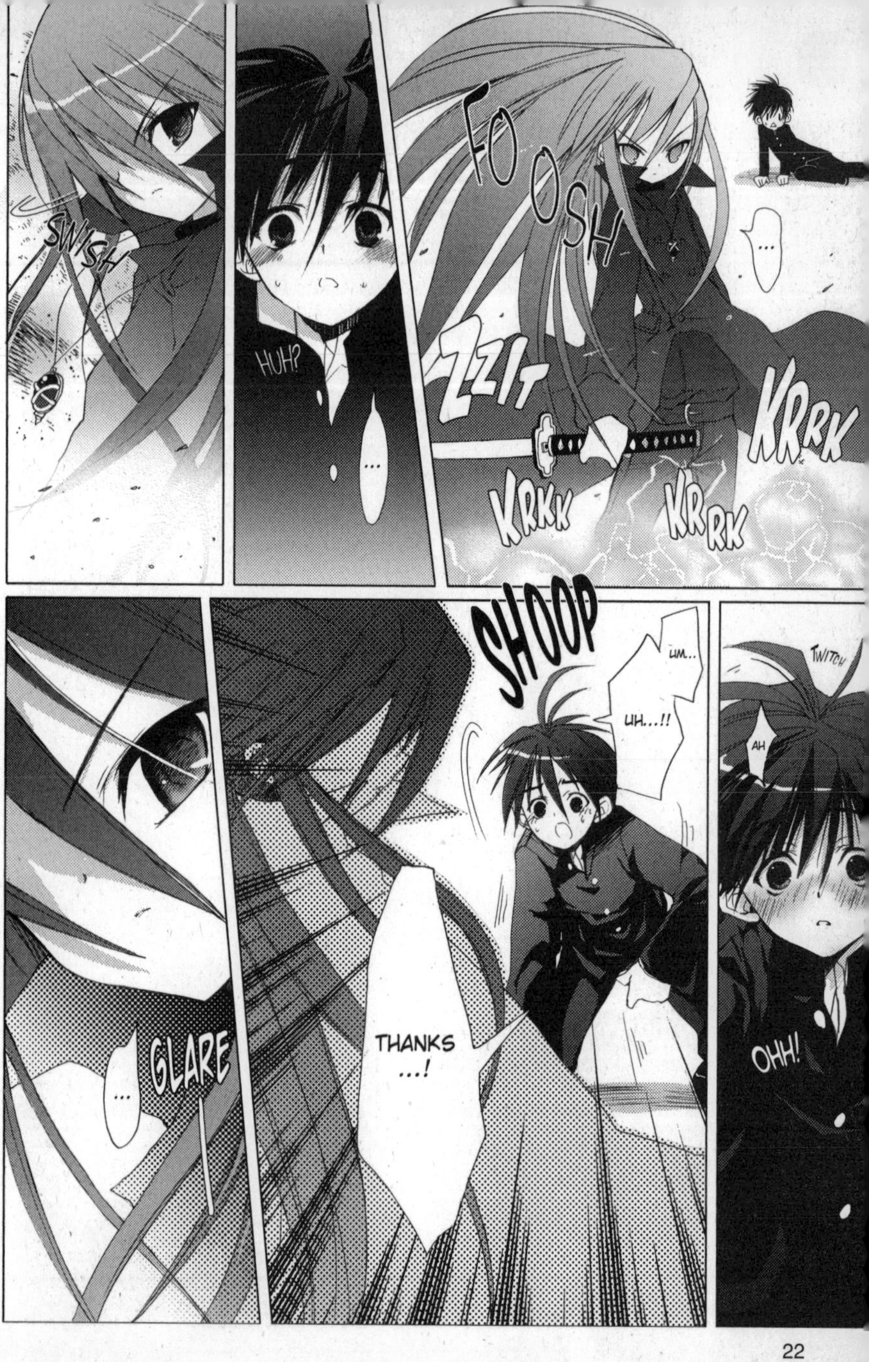
...
FOOSH
ZZIT
KRRK
KRRK
KRRK
HUH?
...
SWISH
TWITCH
AH
OHH!
SHOOP
UM...
UH...!!
THANKS ...!
GLARE
...

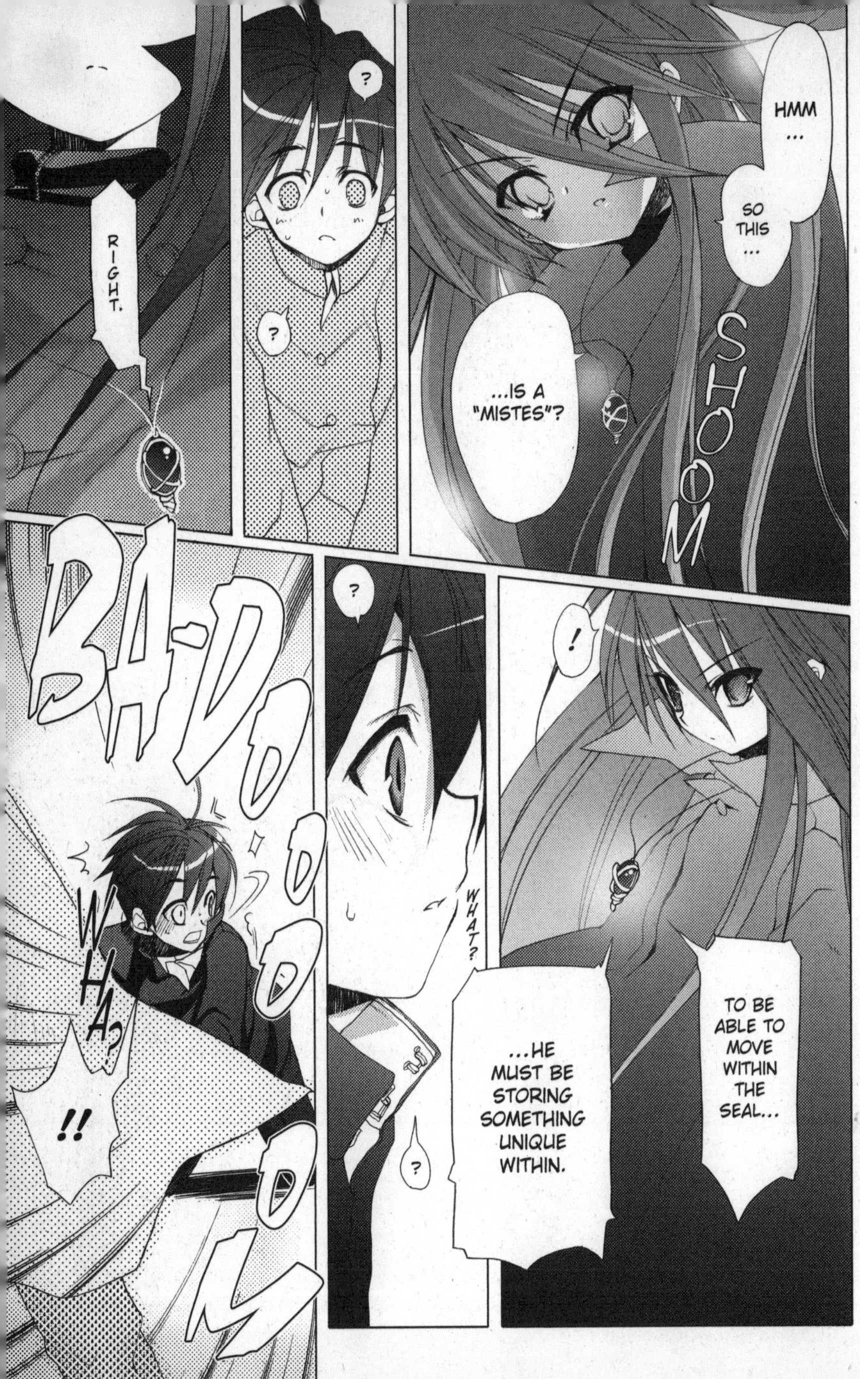
HMM ...
SO THIS ...
SHOOM
...IS A "MISTES"?
?
?
RIGHT.
!
TO BE ABLE TO MOVE WITHIN THE SEAL...
...HE MUST BE STORING SOMETHING UNIQUE WITHIN.
?
WHAT?
?
BA-DOOOOOM
WHA?
!!

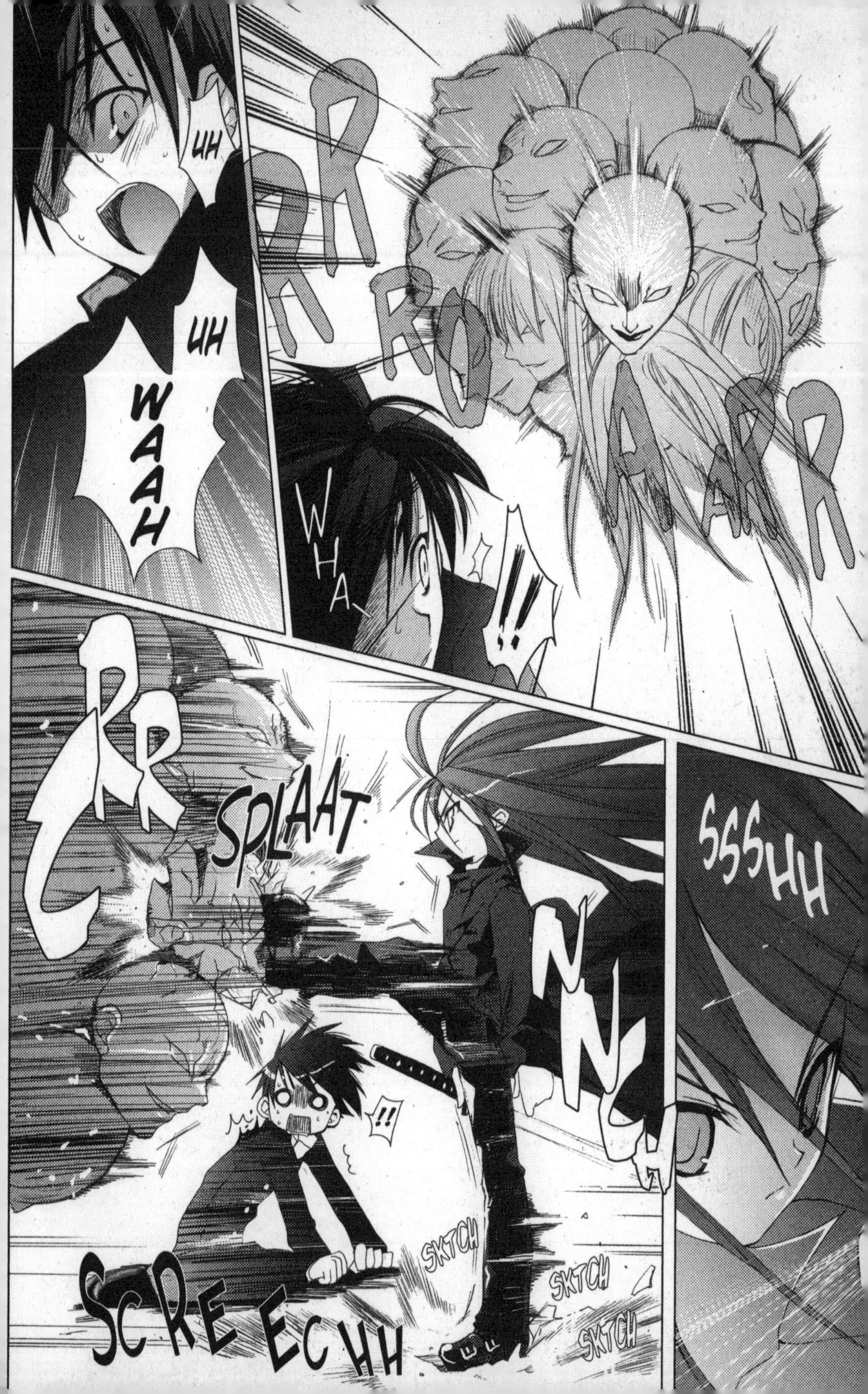

RRRRO
AARR
WHA-
!!
UH
UH
WAAAH
SSSHH
RRC
SPLAAT
NNG
!!
SKTCH
SKTCH
SKTCH
SCREECHH

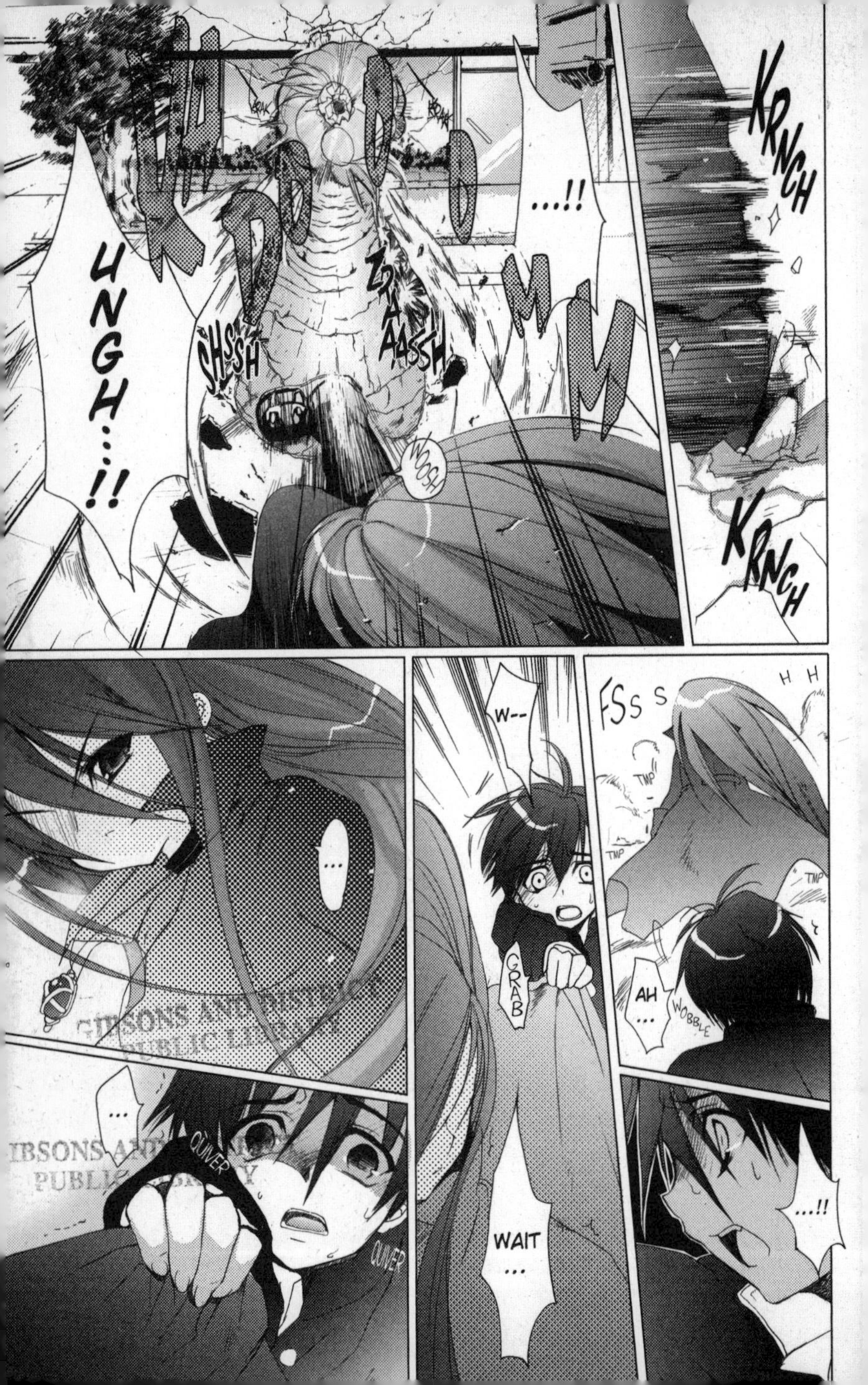
KRNCH
KRNCH
...!!
ZRAAASSH
SHSSH
WOOSH
UNGH...!!
FSSS
H H
TMP
TMP
TMP
AH...
WOBBLE
...!!
W--
GRAB
WAIT...
...
...
QUIVER
QUIVER

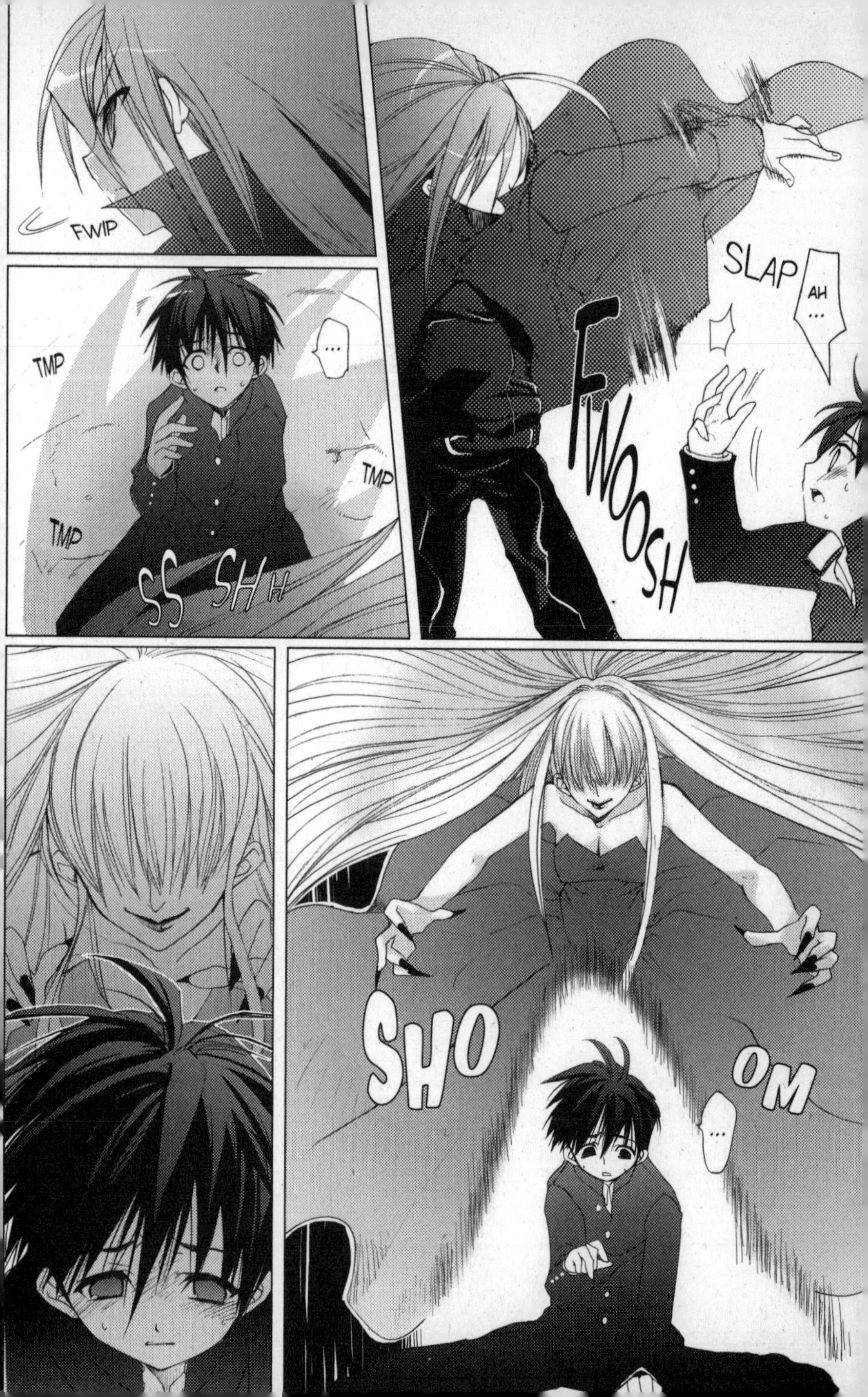
SLAP
AH ...
FWOOSH
FWIP
...
TMP
TMP
TMP
SS SHH
SHO OM
...

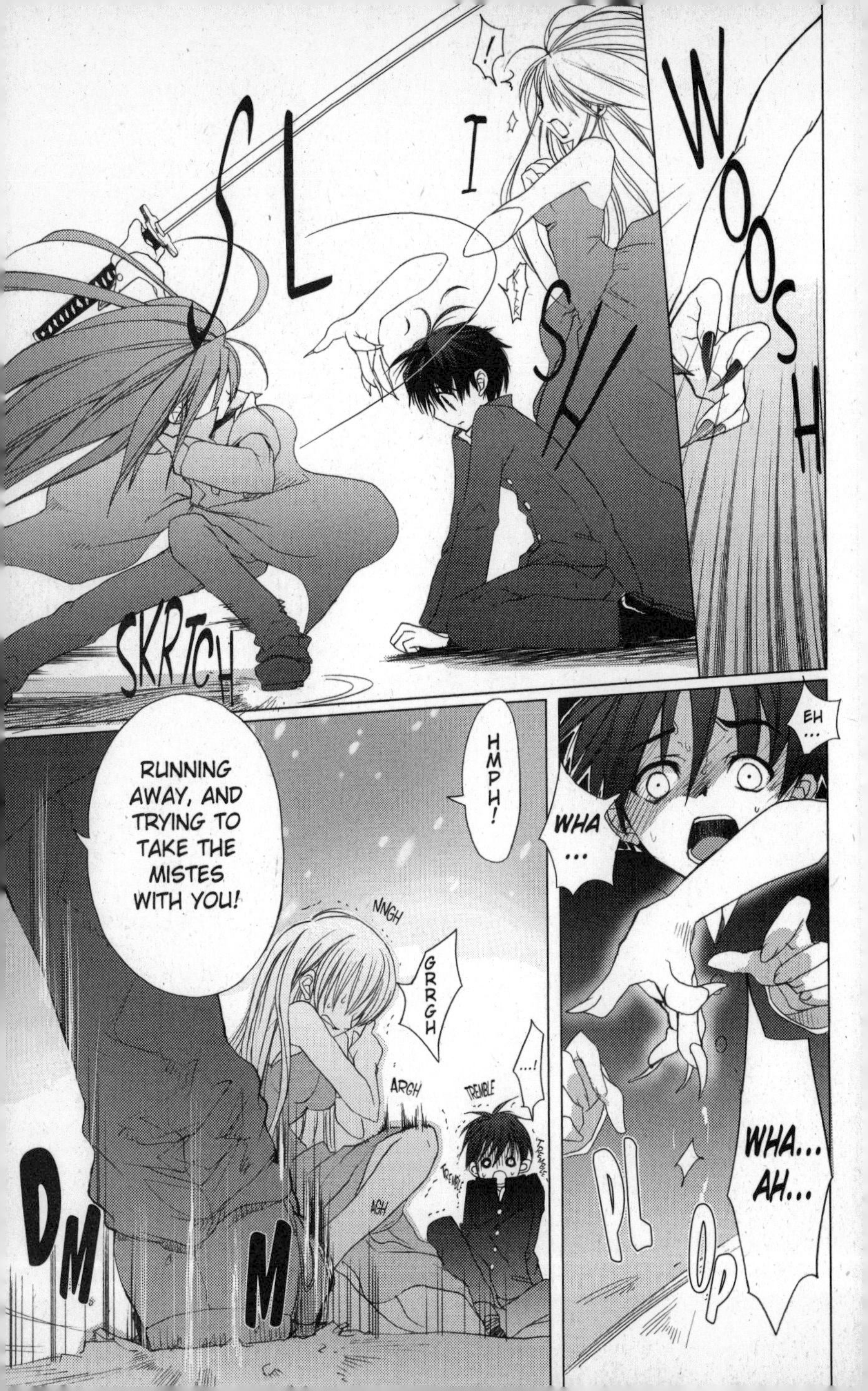
!
WOOSH
SLISH
SKRTCH
EH ...
WHA ...
WHA... AH...
PLOP
HMPH!
RUNNING AWAY, AND TRYING TO TAKE THE MISTES WITH YOU!
NNGH
GRRGH
...!
ARGH
TREMBLE
TREMBLE
TREMBLE
AGH
DMM

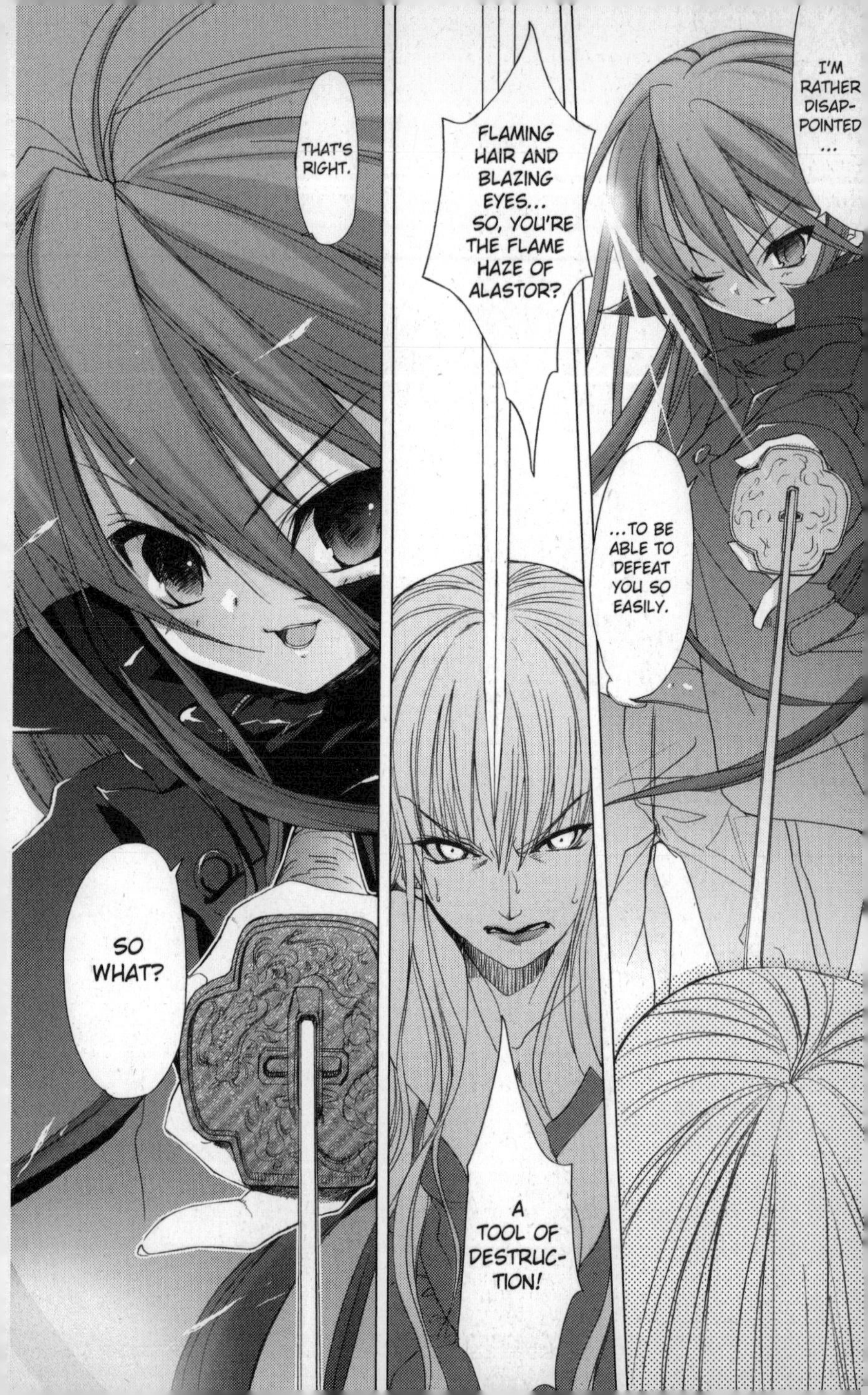
I'M RATHER DISAP-POINTED...
...TO BE ABLE TO DEFEAT YOU SO EASILY.
FLAMING HAIR AND BLAZING EYES... SO, YOU'RE THE FLAME HAZE OF ALASTOR?
A TOOL OF DESTRUC-TION!
THAT'S RIGHT.
SO WHAT?

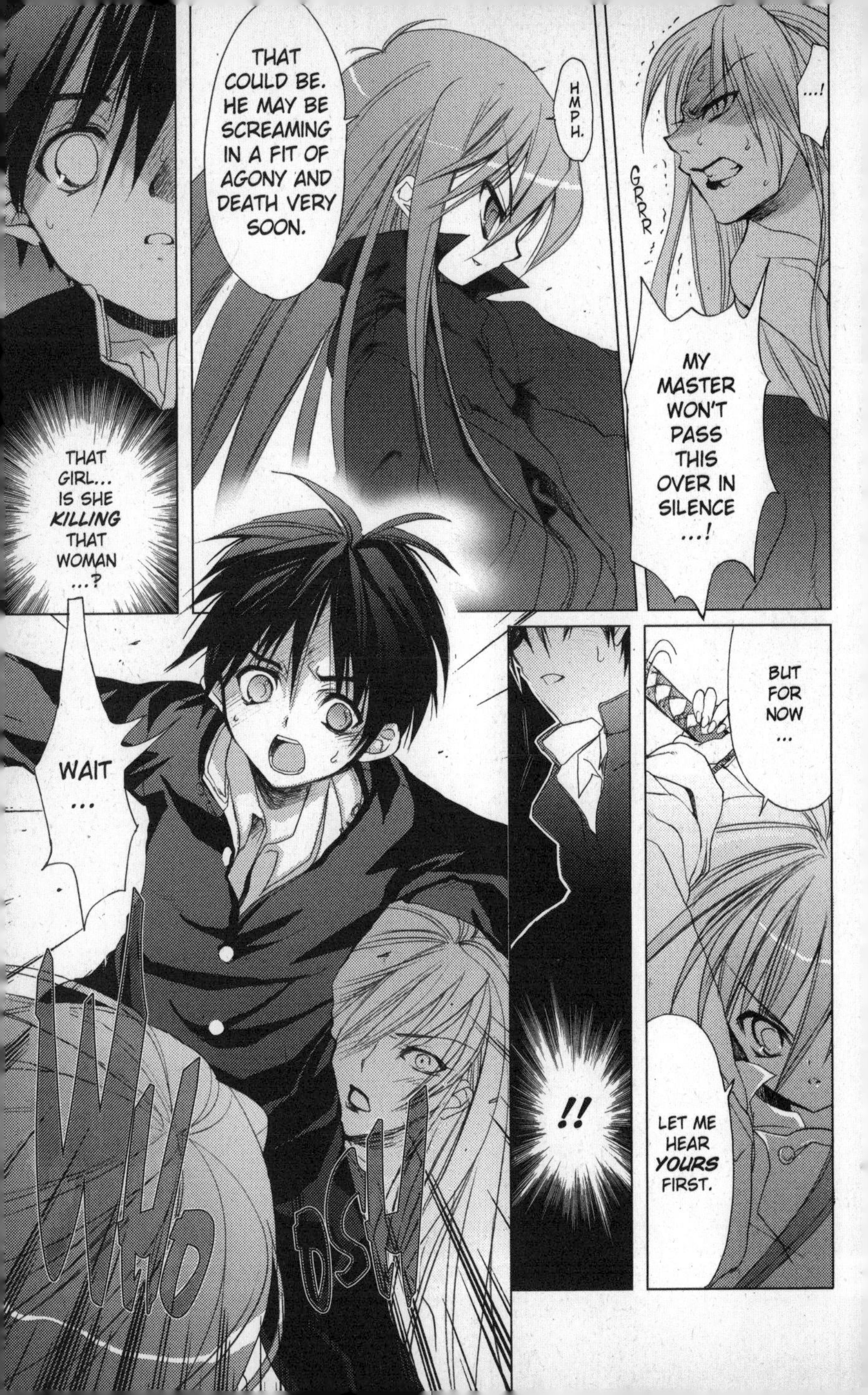
...!
GRRR
MY MASTER WON'T PASS THIS OVER IN SILENCE ...!
THAT COULD BE. HE MAY BE SCREAMING IN A FIT OF AGONY AND DEATH VERY SOON.
HMPH.
THAT GIRL... IS SHE *KILLING* THAT WOMAN ...?
BUT FOR NOW ...
LET ME HEAR ***YOURS*** FIRST.
!!
WAIT ...

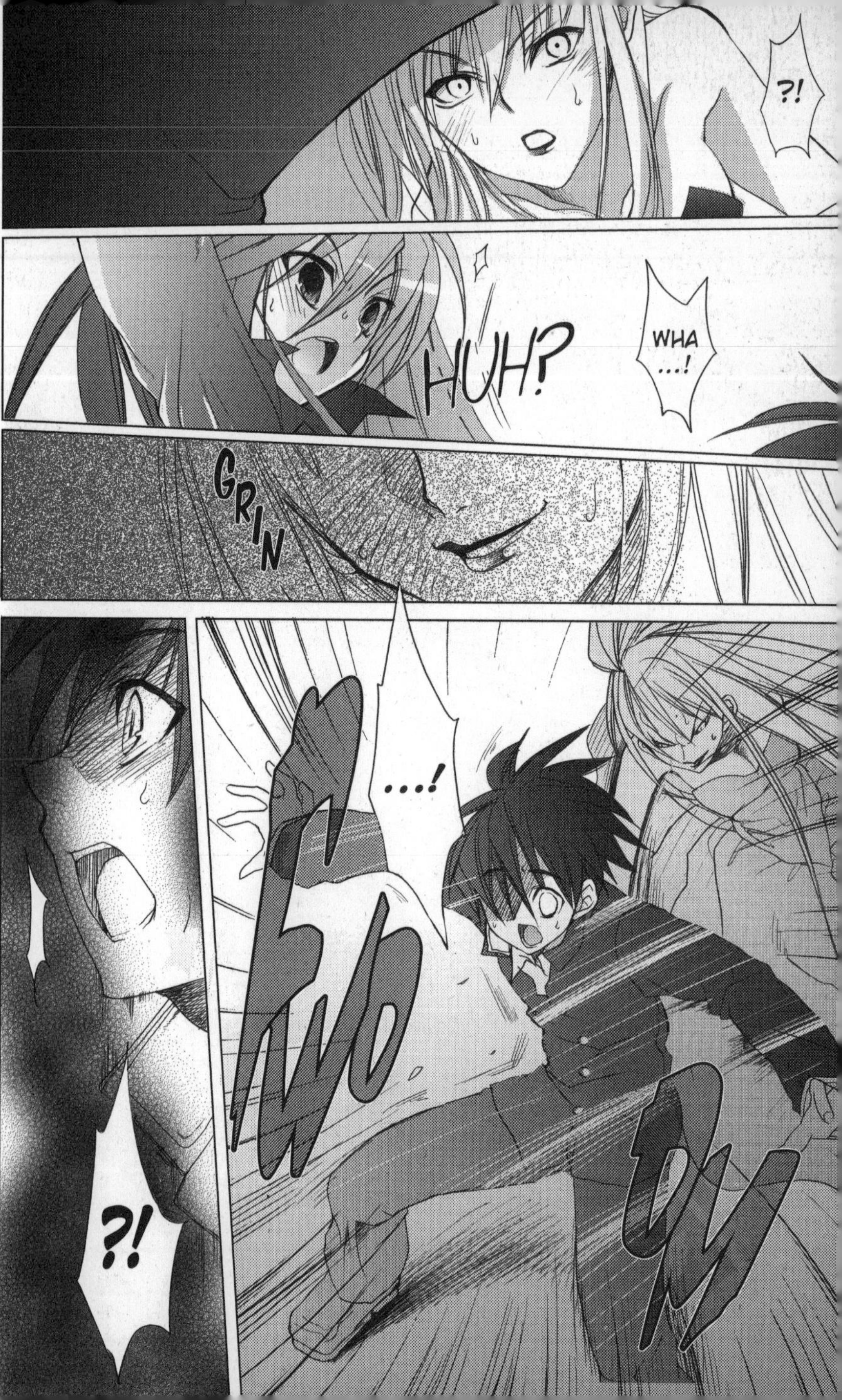
?!
WHA ...!
HUH?
GRIN
...!
?!

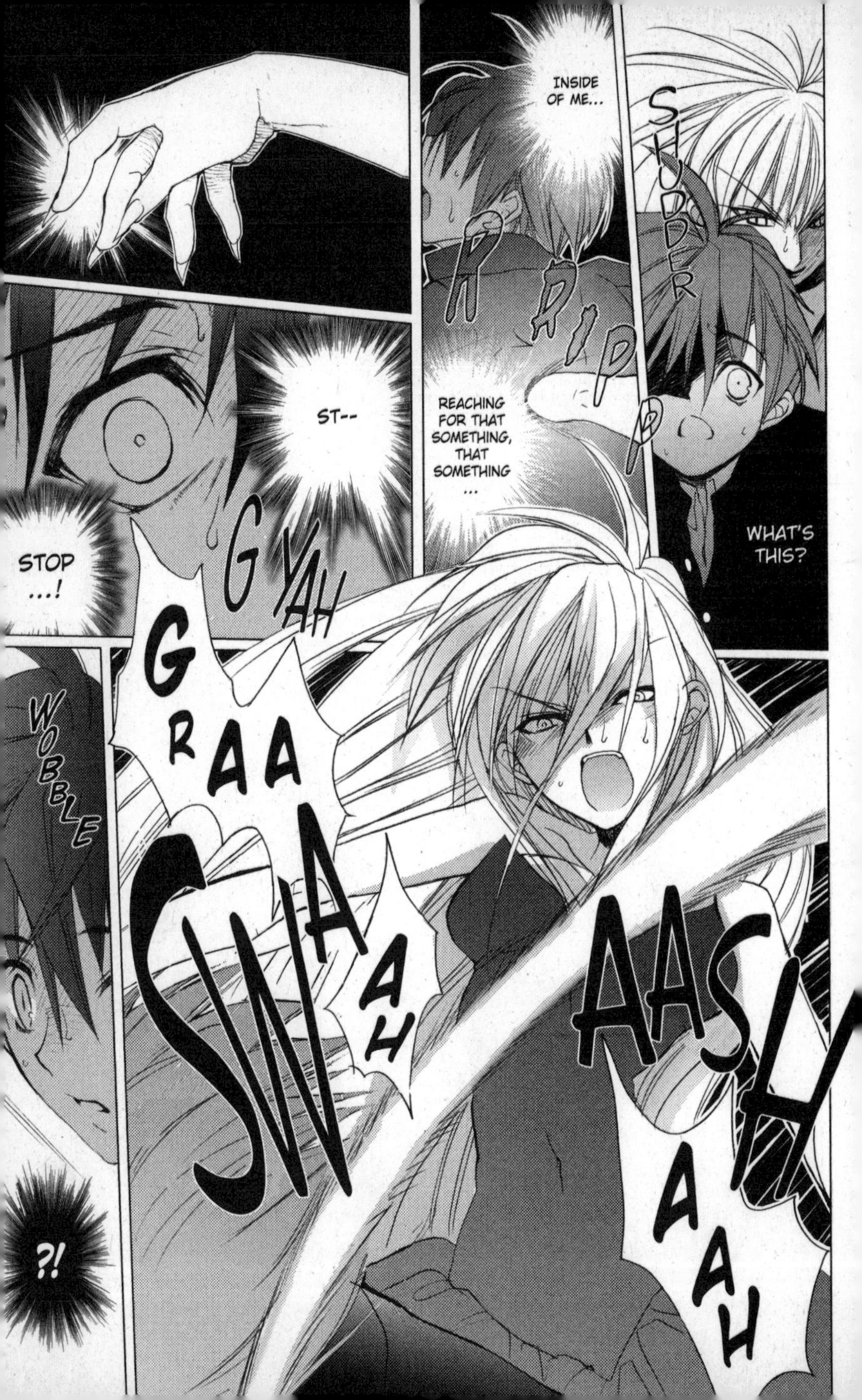
INSIDE OF ME...
SHUDDER
RRIPP
REACHING FOR THAT SOMETHING, THAT SOMETHING ...
WHAT'S THIS?
ST--
STOP ...!
GYAH
GRAAAAH
SWAASH
AAAH
WOBBLE
?!

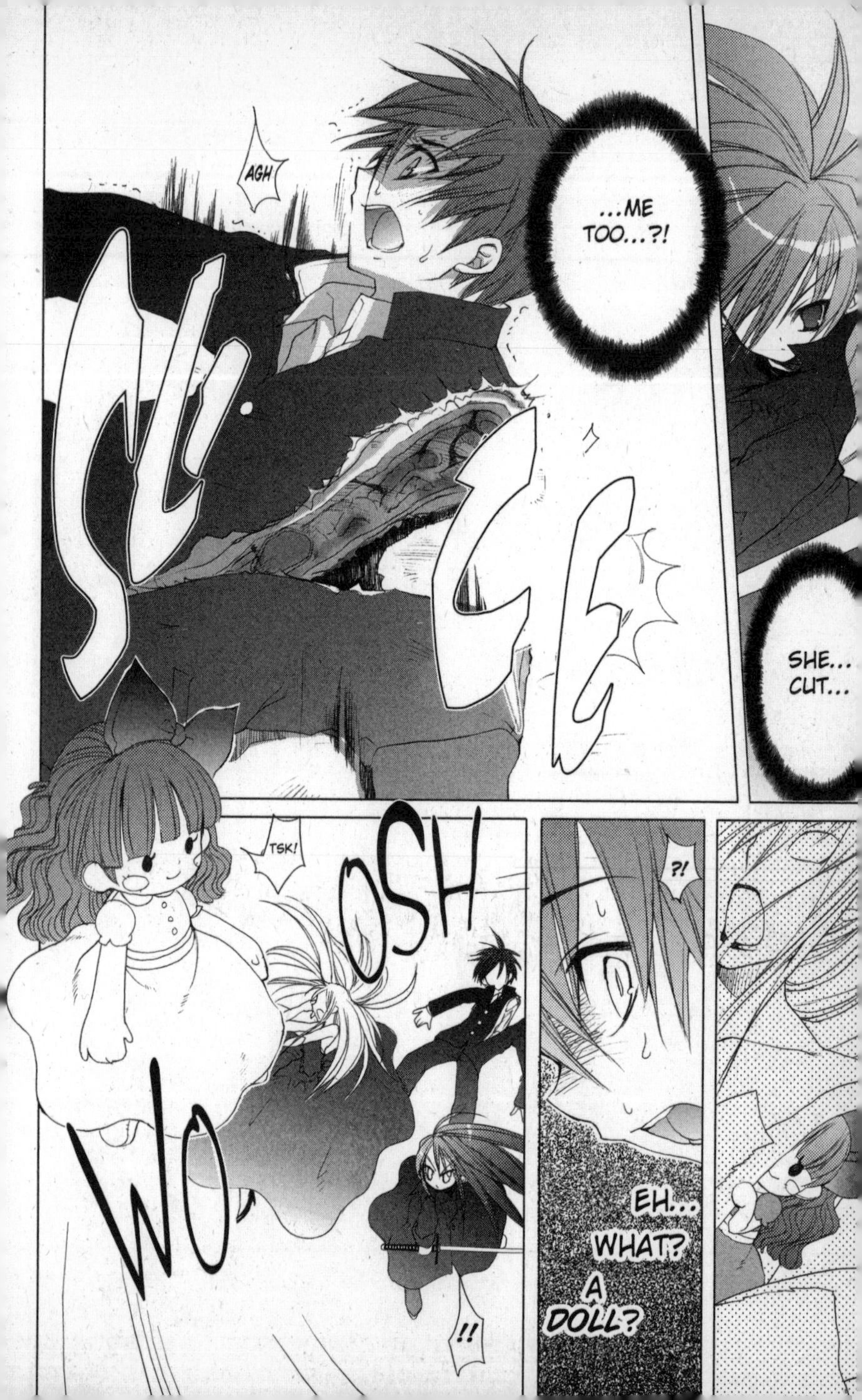
SHE...
CUT...
...ME TOO...?!
AGH
?!
EH... WHAT? A DOLL?
TSK!
WOOSH
!!

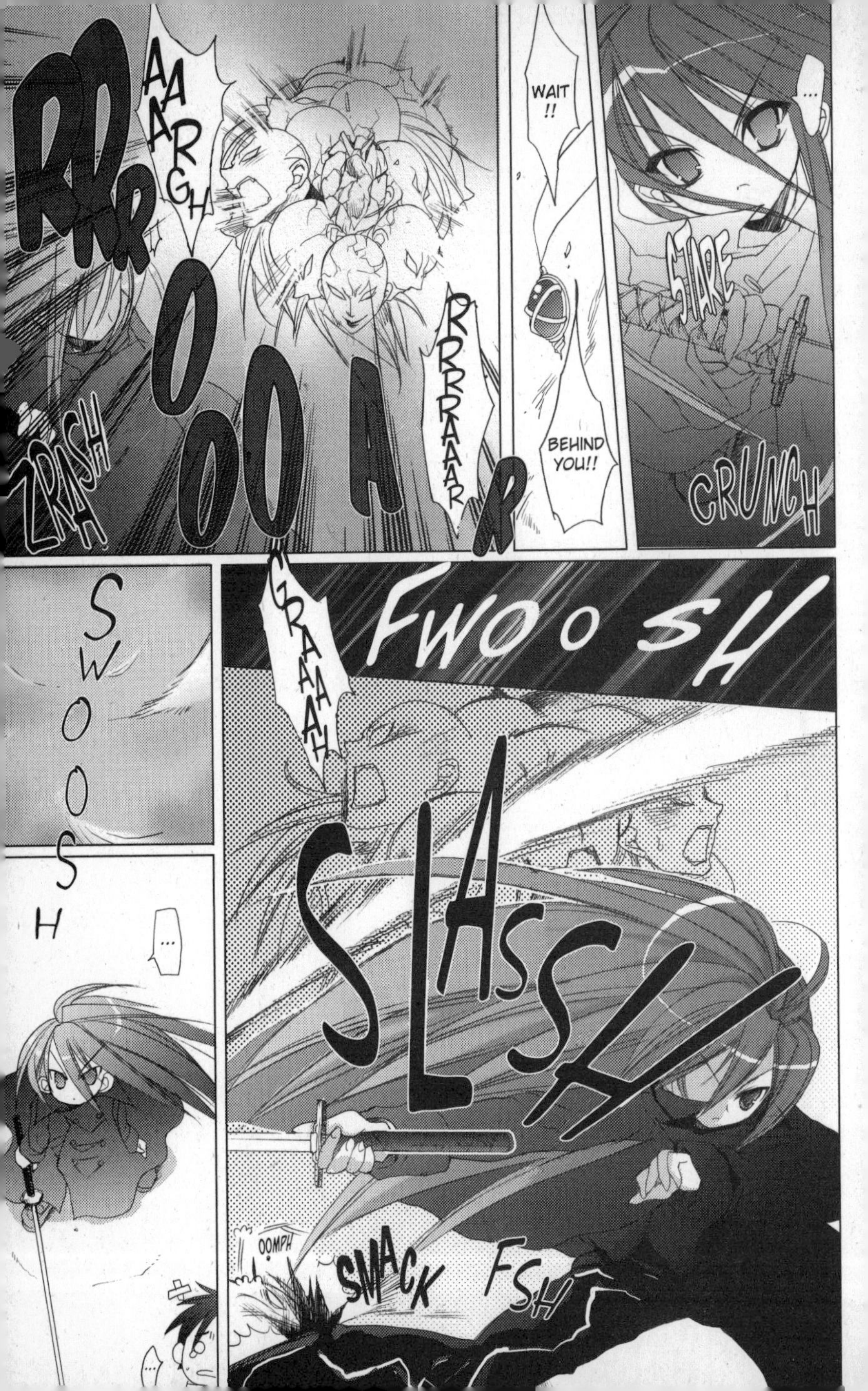
...
STARE
CRUNCH
WAIT !!
BEHIND YOU!!
AAARGH
RRROOOAR
RRRRRAAAR
ZRASH
FWOOSH
GRAAAAH
SLASH
FSH
SMACK
OOMPH
SWOOSH
...
...

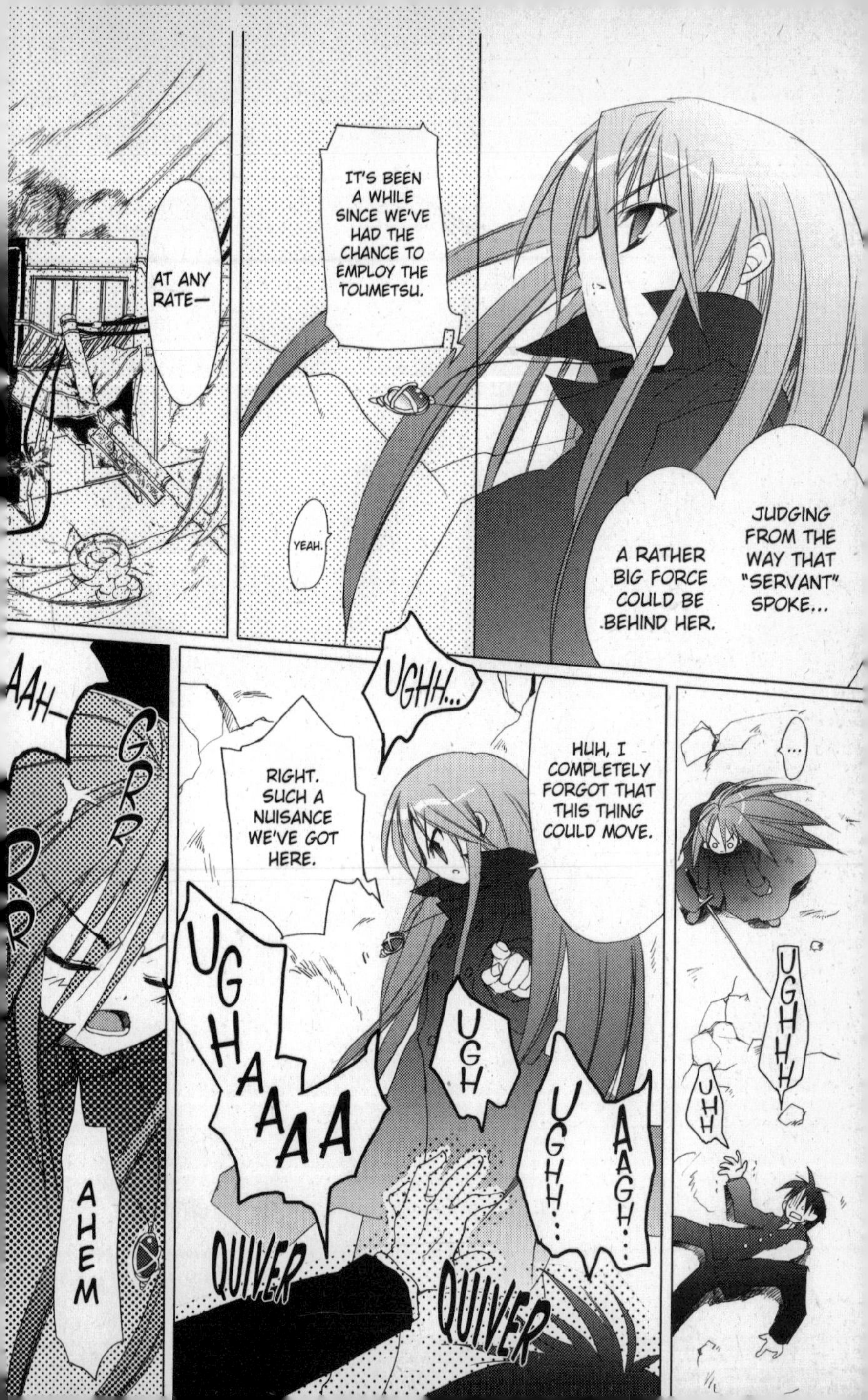
JUDGING FROM THE WAY THAT "SERVANT" SPOKE...
A RATHER BIG FORCE COULD BE BEHIND HER.
IT'S BEEN A WHILE SINCE WE'VE HAD THE CHANCE TO EMPLOY THE TOUMETSU.
YEAH.
AT ANY RATE—
...
UGHHH
UHH
HUH, I COMPLETELY FORGOT THAT THIS THING COULD MOVE.
UGHH...
RIGHT. SUCH A NUISANCE WE'VE GOT HERE.
AAGH...
UGHH...
UGH
UGHAAAAA
QUIVER
QUIVER
AAH—
GRR
RR
AHEM

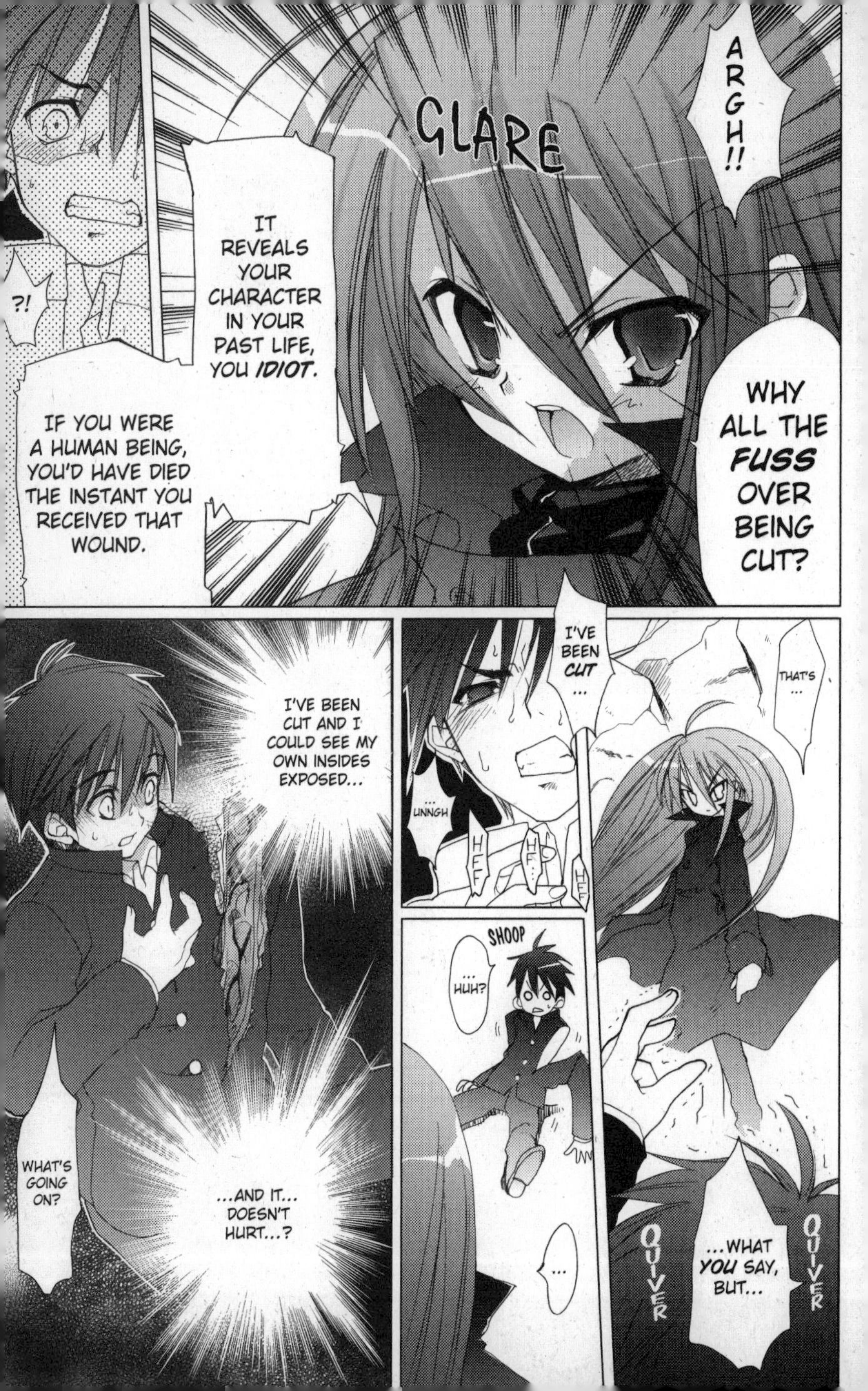
ARGH!!
GLARE
WHY ALL THE *FUSS* OVER BEING CUT?
IT REVEALS YOUR CHARACTER IN YOUR PAST LIFE, YOU *IDIOT*.
IF YOU WERE A HUMAN BEING, YOU'D HAVE DIED THE INSTANT YOU RECEIVED THAT WOUND.
?!
THAT'S ...
I'VE BEEN *CUT* ...
... UNNGH
HFF
HF...
HFF
SHOOP
... HUH?
QUIVER
...WHAT *YOU* SAY, BUT...
QUIVER
...
I'VE BEEN CUT AND I COULD SEE MY OWN INSIDES EXPOSED...
...AND IT... DOESN'T HURT...?
WHAT'S GOING ON?

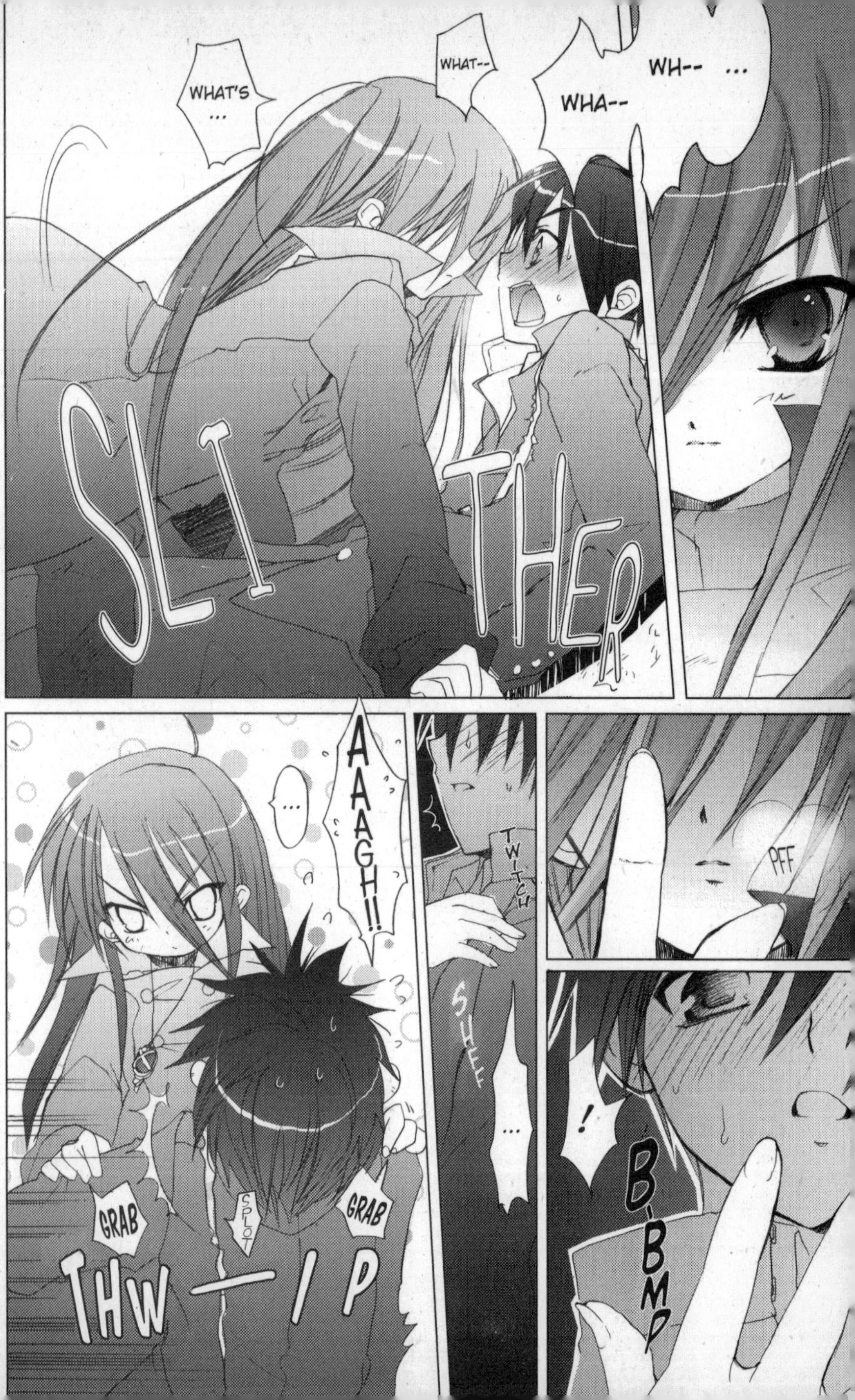
WH-- ...
WHA--
WHAT--
WHAT'S ...
SLITHER
PFF
!
B-BMP
TWITCH
SHEFF
...
AAAAGH!!
...
GRAB
GRAB
SPLOT
THW—IP

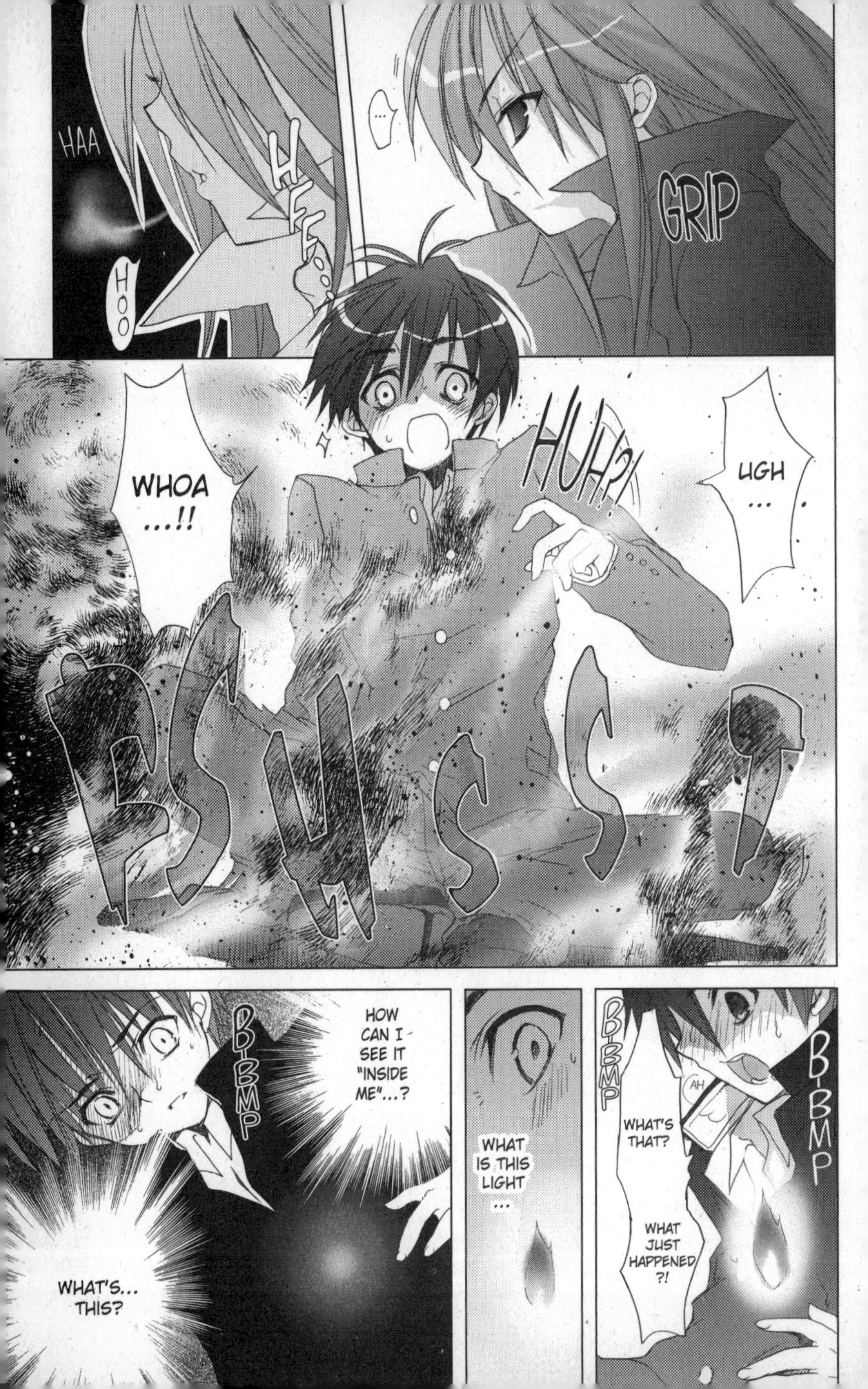

...
GRIP
HFF...
HAA
HOO
UGH ...
HUH?!
WHOA ...!!
B-BMP
AH
B-BMP
WHAT'S THAT?
WHAT JUST HAPPENED ?!
WHAT IS THIS LIGHT ...
B-BMP
HOW CAN I SEE IT "INSIDE ME"...?
WHAT'S... THIS?

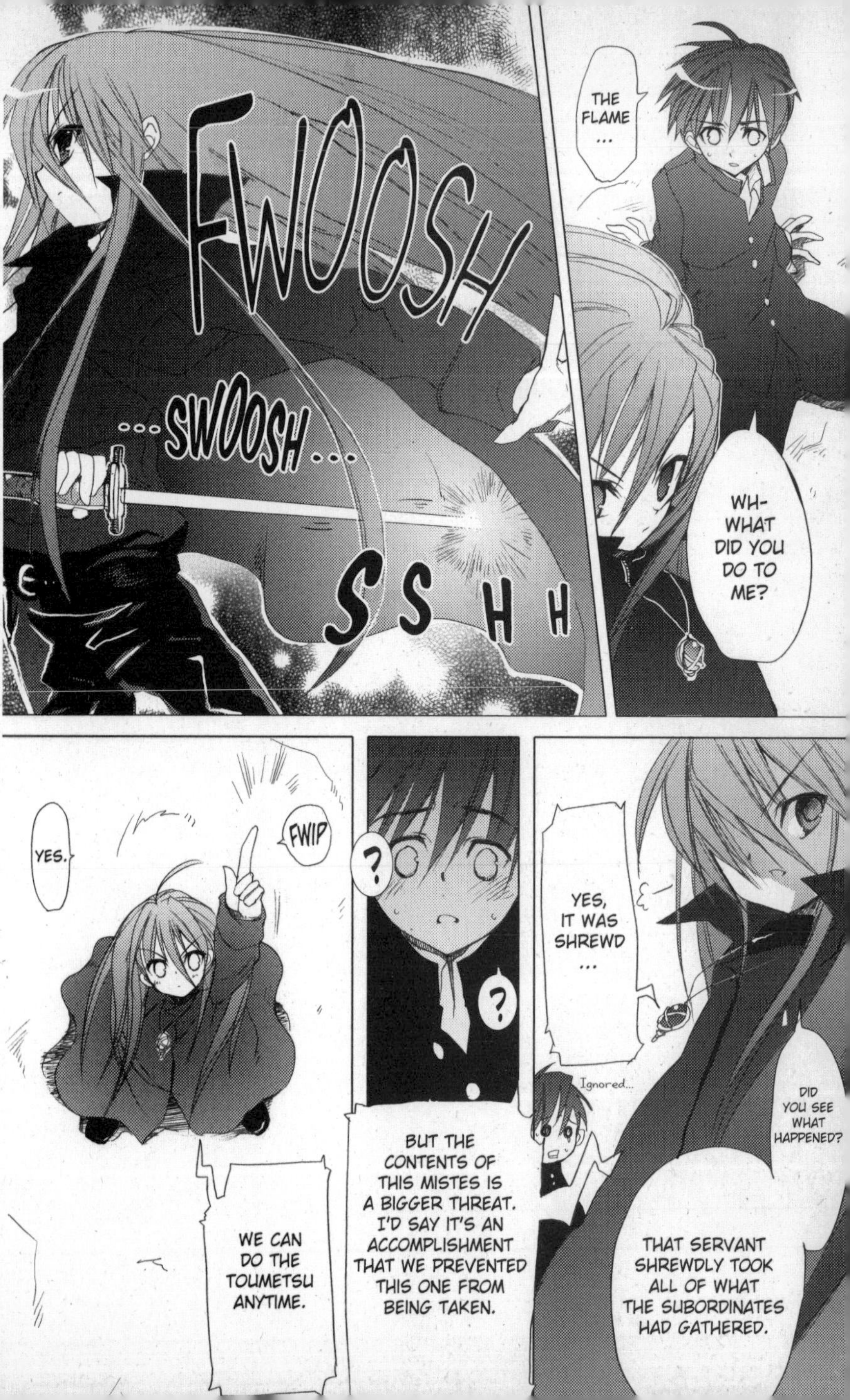
THE FLAME ...
WH- WHAT DID YOU DO TO ME?
FWOOSH
...SWOOSH...
SSHH
DID YOU SEE WHAT HAPPENED?
THAT SERVANT SHREWDLY TOOK ALL OF WHAT THE SUBORDINATES HAD GATHERED.
YES, IT WAS SHREWD ...
Ignored...
?
?
BUT THE CONTENTS OF THIS MISTES IS A BIGGER THREAT. I'D SAY IT'S AN ACCOMPLISHMENT THAT WE PREVENTED THIS ONE FROM BEING TAKEN.
FWIP
YES.
WE CAN DO THE TOUMETSU ANYTIME.

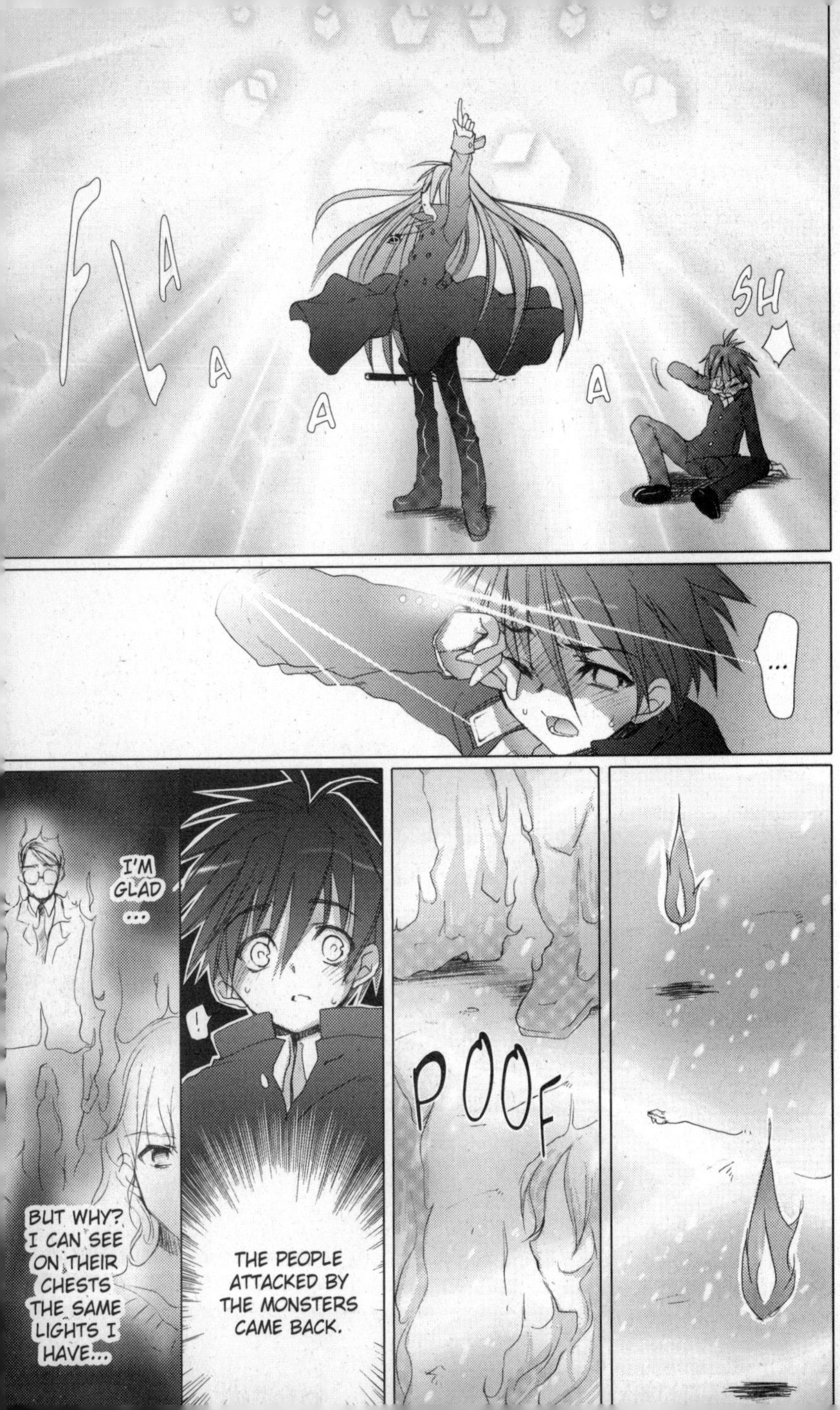

SH
FLAAAA
...
POOF
!
THE PEOPLE ATTACKED BY THE MONSTERS CAME BACK.
I'M GLAD...
BUT WHY? I CAN SEE ON THEIR CHESTS THE SAME LIGHTS I HAVE...

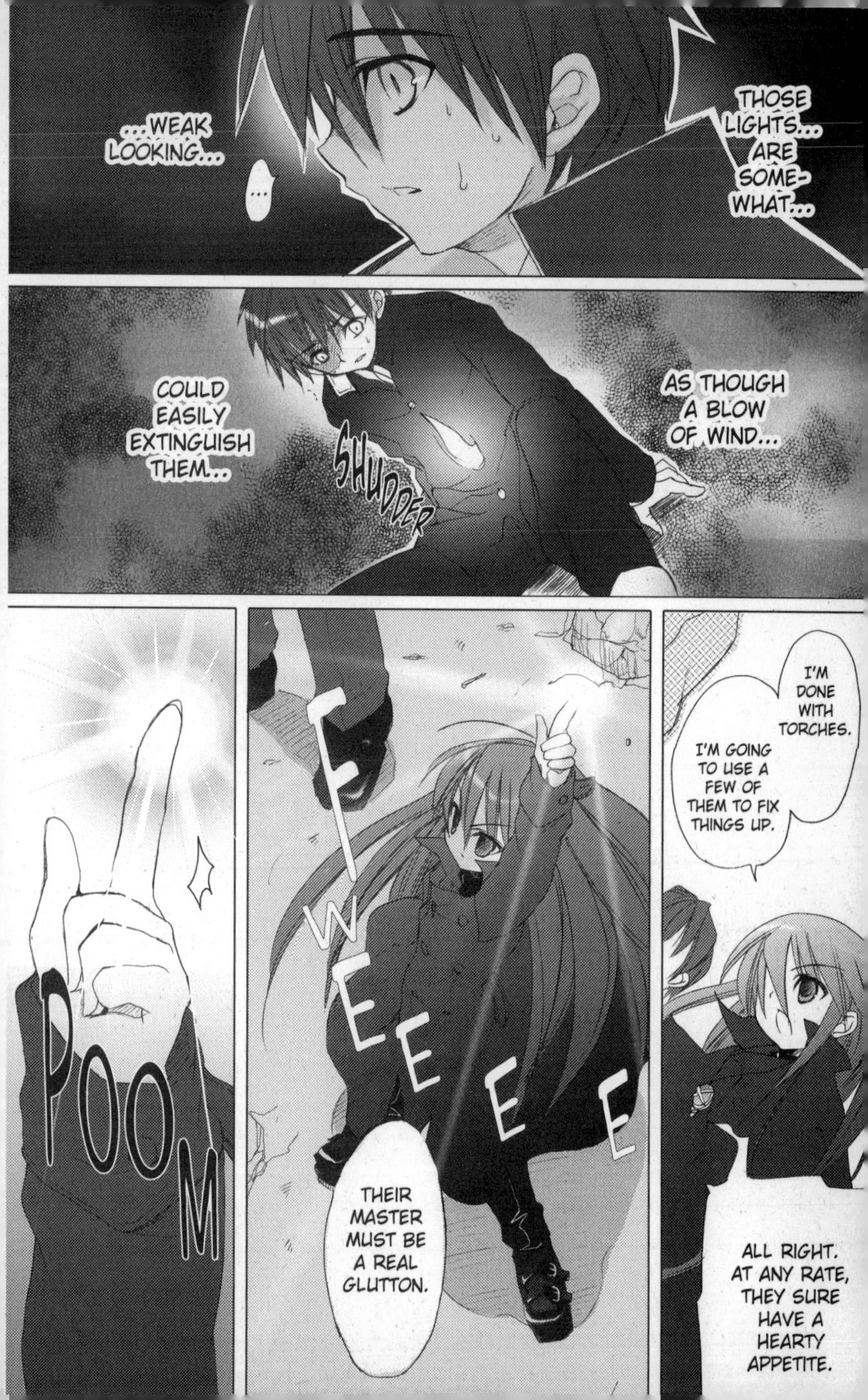
THOSE LIGHTS... ARE SOME-WHAT...
...
...WEAK LOOKING...
AS THOUGH A BLOW OF WIND...
SHUDDER
COULD EASILY EXTINGUISH THEM...
I'M DONE WITH TORCHES.
I'M GOING TO USE A FEW OF THEM TO FIX THINGS UP.
ALL RIGHT. AT ANY RATE, THEY SURE HAVE A HEARTY APPETITE.
FWEEEEE
THEIR MASTER MUST BE A REAL GLUTTON.
POOM

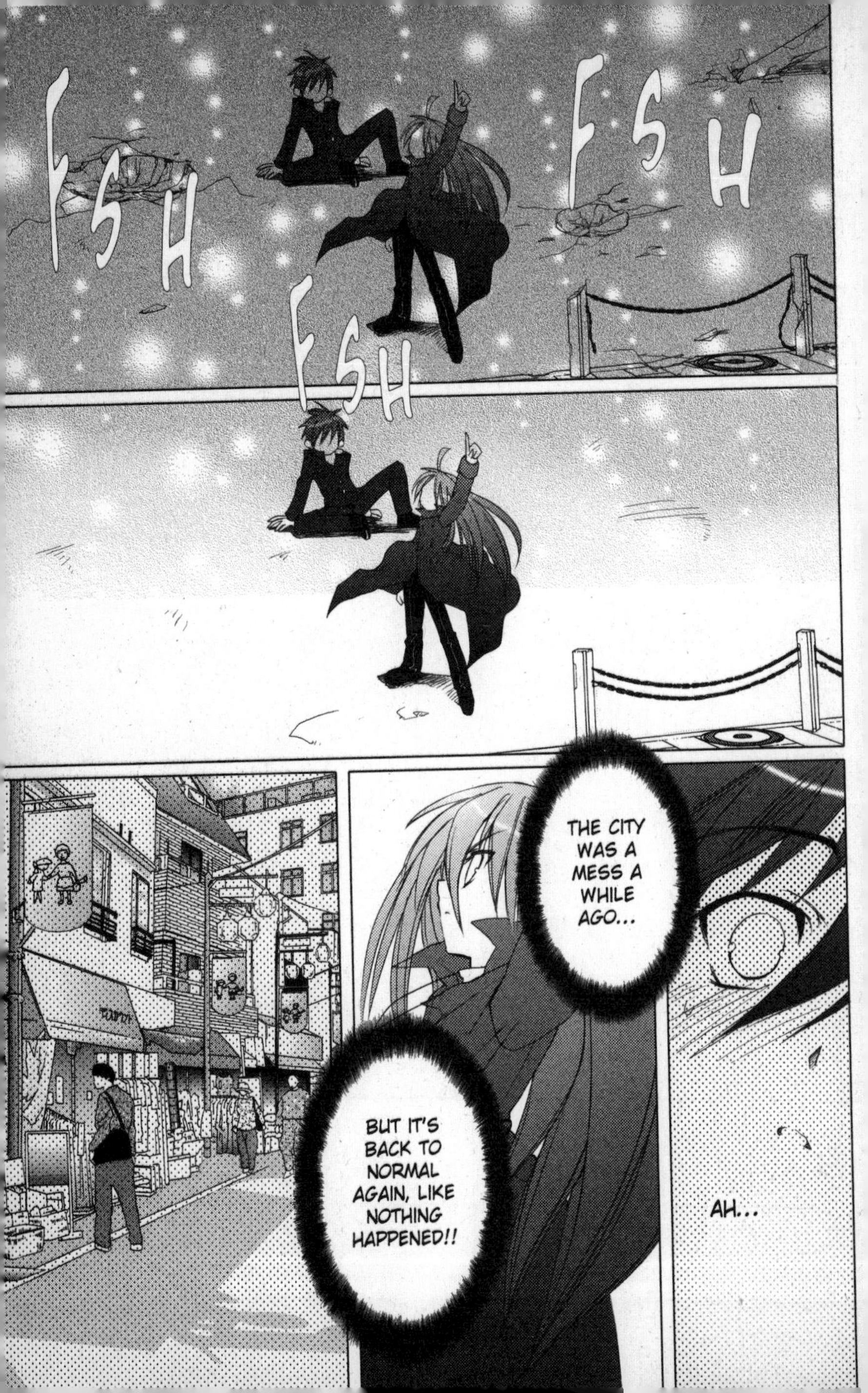
FSH
FSH
FSH
AH...
THE CITY WAS A MESS A WHILE AGO...
BUT IT'S BACK TO NORMAL AGAIN, LIKE NOTHING HAPPENED!!

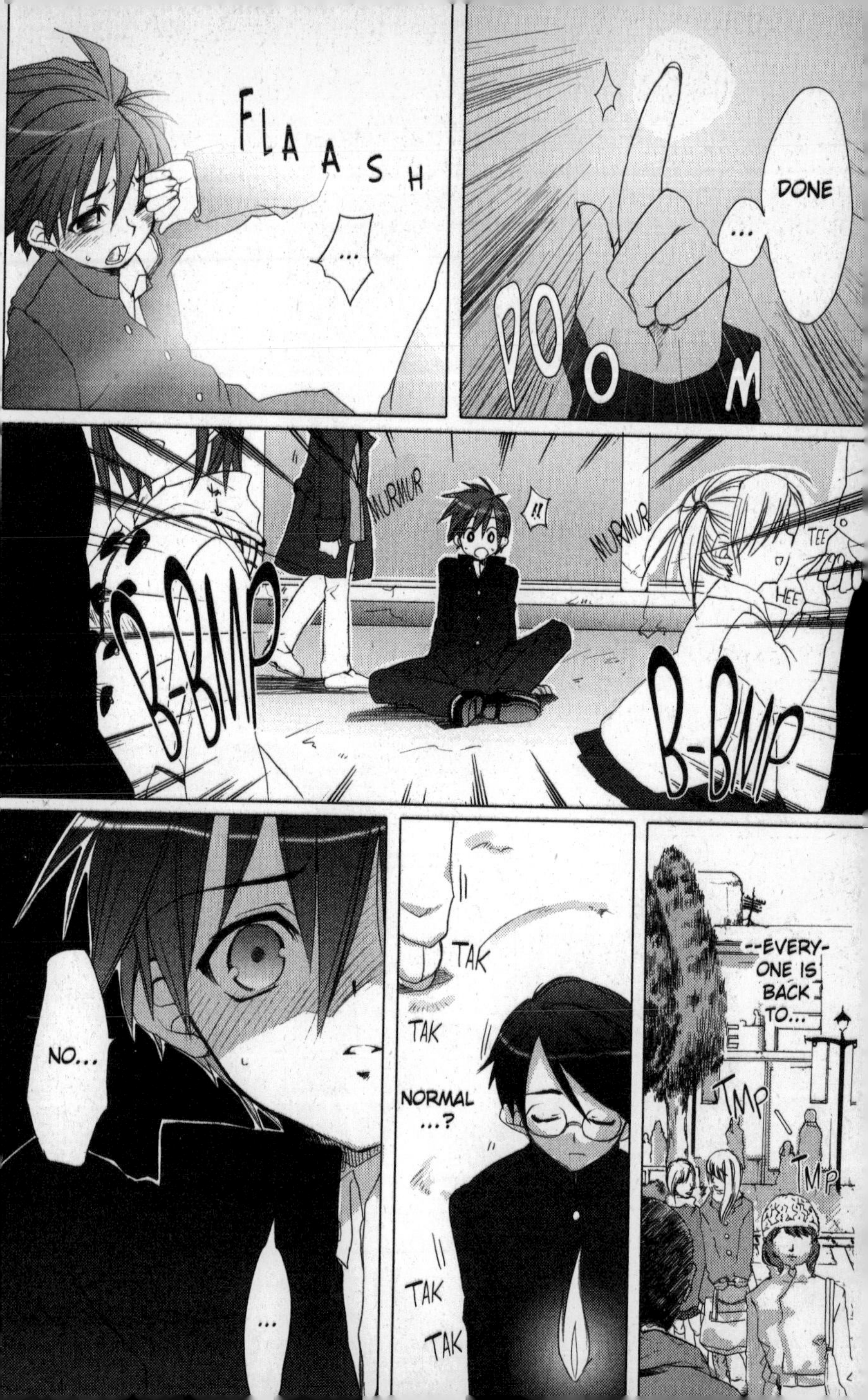
DONE
...
POOM
FLAASH
...
TEE HEE
MURMUR
!!
MURMUR
B-BMP
B-BMP
--EVERY-ONE IS BACK TO...
TMP
TMP
TAK
TAK
NORMAL ...?
TAK
TAK
NO...
...

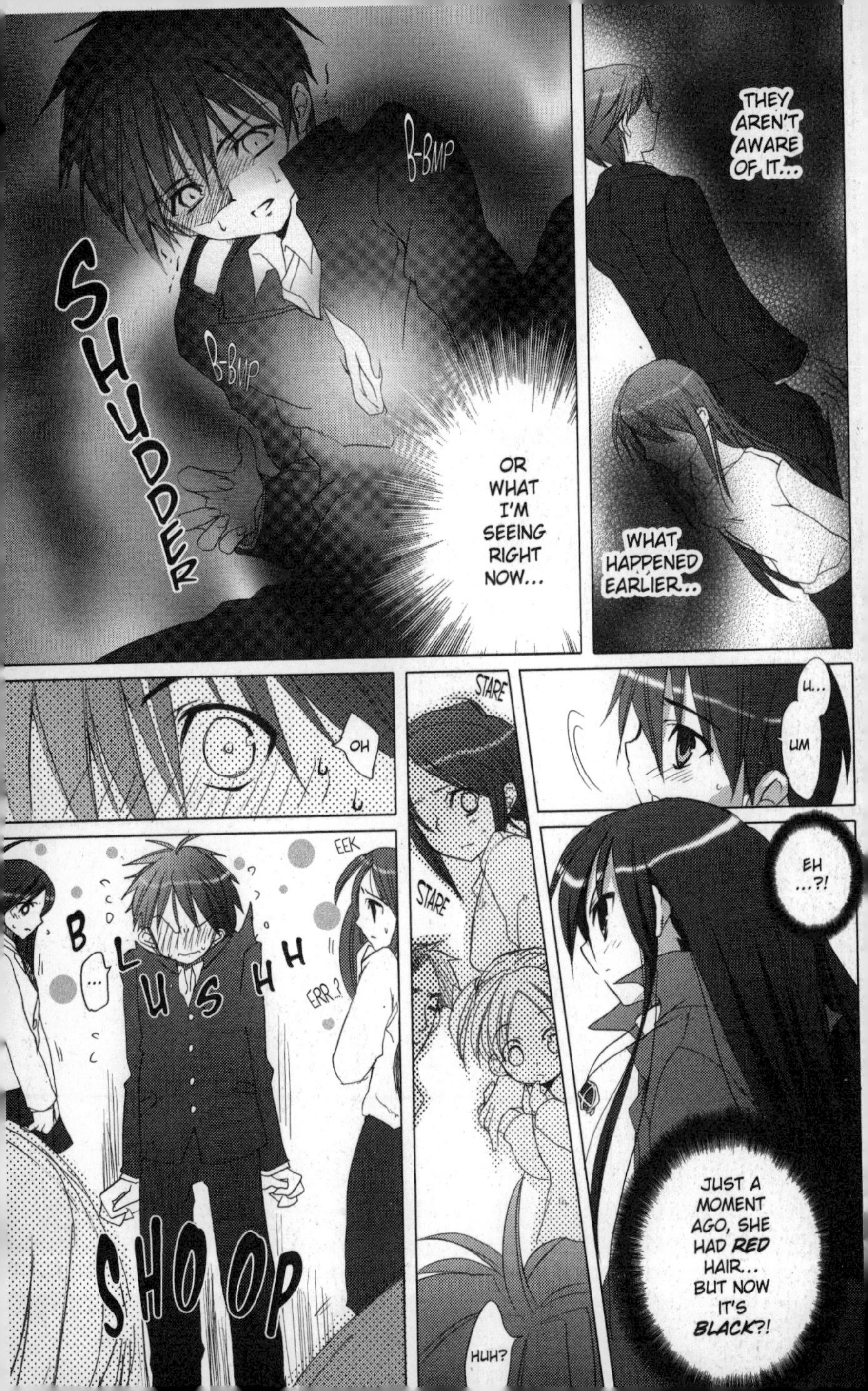
THEY AREN'T AWARE OF IT...
WHAT HAPPENED EARLIER...
B-BMP
B-BMP
SHUDDER
OR WHAT I'M SEEING RIGHT NOW...
U...
UM
EH ...?!
JUST A MOMENT AGO, SHE HAD ***RED*** HAIR... BUT NOW IT'S ***BLACK***?!
STARE
STARE
HUH?
OH
EEK
ERR..?
...
BLUSHH
SHOOP

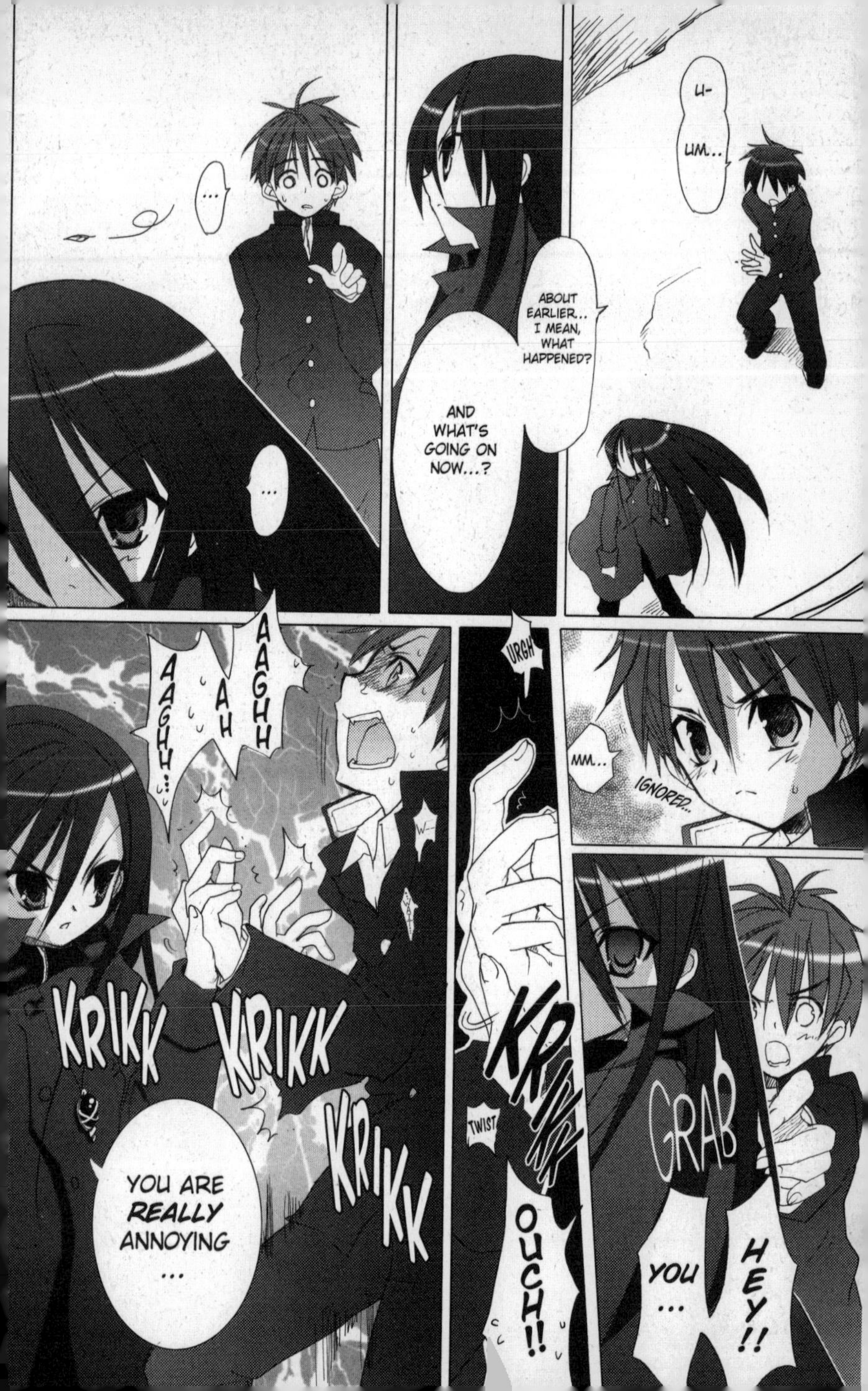
U-
UM...
ABOUT EARLIER... I MEAN, WHAT HAPPENED?
AND WHAT'S GOING ON NOW...?
...
...
MM...
IGNORED...
GRAB
HEY!!
YOU...
URGH
TWIST
OUCH!!
AAGHH
AH
AAGHH!!
W--
KRIKK
KRIKK
KRIKK
YOU ARE *REALLY* ANNOYING...

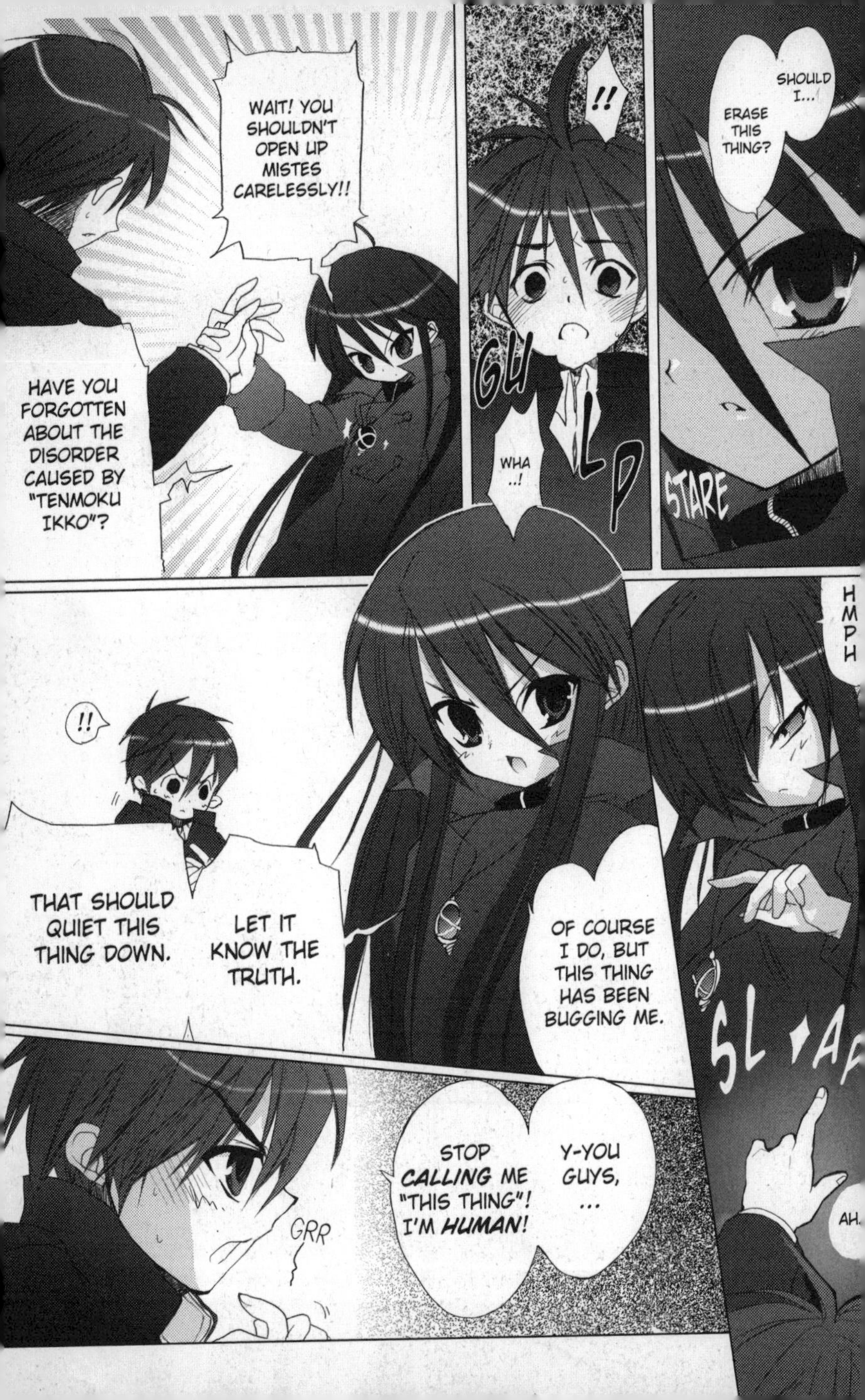
SHOULD I...
ERASE THIS THING?
STARE
!!
GULP
WHA ..!
WAIT! YOU SHOULDN'T OPEN UP MISTES CARELESSLY!!
HAVE YOU FORGOTTEN ABOUT THE DISORDER CAUSED BY "TENMOKU IKKO"?
HMPH
OF COURSE I DO, BUT THIS THING HAS BEEN BUGGING ME.
SLAP
LET IT KNOW THE TRUTH.
THAT SHOULD QUIET THIS THING DOWN.
!!
AH.
Y-YOU GUYS, ...
STOP CALLING ME "THIS THING"! I'M HUMAN!
GRR

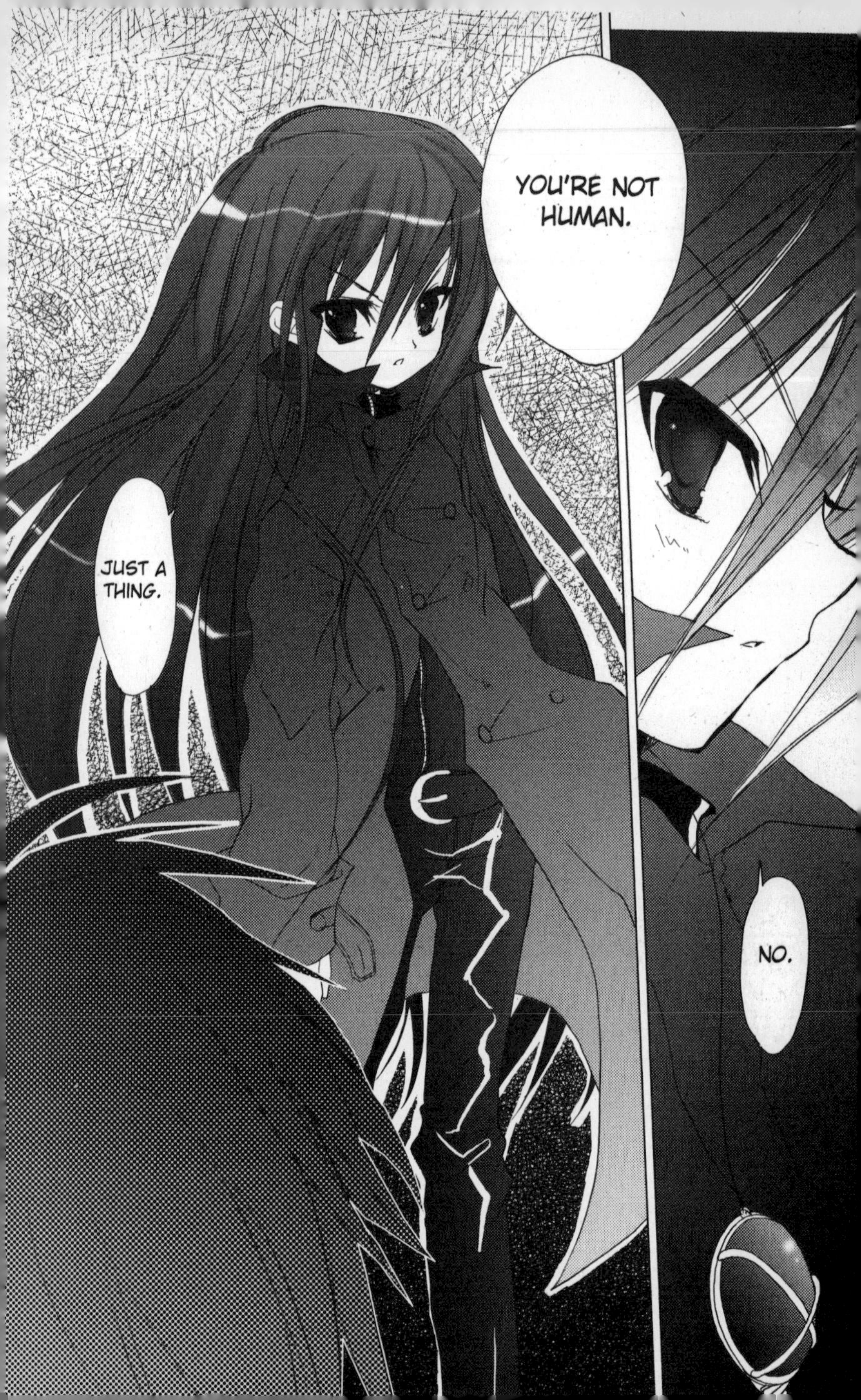
YOU'RE NOT HUMAN.
JUST A THING.
NO.

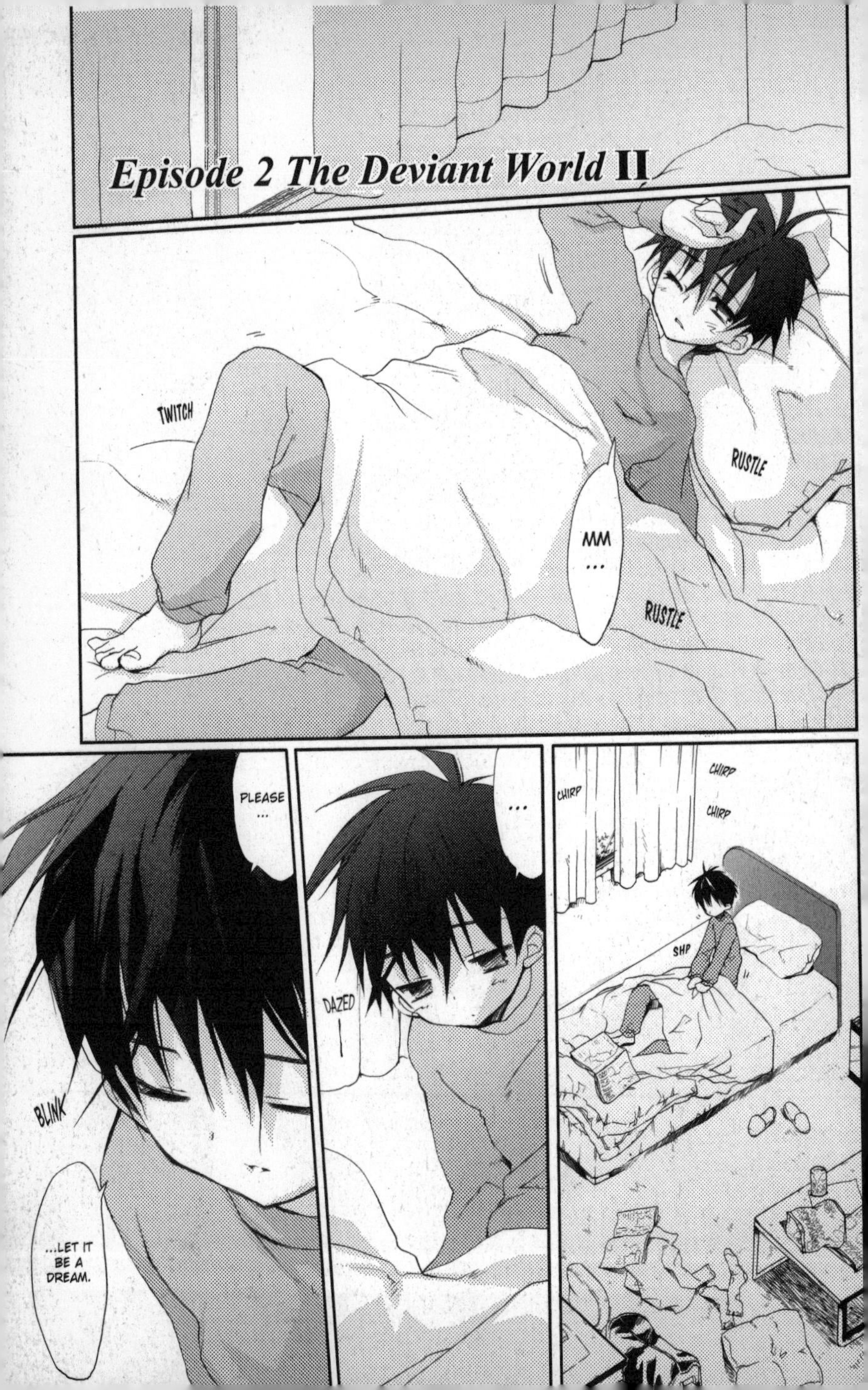
Episode 2 The Deviant World II
RUSTLE
MM...
RUSTLE
TWITCH
CHIRP
CHIRP
CHIRP
SHP
...
DAZED
PLEASE...
BLINK
...LET IT BE A DREAM.

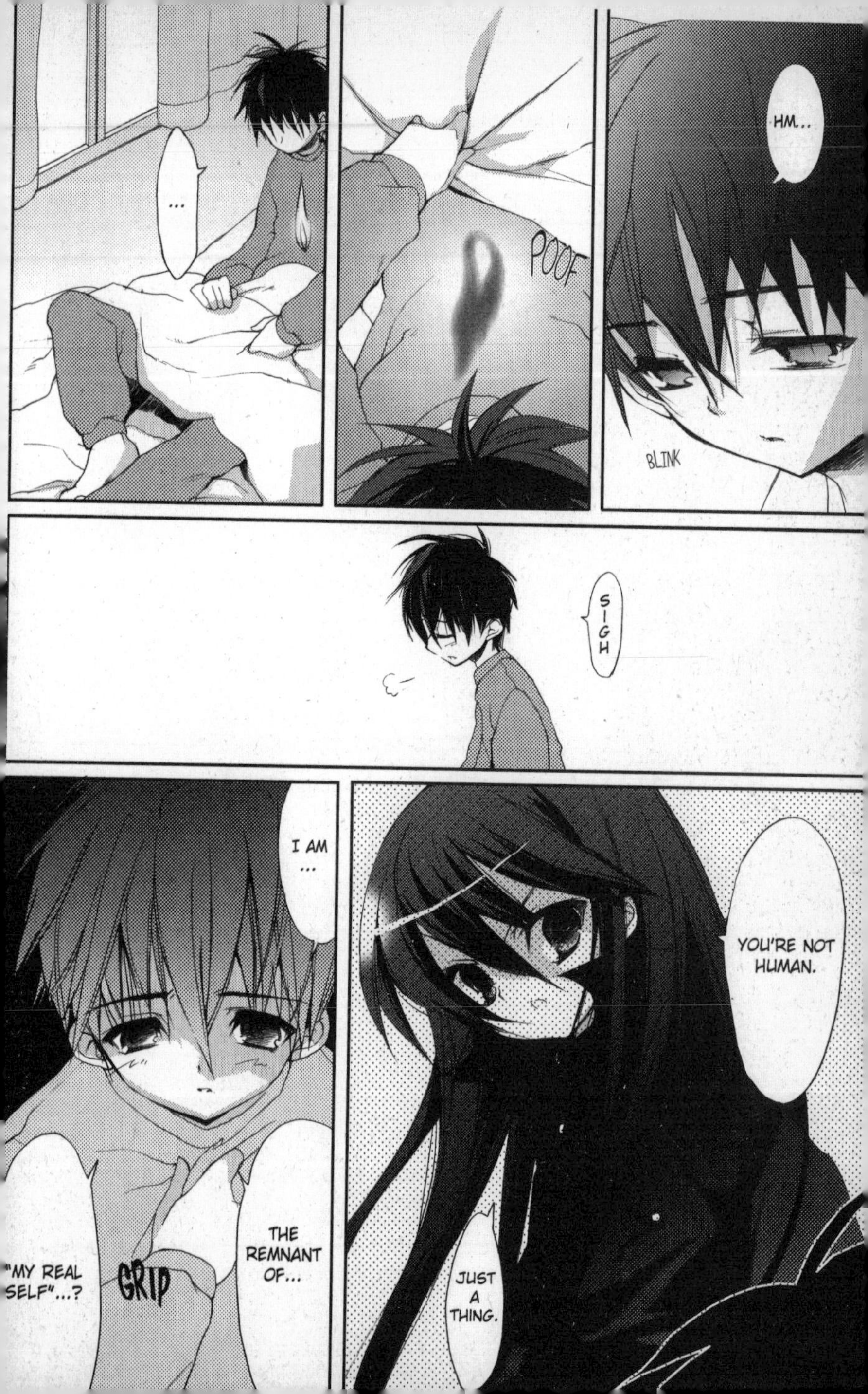
HM...
BLINK
POOF
...
SIGH
YOU'RE NOT HUMAN.
JUST A THING.
I AM ...
THE REMNANT OF...
GRIP
"MY REAL SELF"...?

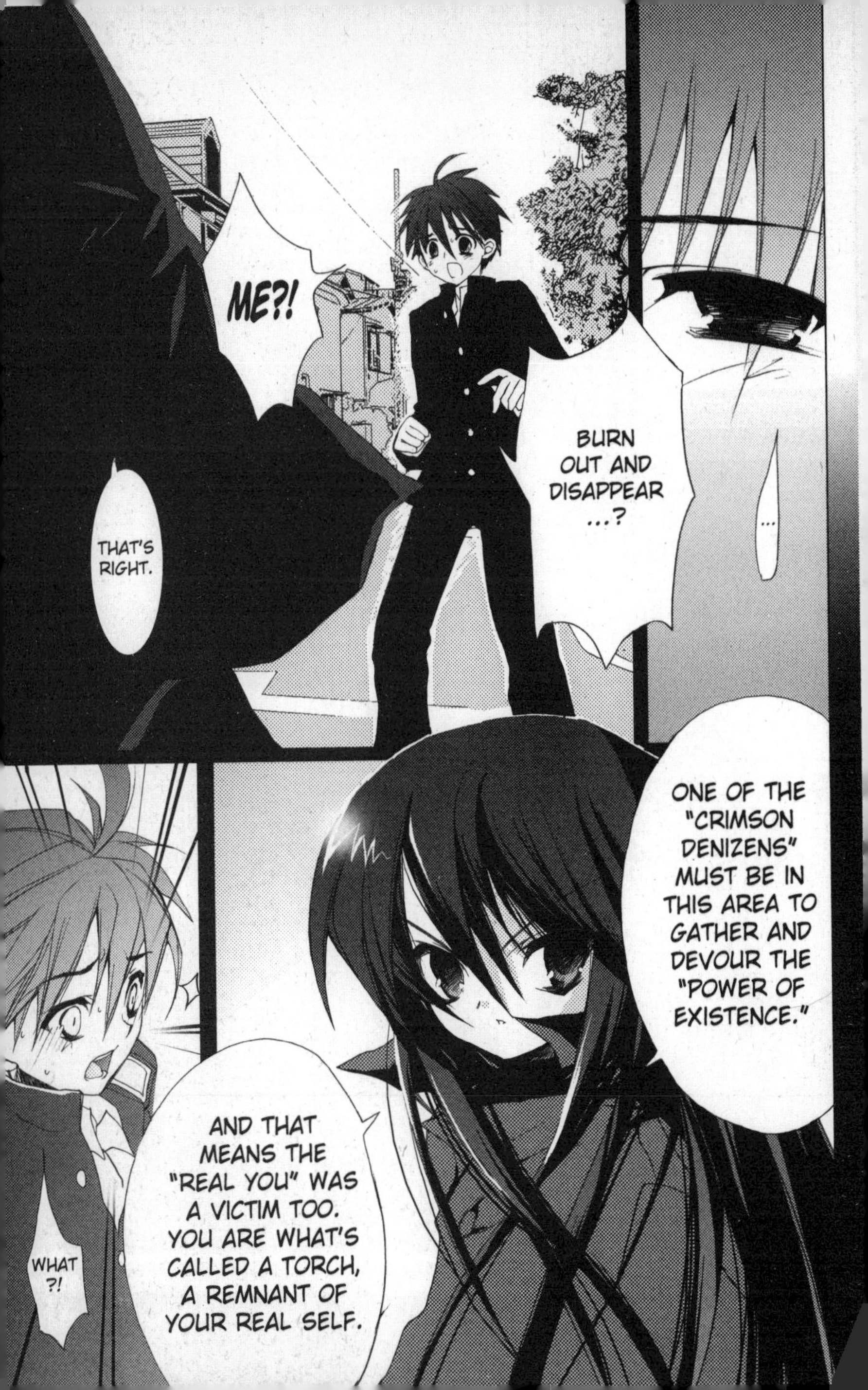
BURN OUT AND DISAPPEAR ...?
...
ME?!
THAT'S RIGHT.
ONE OF THE "CRIMSON DENIZENS" MUST BE IN THIS AREA TO GATHER AND DEVOUR THE "POWER OF EXISTENCE."
AND THAT MEANS THE "REAL YOU" WAS A VICTIM TOO. YOU ARE WHAT'S CALLED A TORCH, A REMNANT OF YOUR REAL SELF.
WHAT ?!

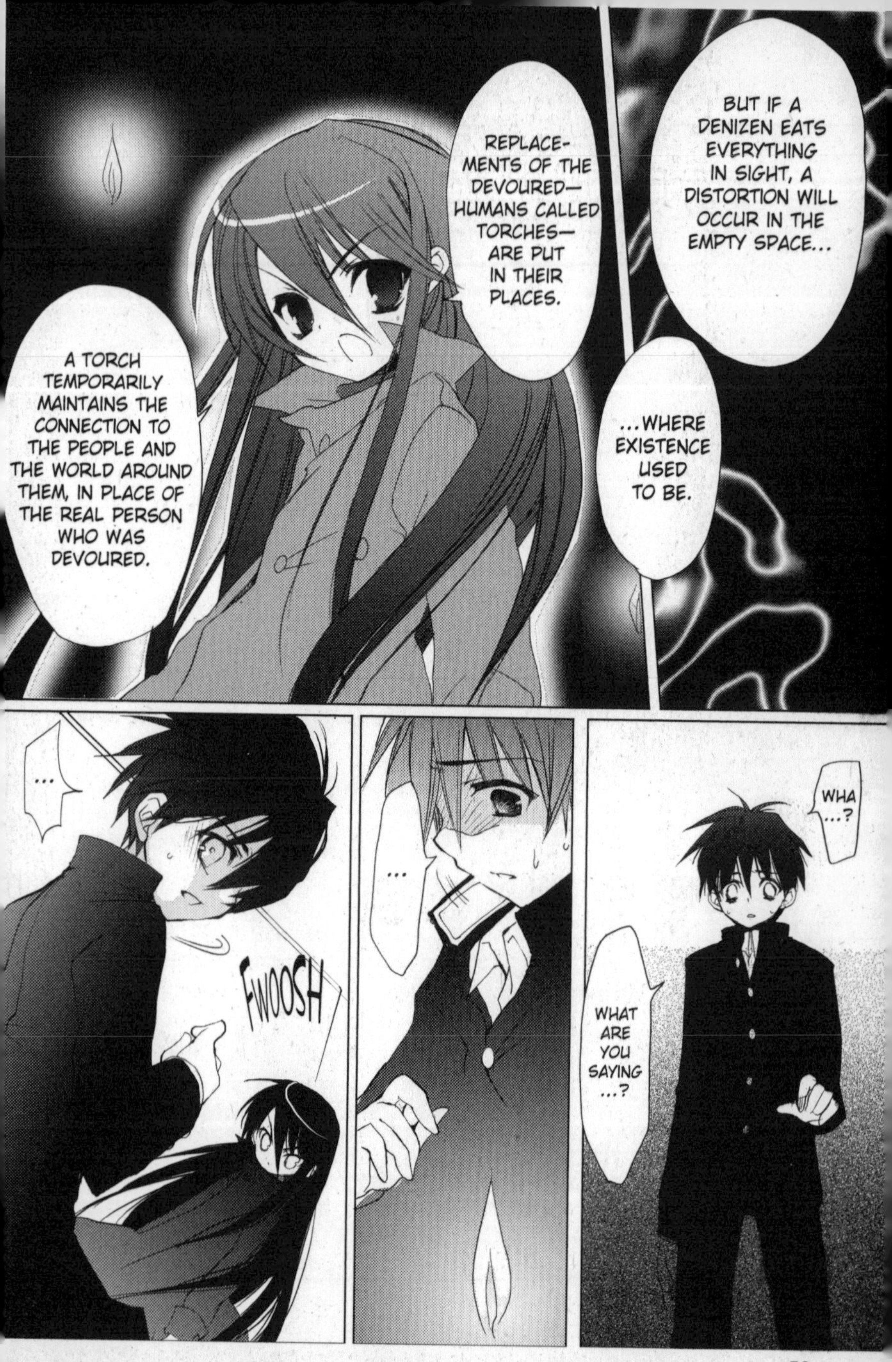
BUT IF A DENIZEN EATS EVERYTHING IN SIGHT, A DISTORTION WILL OCCUR IN THE EMPTY SPACE...
...WHERE EXISTENCE USED TO BE.
REPLACEMENTS OF THE DEVOURED—HUMANS CALLED TORCHES—ARE PUT IN THEIR PLACES.
A TORCH TEMPORARILY MAINTAINS THE CONNECTION TO THE PEOPLE AND THE WORLD AROUND THEM, IN PLACE OF THE REAL PERSON WHO WAS DEVOURED.
WHA ...?
WHAT ARE YOU SAYING ...?
...
...
FWOOSH

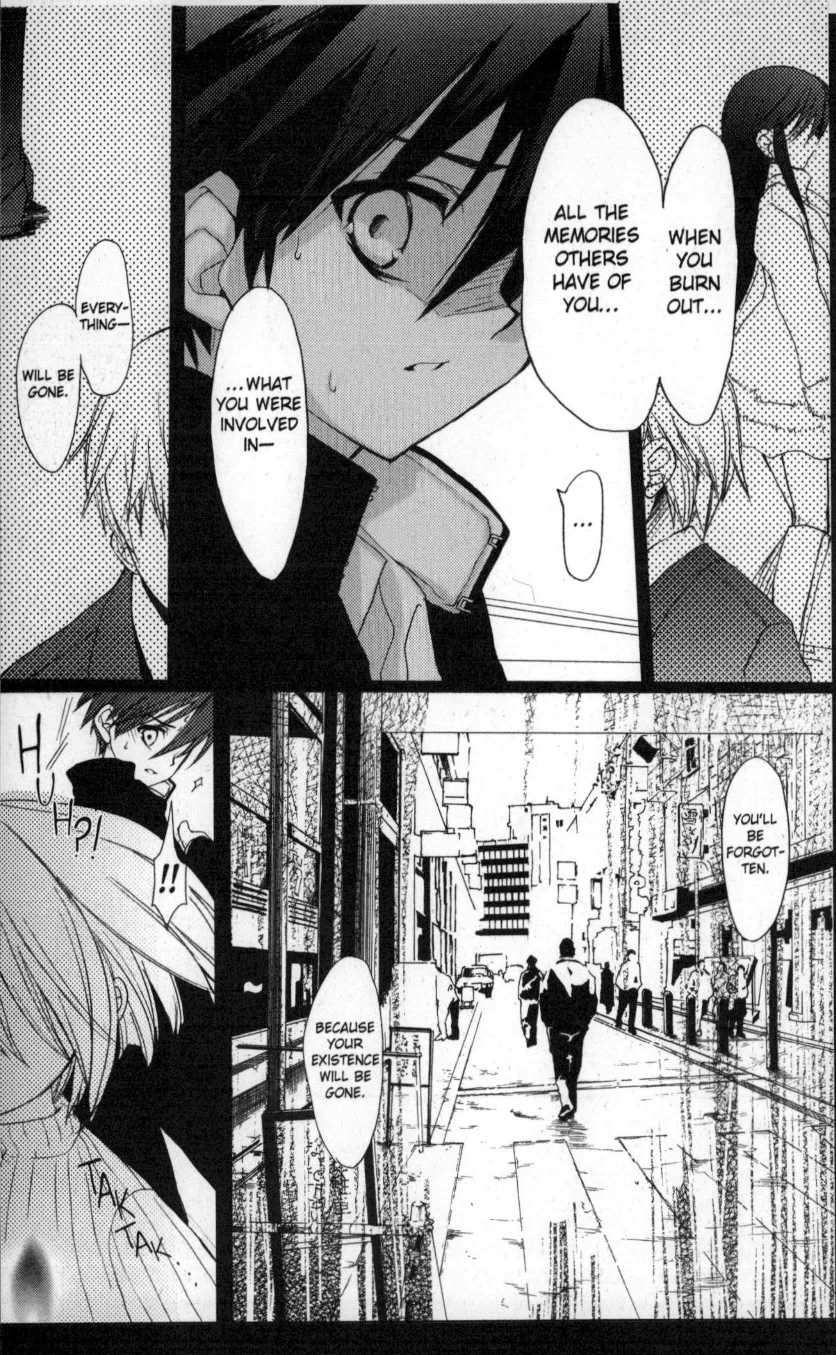
WHEN YOU BURN OUT...
ALL THE MEMORIES OTHERS HAVE OF YOU...
...
...WHAT YOU WERE INVOLVED IN—
EVERY-THING—
WILL BE GONE.
YOU'LL BE FORGOT-TEN.
BECAUSE YOUR EXISTENCE WILL BE GONE.
HUH?!
!!
TAK TAK...

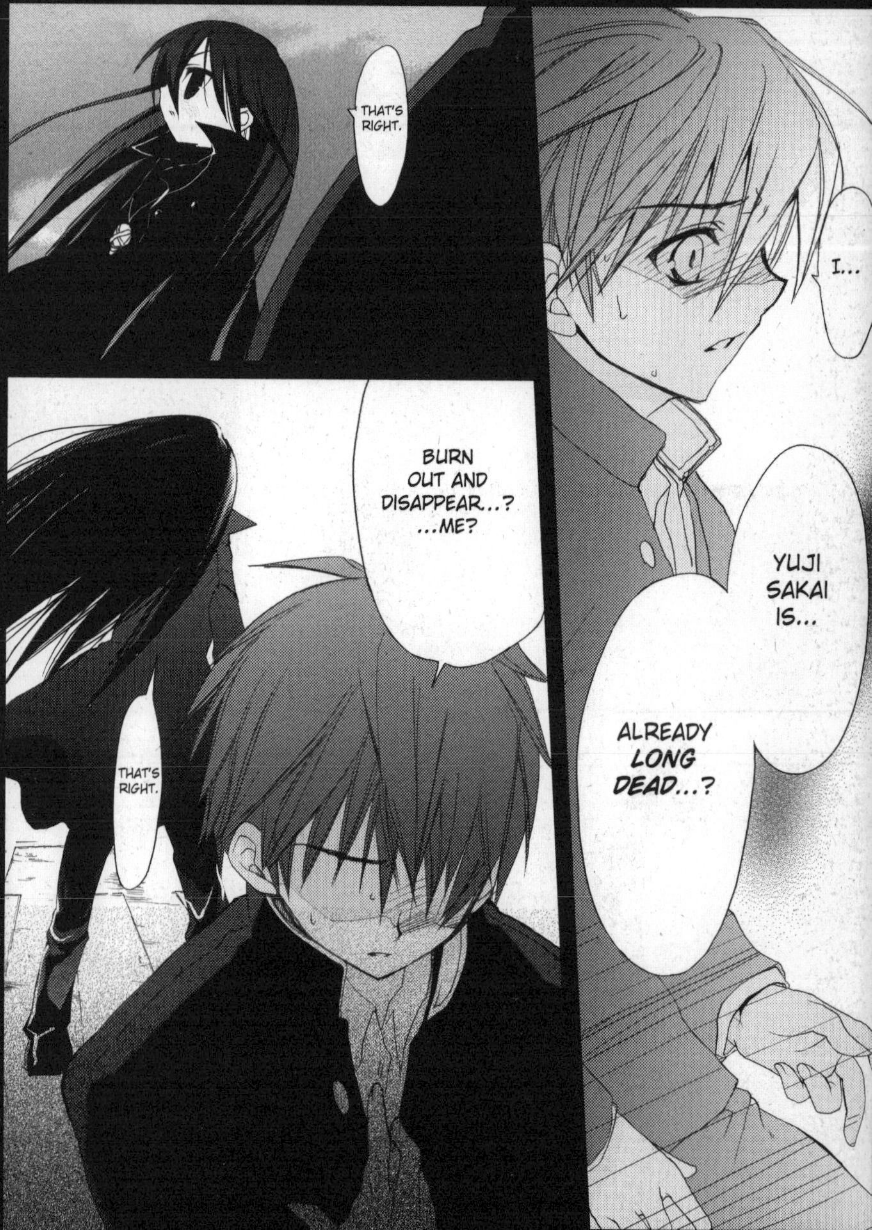
I...
YUJI SAKAI IS...
ALREADY LONG DEAD...?
THAT'S RIGHT.
BURN OUT AND DISAPPEAR...? ...ME?
THAT'S RIGHT.

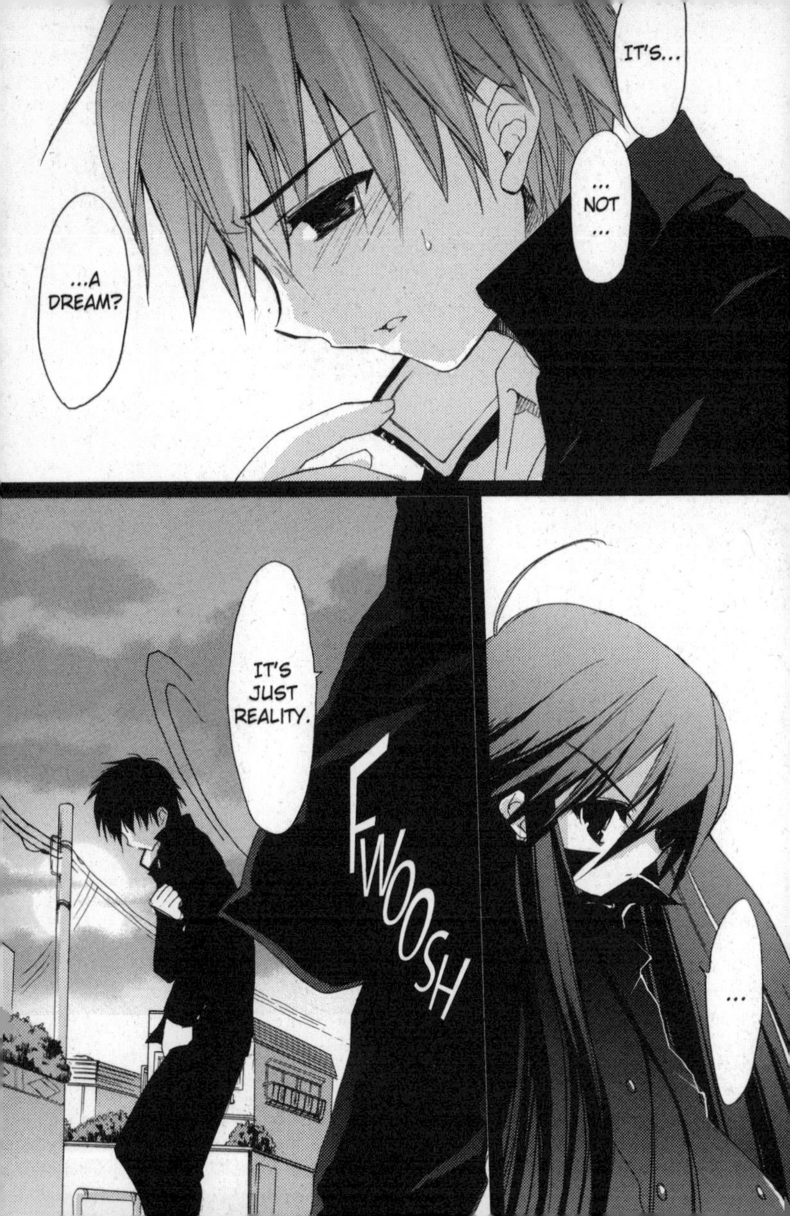
IT'S...
...NOT...
...A DREAM?
...
IT'S JUST REALITY.
FWOOSH

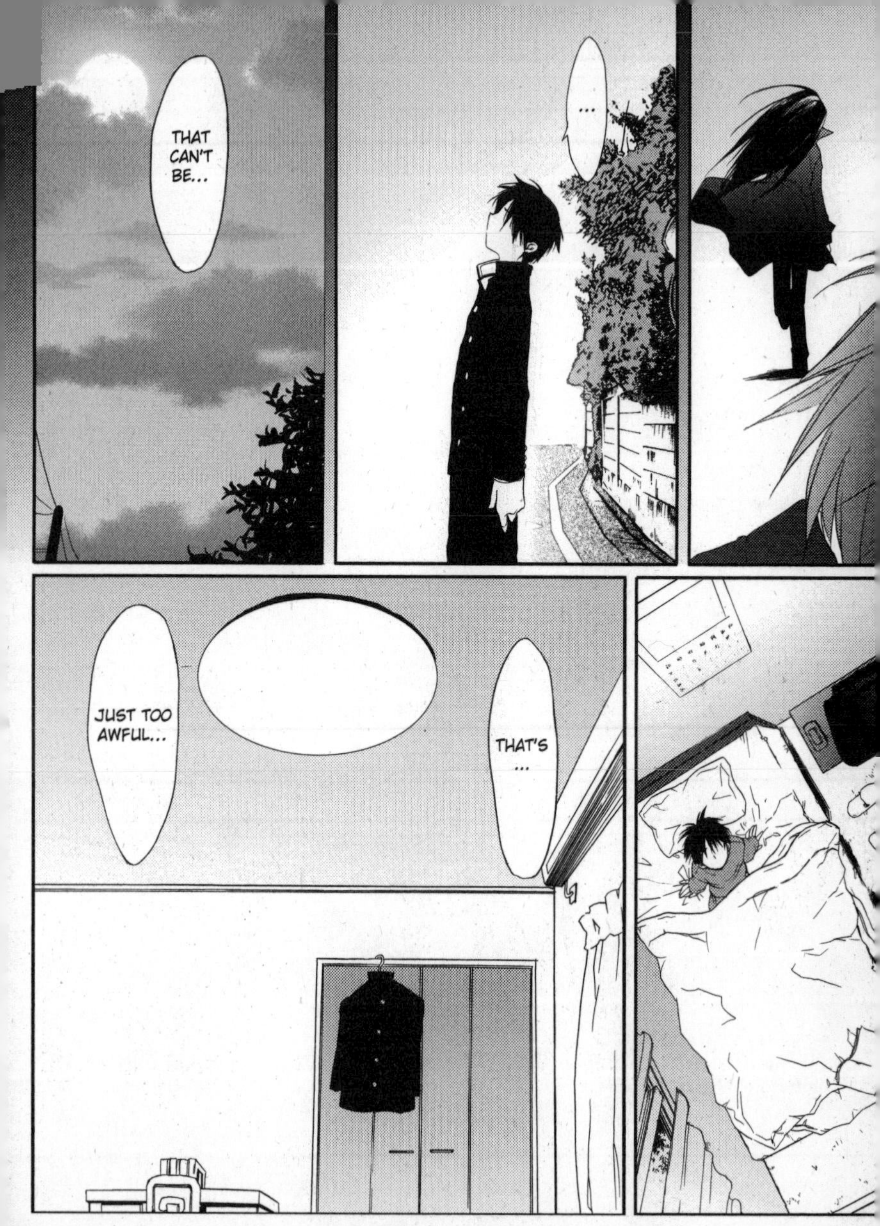
...
THAT CAN'T BE...
THAT'S ...
JUST TOO AWFUL...

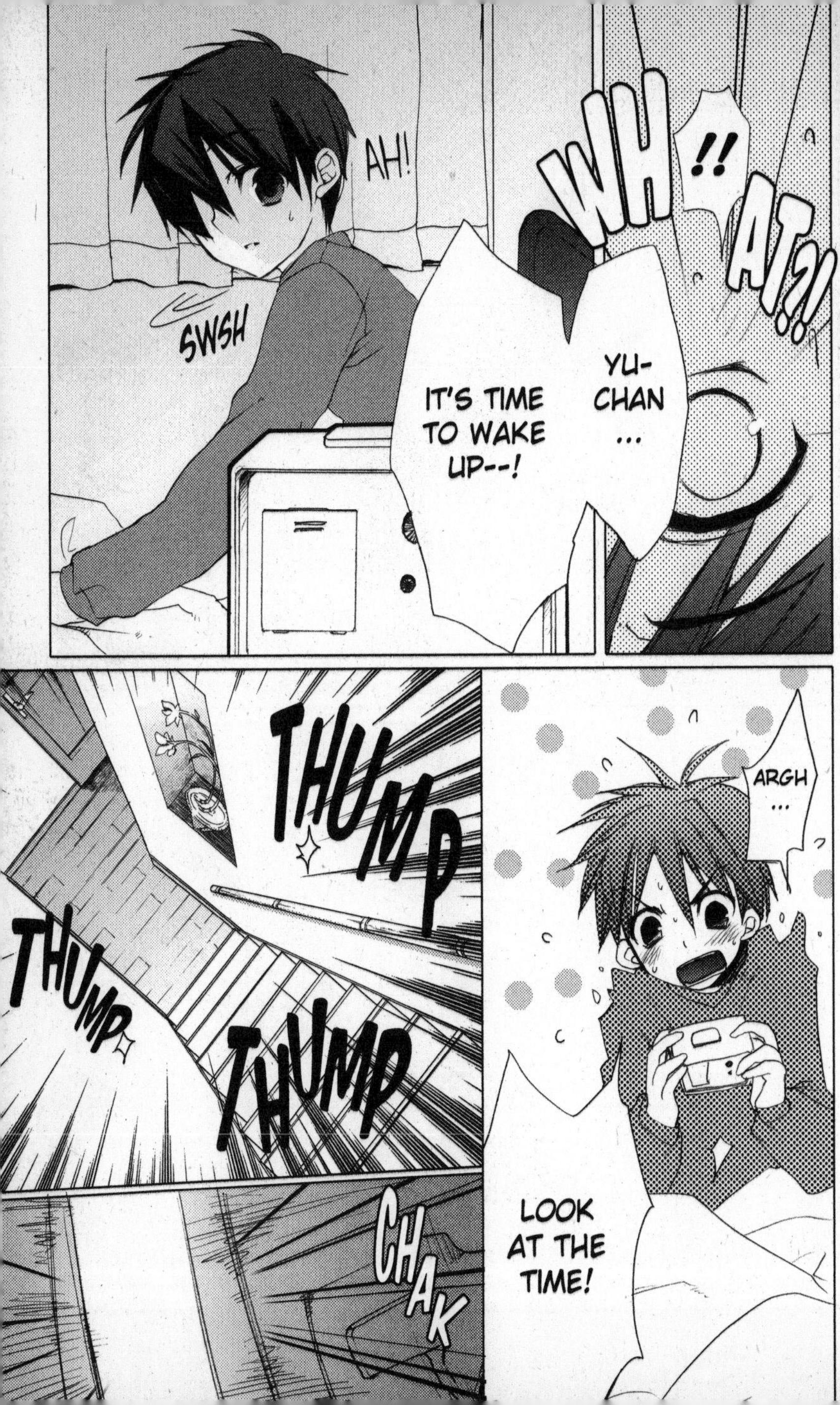
WHAT?!!
YU-CHAN...
IT'S TIME TO WAKE UP--!
AH!
SWSH
ARGH...
LOOK AT THE TIME!
THUMP
THUMP
THUMP
CHAK

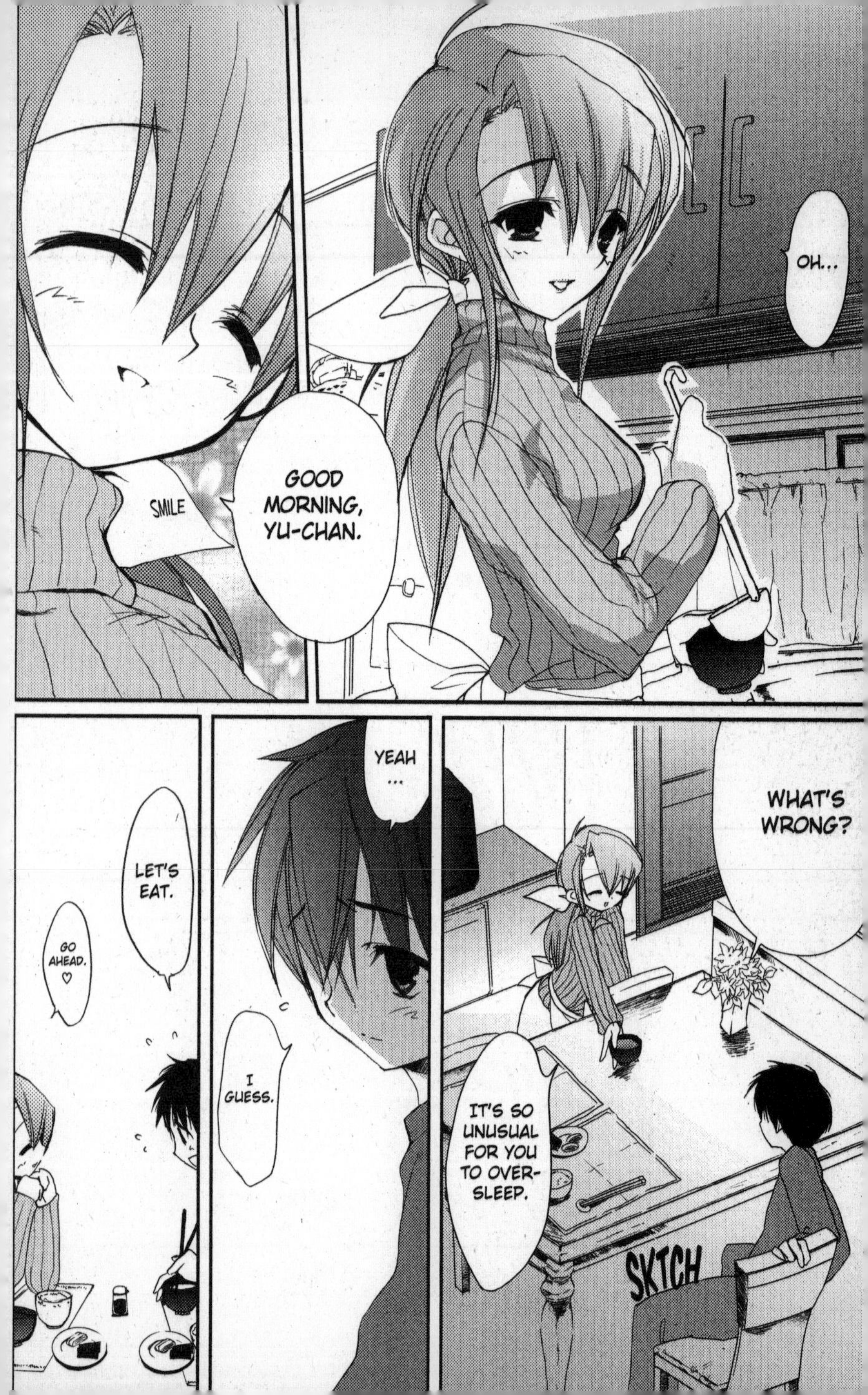
OH...
GOOD MORNING, YU-CHAN.
SMILE
WHAT'S WRONG?
IT'S SO UNUSUAL FOR YOU TO OVER-SLEEP.
SKTCH
YEAH...
I GUESS.
LET'S EAT.
GO AHEAD. ♡

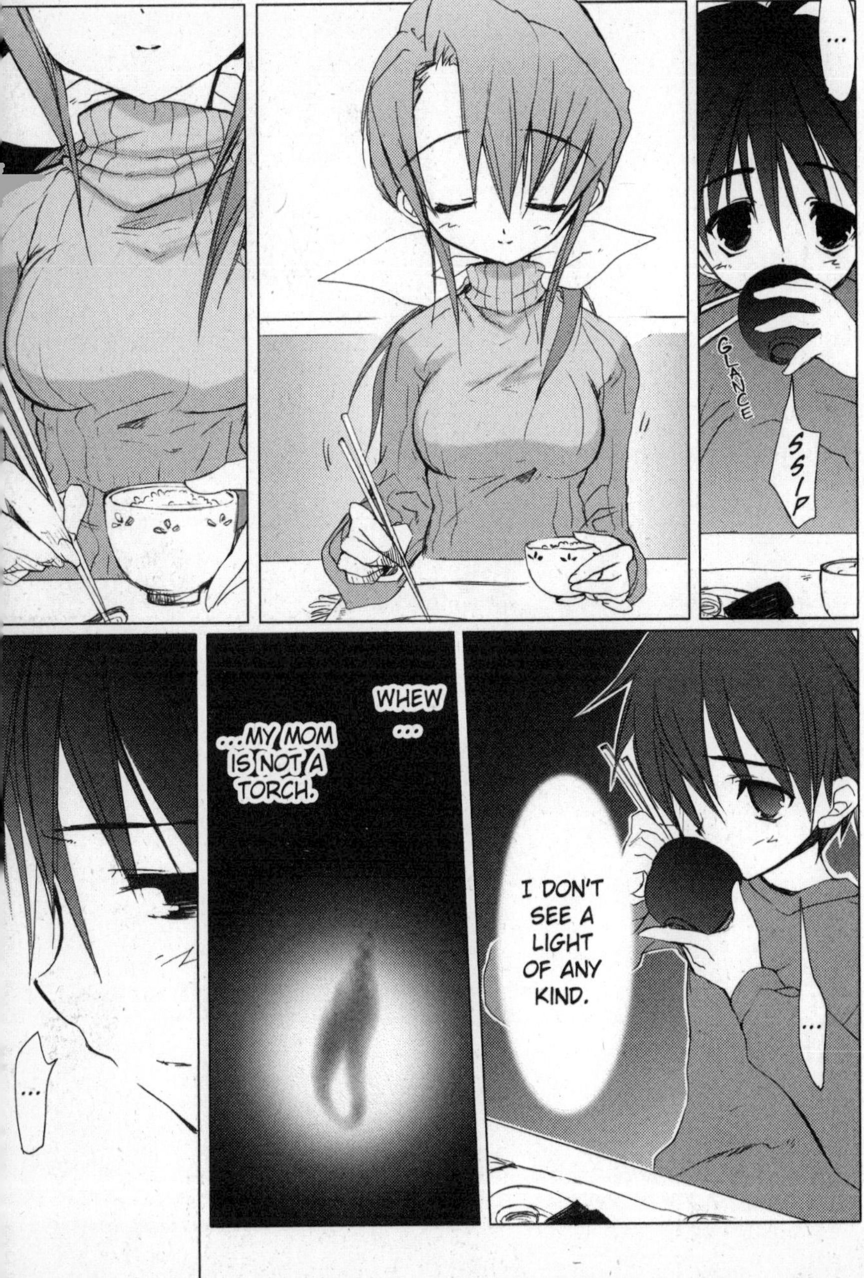
...
GLANCE
SSIP
I DON'T SEE A LIGHT OF ANY KIND.
...
WHEW ...
...MY MOM IS NOT A TORCH.
...

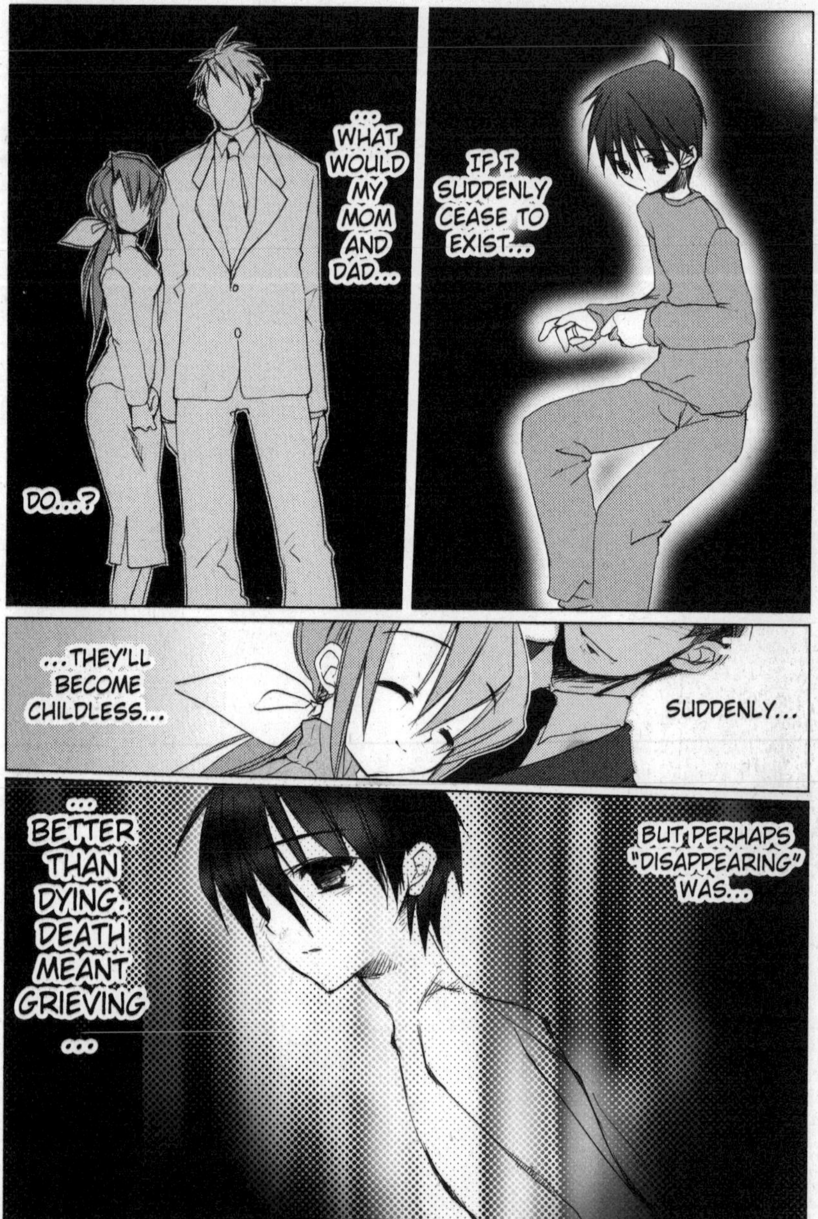
IF I SUDDENLY CEASE TO EXIST...
...WHAT WOULD MY MOM AND DAD...
DO...?
SUDDENLY...
...THEY'LL BECOME CHILDLESS...
BUT PERHAPS "DISAPPEARING" WAS...
...BETTER THAN DYING. DEATH MEANT GRIEVING...

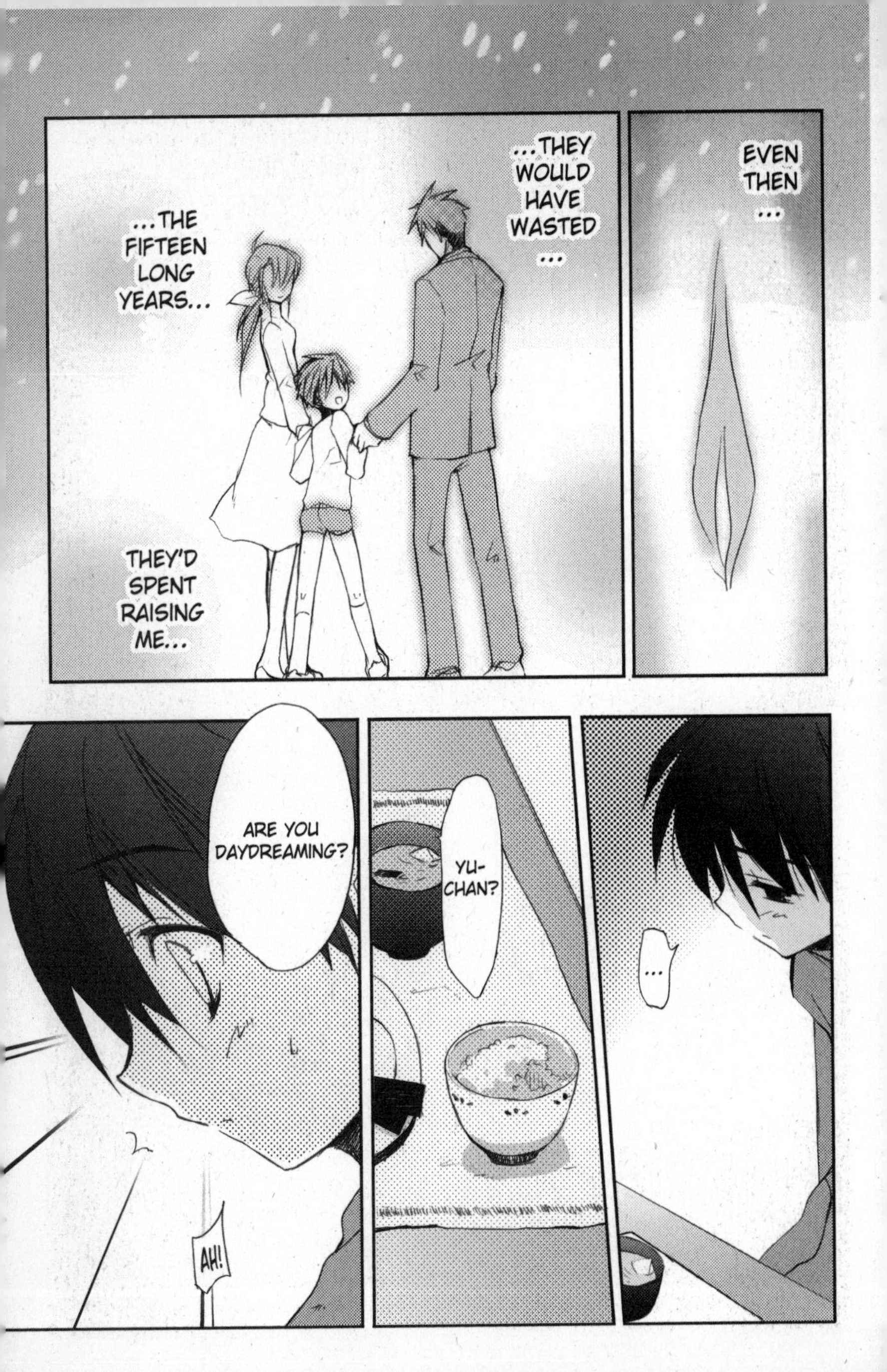
EVEN THEN...
...THEY WOULD HAVE WASTED...
...THE FIFTEEN LONG YEARS...
THEY'D SPENT RAISING ME...
...
YU-CHAN?
ARE YOU DAYDREAMING?
AH!

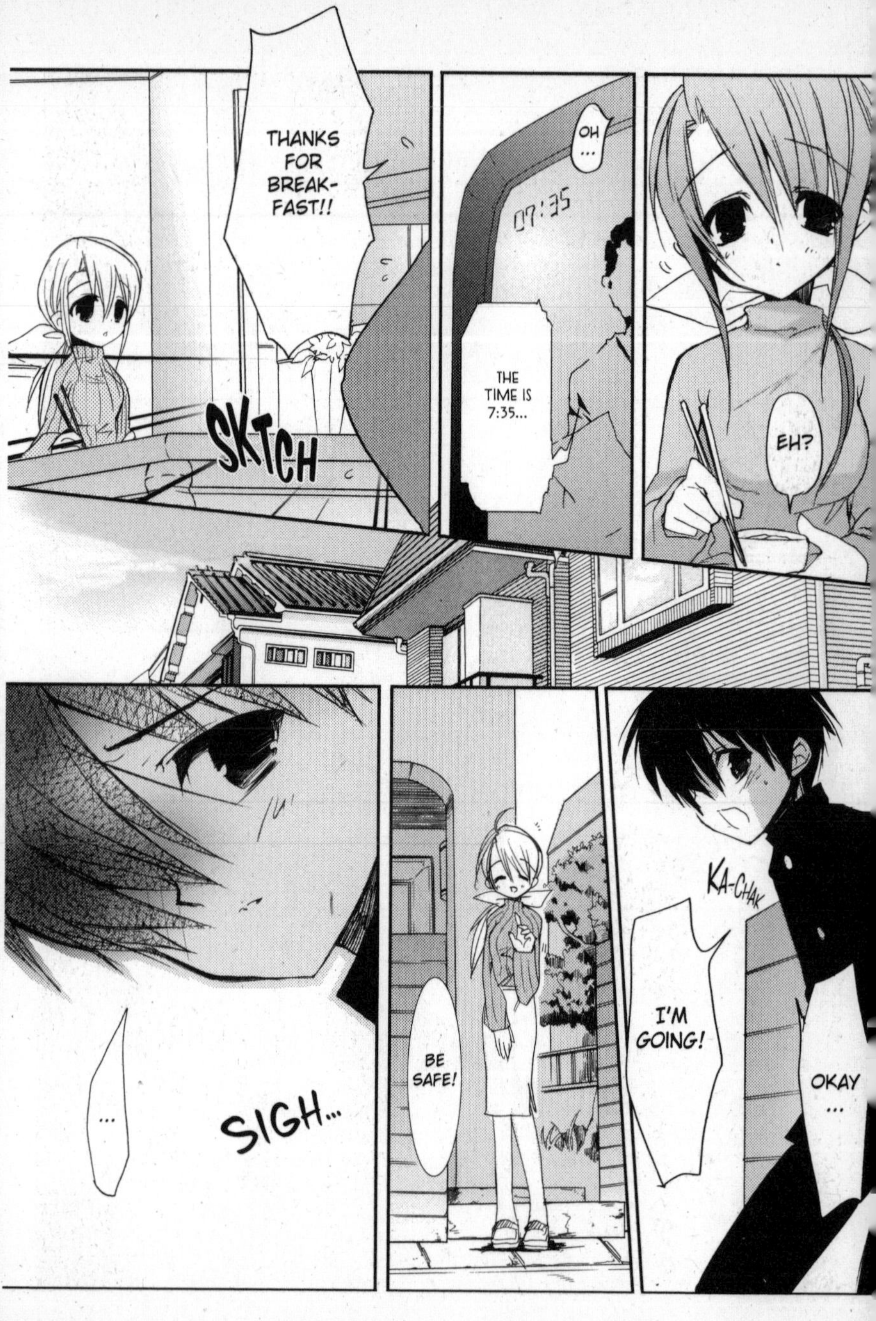
EH?
OH ...
07:35
THE TIME IS 7:35...
THANKS FOR BREAK-FAST!!
SKTCH
KA-CHAK
I'M GOING!
OKAY ...
BE SAFE!
...
SIGH...

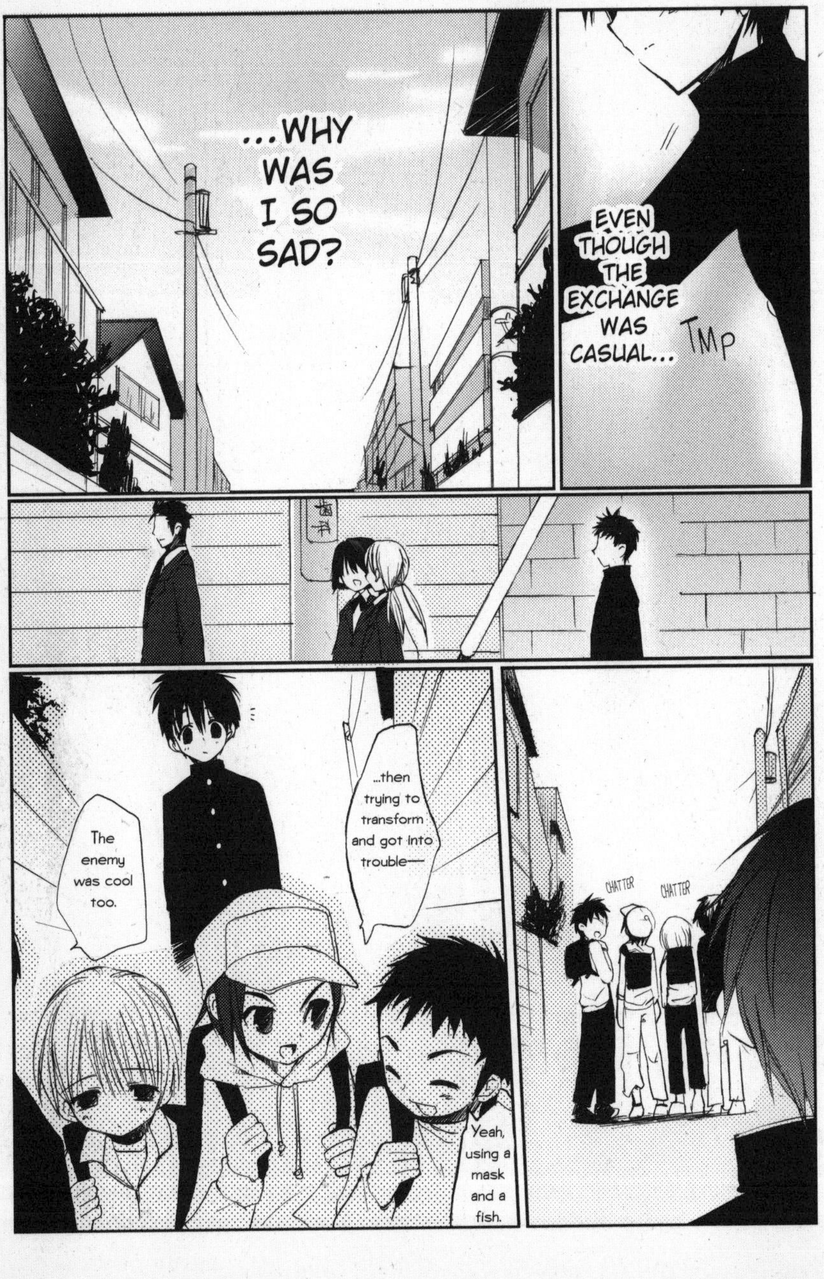
EVEN THOUGH THE EXCHANGE WAS CASUAL...
TMP
...WHY WAS I SO SAD?
CHATTER
CHATTER
...then trying to transform and got into trouble—
The enemy was cool too.
Yeah, using a mask and a fish.

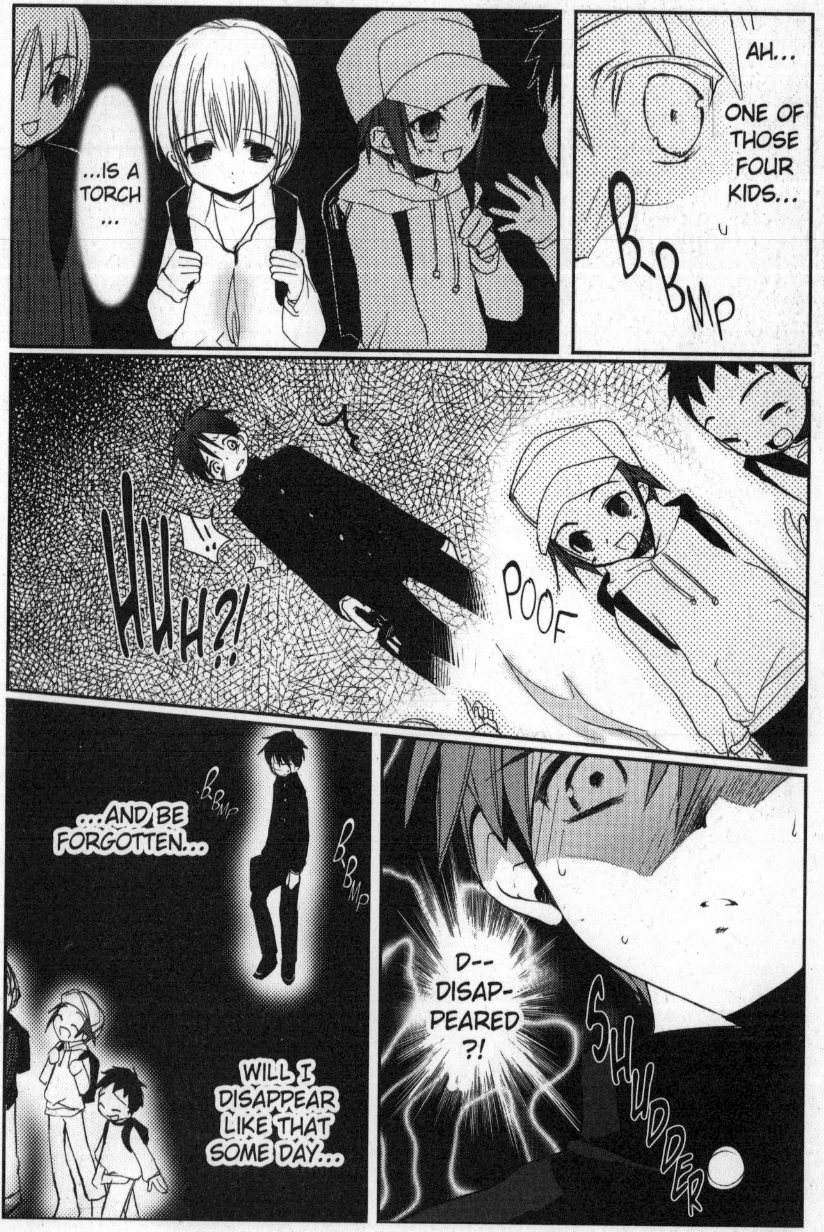
AH...
ONE OF THOSE FOUR KIDS...
B-BMP
...IS A TORCH...
POOF
HUH?!
D--DISAP-PEARED?!
SHUDDER
B-BMP
...AND BE FORGOTTEN...
B-BMP
WILL I DISAPPEAR LIKE THAT SOME DAY...

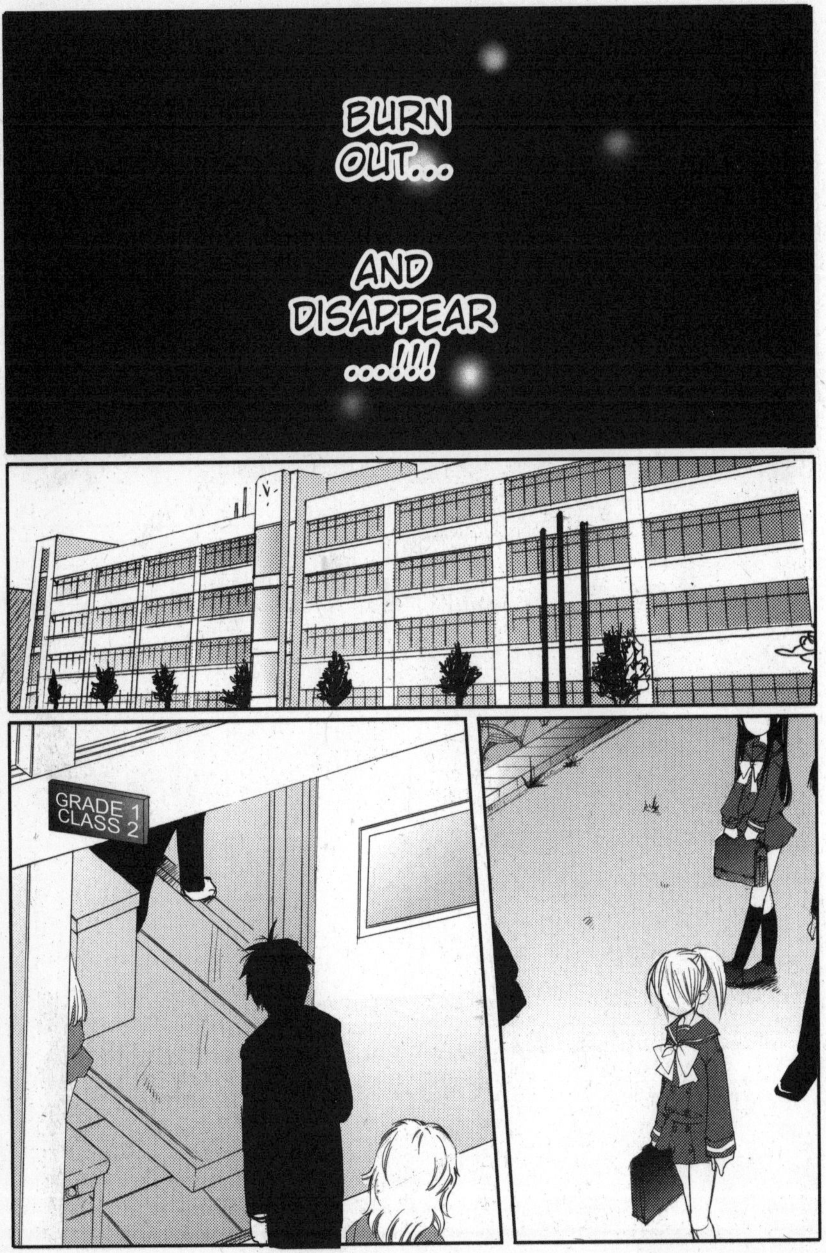
BURN OUT...
AND DISAPPEAR ...!!!!
GRADE 1 CLASS 2

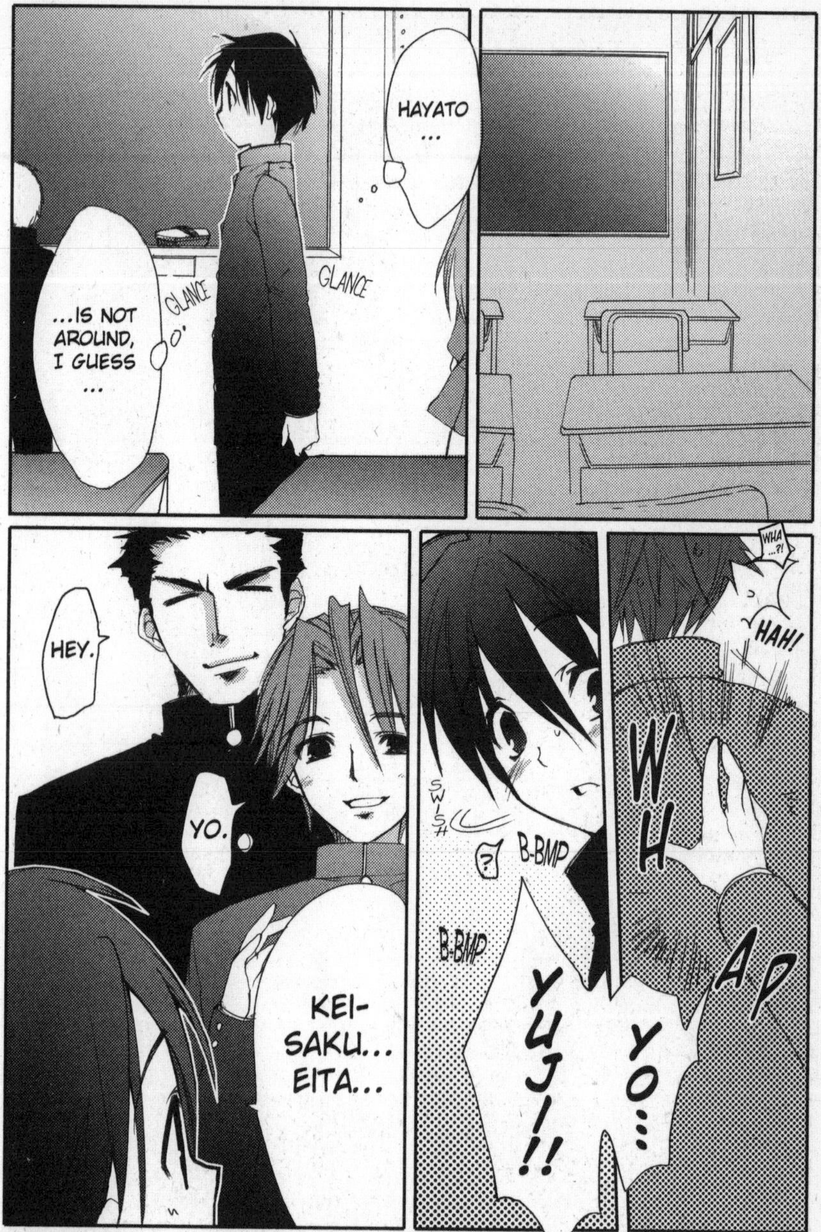
HAYATO...
GLANCE
GLANCE
...IS NOT AROUND, I GUESS...
WHA...?!
HAH!
WHAP
SWISH
?
B-BMP
B-BMP
YO...
YUJI!!
HEY.
YO.
KEI-SAKU... EITA...

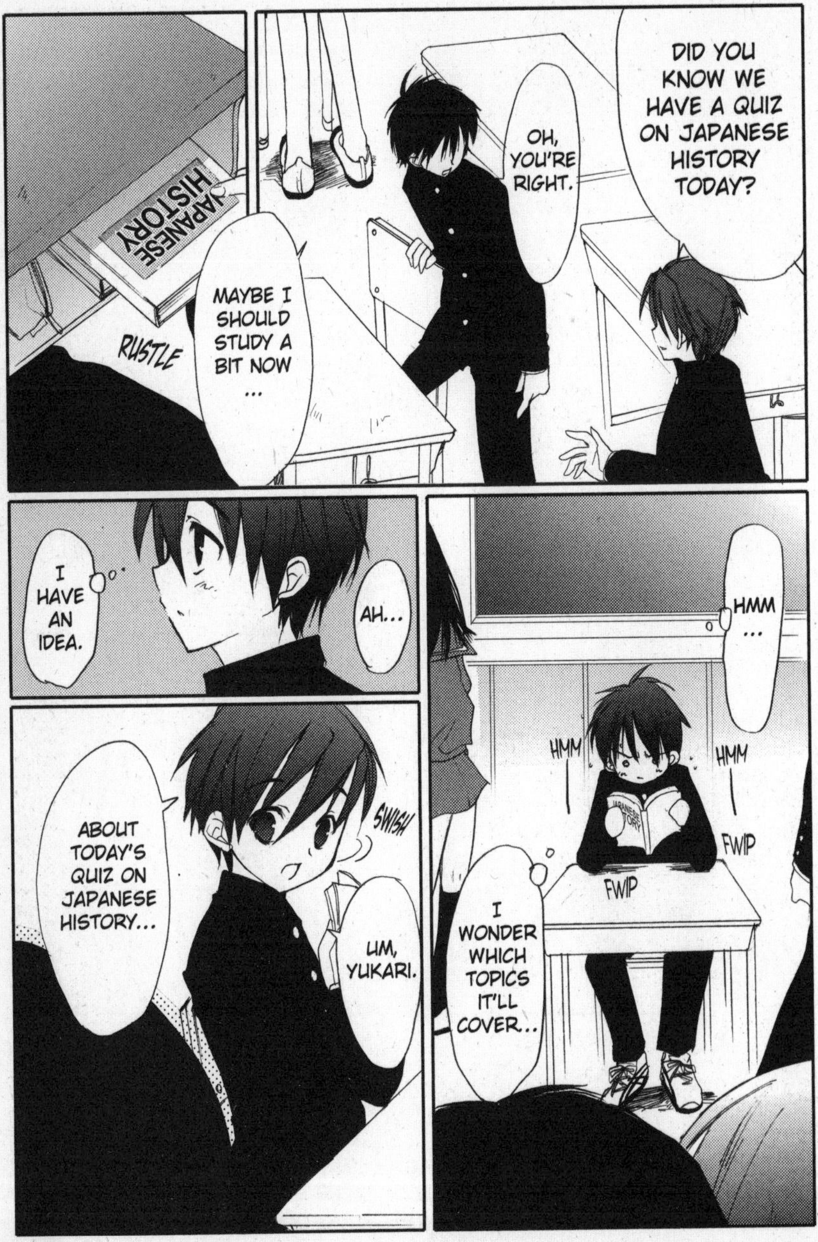
DID YOU KNOW WE HAVE A QUIZ ON JAPANESE HISTORY TODAY?
OH, YOU'RE RIGHT.
MAYBE I SHOULD STUDY A BIT NOW ...
JAPANESE HISTORY
RUSTLE
HMM ...
HMM
HMM
JAPANESE HISTORY
FWIP
FWIP
I WONDER WHICH TOPICS IT'LL COVER...
AH...
I HAVE AN IDEA.
UM, YUKARI.
SWISH
ABOUT TODAY'S QUIZ ON JAPANESE HISTORY...

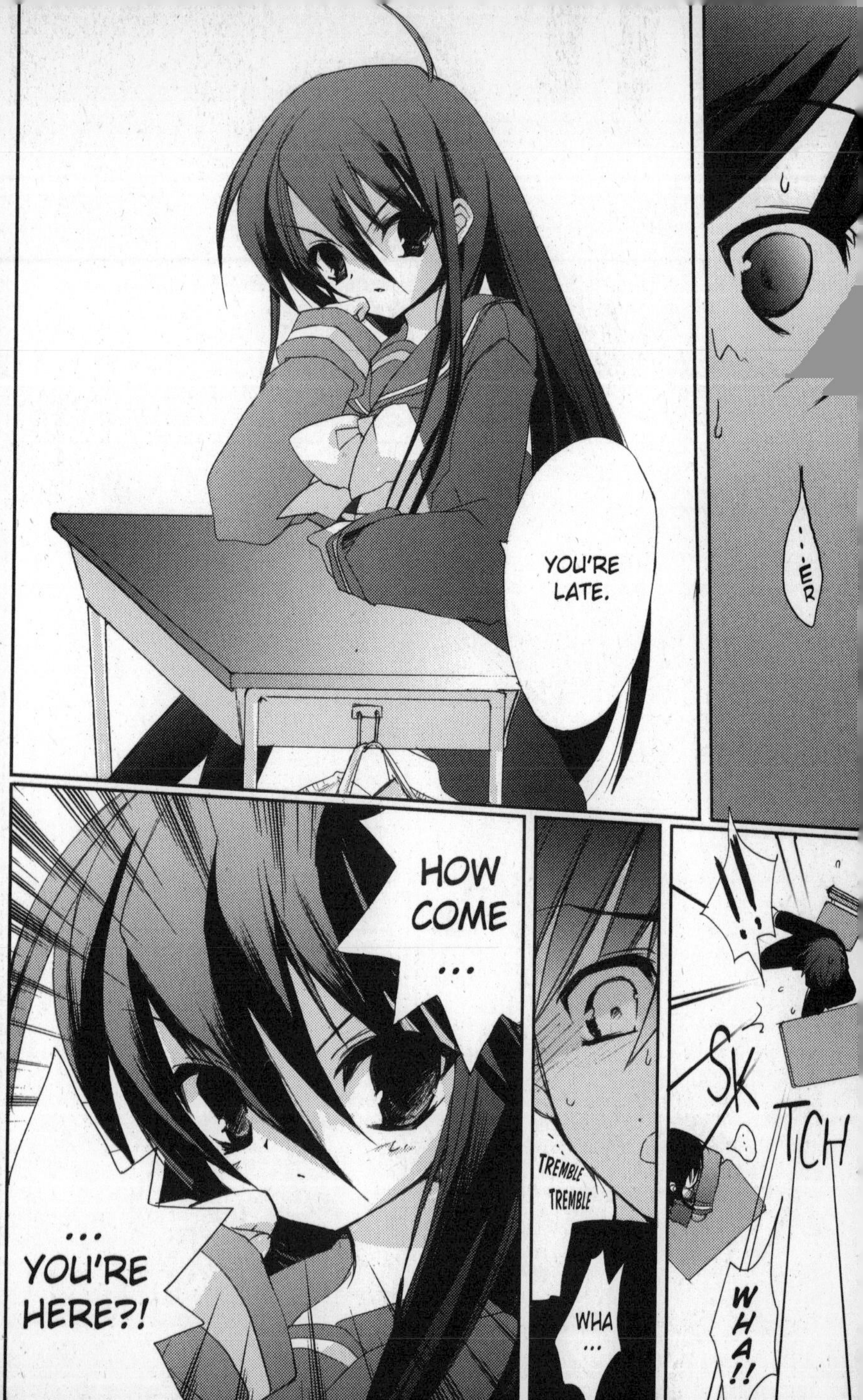
...ER
YOU'RE LATE.
!!
SKTCH
WHA!!
TREMBLE TREMBLE
WHA...
HOW COME...
...YOU'RE HERE?!

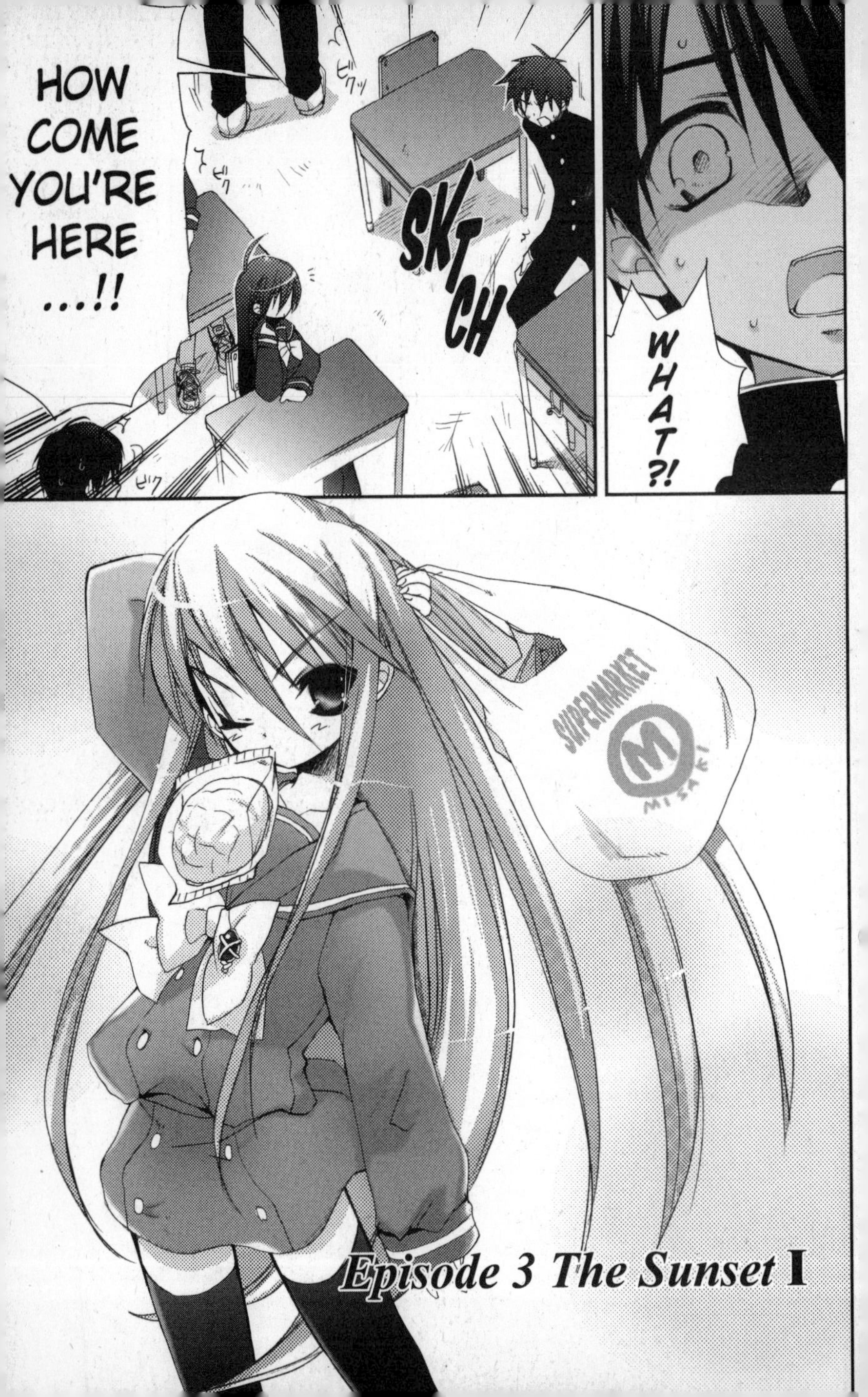
WHAT?!
HOW COME YOU'RE HERE ...!!
ビクッ
ビク
SKTICH
ビク
SUPERMARKET
M
MISAKI

Episode 3 The Sunset I

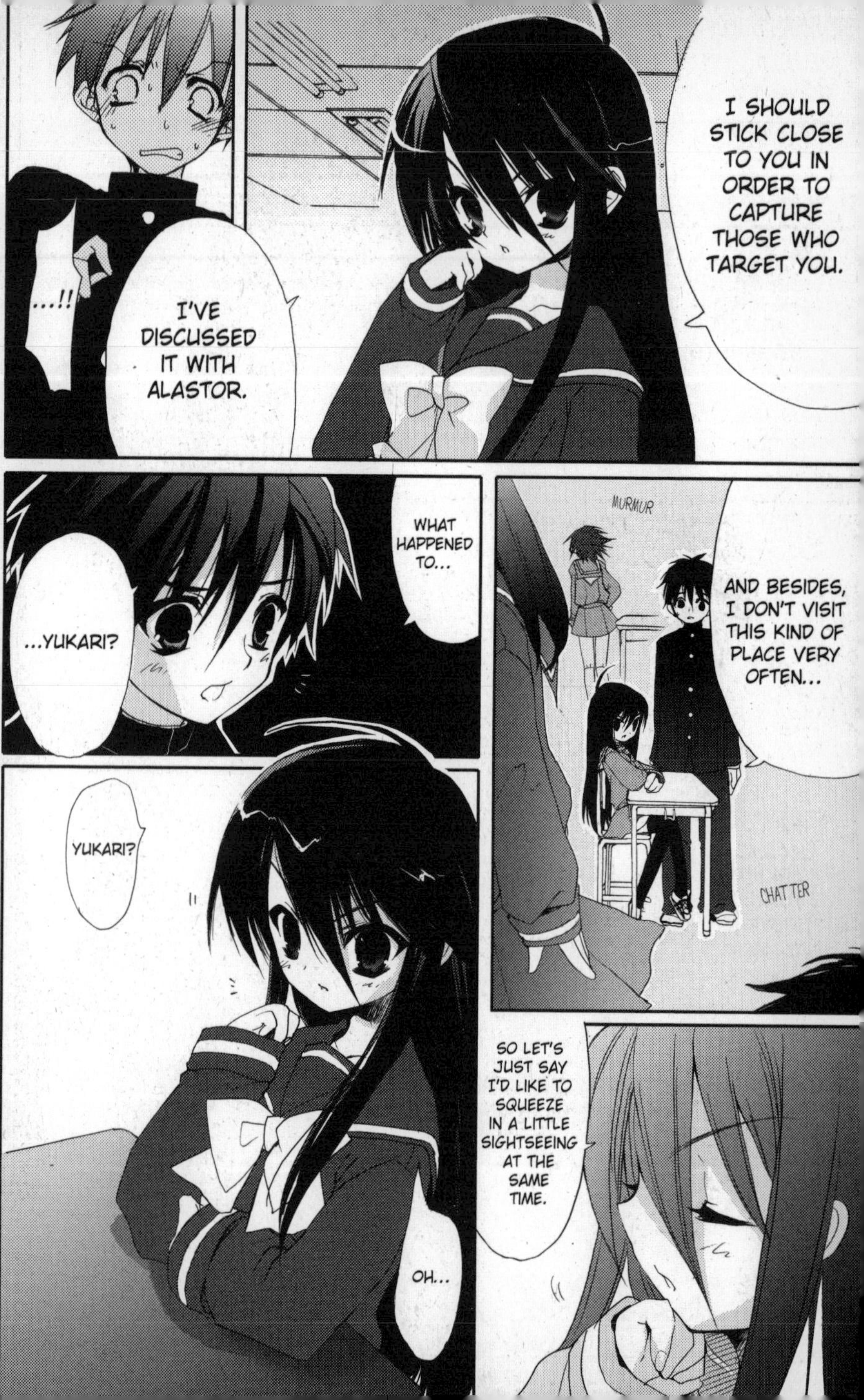
I SHOULD STICK CLOSE TO YOU IN ORDER TO CAPTURE THOSE WHO TARGET YOU.
I'VE DISCUSSED IT WITH ALASTOR.
...!!
MURMUR
AND BESIDES, I DON'T VISIT THIS KIND OF PLACE VERY OFTEN...
CHATTER
SO LET'S JUST SAY I'D LIKE TO SQUEEZE IN A LITTLE SIGHTSEEING AT THE SAME TIME.
WHAT HAPPENED TO...
...YUKARI?
YUKARI?
OH...

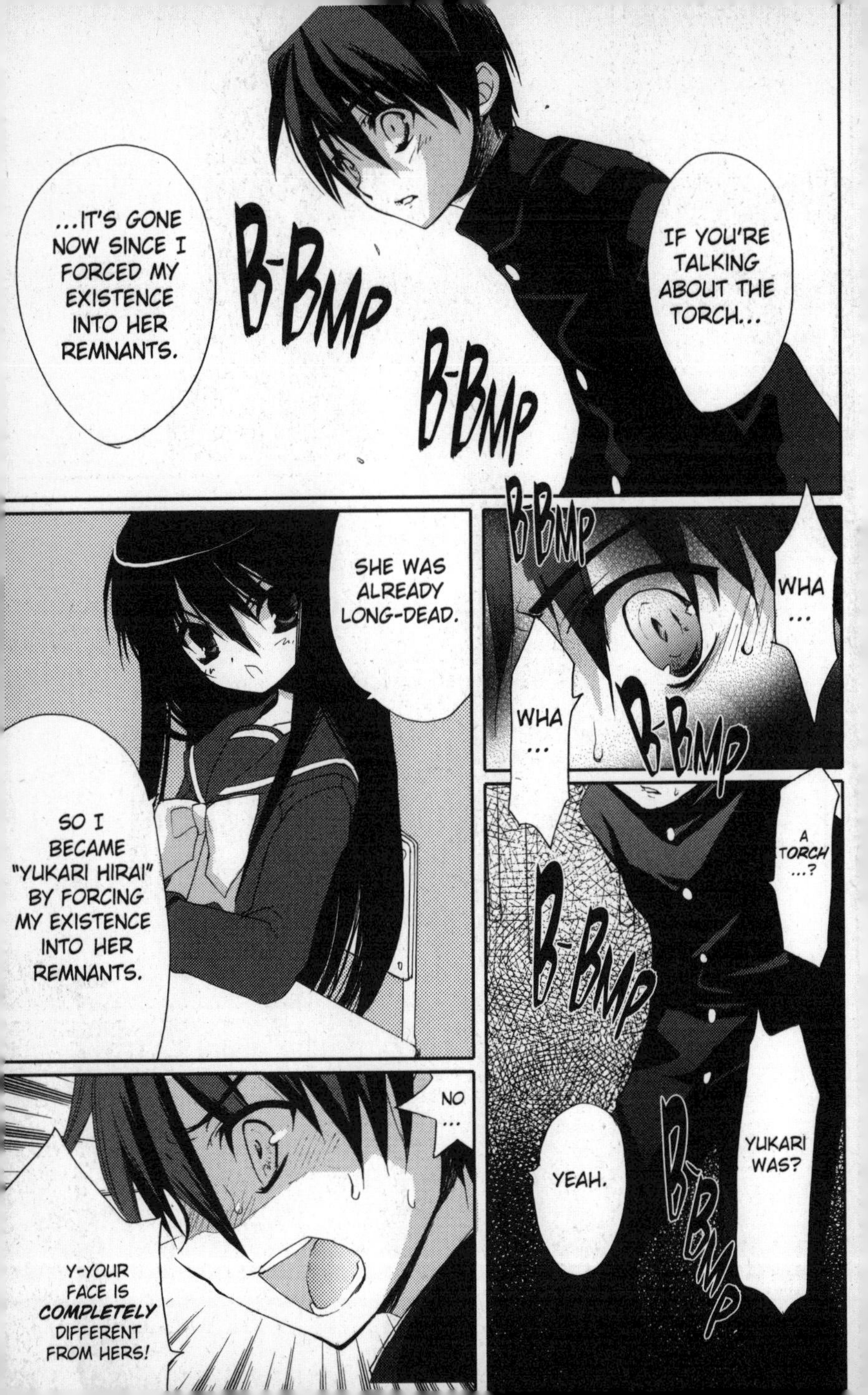
IF YOU'RE TALKING ABOUT THE TORCH...
B-BMP
B-BMP
...IT'S GONE NOW SINCE I FORCED MY EXISTENCE INTO HER REMNANTS.
B-BMP
WHA...
WHA...
B-BMP
SHE WAS ALREADY LONG-DEAD.
SO I BECAME "YUKARI HIRAI" BY FORCING MY EXISTENCE INTO HER REMNANTS.
A TORCH...?
B-BMP
YUKARI WAS?
B-BMP
YEAH.
NO...
Y-YOUR FACE IS COMPLETELY DIFFERENT FROM HERS!

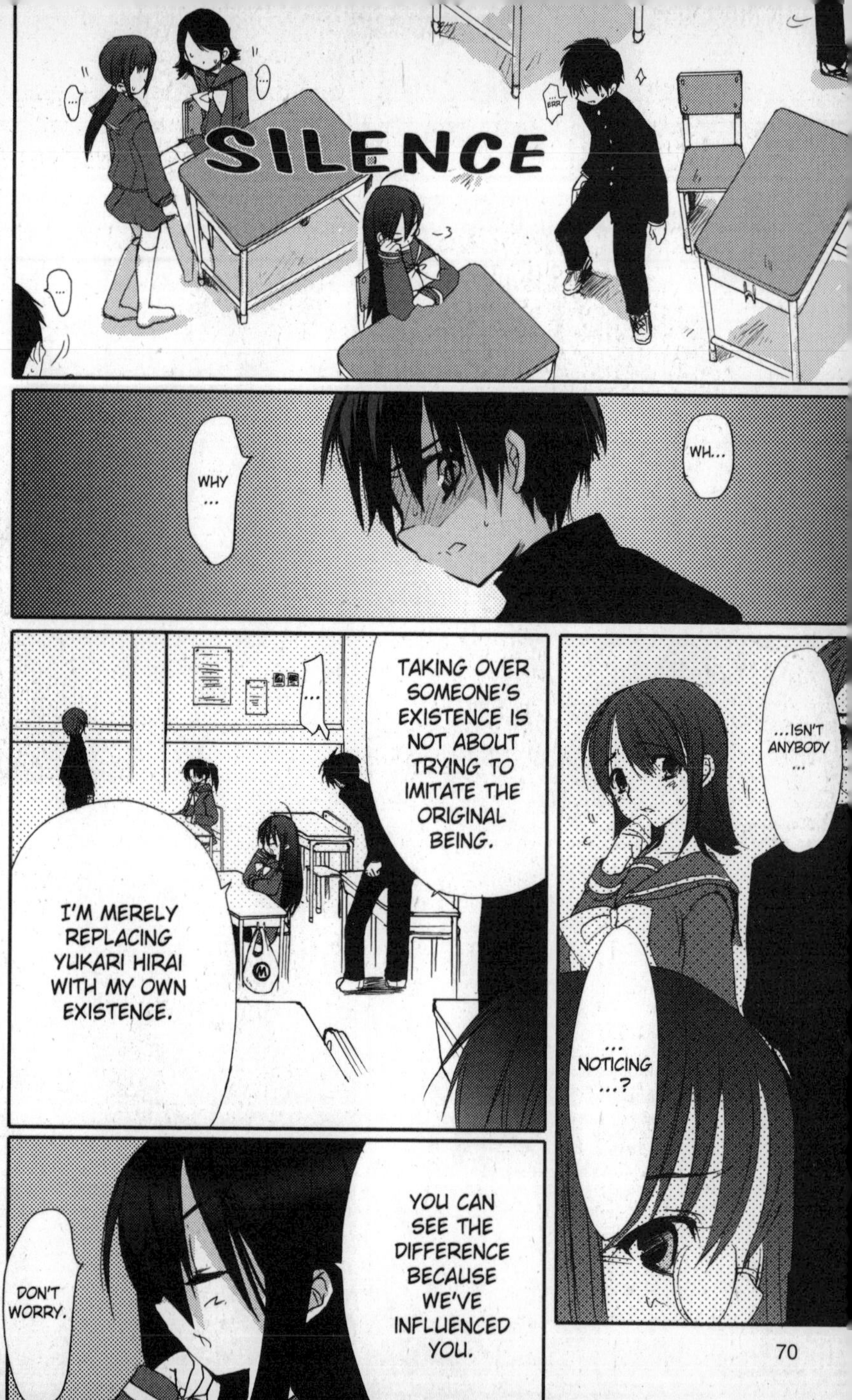

... ERR
...
...
SILENCE
...
WH...
WHY ...
...ISN'T ANYBODY ...
... NOTICING ...?
TAKING OVER SOMEONE'S EXISTENCE IS NOT ABOUT TRYING TO IMITATE THE ORIGINAL BEING.
...
I'M MERELY REPLACING YUKARI HIRAI WITH MY OWN EXISTENCE.
YOU CAN SEE THE DIFFERENCE BECAUSE WE'VE INFLUENCED YOU.
DON'T WORRY.

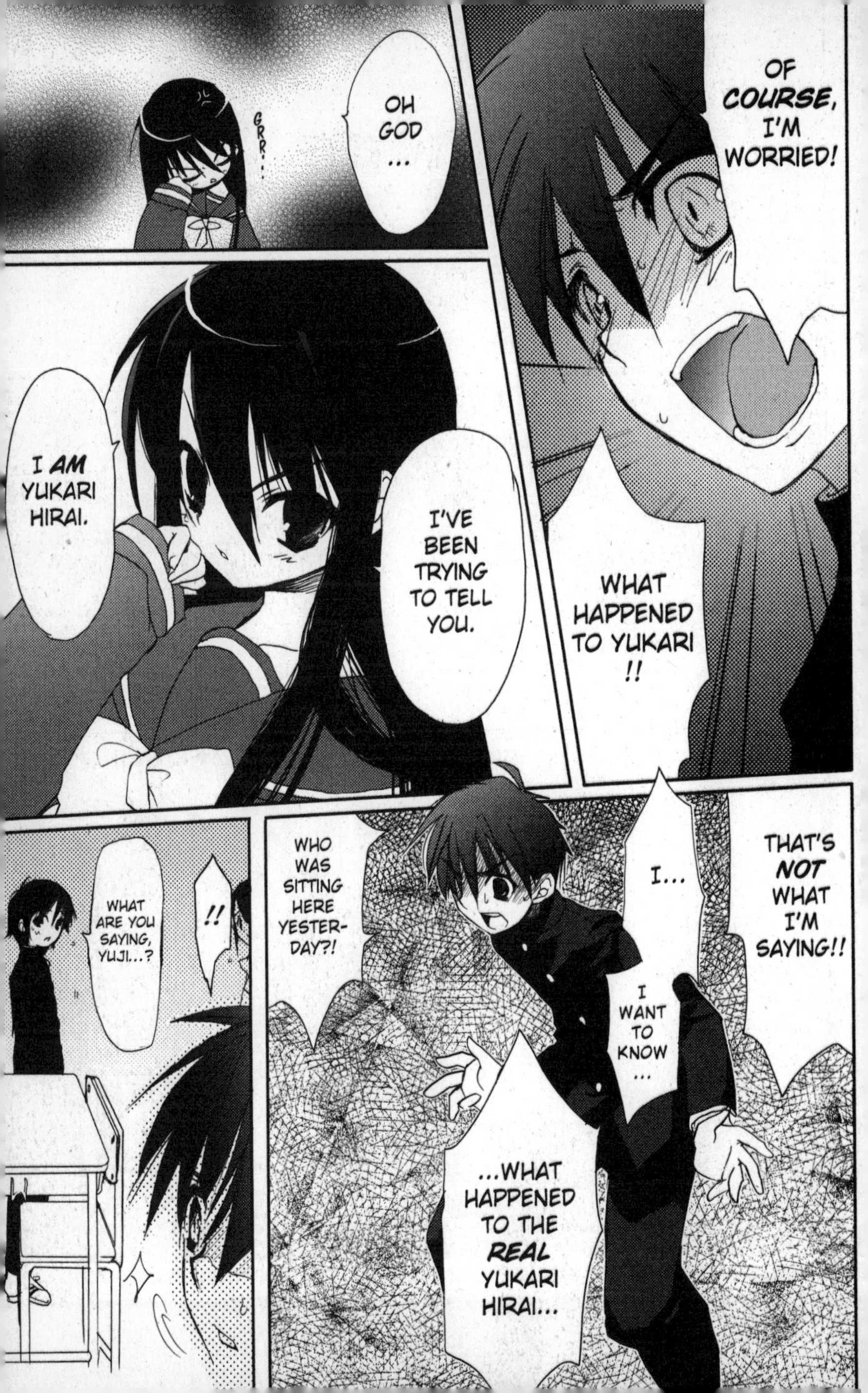
OF COURSE, I'M WORRIED!
OH GOD ...
GRR..
WHAT HAPPENED TO YUKARI !!
I'VE BEEN TRYING TO TELL YOU.
I AM YUKARI HIRAI.
THAT'S NOT WHAT I'M SAYING!!
I...
I WANT TO KNOW ...
...WHAT HAPPENED TO THE REAL YUKARI HIRAI...
WHO WAS SITTING HERE YESTER-DAY?!
!!
WHAT ARE YOU SAYING, YUJI...?

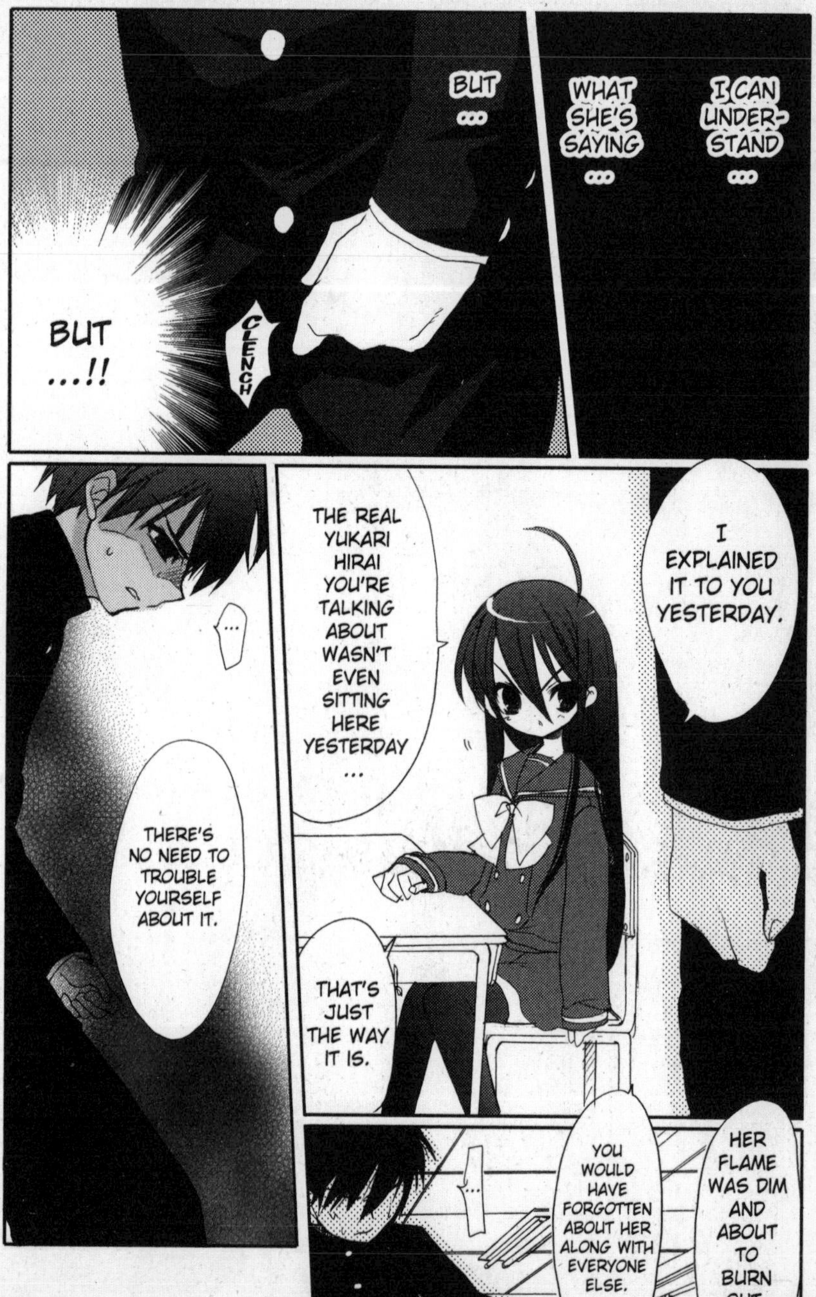
I CAN UNDER-STAND ...
WHAT SHE'S SAYING ...
BUT ...
BUT ...!!
CLENCH
I EXPLAINED IT TO YOU YESTERDAY.
THE REAL YUKARI HIRAI YOU'RE TALKING ABOUT WASN'T EVEN SITTING HERE YESTERDAY ...
THAT'S JUST THE WAY IT IS.
HER FLAME WAS DIM AND ABOUT TO BURN OUT.
YOU WOULD HAVE FORGOTTEN ABOUT HER ALONG WITH EVERYONE ELSE.
...
...
THERE'S NO NEED TO TROUBLE YOURSELF ABOUT IT.

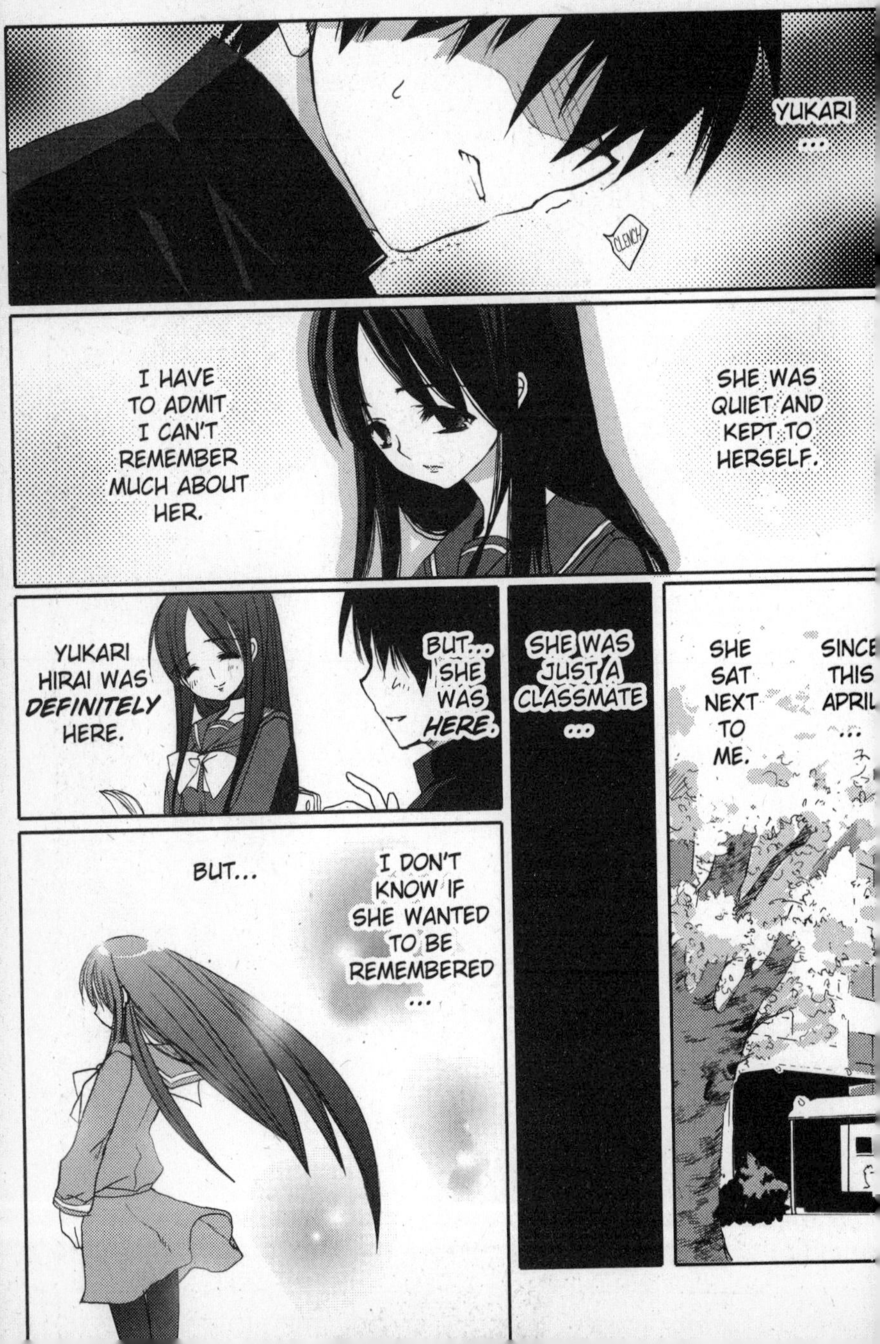
YUKARI ...
CLENCH
SHE WAS QUIET AND KEPT TO HERSELF.
I HAVE TO ADMIT I CAN'T REMEMBER MUCH ABOUT HER.
SINCE THIS APRIL ...
SHE SAT NEXT TO ME.
SHE WAS JUST A CLASSMATE ...
BUT... SHE WAS *HERE.*
YUKARI HIRAI WAS *DEFINITELY* HERE.
BUT...
I DON'T KNOW IF SHE WANTED TO BE REMEMBERED ...

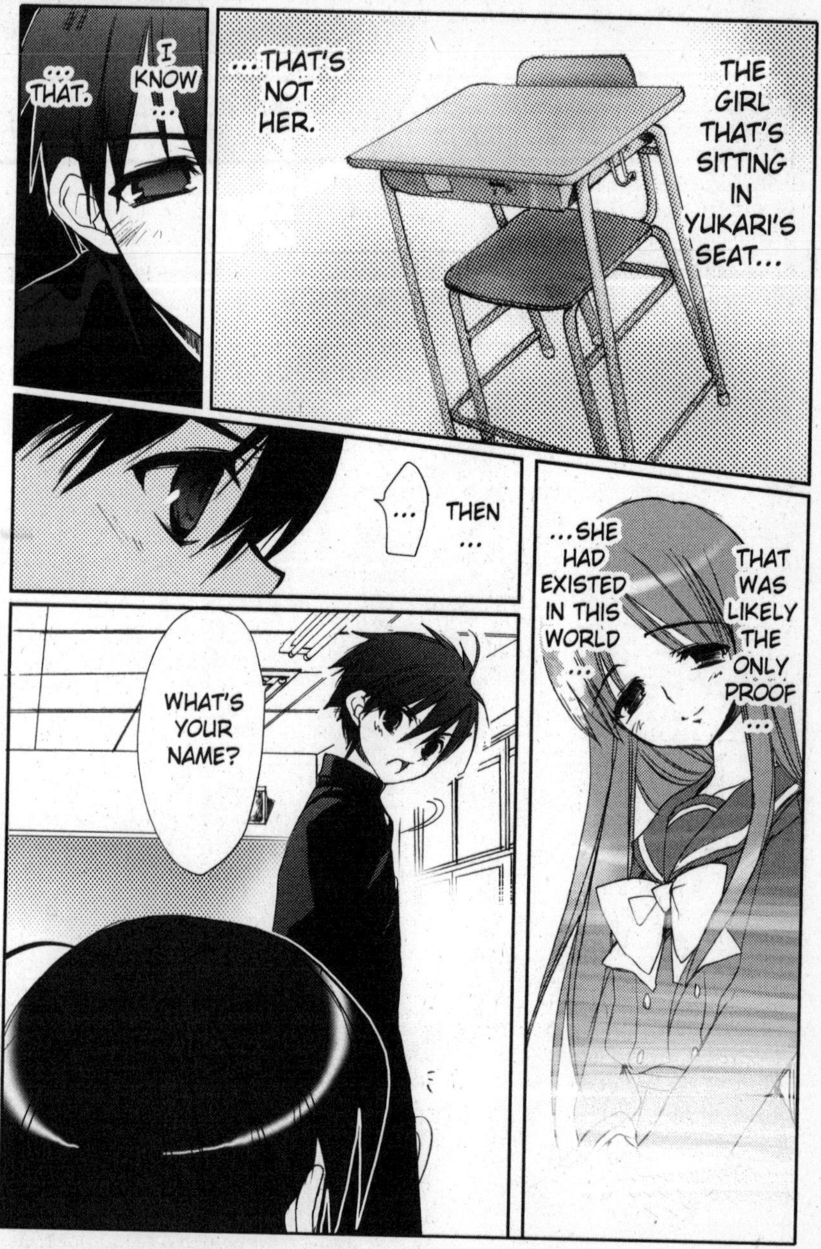
THE GIRL THAT'S SITTING IN YUKARI'S SEAT...
...THAT'S NOT HER.
I KNOW...
...THAT.
THAT WAS LIKELY THE ONLY PROOF...
...SHE HAD EXISTED IN THIS WORLD...
THEN...
...
WHAT'S YOUR NAME?

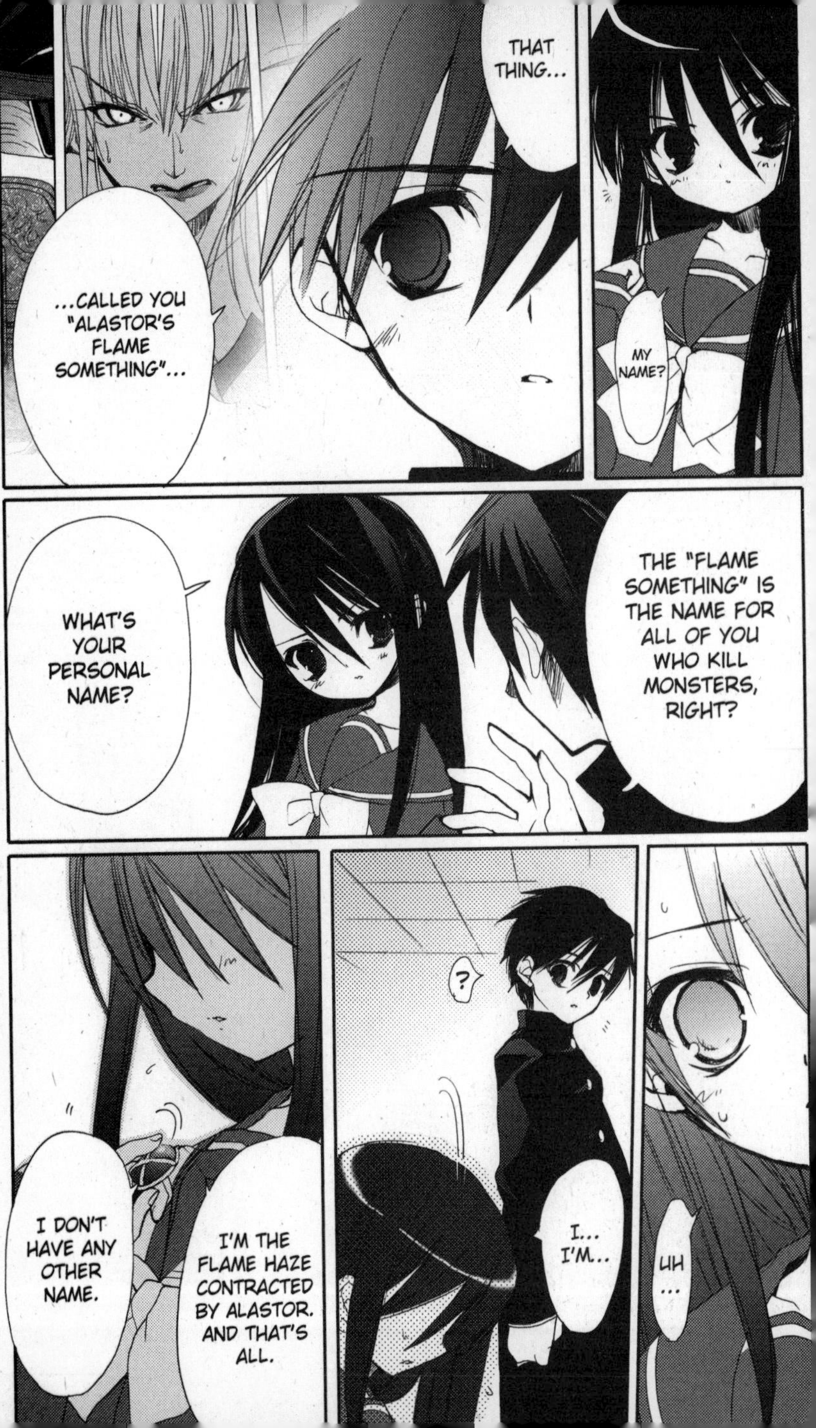
MY NAME?
THAT THING...
...CALLED YOU "ALASTOR'S FLAME SOMETHING"...
THE "FLAME SOMETHING" IS THE NAME FOR ALL OF YOU WHO KILL MONSTERS, RIGHT?
WHAT'S YOUR PERSONAL NAME?
UH ...
?
I... I'M...
I'M THE FLAME HAZE CONTRACTED BY ALASTOR. AND THAT'S ALL.
I DON'T HAVE ANY OTHER NAME.

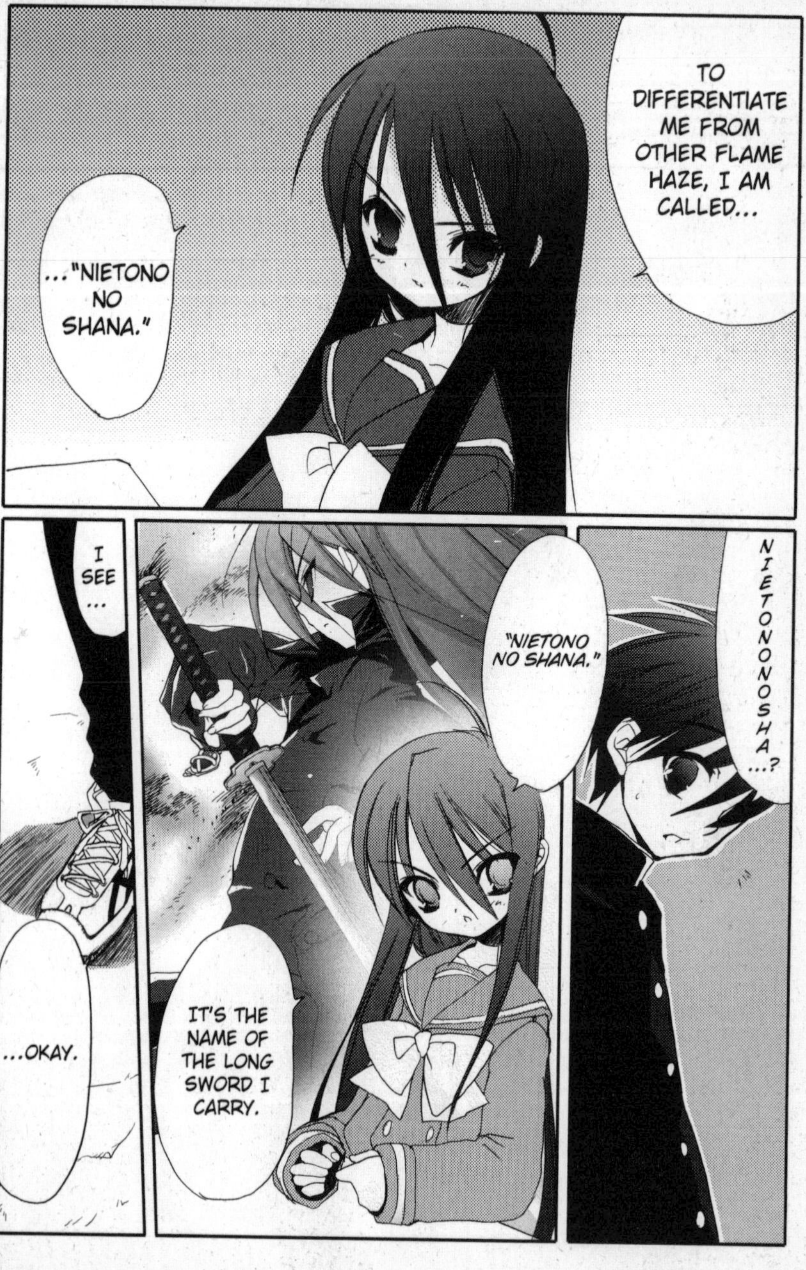
TO DIFFERENTIATE ME FROM OTHER FLAME HAZE, I AM CALLED...
..."NIETONO NO SHANA."
NIETONONOSHA...?
"NIETONO NO SHANA."
IT'S THE NAME OF THE LONG SWORD I CARRY.
I SEE...
...OKAY.

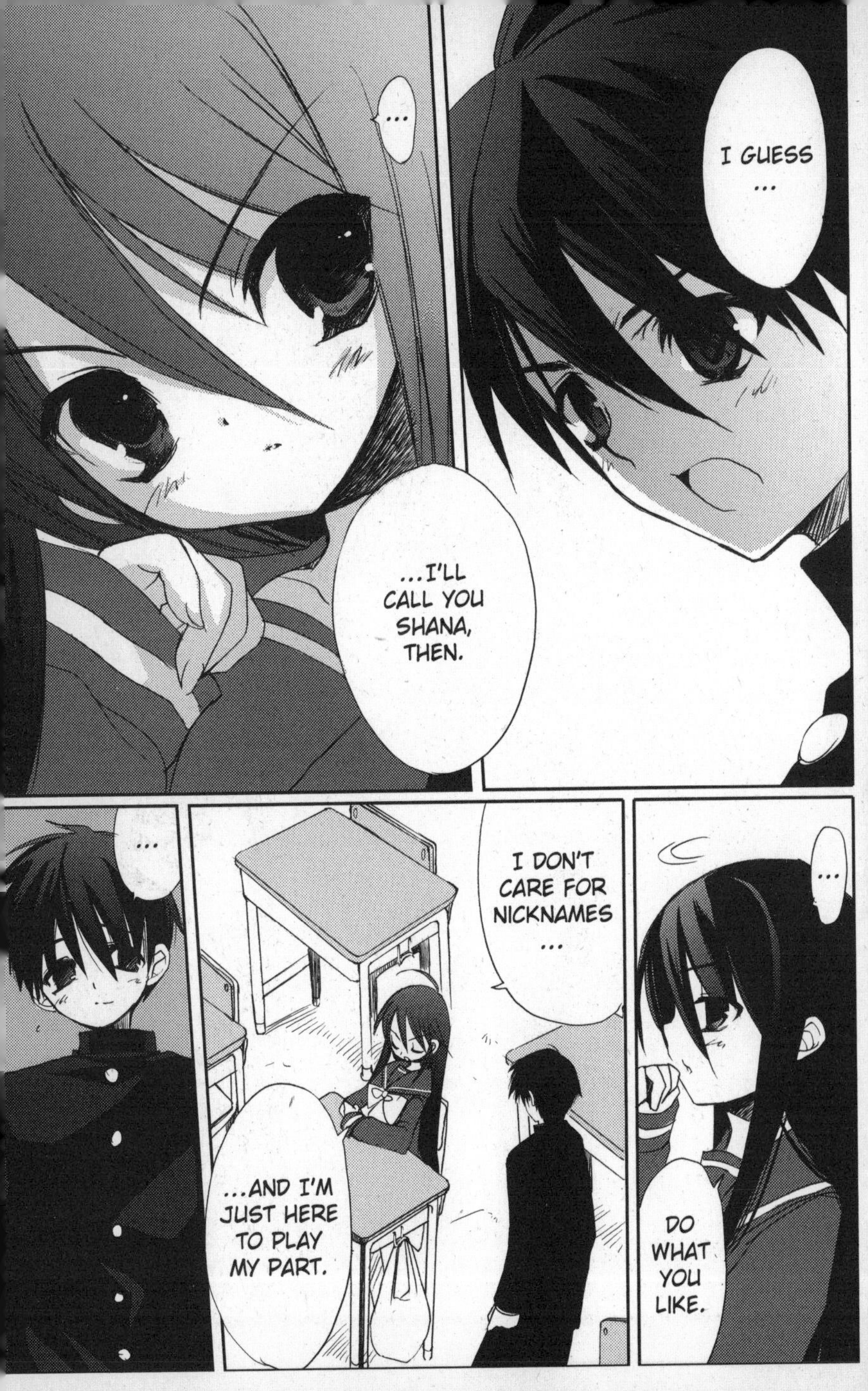
I GUESS ...
...
...I'LL CALL YOU SHANA, THEN.
...
DO WHAT YOU LIKE.
I DON'T CARE FOR NICKNAMES ...
...AND I'M JUST HERE TO PLAY MY PART.
...

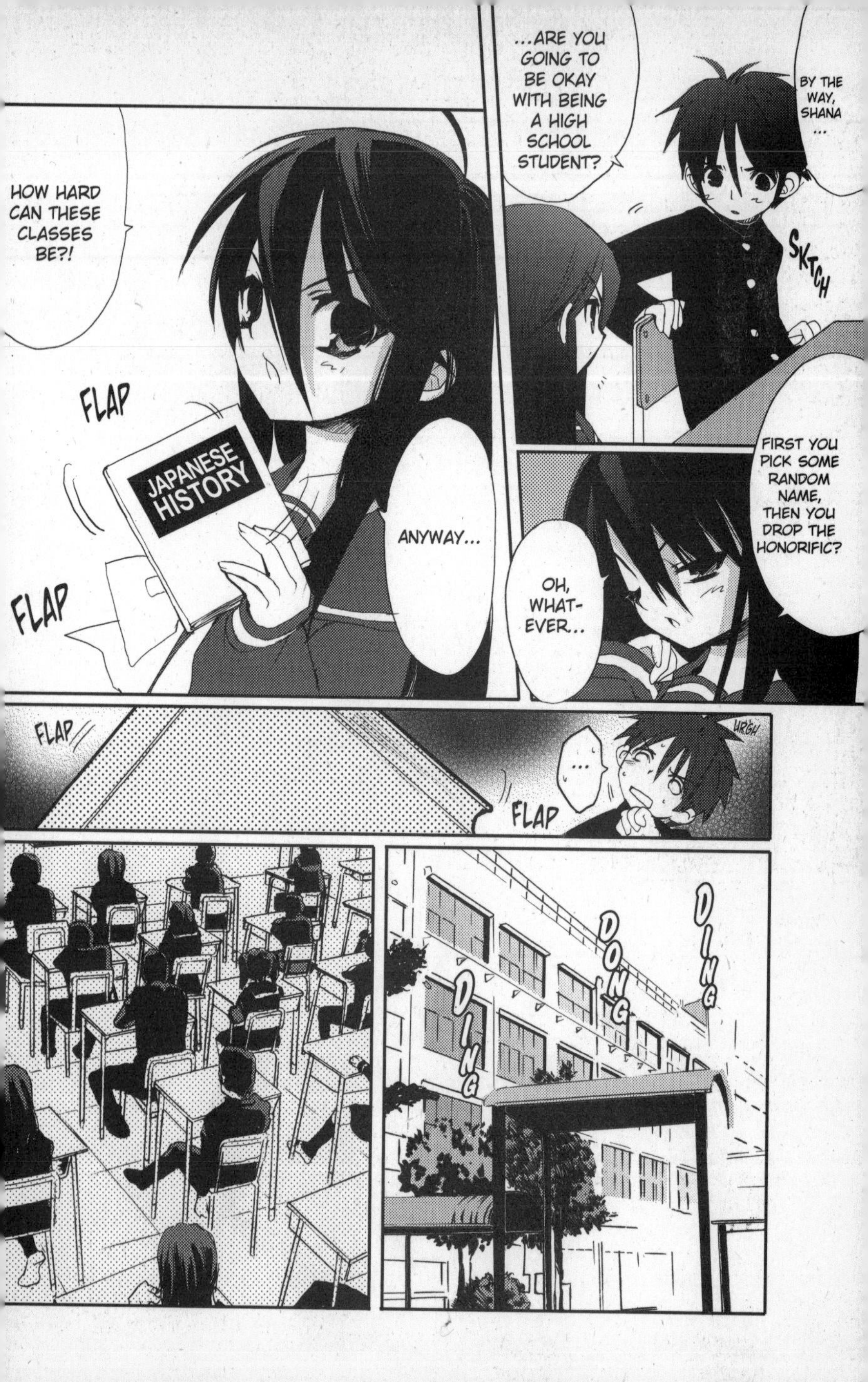
BY THE WAY, SHANA...
...ARE YOU GOING TO BE OKAY WITH BEING A HIGH SCHOOL STUDENT?
SKTCH
FIRST YOU PICK SOME RANDOM NAME, THEN YOU DROP THE HONORIFIC?
OH, WHATEVER...
ANYWAY...
HOW HARD CAN THESE CLASSES BE?!
FLAP
JAPANESE HISTORY
FLAP
URGH
...
FLAP
FLAP
DING
DONG
DING
DING

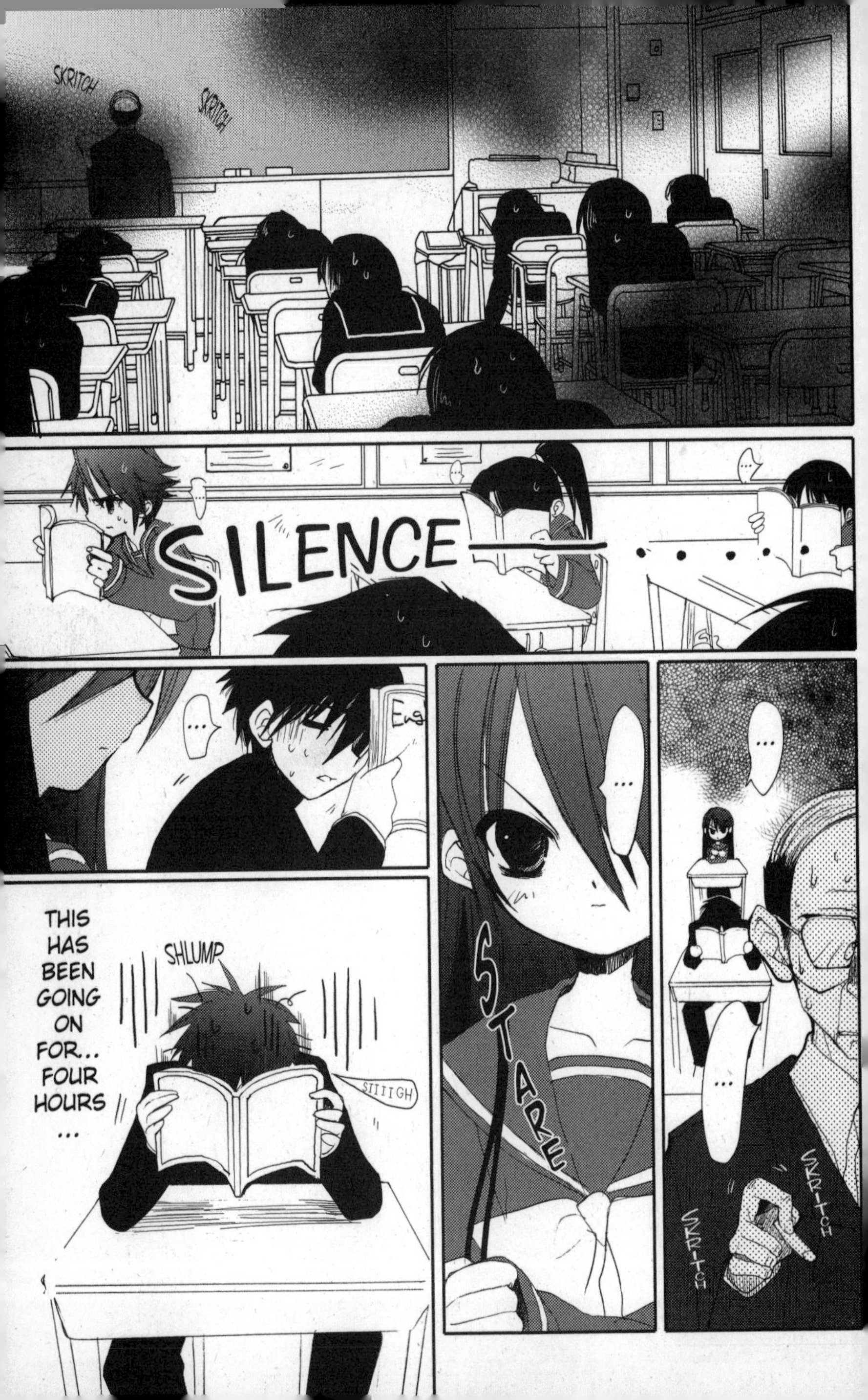
SKRITCH
SKRITCH
SILENCE—
...
...
...
...
...
SKRITCH
SKRITCH
...
STARE
...
Eng
THIS HAS BEEN GOING ON FOR... FOUR HOURS...
SHLUMP
SIIIIGH

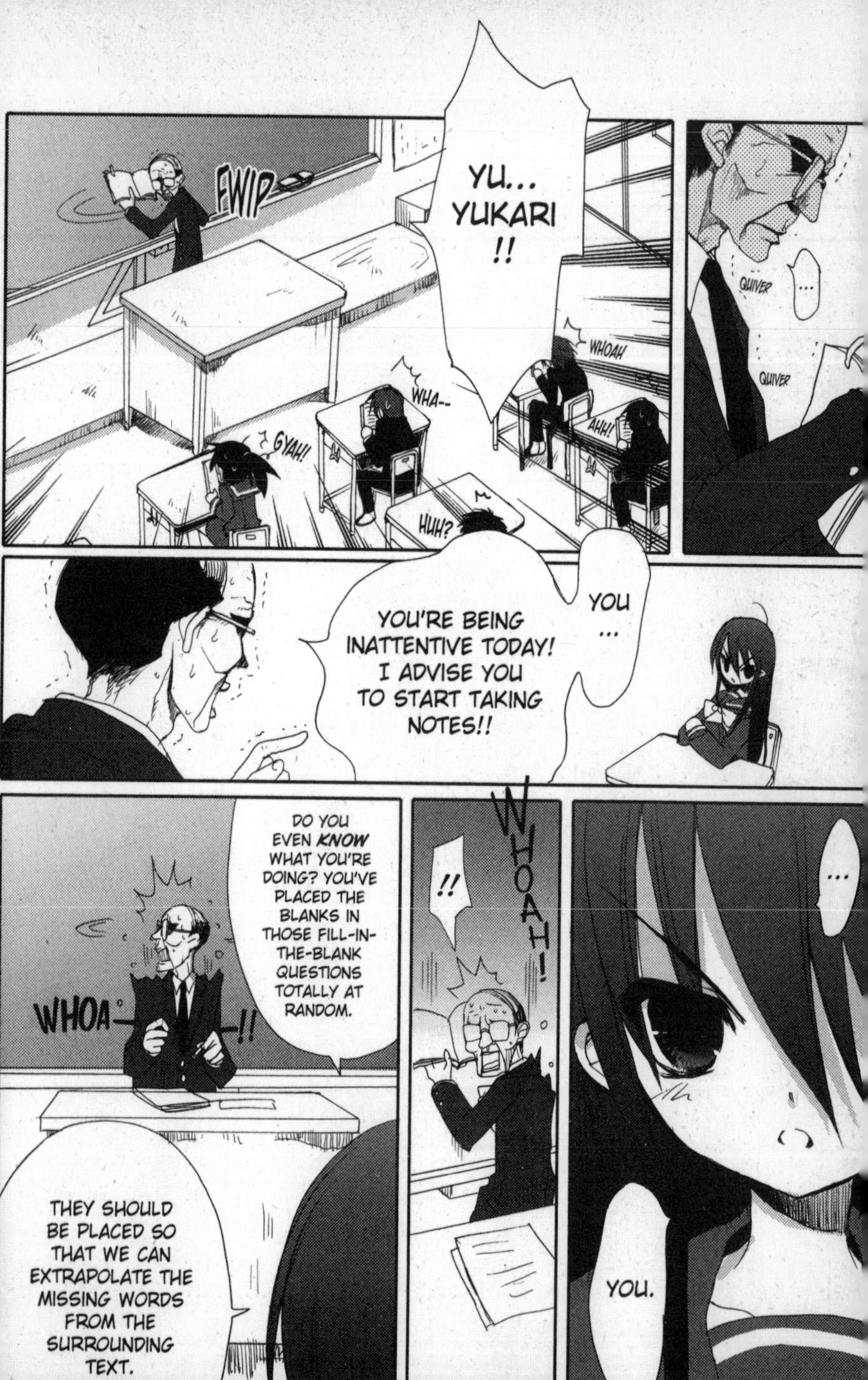
QUIVER
...
QUIVER
YU... YUKARI !!
FWIP
WHOAH
AHH!
WHA--
GYAH!
HUH?
YOU ...
YOU'RE BEING INATTENTIVE TODAY! I ADVISE YOU TO START TAKING NOTES!!
...
YOU.
WHOAH!
!!
DO YOU EVEN KNOW WHAT YOU'RE DOING? YOU'VE PLACED THE BLANKS IN THOSE FILL-IN-THE-BLANK QUESTIONS TOTALLY AT RANDOM.
WHOA--!!
THEY SHOULD BE PLACED SO THAT WE CAN EXTRAPOLATE THE MISSING WORDS FROM THE SURROUNDING TEXT.

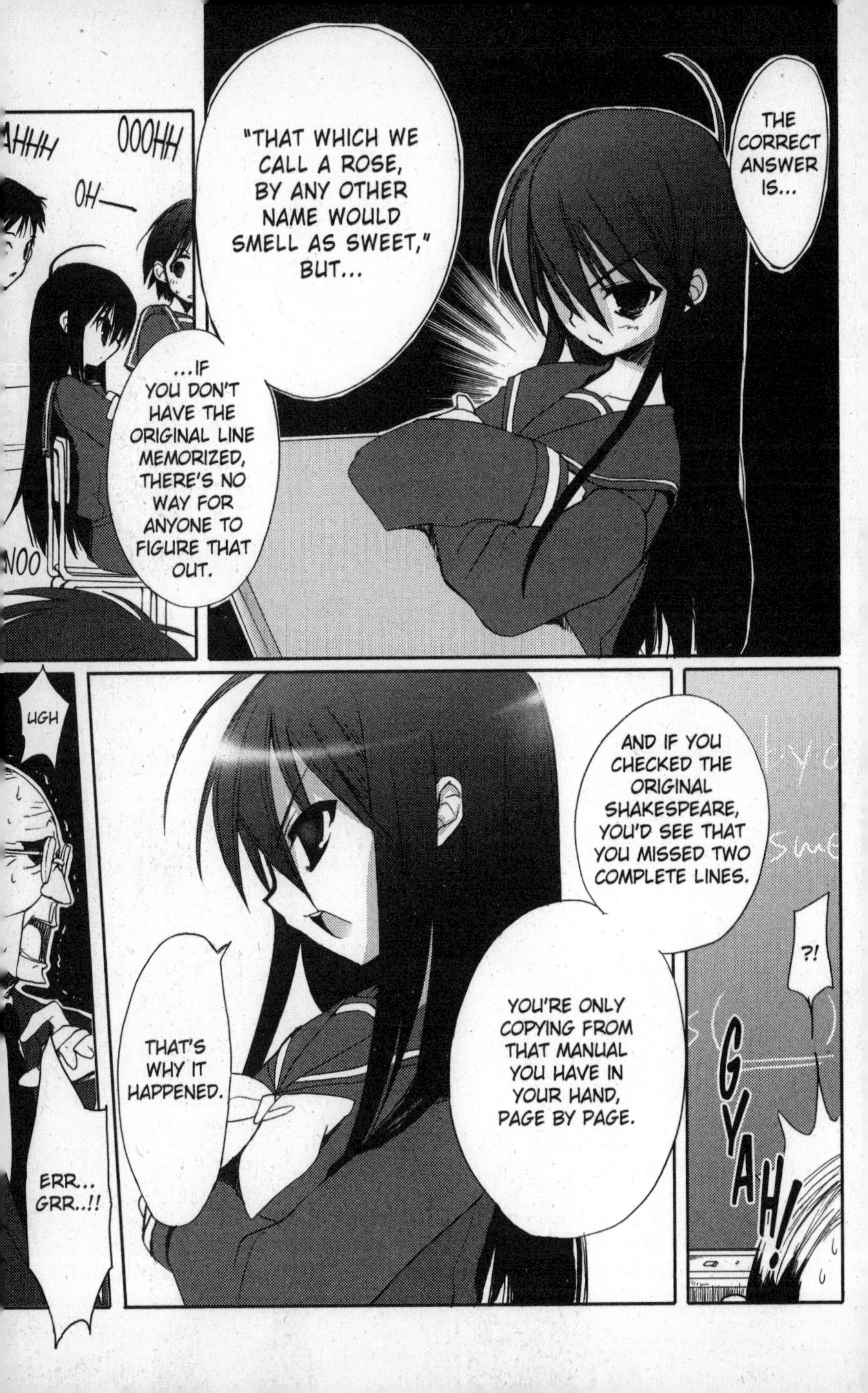
THE CORRECT ANSWER IS...
"THAT WHICH WE CALL A ROSE, BY ANY OTHER NAME WOULD SMELL AS SWEET," BUT...
...IF YOU DON'T HAVE THE ORIGINAL LINE MEMORIZED, THERE'S NO WAY FOR ANYONE TO FIGURE THAT OUT.
OOOHH
AHHH
OH—
NOO
?!
GYAH!
AND IF YOU CHECKED THE ORIGINAL SHAKESPEARE, YOU'D SEE THAT YOU MISSED TWO COMPLETE LINES.
YOU'RE ONLY COPYING FROM THAT MANUAL YOU HAVE IN YOUR HAND, PAGE BY PAGE.
THAT'S WHY IT HAPPENED.
UGH
ERR... GRR..!!

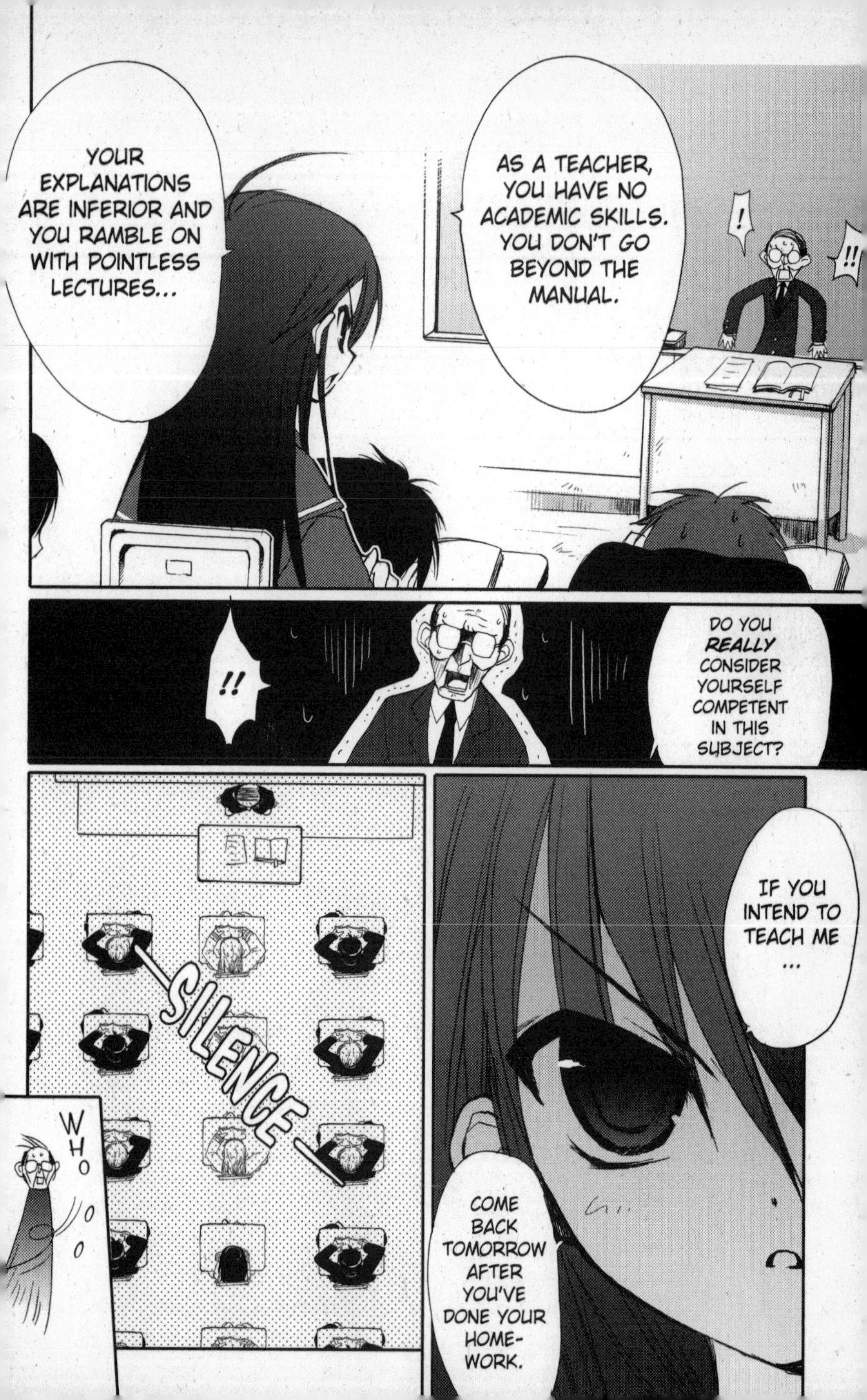
!
!!
AS A TEACHER, YOU HAVE NO ACADEMIC SKILLS. YOU DON'T GO BEYOND THE MANUAL.
YOUR EXPLANATIONS ARE INFERIOR AND YOU RAMBLE ON WITH POINTLESS LECTURES...
DO YOU *REALLY* CONSIDER YOURSELF COMPETENT IN THIS SUBJECT?
!!
IF YOU INTEND TO TEACH ME ...
COME BACK TOMORROW AFTER YOU'VE DONE YOUR HOME-WORK.
SILENCE
WHOOO

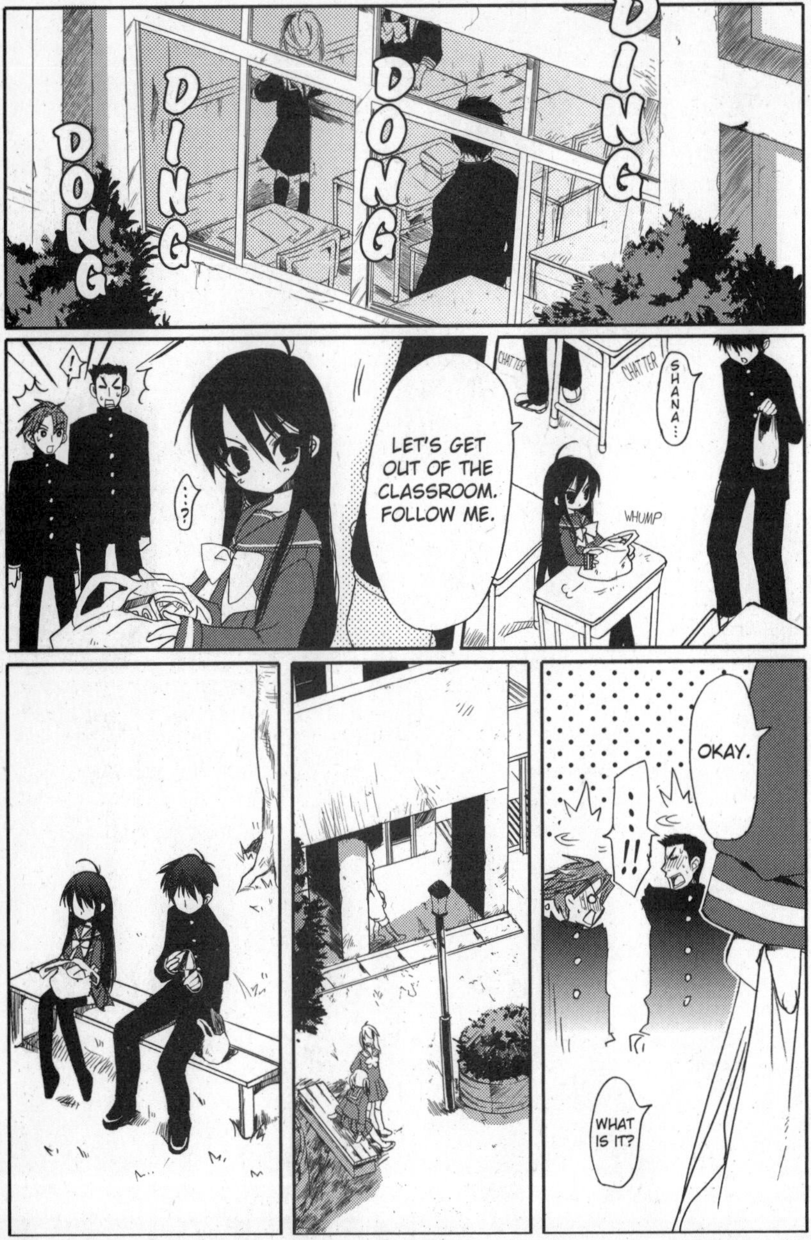
DING
DONG
DING
DONG
CHATTER
CHATTER
SHANA...
WHUMP
LET'S GET OUT OF THE CLASSROOM. FOLLOW ME.
...?
!
OKAY.
...!!
WHAT IS IT?

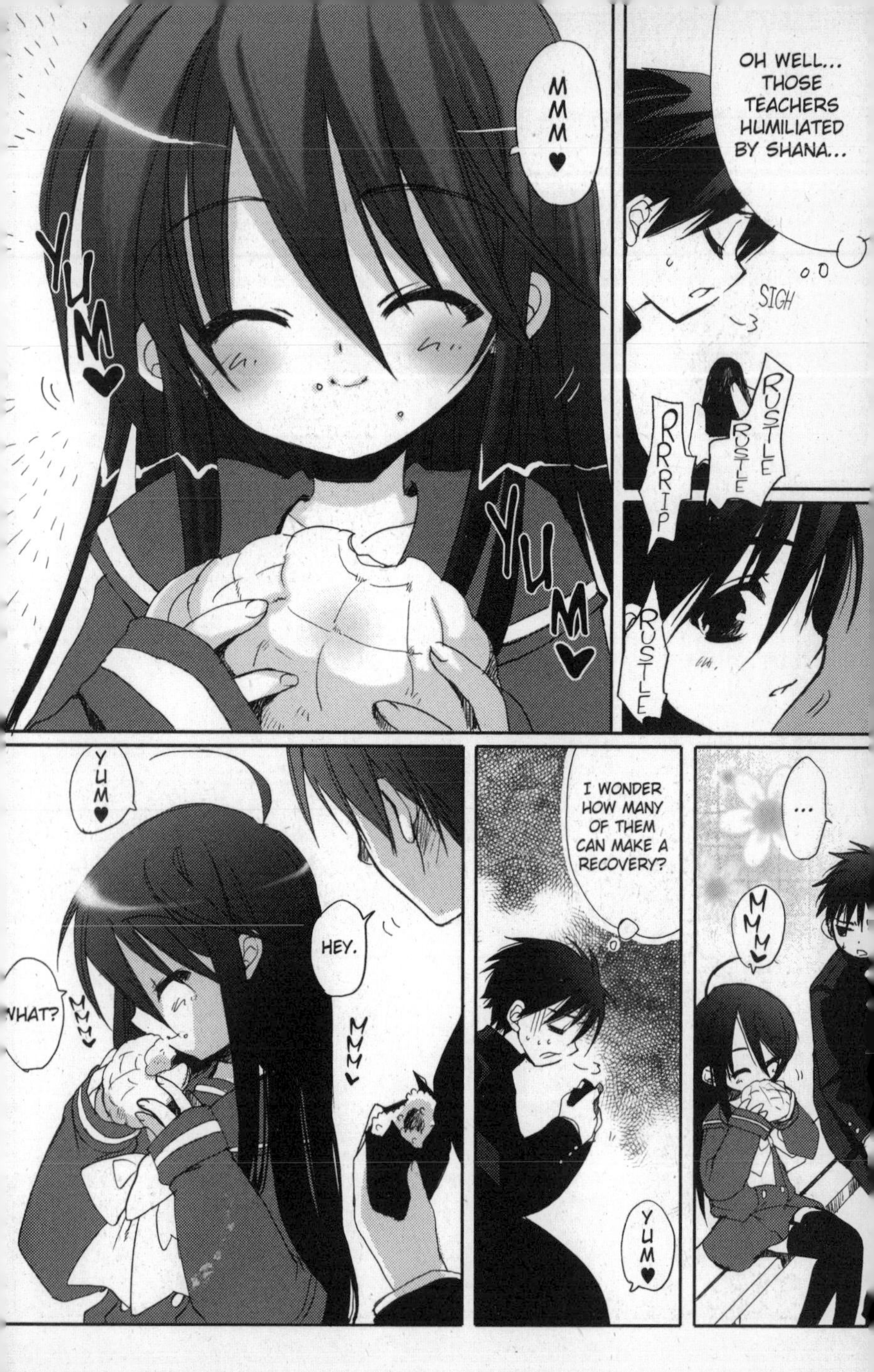
OH WELL... THOSE TEACHERS HUMILIATED BY SHANA...
SIGH
RUSTLE RUSTLE
RRRIP
RUSTLE
MMM♥
YUM YUM♥
YUM YUM♥
...
MMM♥
I WONDER HOW MANY OF THEM CAN MAKE A RECOVERY?
YUM♥
YUM♥
HEY.
MMM♥
WHAT?
MMM♥

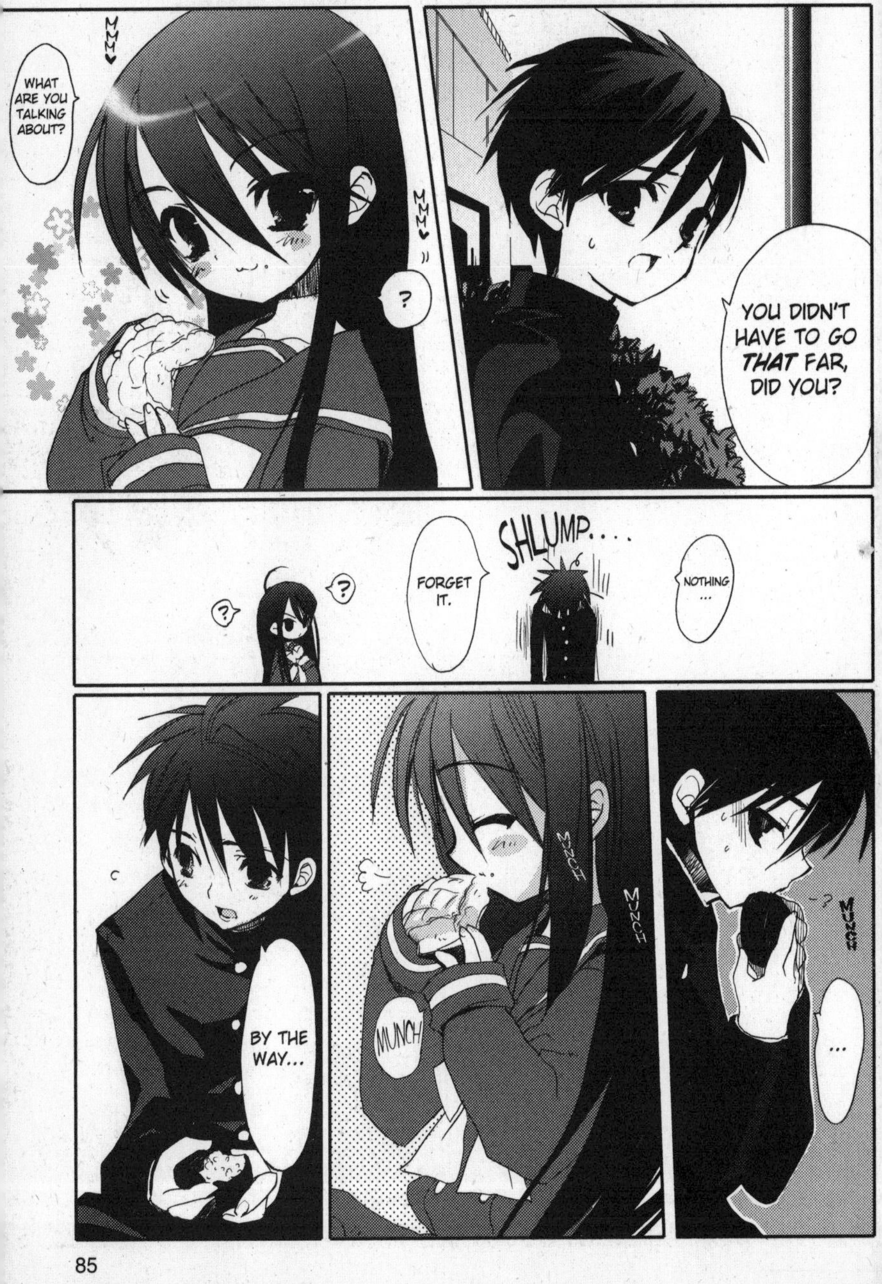
YOU DIDN'T HAVE TO GO *THAT* FAR, DID YOU?
MMM♥
?
MMM♥
WHAT ARE YOU TALKING ABOUT?
NOTHING ...
SHLUMP....
FORGET IT.
?
?
MUNCH
...
MUNCH
MUNCH
MUNCH
BY THE WAY...

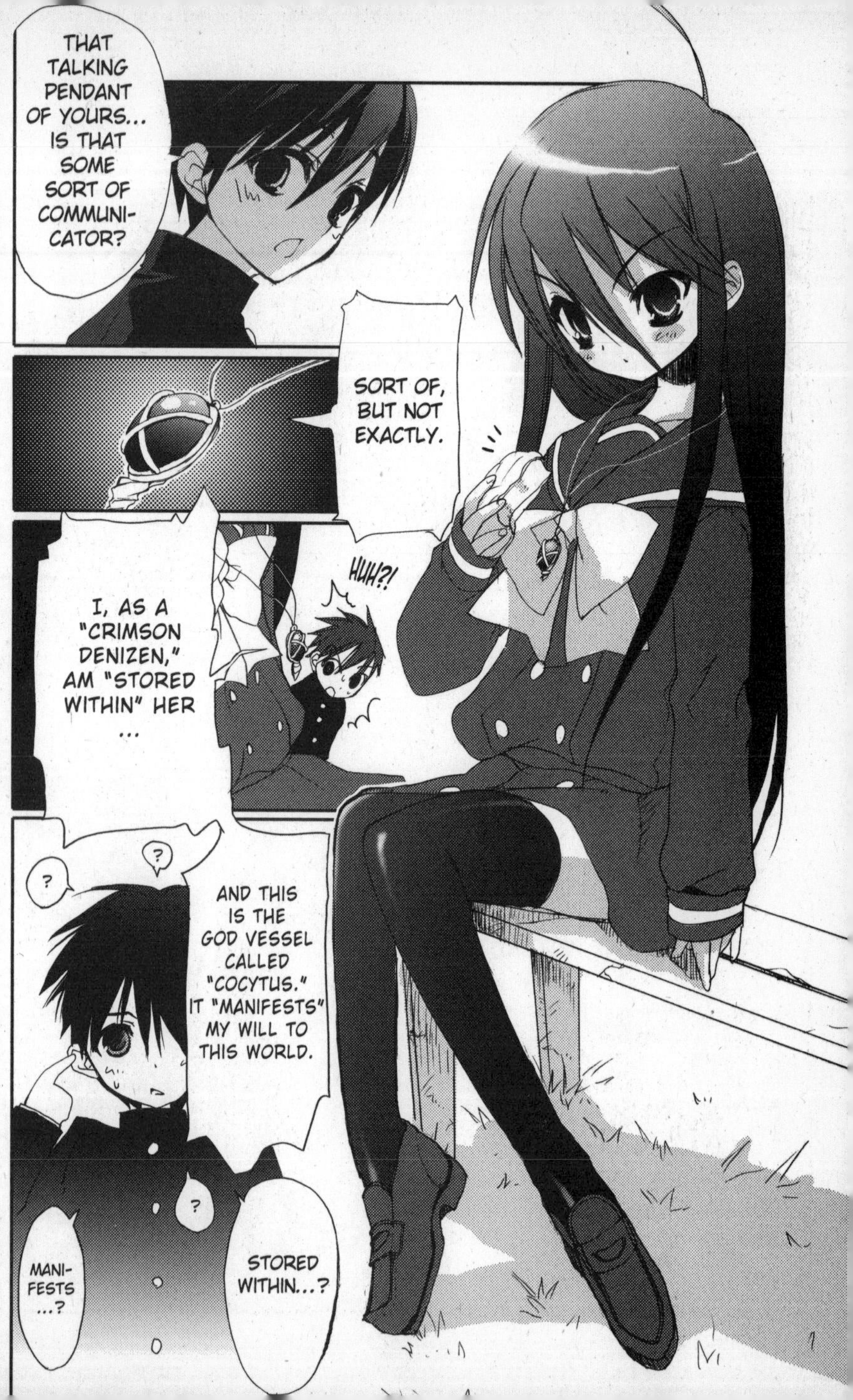
THAT TALKING PENDANT OF YOURS... IS THAT SOME SORT OF COMMUNICATOR?
SORT OF, BUT NOT EXACTLY.
HUH?!
I, AS A "CRIMSON DENIZEN," AM "STORED WITHIN" HER ...
AND THIS IS THE GOD VESSEL CALLED "COCYTUS." IT "MANIFESTS" MY WILL TO THIS WORLD.
?
?
STORED WITHIN...?
?
MANI-FESTS ...?

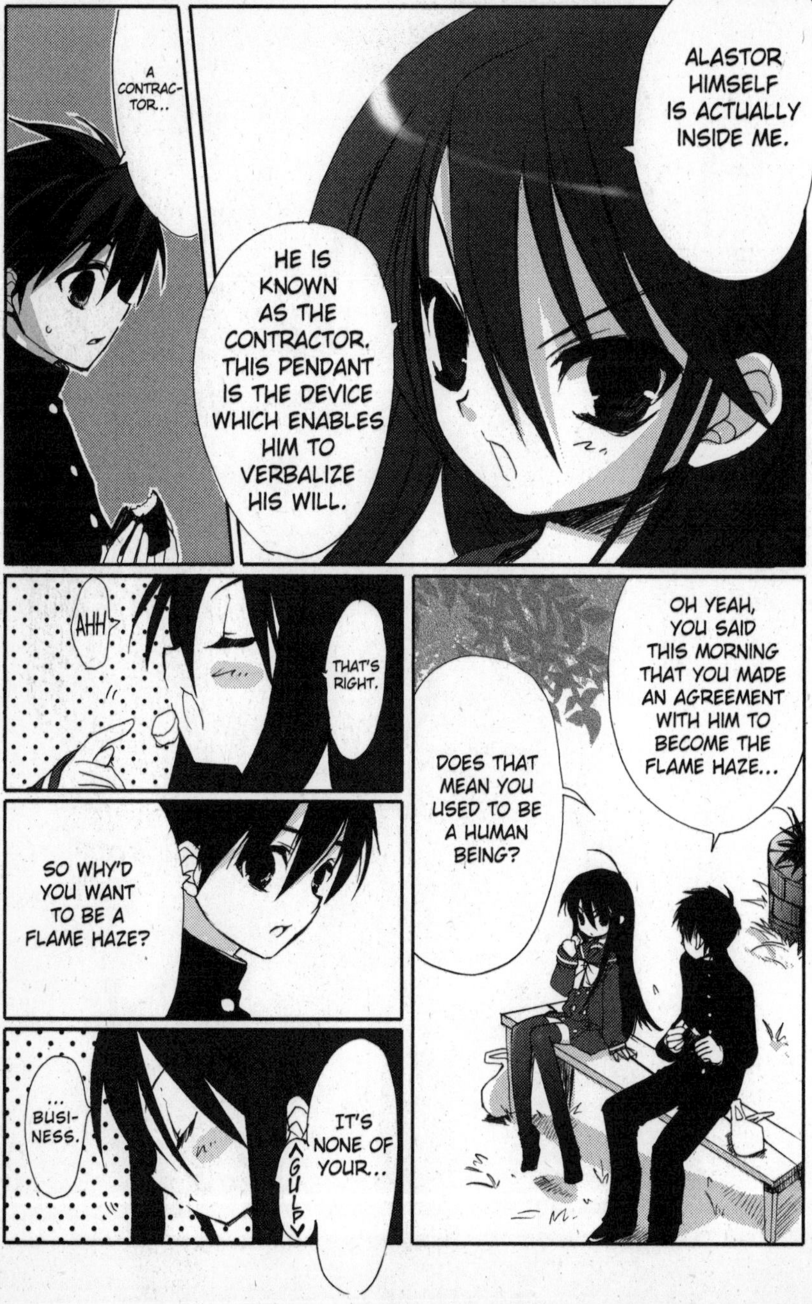
ALASTOR HIMSELF IS ACTUALLY INSIDE ME.
HE IS KNOWN AS THE CONTRACTOR. THIS PENDANT IS THE DEVICE WHICH ENABLES HIM TO VERBALIZE HIS WILL.
A CONTRAC-TOR...
OH YEAH, YOU SAID THIS MORNING THAT YOU MADE AN AGREEMENT WITH HIM TO BECOME THE FLAME HAZE...
DOES THAT MEAN YOU USED TO BE A HUMAN BEING?
THAT'S RIGHT.
AHH
SO WHY'D YOU WANT TO BE A FLAME HAZE?
IT'S NONE OF YOUR...
<GULP>
...BUSI-NESS.

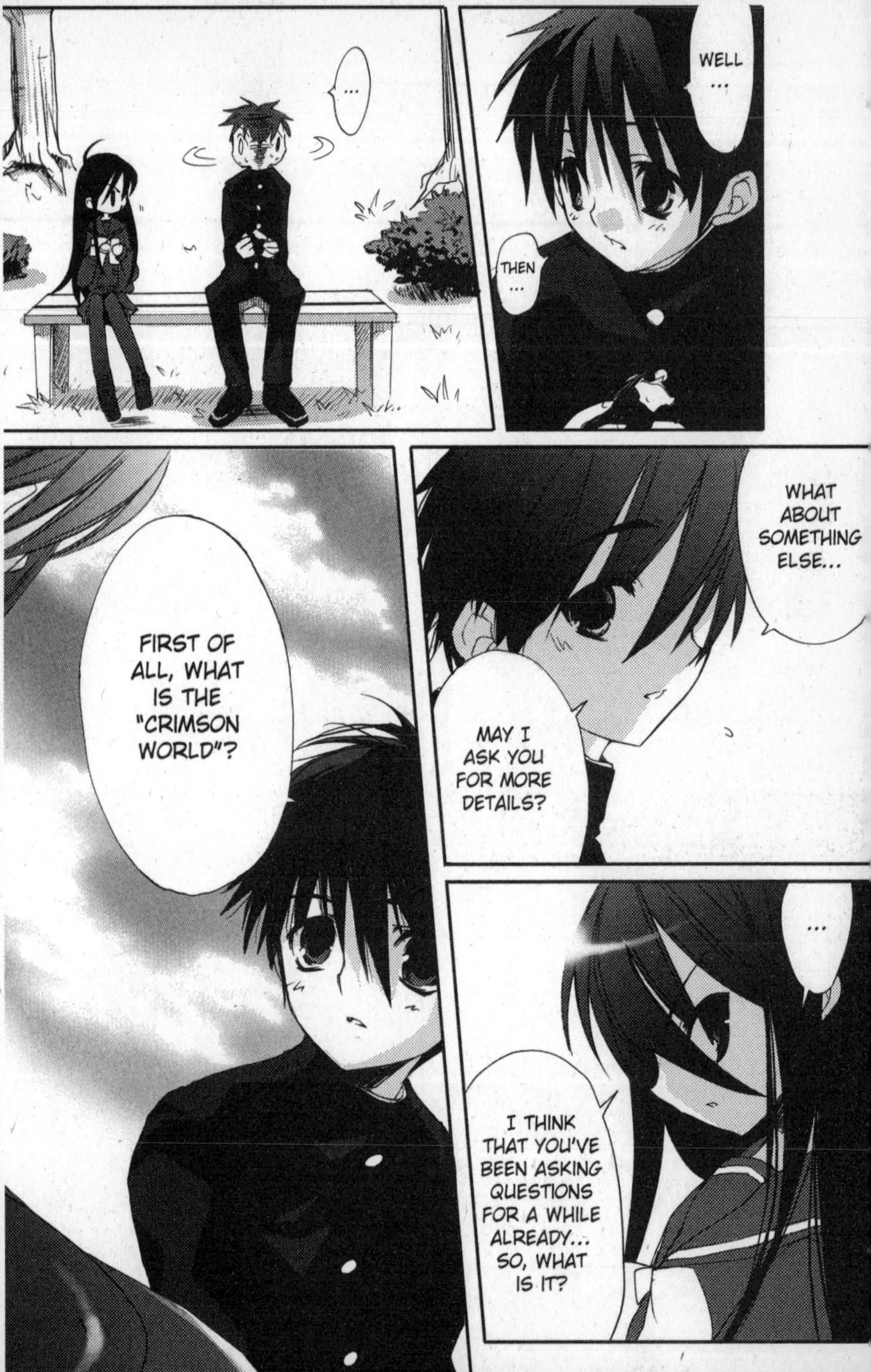
WELL ...
THEN ...
...
WHAT ABOUT SOMETHING ELSE...
MAY I ASK YOU FOR MORE DETAILS?
...
I THINK THAT YOU'VE BEEN ASKING QUESTIONS FOR A WHILE ALREADY... SO, WHAT IS IT?
FIRST OF ALL, WHAT IS THE "CRIMSON WORLD"?

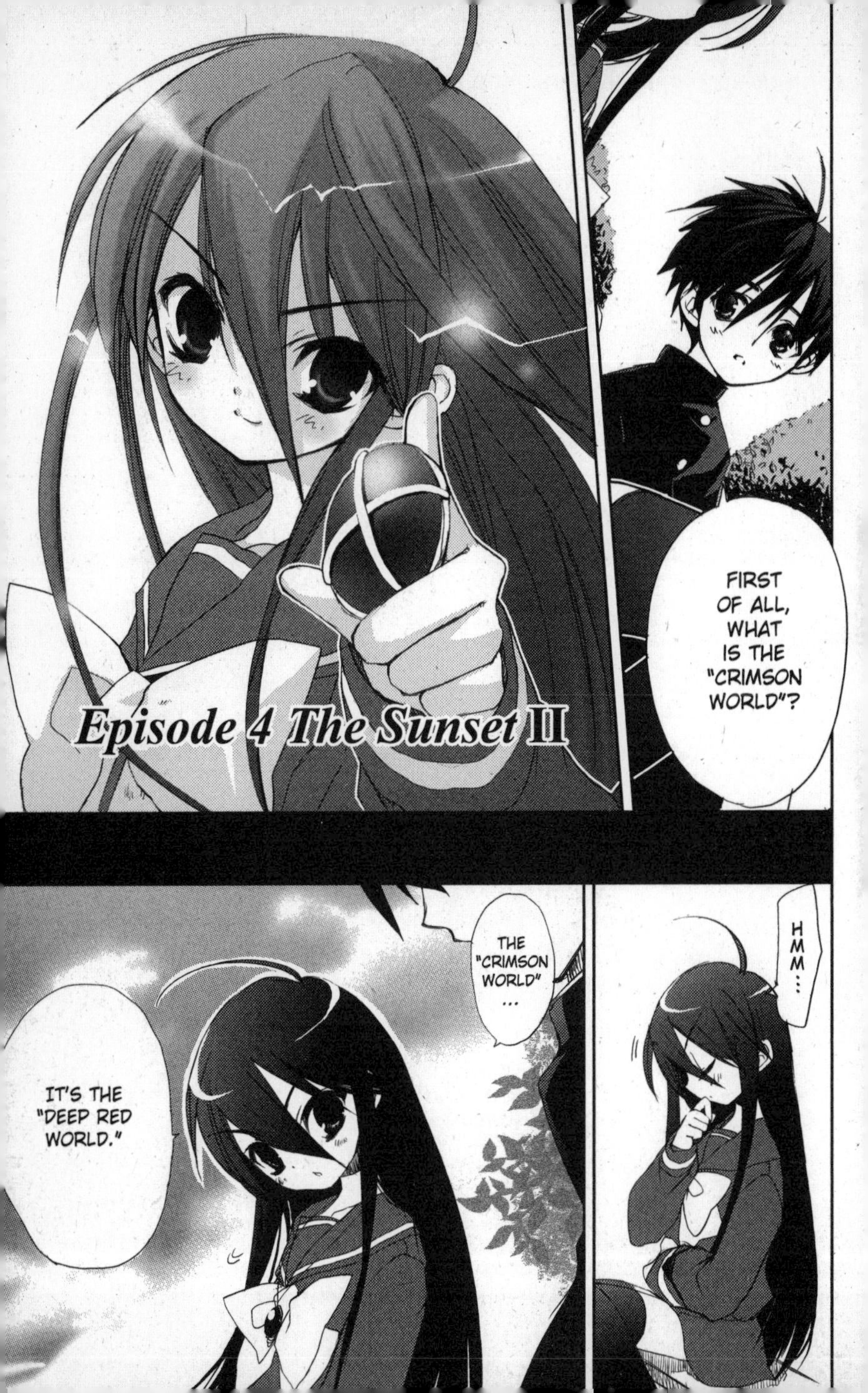
FIRST OF ALL, WHAT IS THE "CRIMSON WORLD"?
Episode 4 The Sunset II
HMM...
THE "CRIMSON WORLD"...
IT'S THE "DEEP RED WORLD."

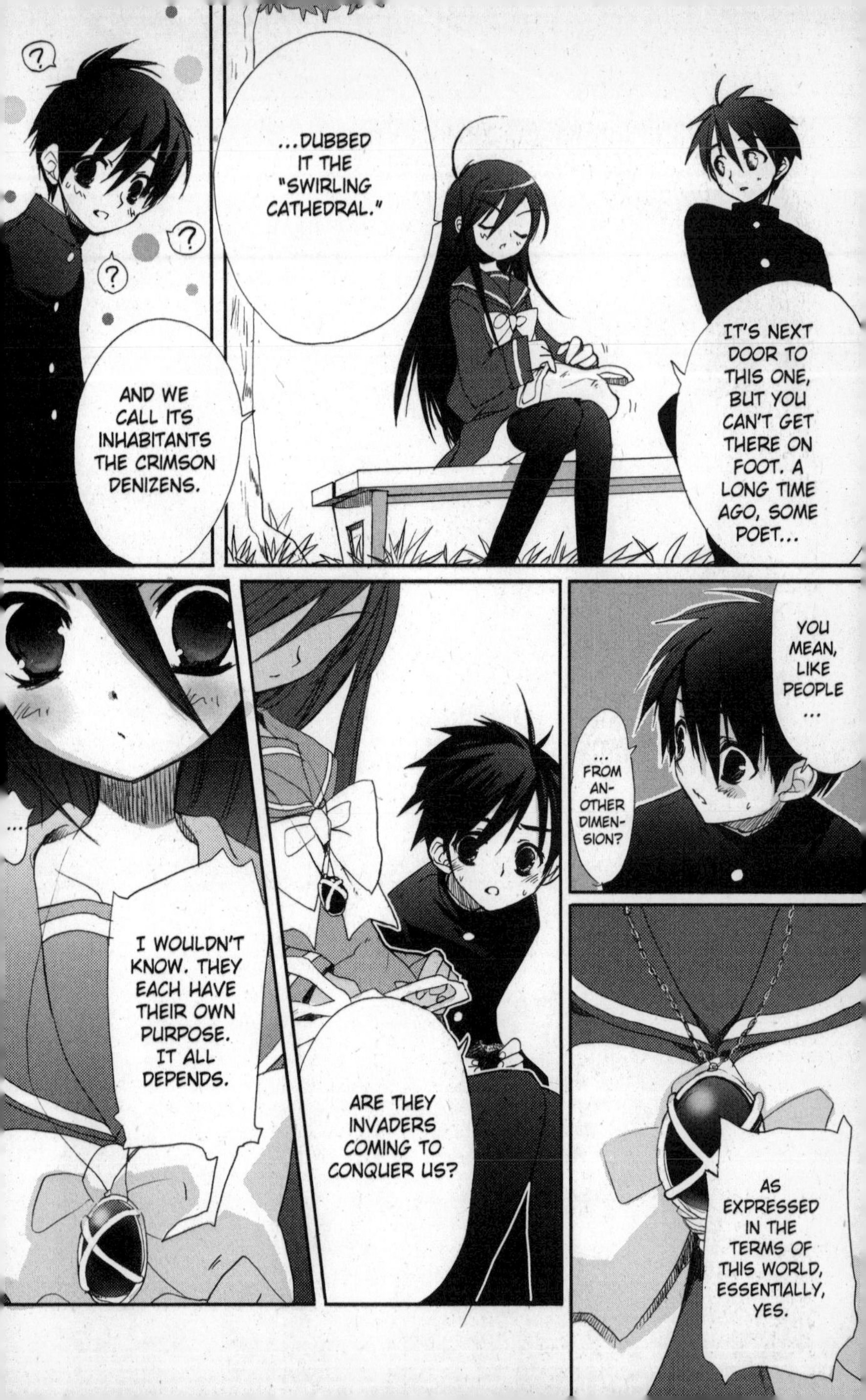
IT'S NEXT DOOR TO THIS ONE, BUT YOU CAN'T GET THERE ON FOOT. A LONG TIME AGO, SOME POET...
...DUBBED IT THE "SWIRLING CATHEDRAL."
?
?
?
AND WE CALL ITS INHABITANTS THE CRIMSON DENIZENS.
YOU MEAN, LIKE PEOPLE...
...FROM AN-OTHER DIMEN-SION?
AS EXPRESSED IN THE TERMS OF THIS WORLD, ESSENTIALLY, YES.
ARE THEY INVADERS COMING TO CONQUER US?
...
I WOULDN'T KNOW. THEY EACH HAVE THEIR OWN PURPOSE. IT ALL DEPENDS.

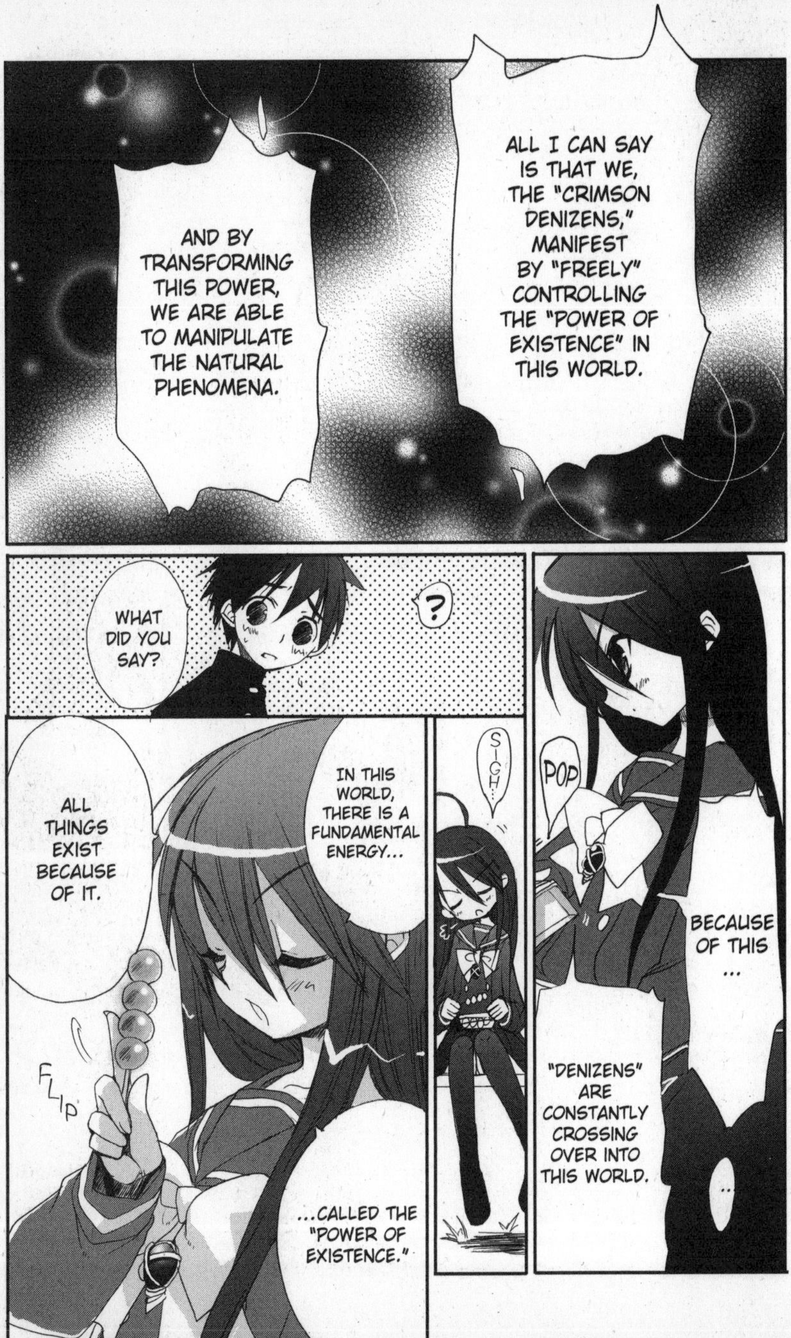
ALL I CAN SAY IS THAT WE, THE "CRIMSON DENIZENS," MANIFEST BY "FREELY" CONTROLLING THE "POWER OF EXISTENCE" IN THIS WORLD.
AND BY TRANSFORMING THIS POWER, WE ARE ABLE TO MANIPULATE THE NATURAL PHENOMENA.
POP
BECAUSE OF THIS ...
"DENIZENS" ARE CONSTANTLY CROSSING OVER INTO THIS WORLD.
...
?
WHAT DID YOU SAY?
SIGH...
IN THIS WORLD, THERE IS A FUNDAMENTAL ENERGY...
...CALLED THE "POWER OF EXISTENCE."
ALL THINGS EXIST BECAUSE OF IT.
FLIP

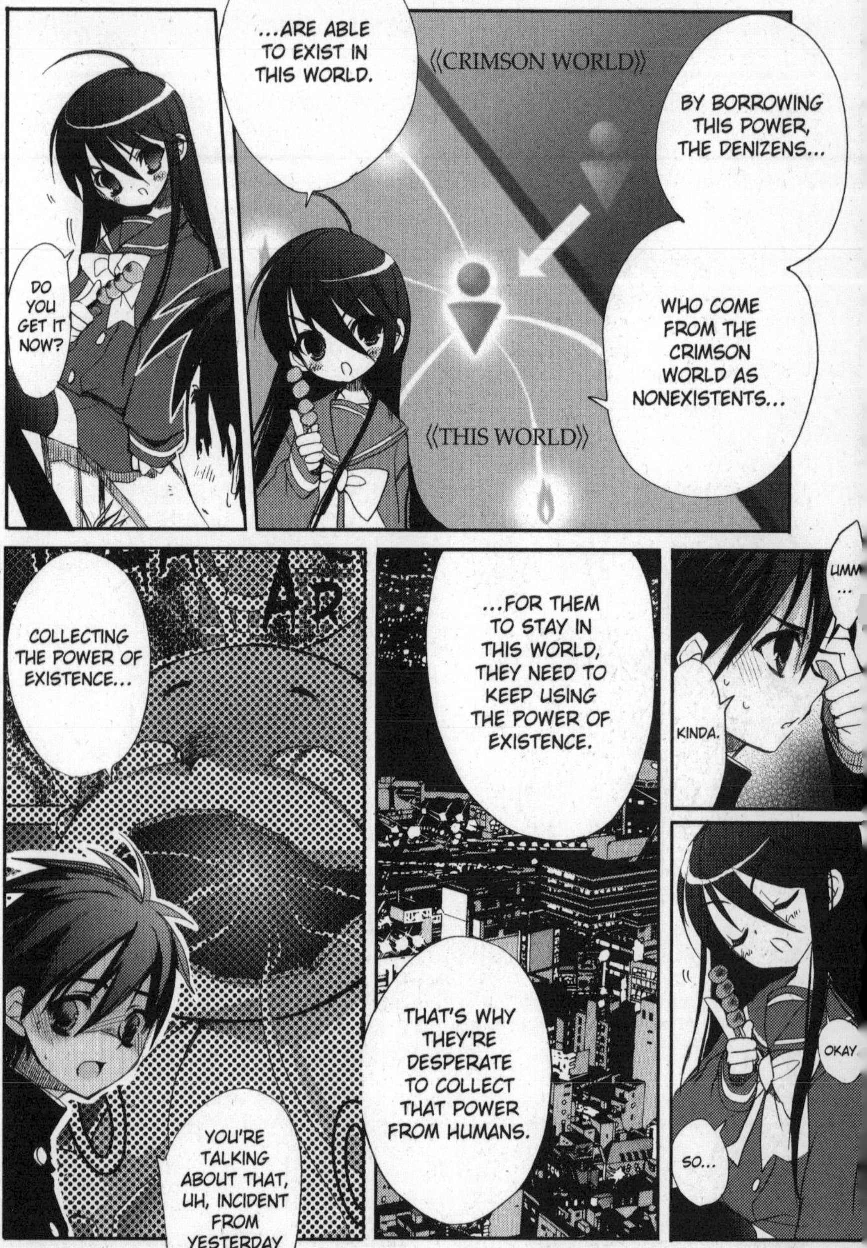
《CRIMSON WORLD》
BY BORROWING THIS POWER, THE DENIZENS...
WHO COME FROM THE CRIMSON WORLD AS NONEXISTENTS...
...ARE ABLE TO EXIST IN THIS WORLD.
《THIS WORLD》
DO YOU GET IT NOW?
UMM...
KINDA.
OKAY
SO...
...FOR THEM TO STAY IN THIS WORLD, THEY NEED TO KEEP USING THE POWER OF EXISTENCE.
THAT'S WHY THEY'RE DESPERATE TO COLLECT THAT POWER FROM HUMANS.
COLLECTING THE POWER OF EXISTENCE...
YOU'RE TALKING ABOUT THAT, UH, INCIDENT FROM YESTERDAY...

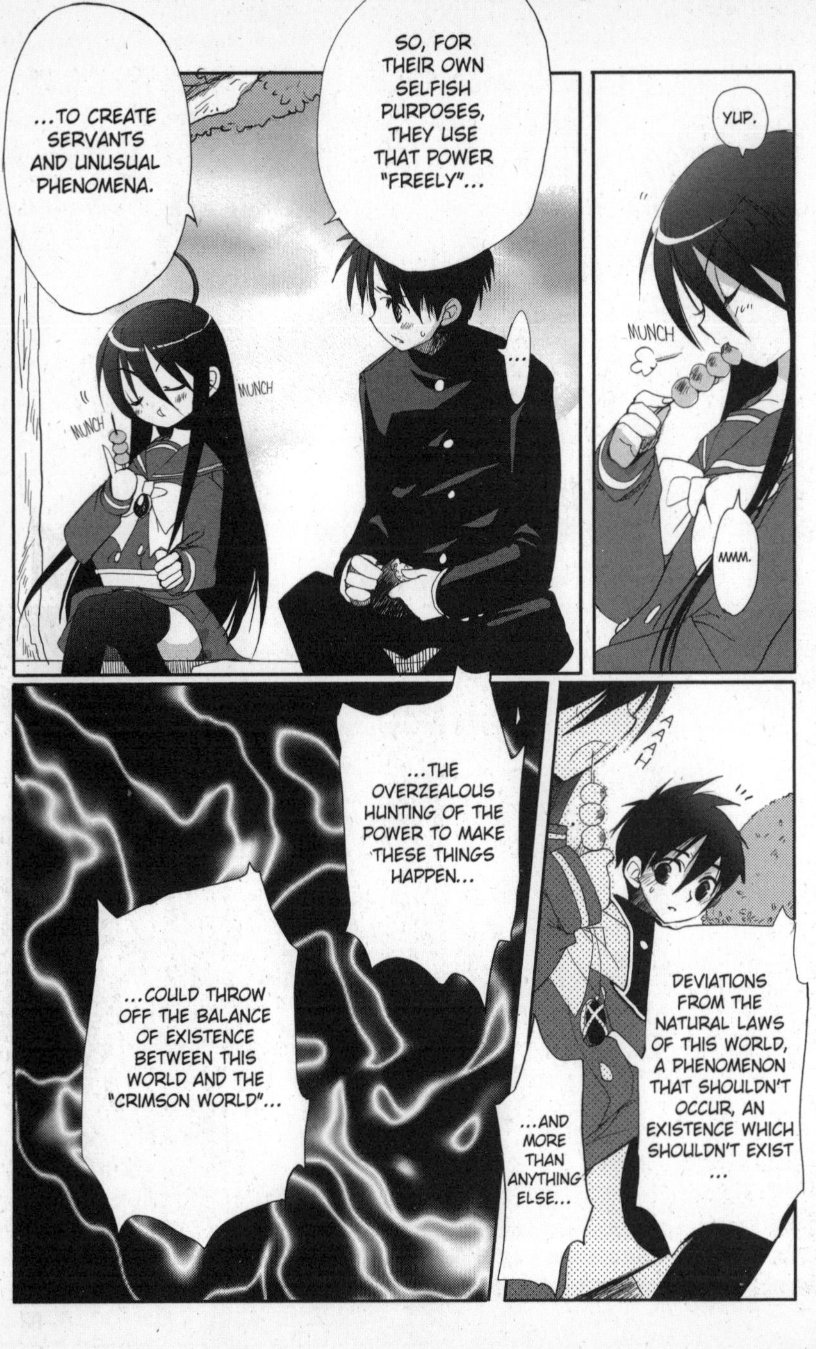
YUP.
MUNCH
MMM.
SO, FOR THEIR OWN SELFISH PURPOSES, THEY USE THAT POWER "FREELY"...
...TO CREATE SERVANTS AND UNUSUAL PHENOMENA.
...
MUNCH
MUNCH
AAAH
DEVIATIONS FROM THE NATURAL LAWS OF THIS WORLD, A PHENOMENON THAT SHOULDN'T OCCUR, AN EXISTENCE WHICH SHOULDN'T EXIST ...
...AND MORE THAN ANYTHING ELSE...
...THE OVERZEALOUS HUNTING OF THE POWER TO MAKE THESE THINGS HAPPEN...
...COULD THROW OFF THE BALANCE OF EXISTENCE BETWEEN THIS WORLD AND THE "CRIMSON WORLD"...

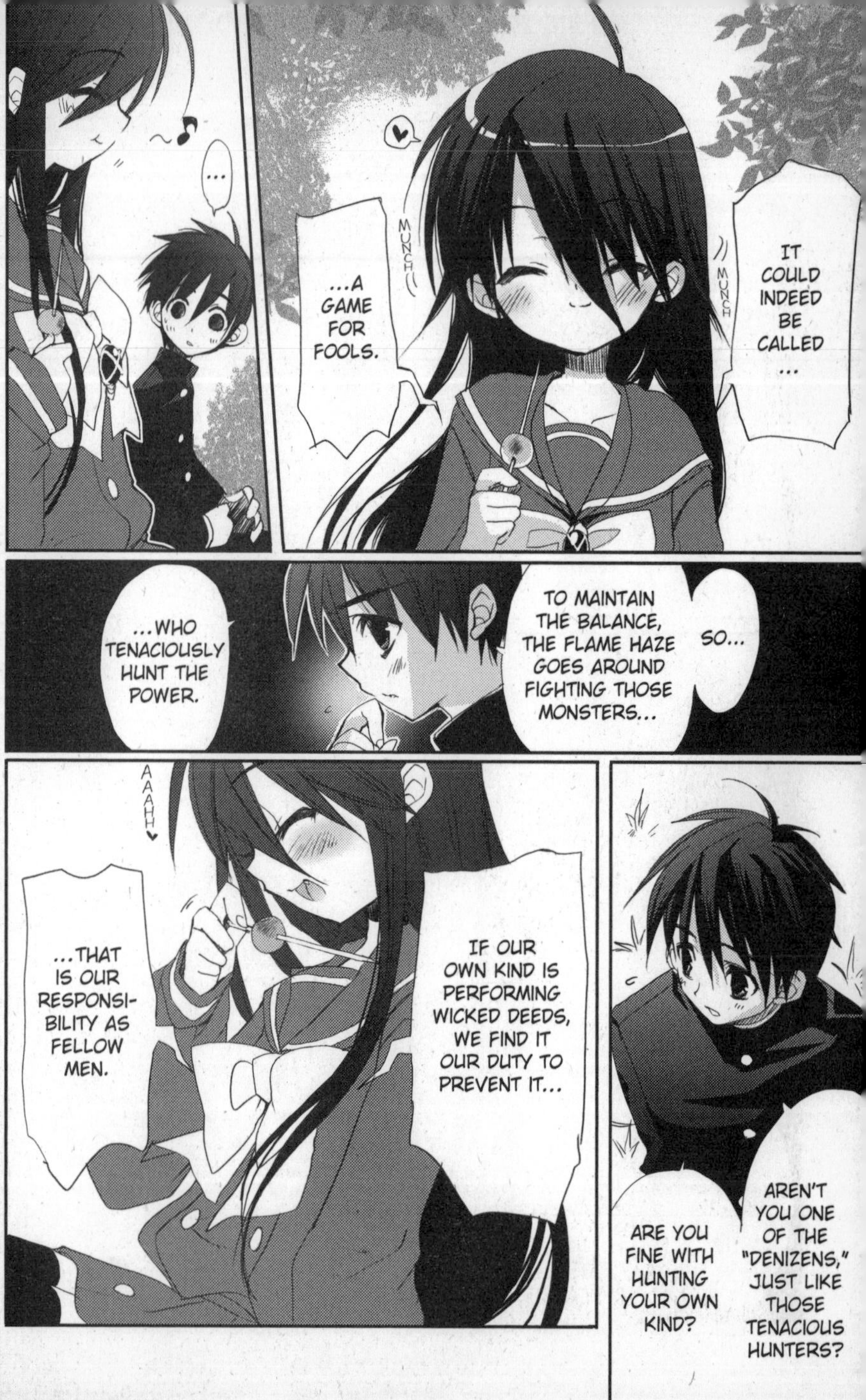

IT COULD INDEED BE CALLED...
MUNCH
MUNCH
...A GAME FOR FOOLS.
...
SO...
TO MAINTAIN THE BALANCE, THE FLAME HAZE GOES AROUND FIGHTING THOSE MONSTERS...
...WHO TENACIOUSLY HUNT THE POWER.
AREN'T YOU ONE OF THE "DENIZENS," JUST LIKE THOSE TENACIOUS HUNTERS?
ARE YOU FINE WITH HUNTING YOUR OWN KIND?
AAAH
IF OUR OWN KIND IS PERFORMING WICKED DEEDS, WE FIND IT OUR DUTY TO PREVENT IT...
...THAT IS OUR RESPONSI-BILITY AS FELLOW MEN.

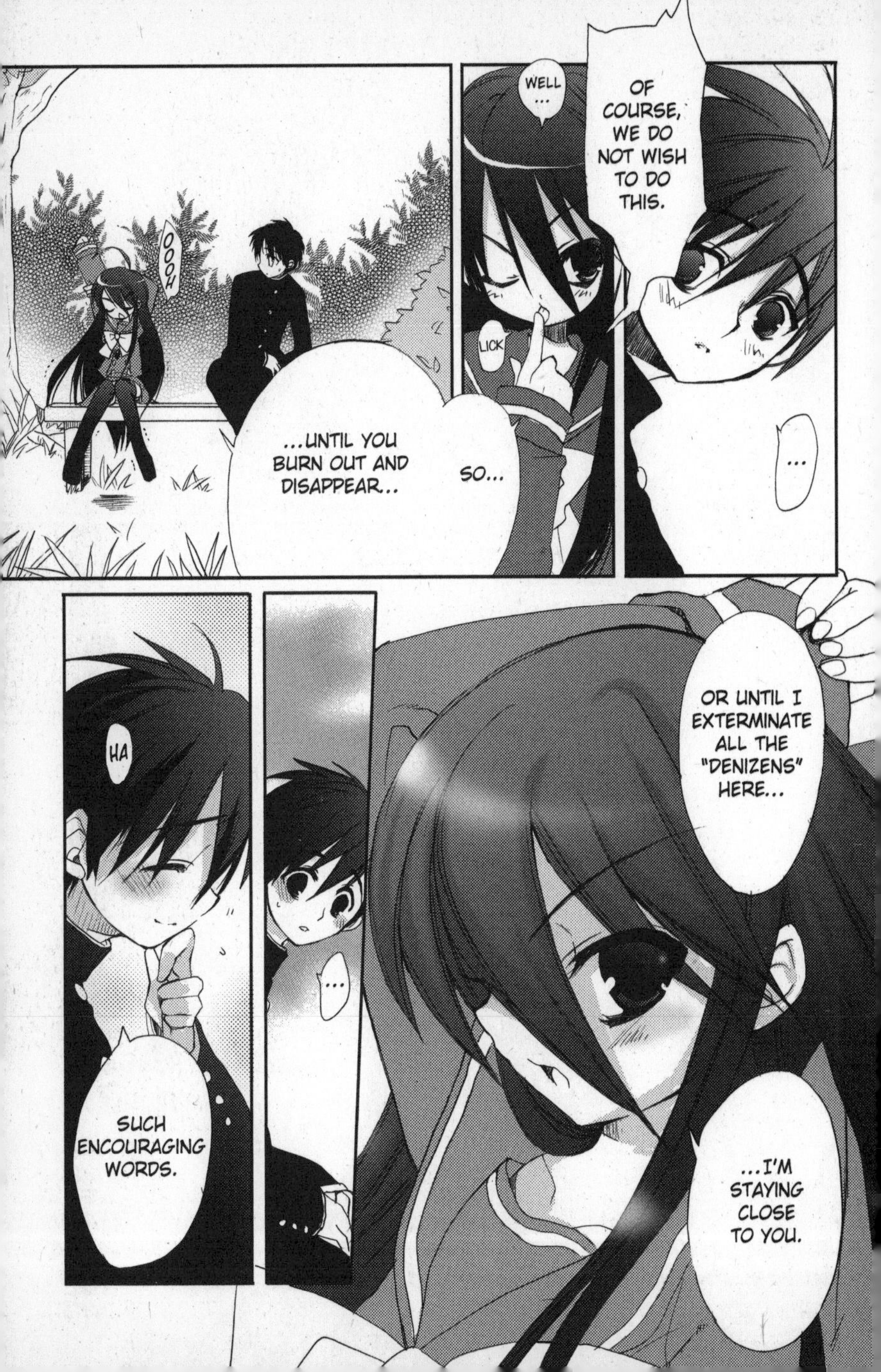
OF COURSE, WE DO NOT WISH TO DO THIS.
...
WELL...
LICK
SO...
...UNTIL YOU BURN OUT AND DISAPPEAR...
OOOH
OR UNTIL I EXTERMINATE ALL THE "DENIZENS" HERE...
...I'M STAYING CLOSE TO YOU.
...
HA
SUCH ENCOURAGING WORDS.

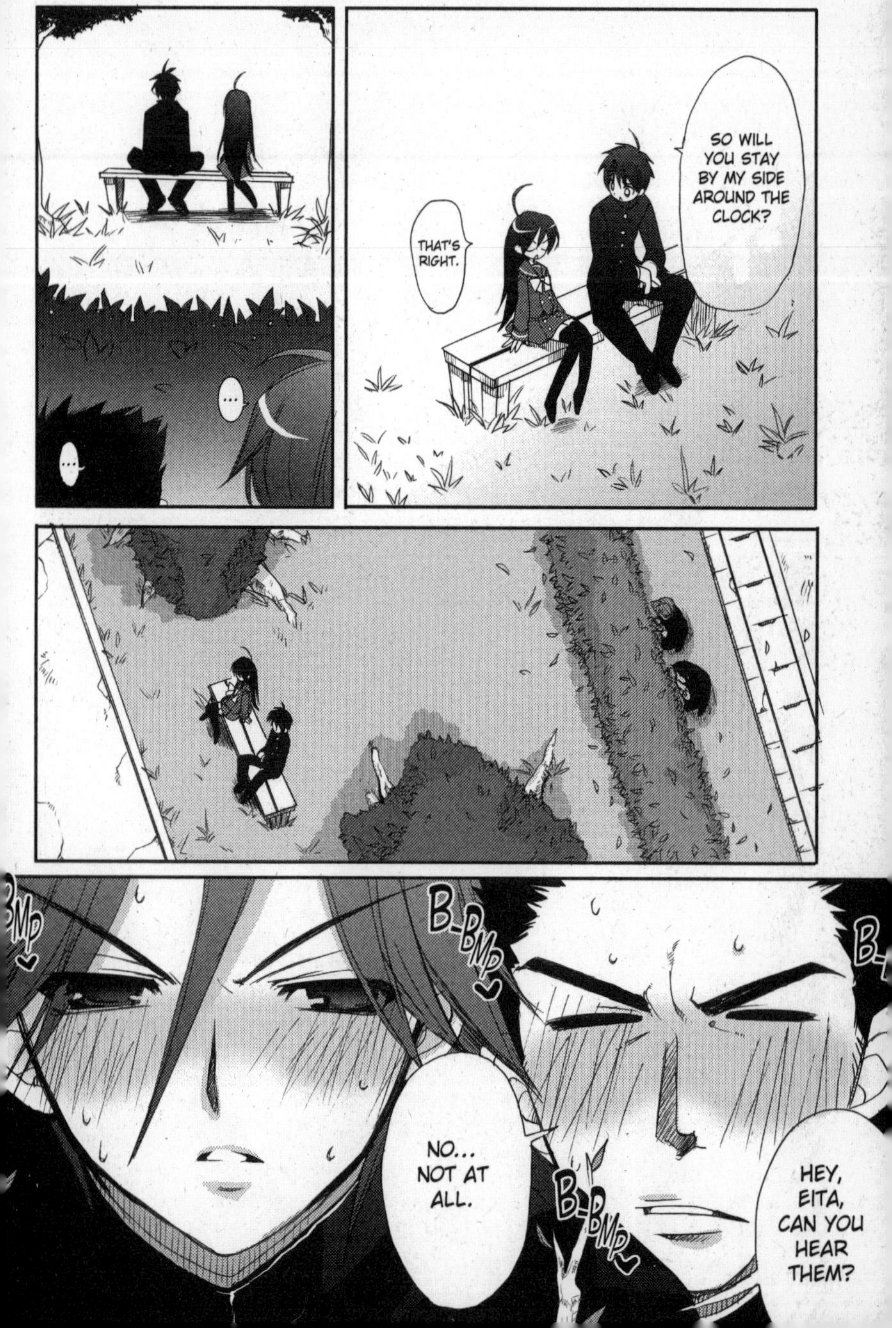
SO WILL YOU STAY BY MY SIDE AROUND THE CLOCK?
THAT'S RIGHT.
...
...
B-BMP
HEY, EITA, CAN YOU HEAR THEM?
B-BMP
NO... NOT AT ALL.

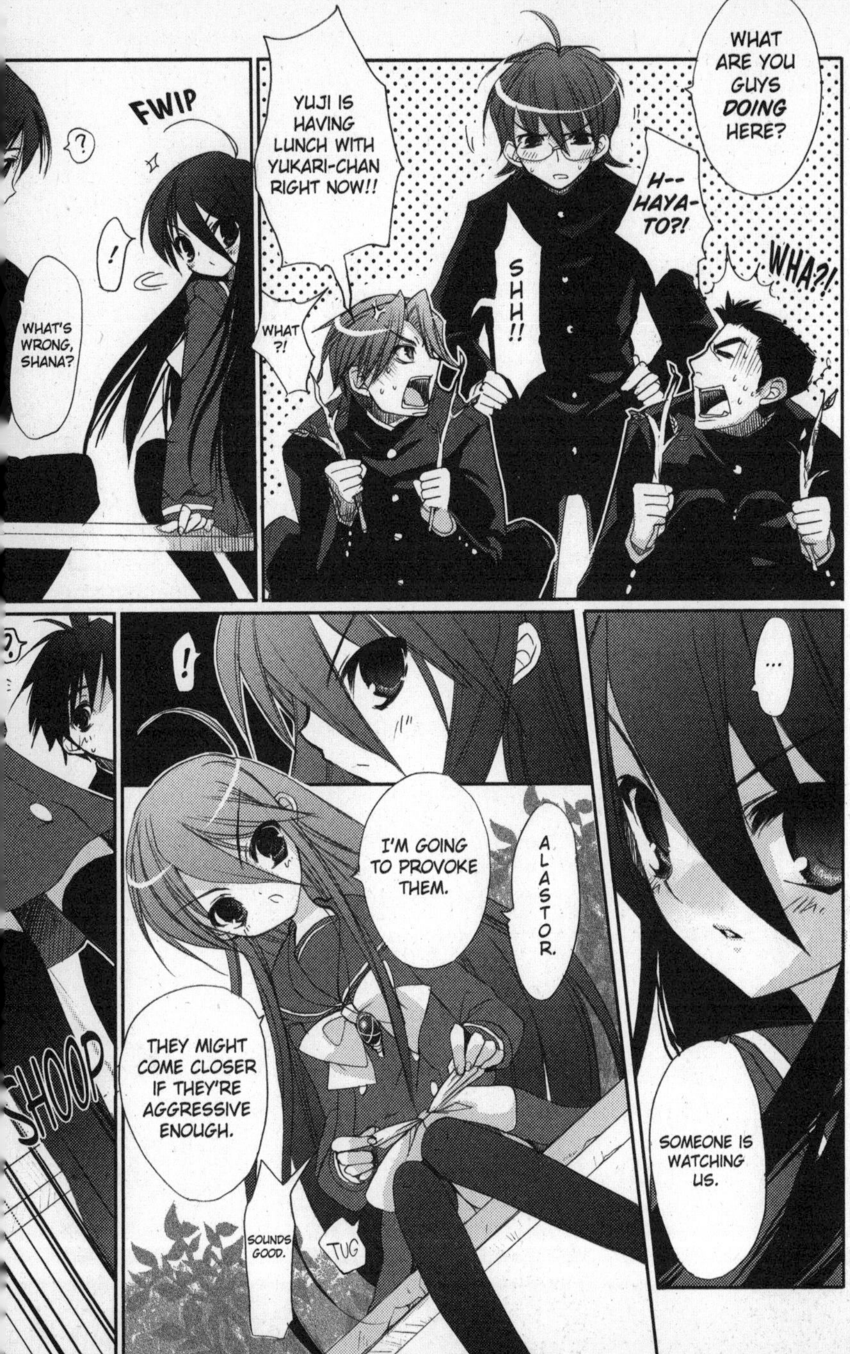
WHAT ARE YOU GUYS DOING HERE?
H--HAYATO?!
WHA?!
YUJI IS HAVING LUNCH WITH YUKARI-CHAN RIGHT NOW!!
SHH!!
WHAT?!
FWIP
?
!
WHAT'S WRONG, SHANA?
...
SOMEONE IS WATCHING US.
!
ALASTOR.
I'M GOING TO PROVOKE THEM.
THEY MIGHT COME CLOSER IF THEY'RE AGGRESSIVE ENOUGH.
TUG
SOUNDS GOOD.
?
SHOOP

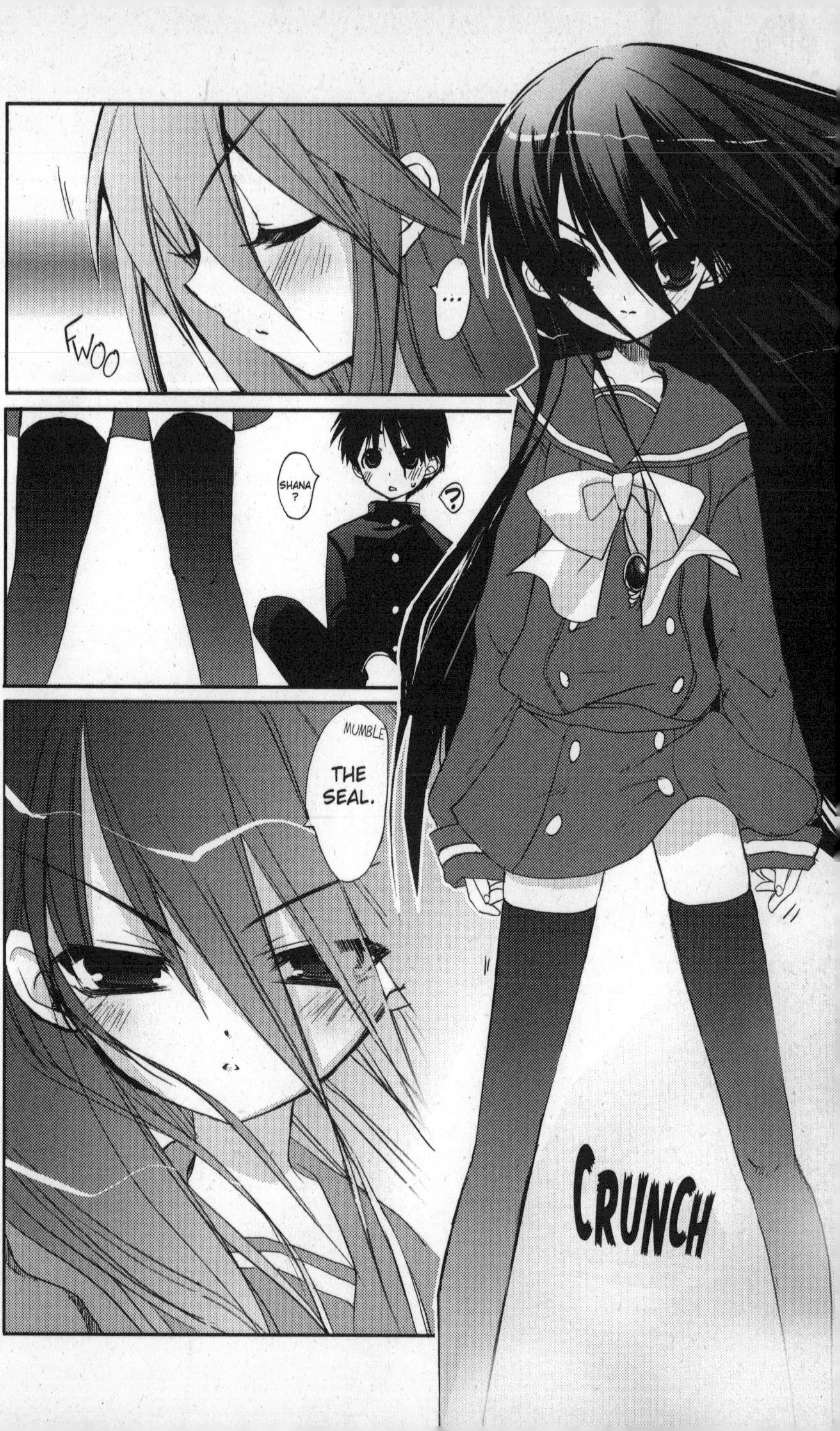
...
FWOO
SHANA?
?
MUMBLE
THE SEAL.
CRUNCH

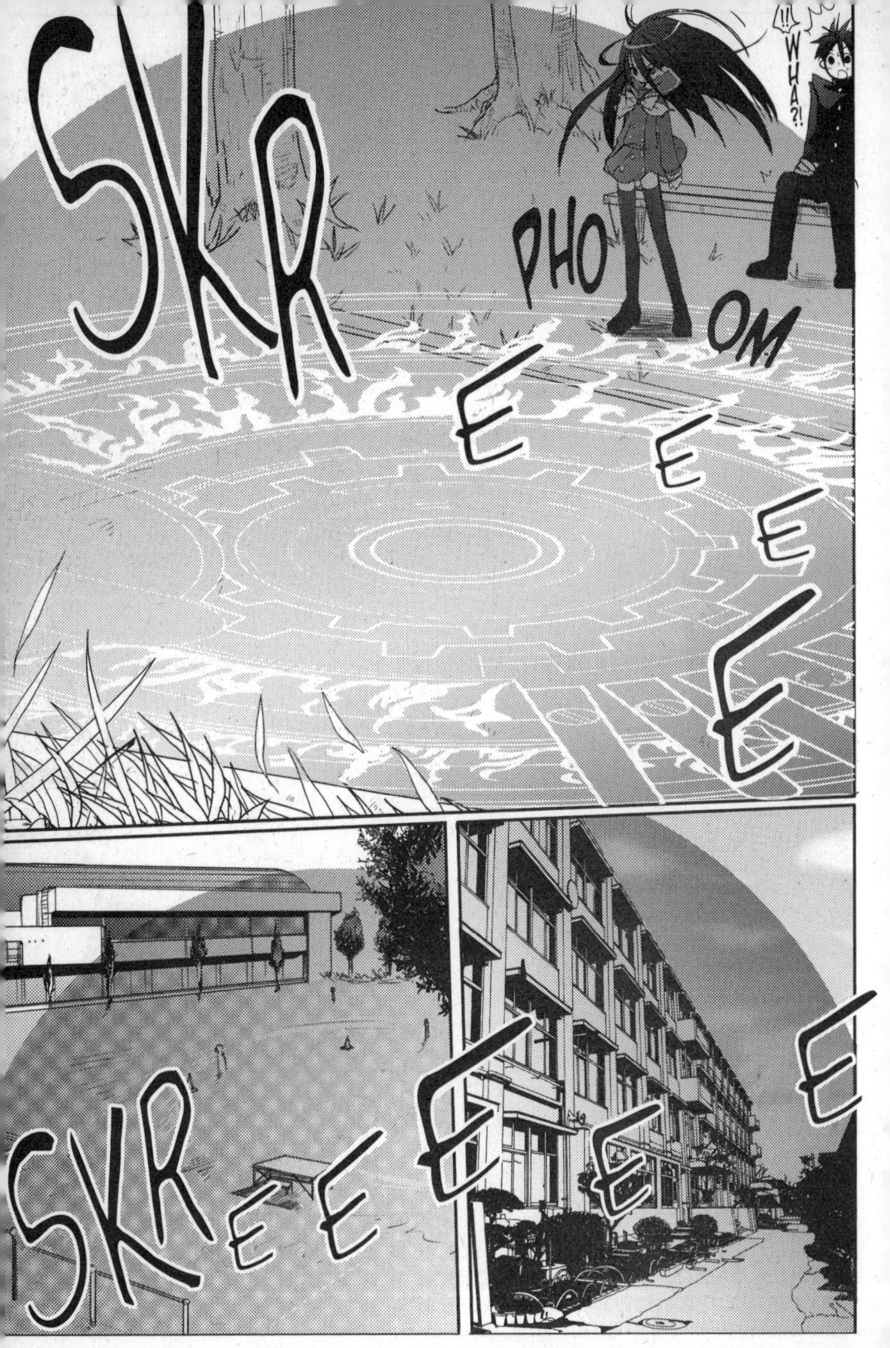
!!
WHA?!
PHOOM
SKREEEEE
SKREEEEEEE

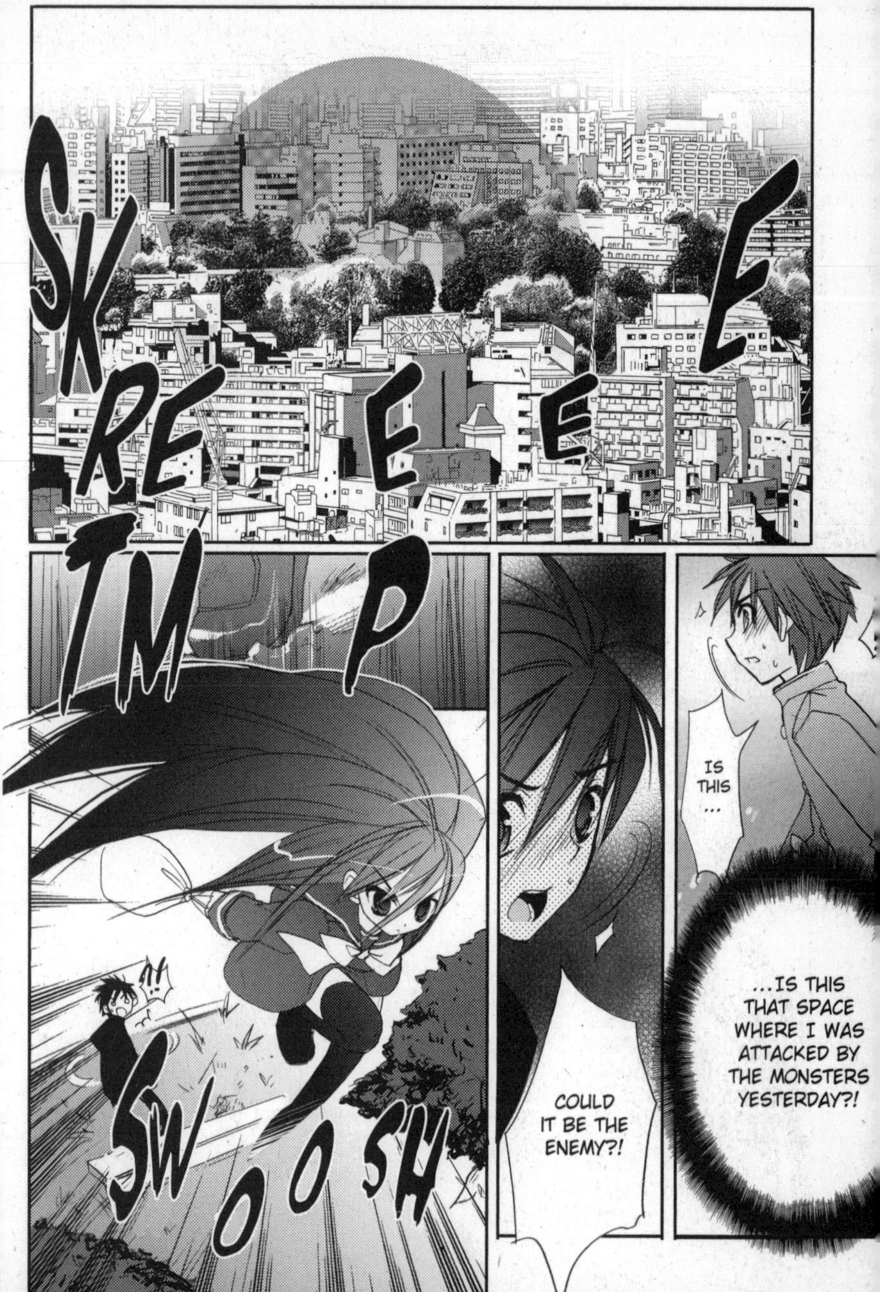
SKREEEE
IS THIS...
...IS THIS THAT SPACE WHERE I WAS ATTACKED BY THE MONSTERS YESTERDAY?!
COULD IT BE THE ENEMY?!
TMP
?!
SWOOSH

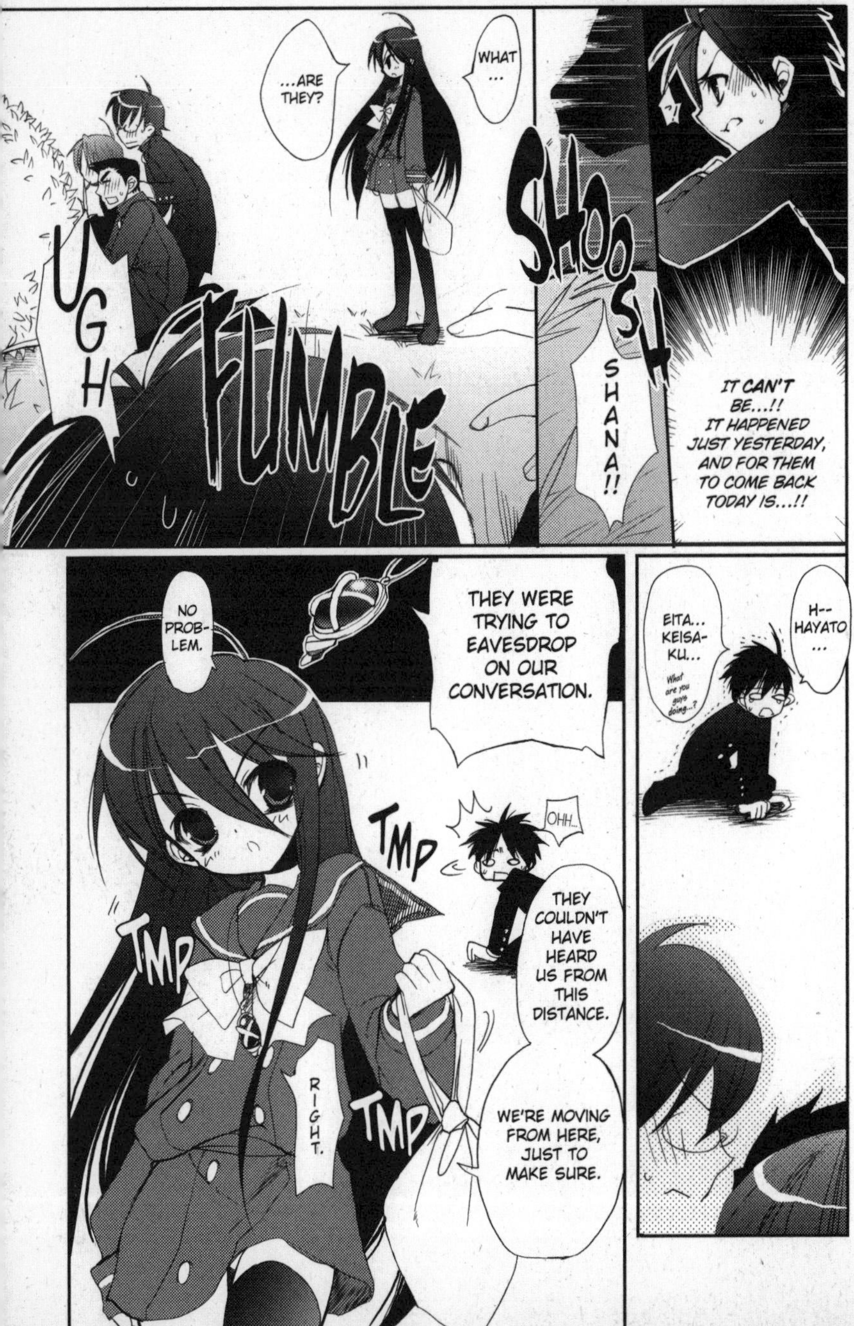
IT CAN'T BE...!! IT HAPPENED JUST YESTERDAY, AND FOR THEM TO COME BACK TODAY IS...!!
SHOOSH
SHANA!!
WHAT ...
...ARE THEY?
FUMBLE
UGH
H-- HAYATO ...
EITA... KEISA-KU...
What are you guys doing...?
THEY WERE TRYING TO EAVESDROP ON OUR CONVERSATION.
NO PROB-LEM.
OHH...
TMP
THEY COULDN'T HAVE HEARD US FROM THIS DISTANCE.
TMP
WE'RE MOVING FROM HERE, JUST TO MAKE SURE.
RIGHT.
TMP

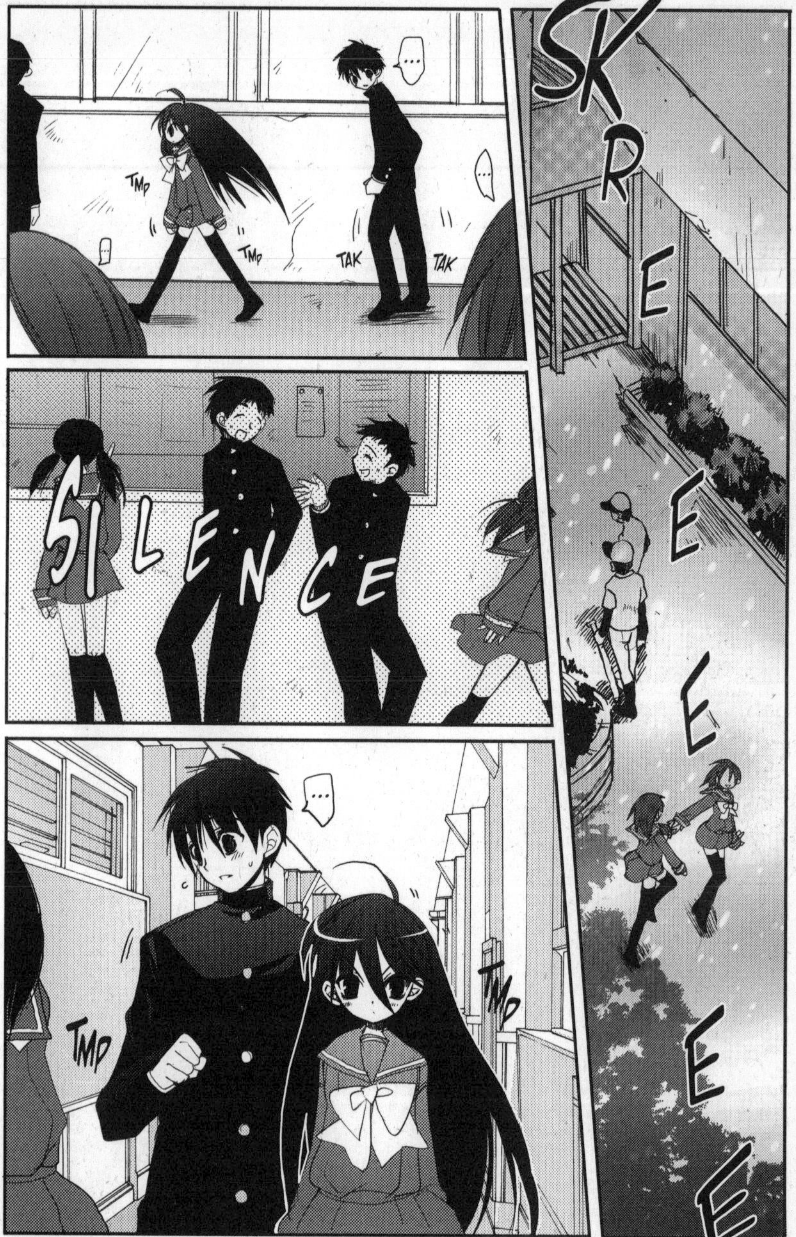
SKREEEEE
...
...
TAK
TAK
TMP
TMP
...
SILENCE
...
TMP
TMP

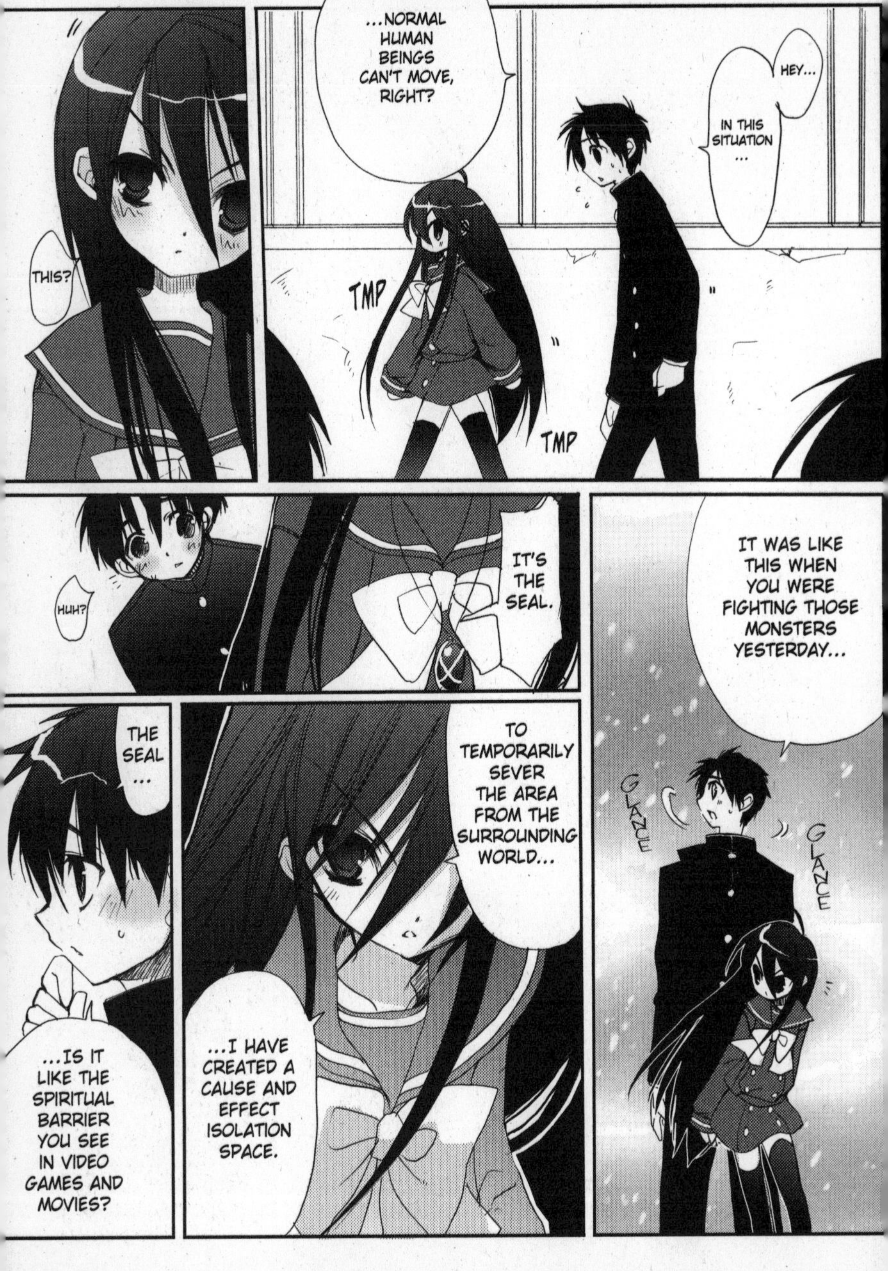
HEY...
IN THIS SITUATION ...
...NORMAL HUMAN BEINGS CAN'T MOVE, RIGHT?
TMP
TMP
THIS?
IT WAS LIKE THIS WHEN YOU WERE FIGHTING THOSE MONSTERS YESTERDAY...
GLANCE
GLANCE
IT'S THE SEAL.
HUH?
TO TEMPORARILY SEVER THE AREA FROM THE SURROUNDING WORLD...
...I HAVE CREATED A CAUSE AND EFFECT ISOLATION SPACE.
THE SEAL ...
...IS IT LIKE THE SPIRITUAL BARRIER YOU SEE IN VIDEO GAMES AND MOVIES?

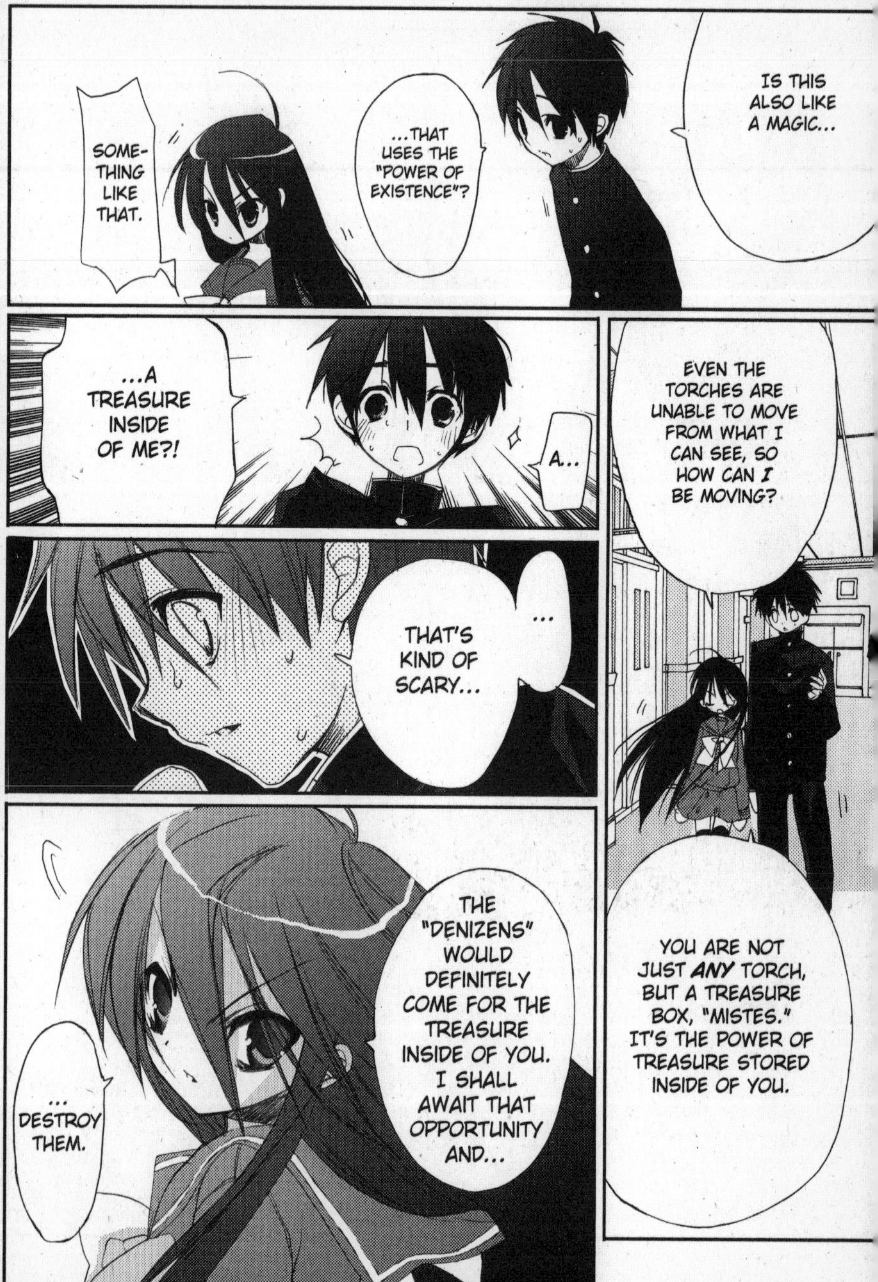
IS THIS ALSO LIKE A MAGIC...
...THAT USES THE "POWER OF EXISTENCE"?
SOME-THING LIKE THAT.
EVEN THE TORCHES ARE UNABLE TO MOVE FROM WHAT I CAN SEE, SO HOW CAN *I* BE MOVING?
YOU ARE NOT JUST ***ANY*** TORCH, BUT A TREASURE BOX, "MISTES." IT'S THE POWER OF TREASURE STORED INSIDE OF YOU.
A...
...A TREASURE INSIDE OF ME?!
...
THAT'S KIND OF SCARY...
THE "DENIZENS" WOULD DEFINITELY COME FOR THE TREASURE INSIDE OF YOU. I SHALL AWAIT THAT OPPORTUNITY AND...
... DESTROY THEM.

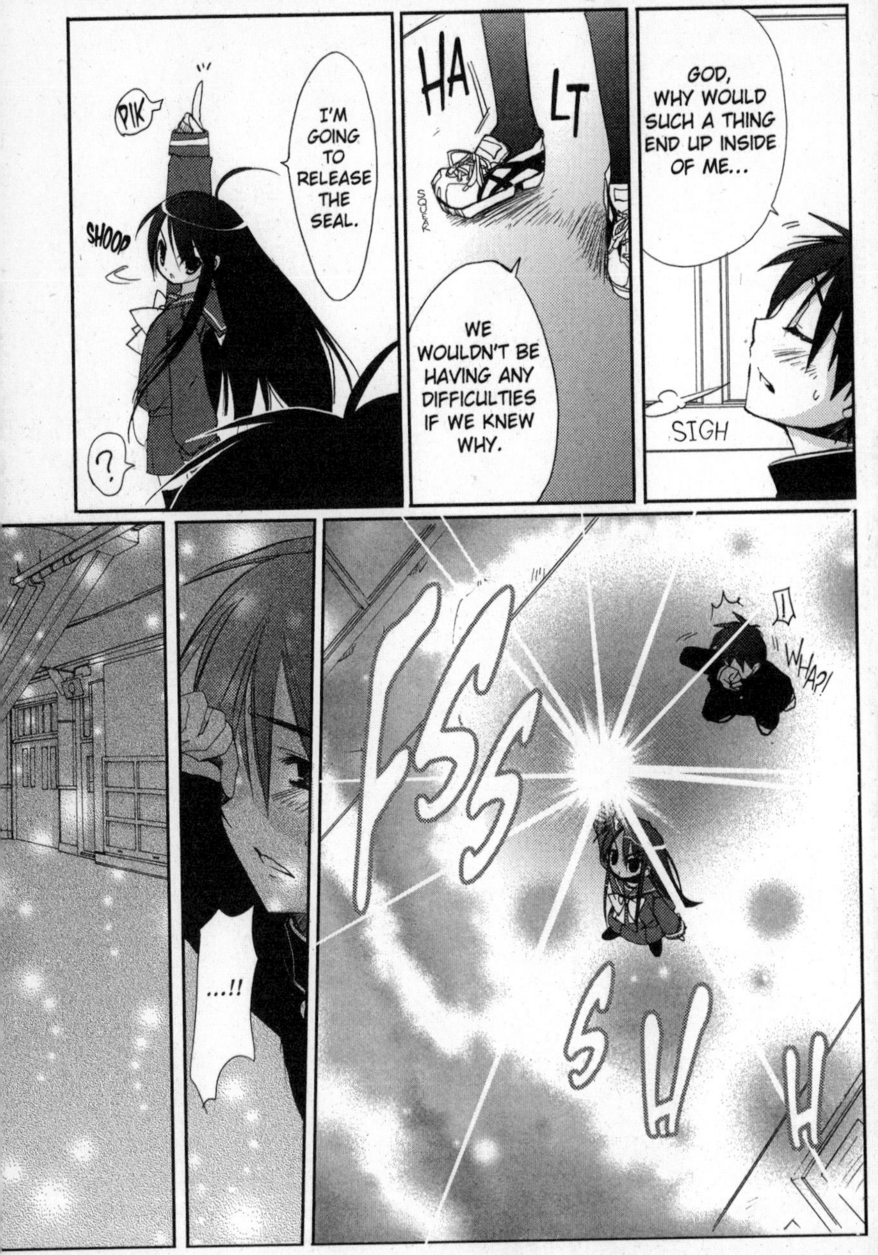
GOD, WHY WOULD SUCH A THING END UP INSIDE OF ME...
SIGH
HALT
SQUEAK
WE WOULDN'T BE HAVING ANY DIFFICULTIES IF WE KNEW WHY.
I'M GOING TO RELEASE THE SEAL.
PIK
SHOOP
?
!
WHA?!
FSSS
SHH
...!!

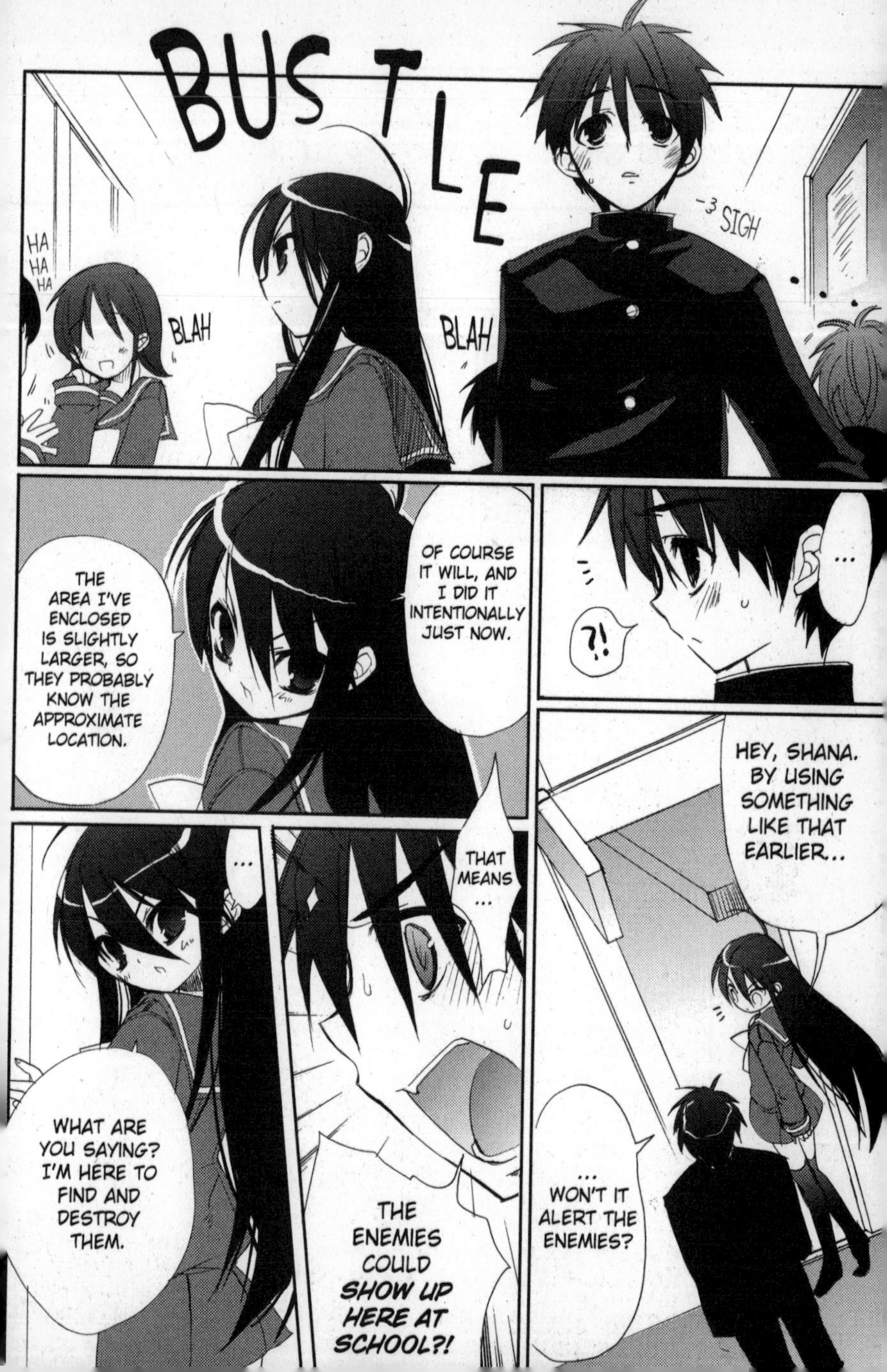
BUSTLE
-3 SIGH
BLAH
BLAH
HA HA HA
HEY, SHANA. BY USING SOMETHING LIKE THAT EARLIER...
... WON'T IT ALERT THE ENEMIES?
OF COURSE IT WILL, AND I DID IT INTENTIONALLY JUST NOW.
THE AREA I'VE ENCLOSED IS SLIGHTLY LARGER, SO THEY PROBABLY KNOW THE APPROXIMATE LOCATION.
...
?!
THAT MEANS ...
THE ENEMIES COULD ***SHOW UP HERE AT SCHOOL?!***
...
WHAT ARE YOU SAYING? I'M HERE TO FIND AND DESTROY THEM.

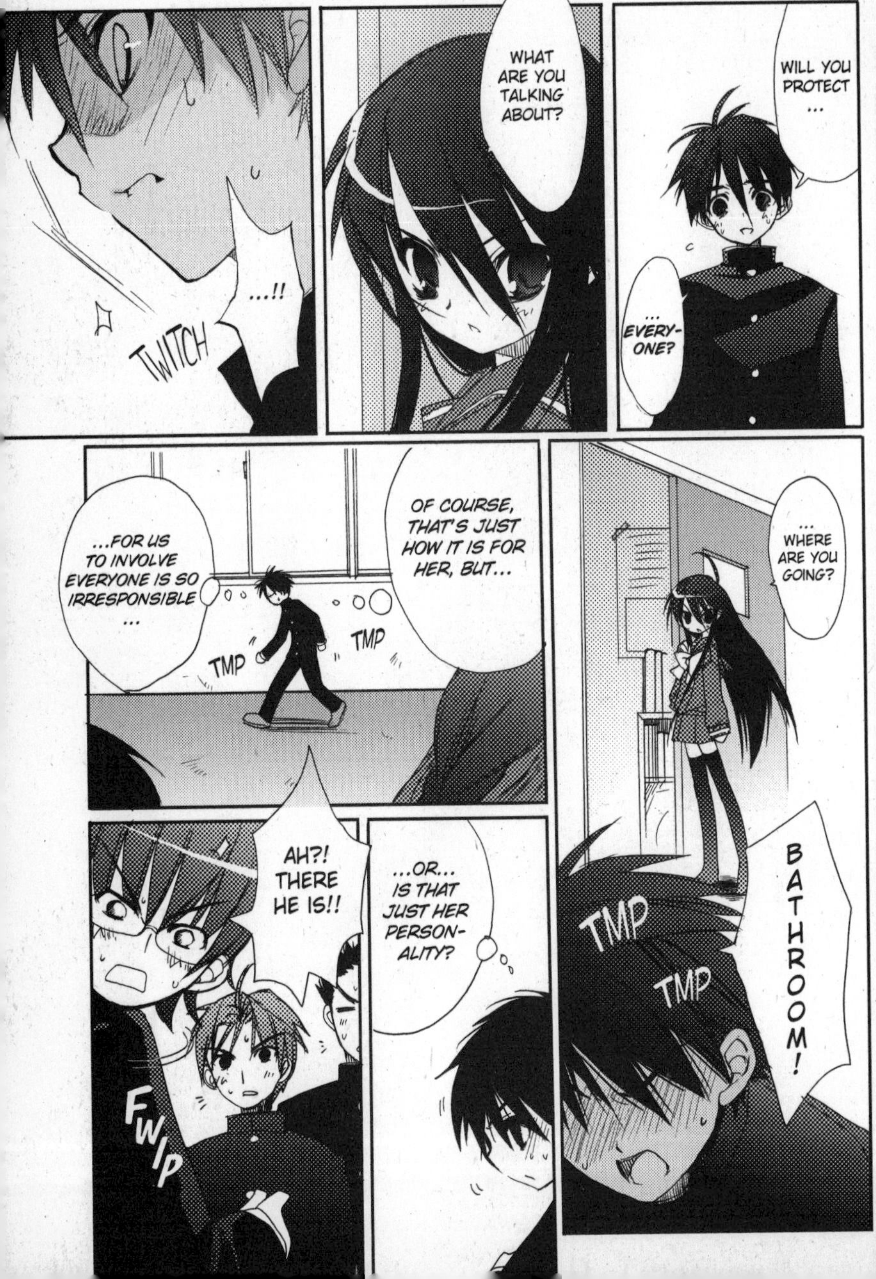
WILL YOU PROTECT ...
... EVERY-ONE?
WHAT ARE YOU TALKING ABOUT?
...!!
TWITCH
... WHERE ARE YOU GOING?
BATHROOM!
TMP
TMP
OF COURSE, THAT'S JUST HOW IT IS FOR HER, BUT...
...FOR US TO INVOLVE EVERYONE IS SO IRRESPONSIBLE ...
TMP
TMP
...OR... IS THAT JUST HER PERSONALITY?
AH?! THERE HE IS!!
FWIP

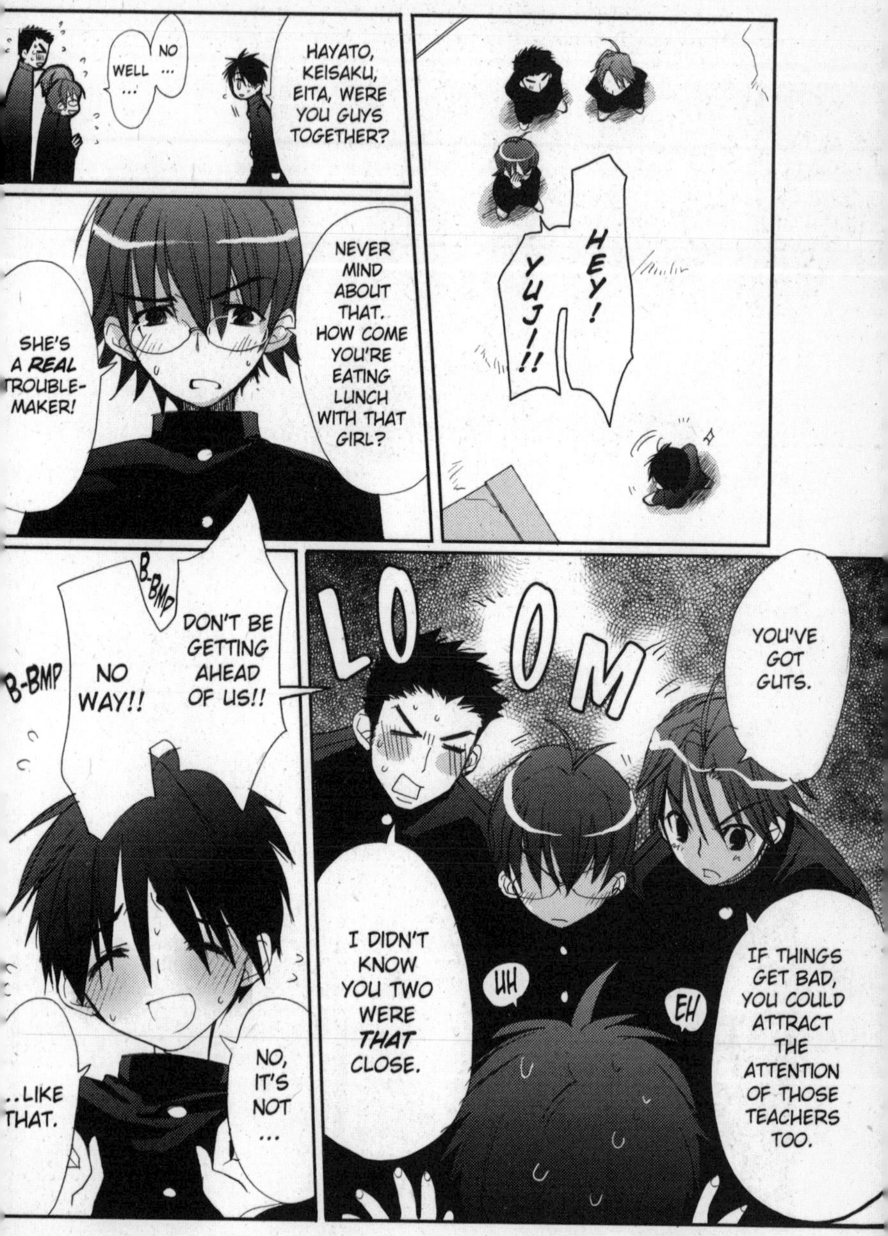
HEY! YUJI!!
HAYATO, KEISAKU, EITA, WERE YOU GUYS TOGETHER?
NO ...
WELL ...
NEVER MIND ABOUT THAT. HOW COME YOU'RE EATING LUNCH WITH THAT GIRL?
SHE'S A REAL TROUBLE-MAKER!
LOOM
YOU'VE GOT GUTS.
IF THINGS GET BAD, YOU COULD ATTRACT THE ATTENTION OF THOSE TEACHERS TOO.
EH
UH
I DIDN'T KNOW YOU TWO WERE THAT CLOSE.
DON'T BE GETTING AHEAD OF US!!
B-BMP
NO WAY!!
B-BMP
NO, IT'S NOT ...
..LIKE THAT.

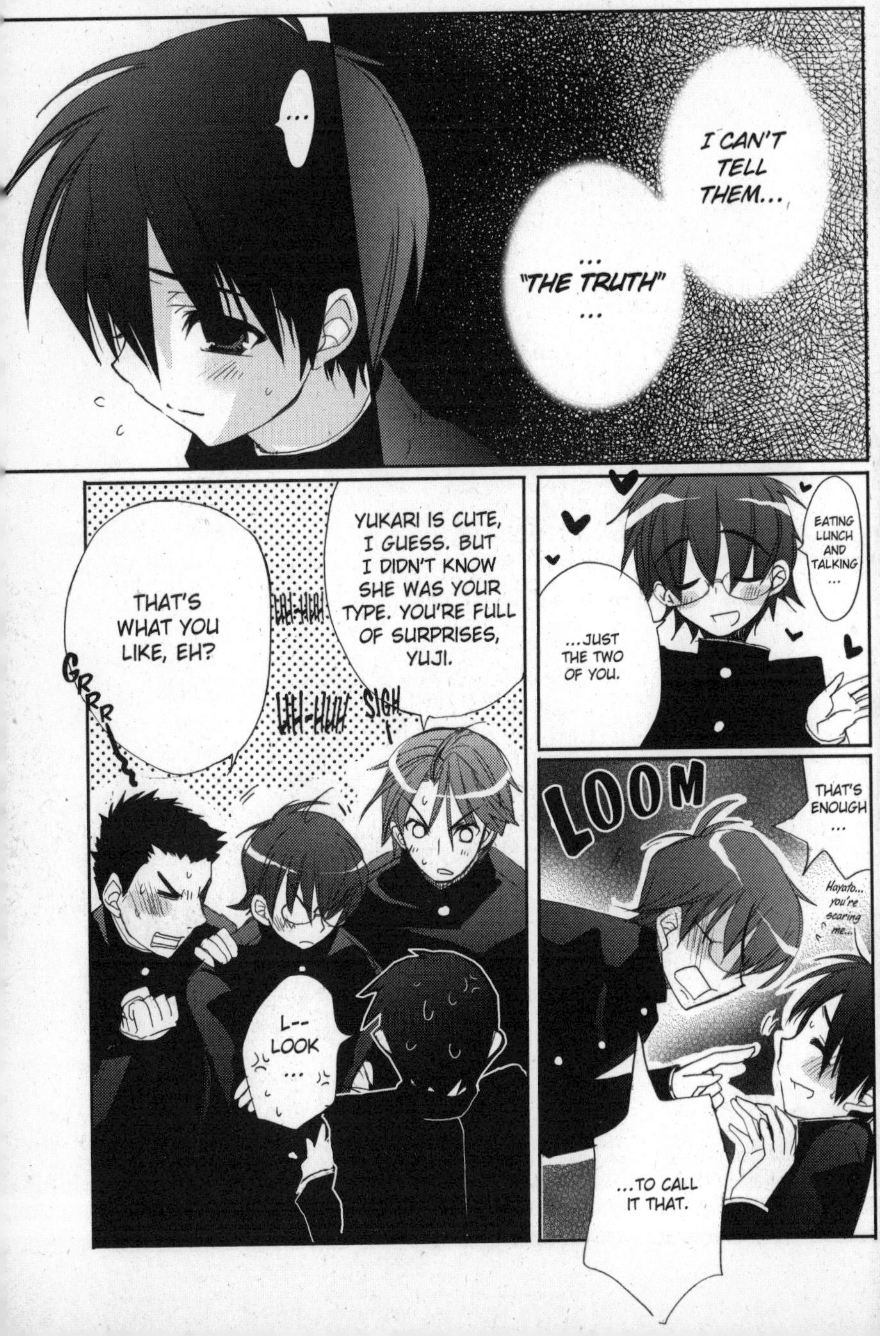
...
I CAN'T TELL THEM...
... "THE TRUTH" ...
EATING LUNCH AND TALKING ...
...JUST THE TWO OF YOU.
LOOM
THAT'S ENOUGH ...
Hayato... you're scaring me...
...TO CALL IT THAT.
YUKARI IS CUTE, I GUESS. BUT I DIDN'T KNOW SHE WAS YOUR TYPE. YOU'RE FULL OF SURPRISES, YUJI.
SIGH
THAT'S WHAT YOU LIKE, EH?
GRRR
L-- LOOK ...

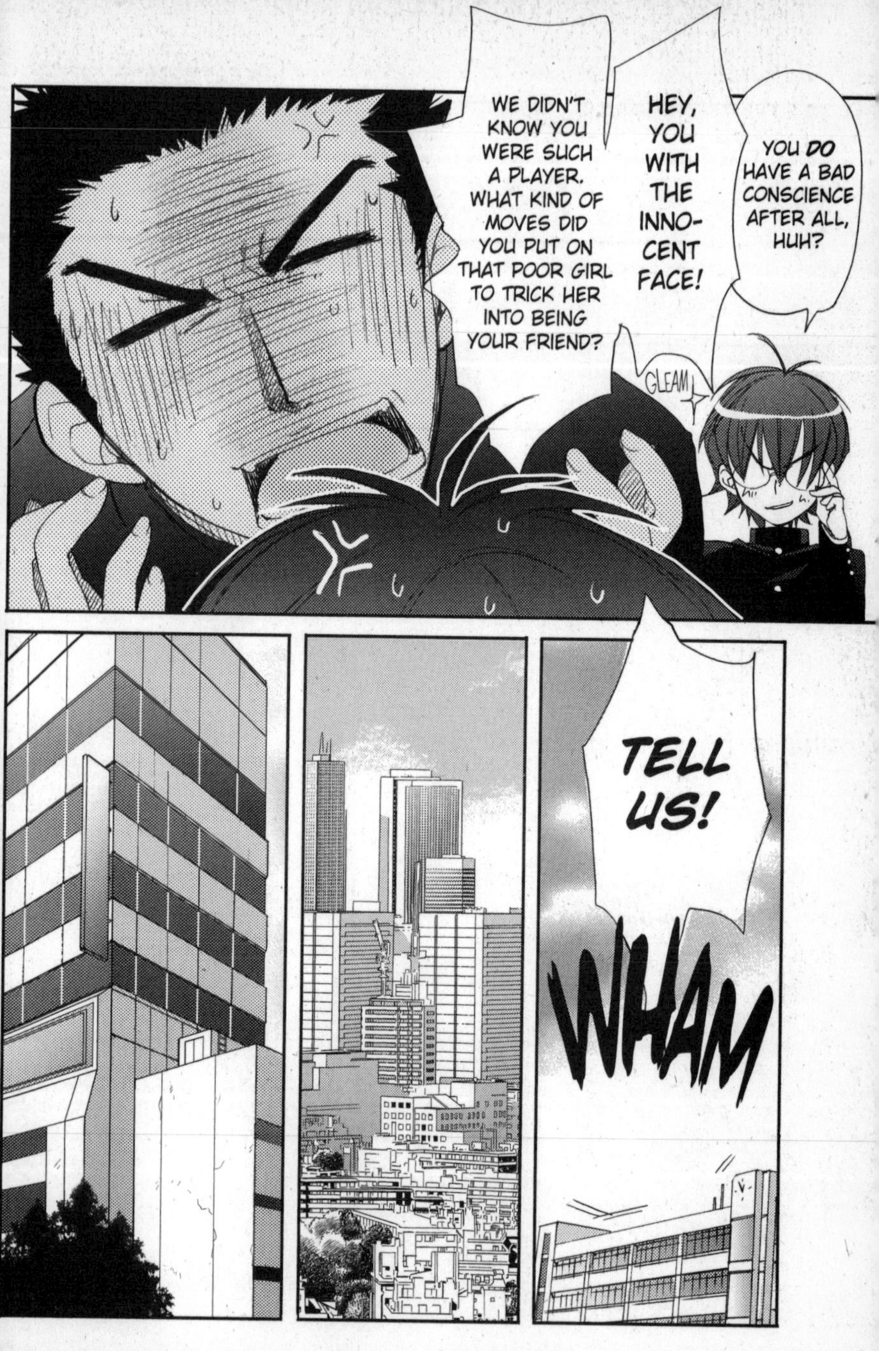
YOU DO HAVE A BAD CONSCIENCE AFTER ALL, HUH?
HEY, YOU WITH THE INNO-CENT FACE!
WE DIDN'T KNOW YOU WERE SUCH A PLAYER. WHAT KIND OF MOVES DID YOU PUT ON THAT POOR GIRL TO TRICK HER INTO BEING YOUR FRIEND?
GLEAM
TELL US!
WHAM

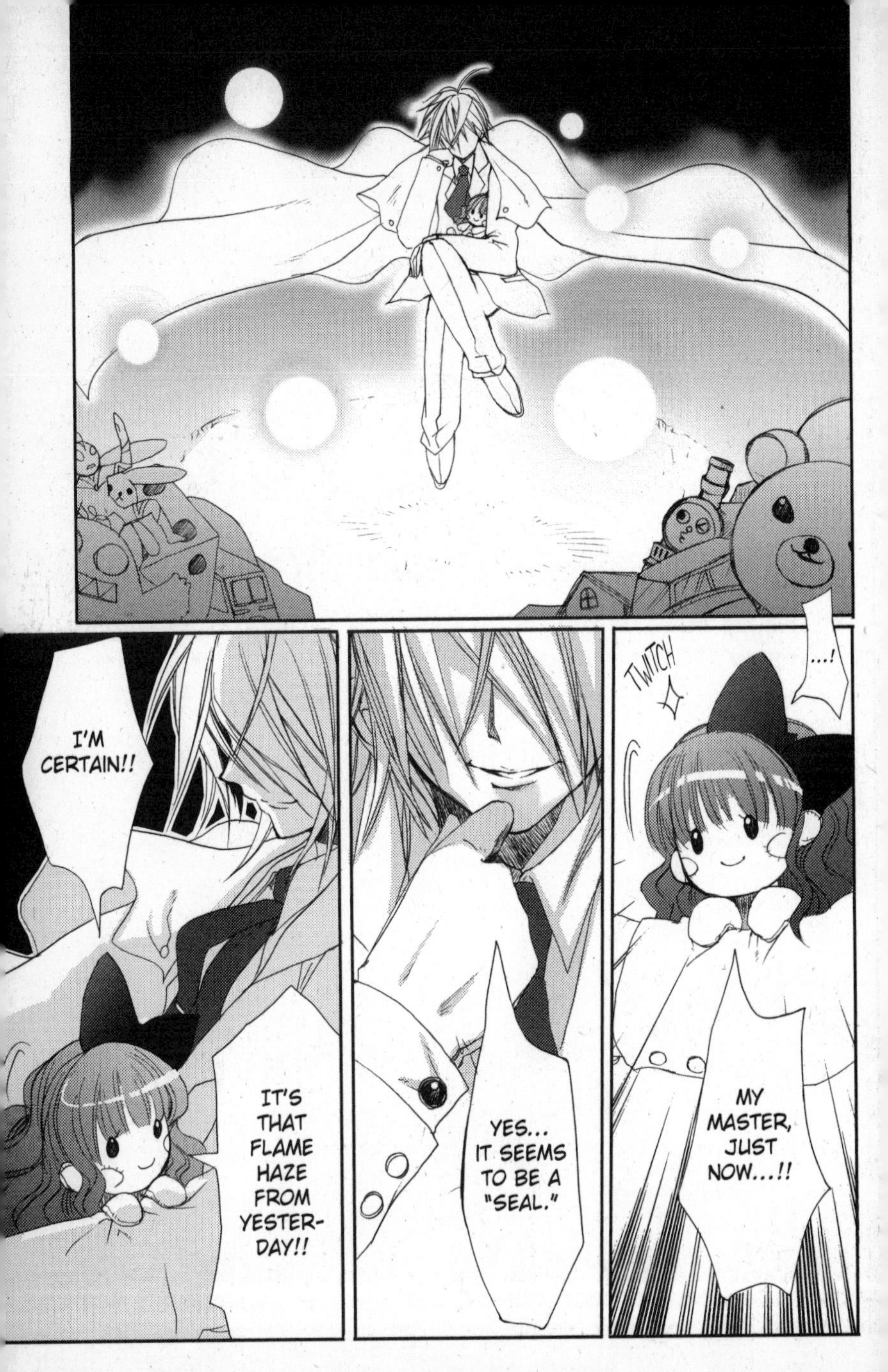
...!
TWITCH
MY MASTER, JUST NOW...!!
YES... IT SEEMS TO BE A "SEAL."
IT'S THAT FLAME HAZE FROM YESTER-DAY!!
I'M CERTAIN!!

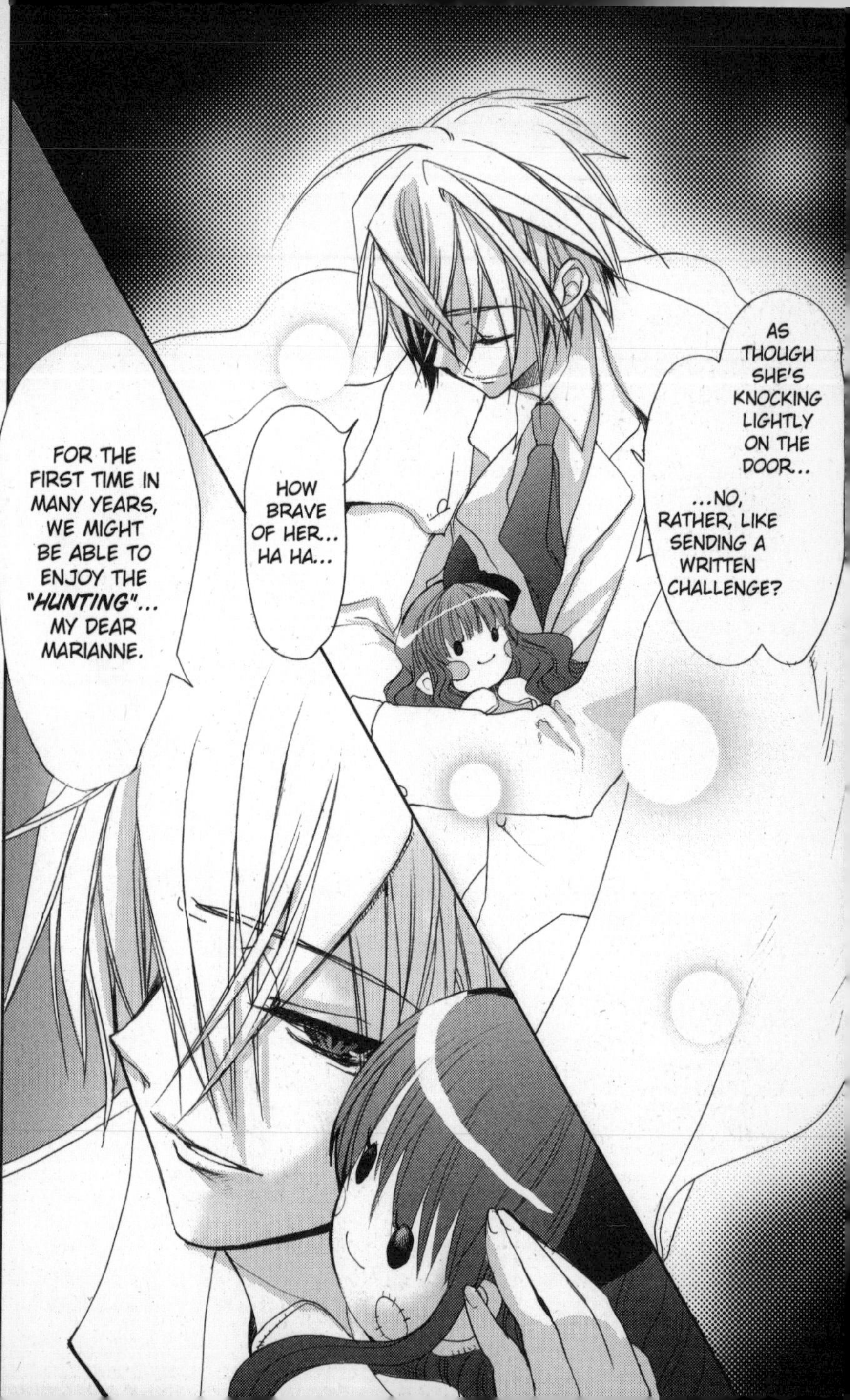
AS THOUGH SHE'S KNOCKING LIGHTLY ON THE DOOR...
...NO, RATHER, LIKE SENDING A WRITTEN CHALLENGE?
HOW BRAVE OF HER... HA HA...
FOR THE FIRST TIME IN MANY YEARS, WE MIGHT BE ABLE TO ENJOY THE "*HUNTING*"... MY DEAR MARIANNE.

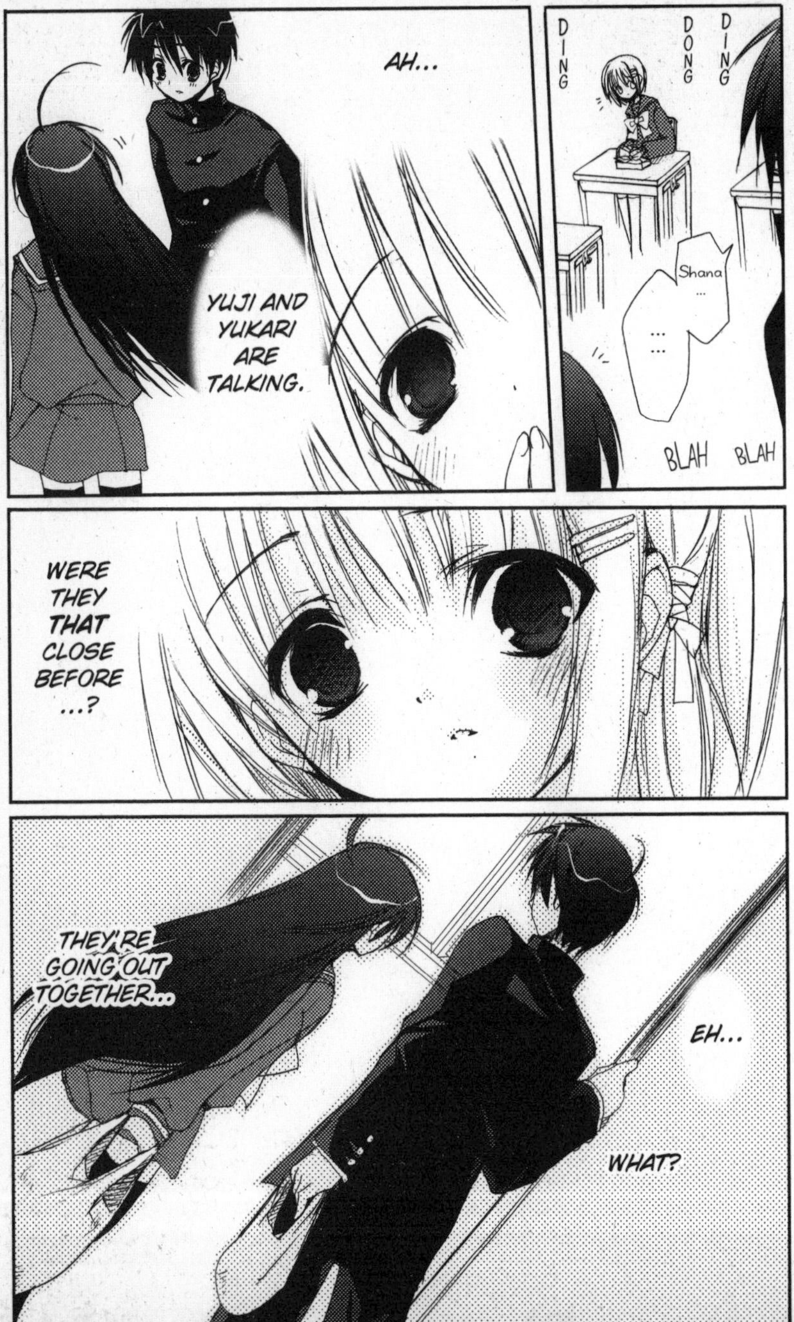
DING
DONG
DING
Shana...
......
BLAH BLAH
AH...
YUJI AND YUKARI ARE TALKING.
WERE THEY THAT CLOSE BEFORE ...?
EH...
WHAT?
THEY'RE GOING OUT TOGETHER...

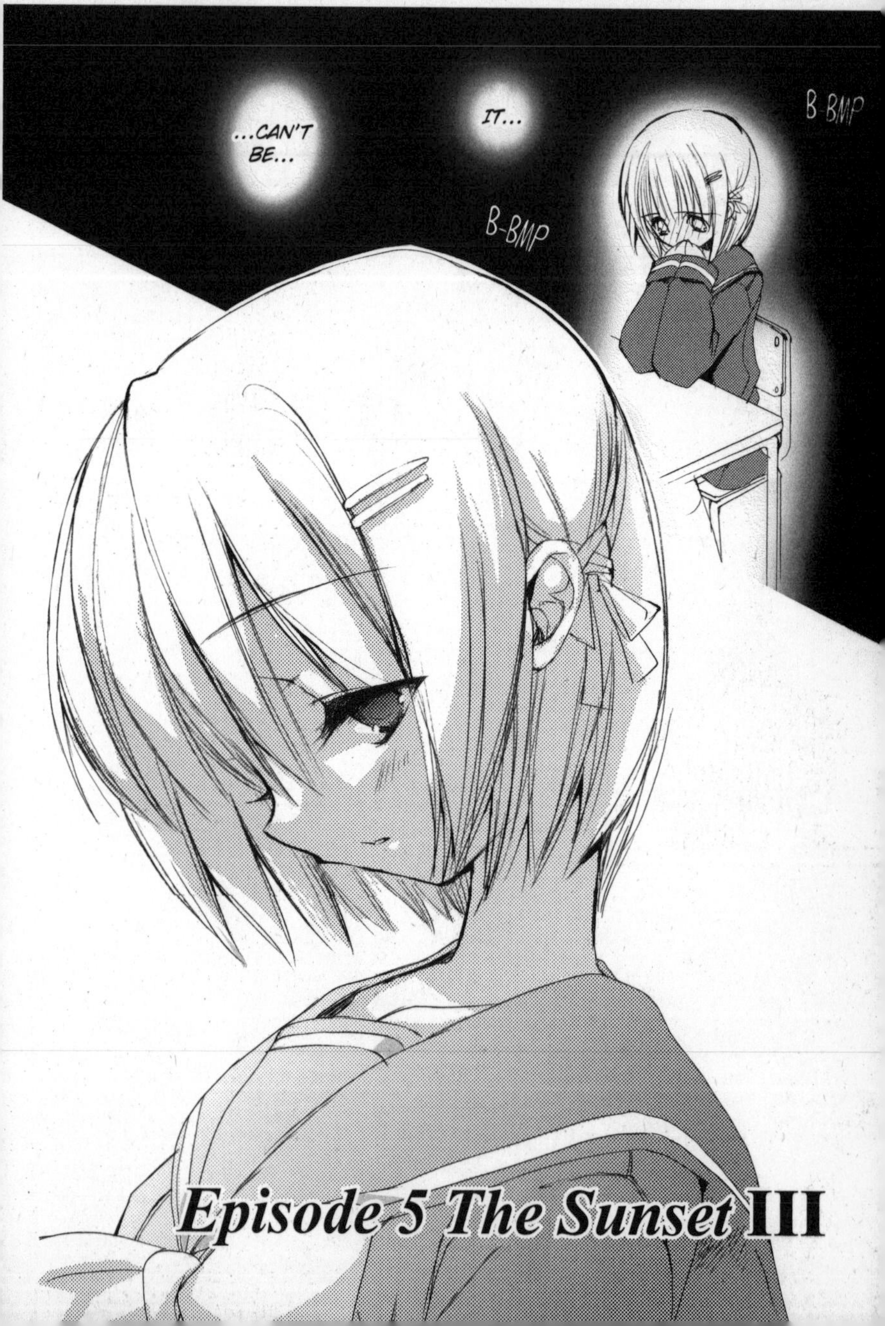
B-BMP
IT...
...CAN'T BE...
B-BMP
Episode 5 The Sunset III

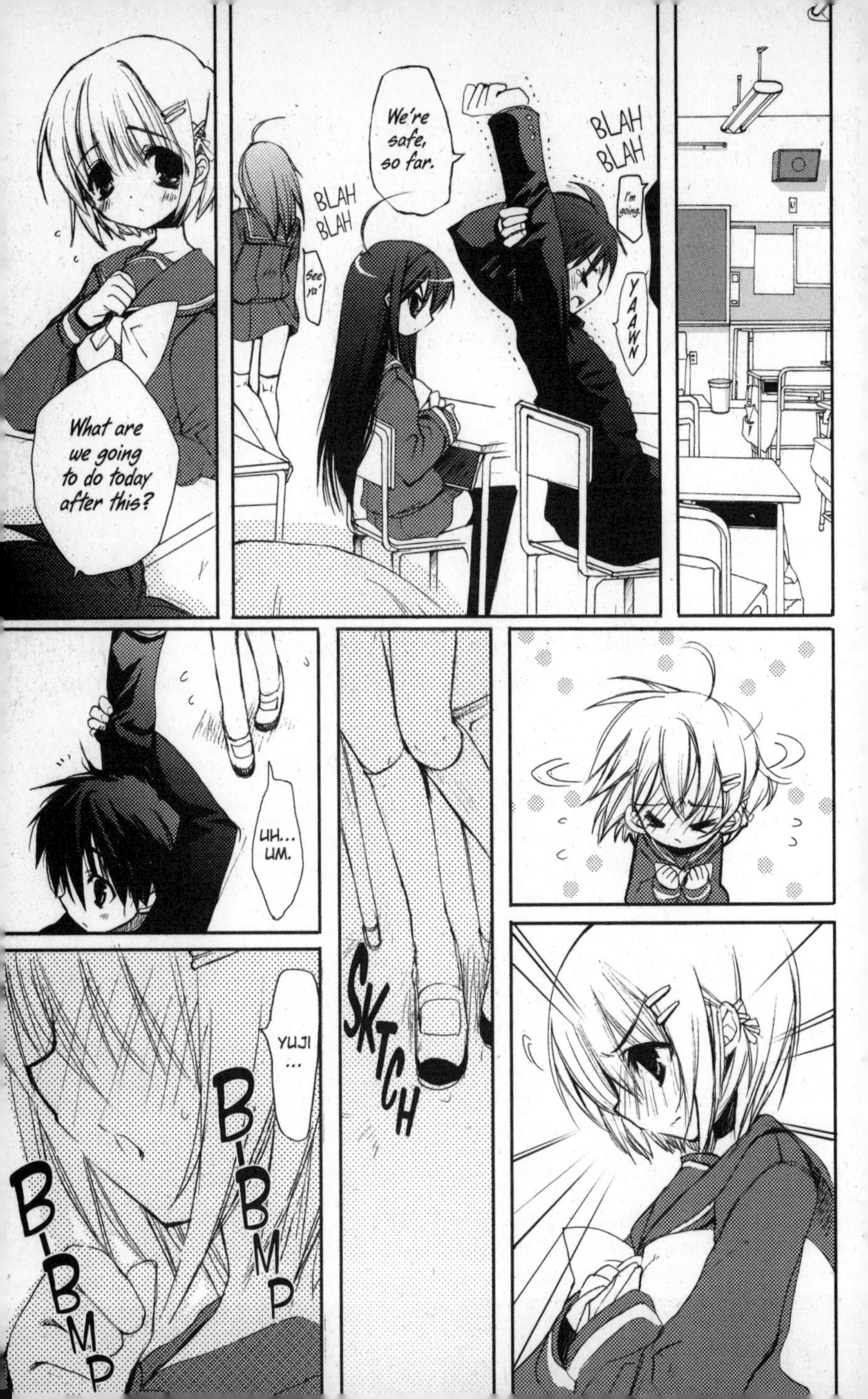
BLAH BLAH
I'm going.
YAAAWN
We're safe, so far.
BLAH BLAH
See ya'
What are we going to do today after this?
SKTCH
UH... UM.
YUJI...
BIBMP
BIBMP

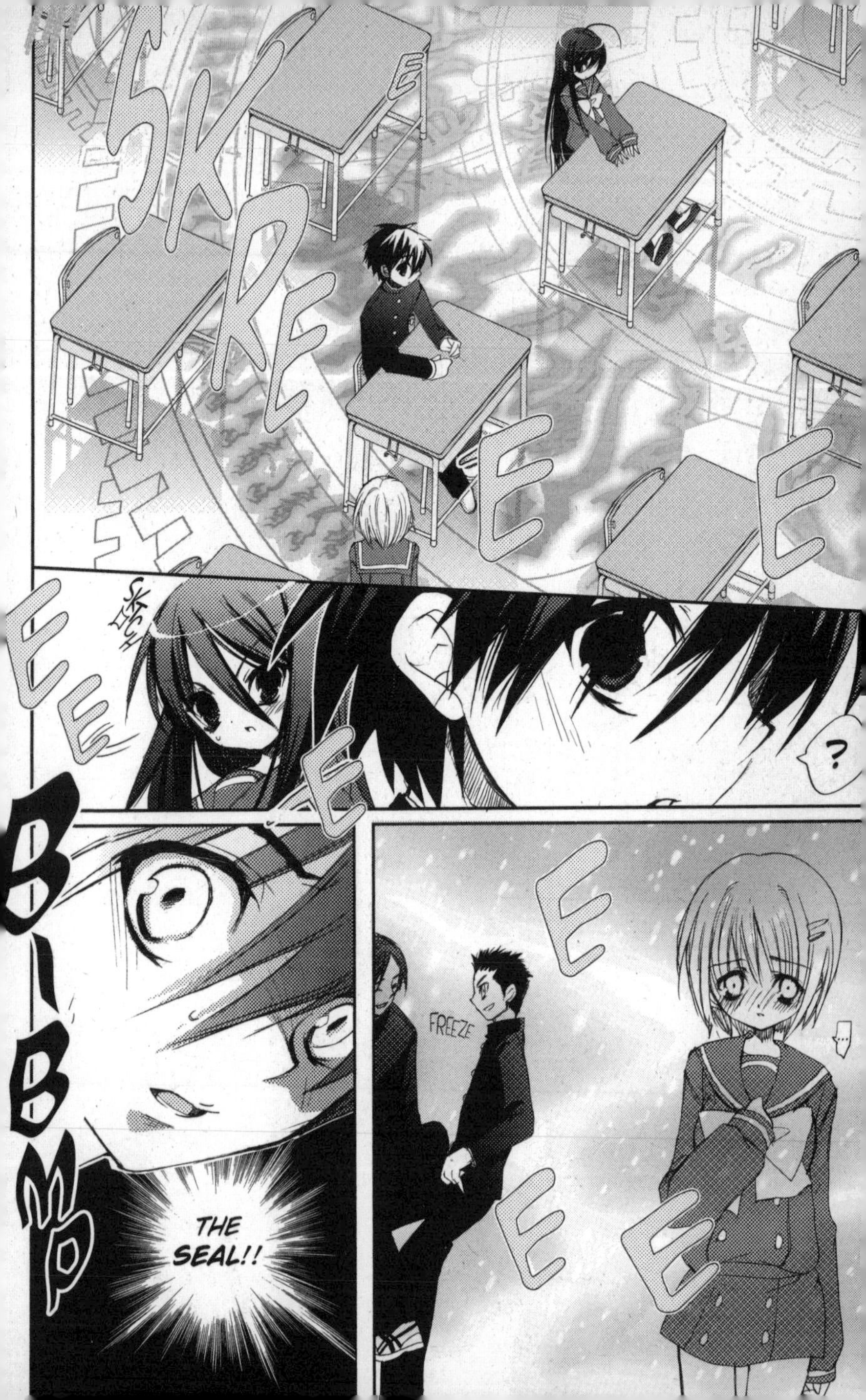
SKREEEEEEEEEEEEE
?
...
FREEZE
B-BMP
THE SEAL!!

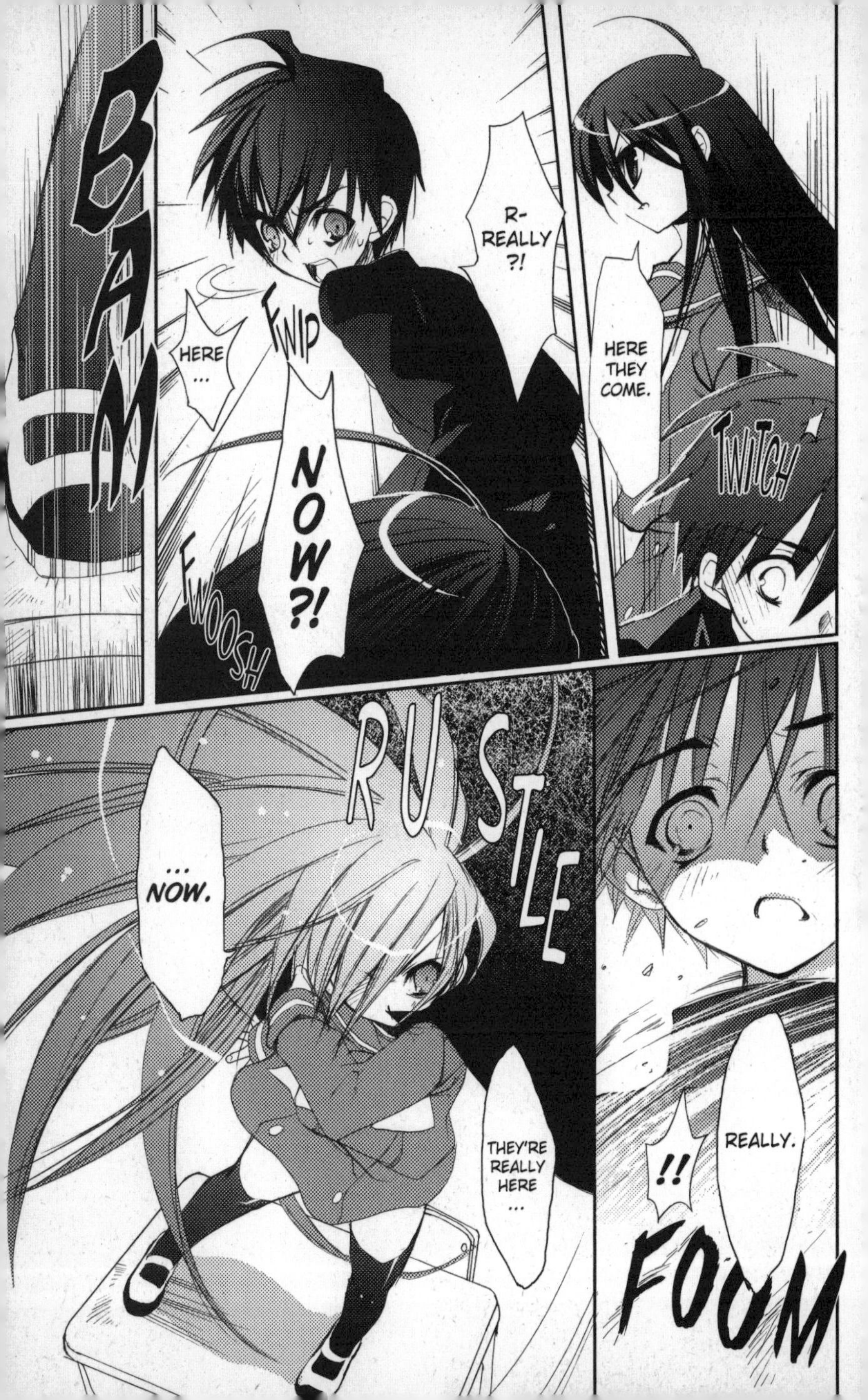
HERE THEY COME.
TWITCH
R-REALLY?!
FWIP
HERE...
NOW?!
FWOOSH
BAM
REALLY.
!!
FOOM
RUSTLE
...NOW.
THEY'RE REALLY HERE...

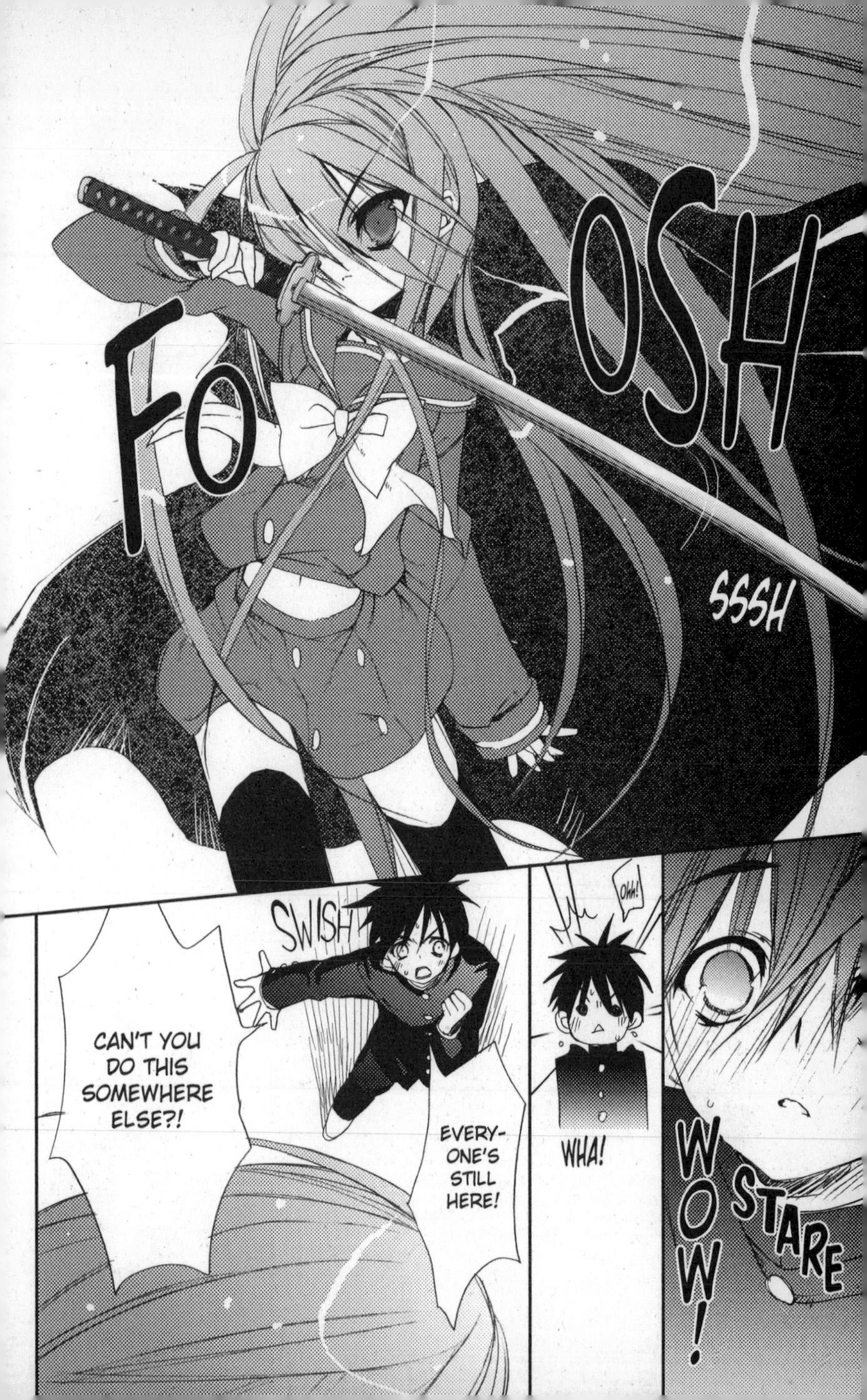
FO
OSH
SSSH
WOW!
STARE
OHH!
WHA!
SWISH
CAN'T YOU DO THIS SOMEWHERE ELSE?!
EVERY-ONE'S STILL HERE!

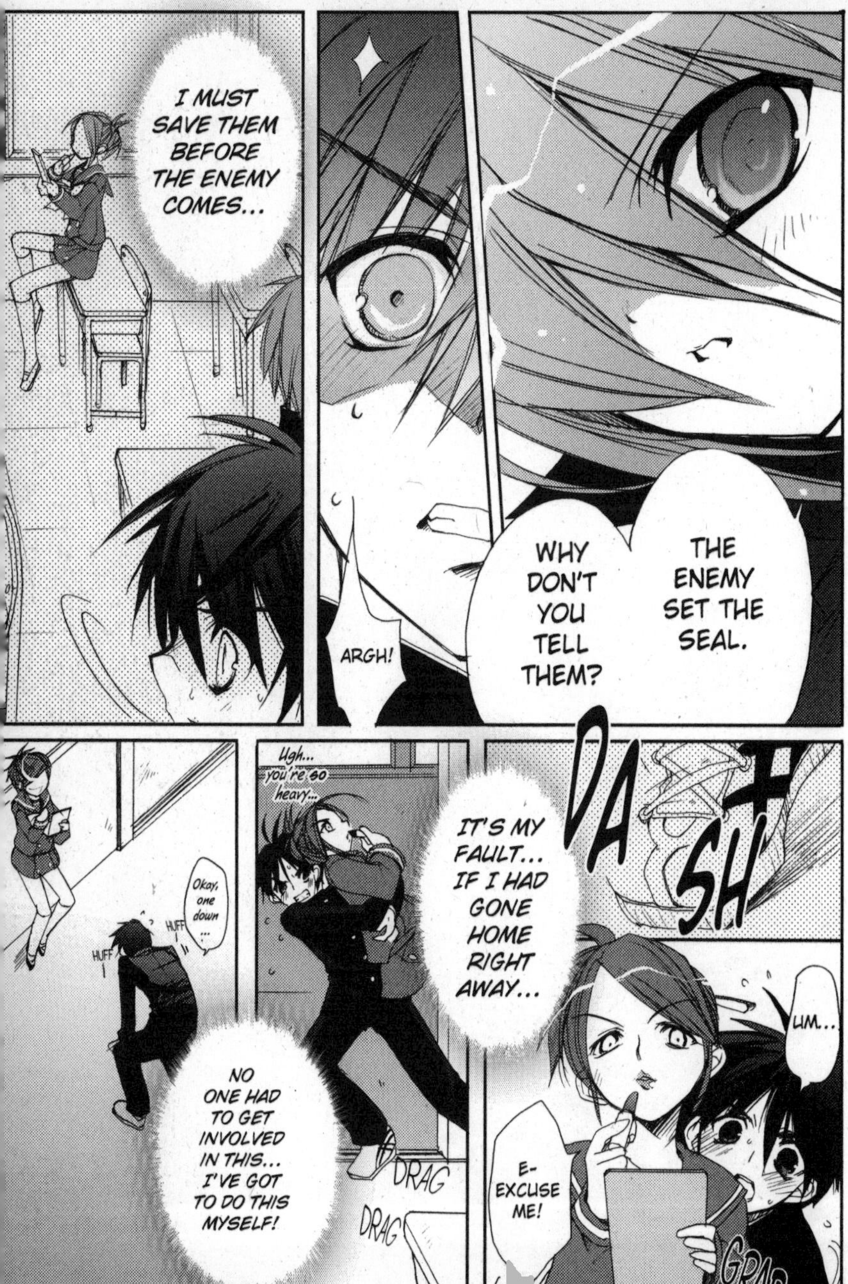
THE ENEMY SET THE SEAL.
WHY DON'T YOU TELL THEM?
ARGH!
I MUST SAVE THEM BEFORE THE ENEMY COMES...
DASH
UM...
E-EXCUSE ME!
GRAB
Ugh... you're so heavy...
IT'S MY FAULT... IF I HAD GONE HOME RIGHT AWAY...
DRAG
DRAG
Okay, one down...
HUFF
HUFF
NO ONE HAD TO GET INVOLVED IN THIS... I'VE GOT TO DO THIS MYSELF!

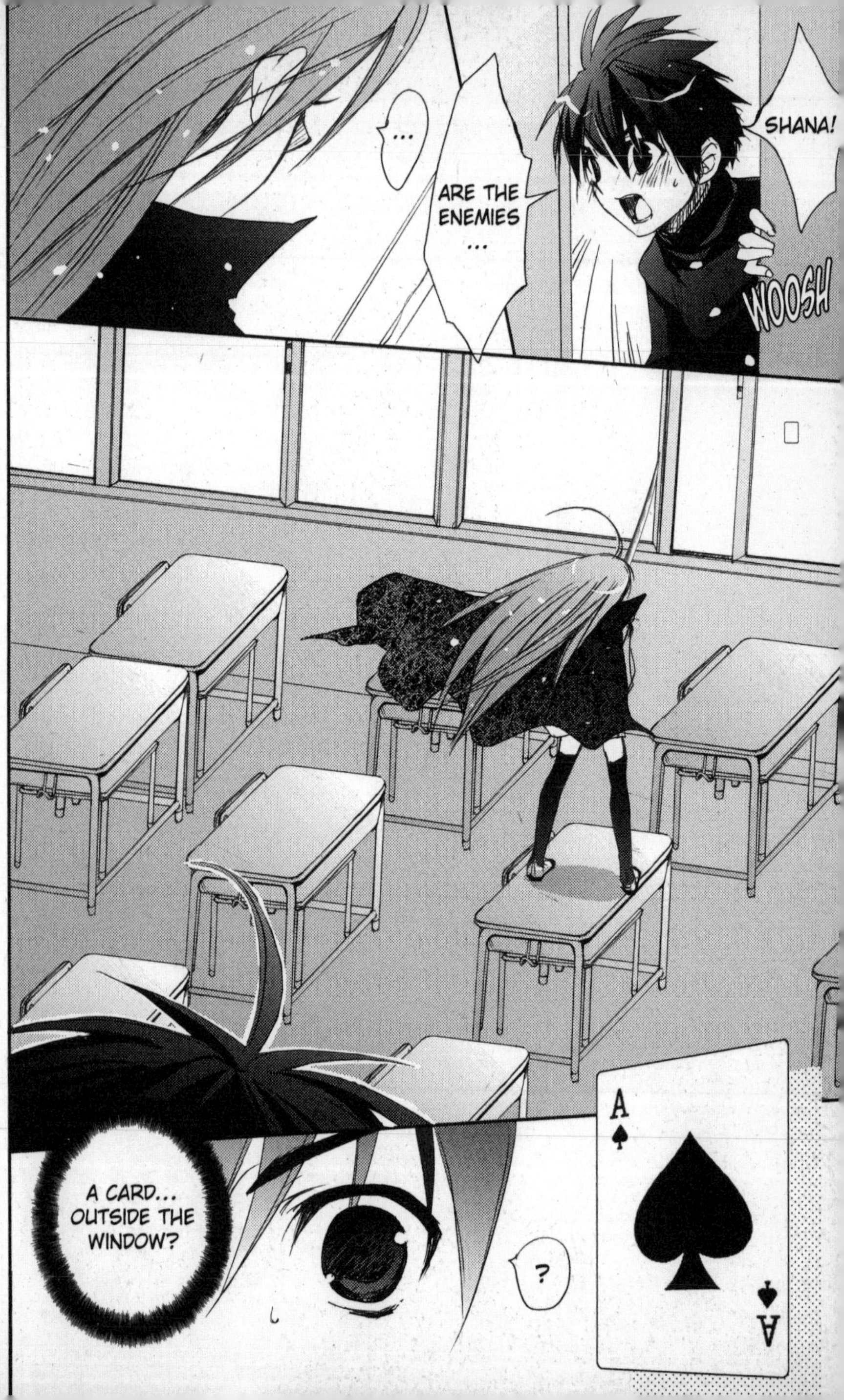
SHANA!
WOOSH
ARE THE ENEMIES ...
...
?
A CARD... OUTSIDE THE WINDOW?

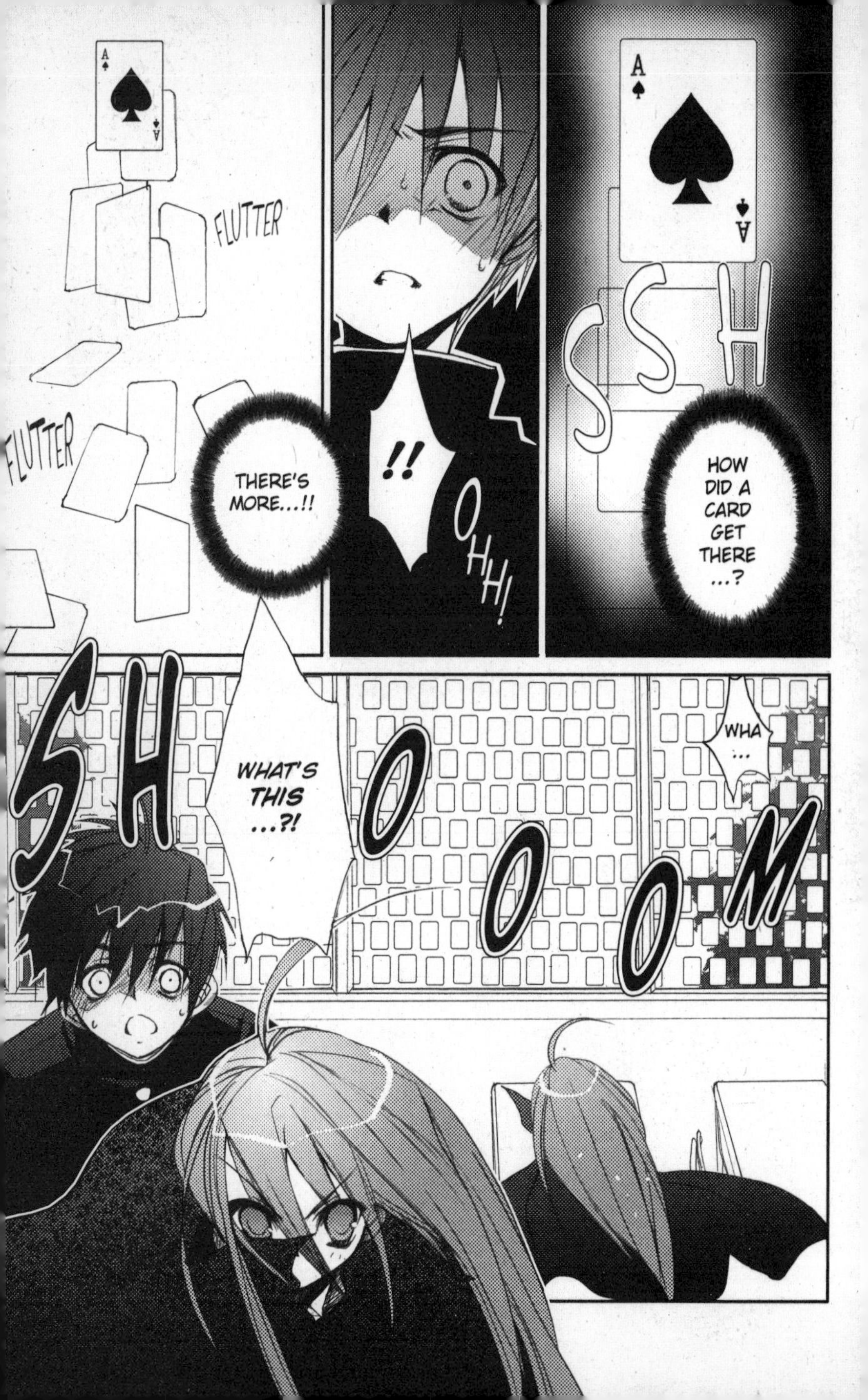
SSH
HOW DID A CARD GET THERE...?
!!
OHHH!
FLUTTER
FLUTTER
THERE'S MORE...!!
WHA...
SHOOOOM
WHAT'S THIS...?!

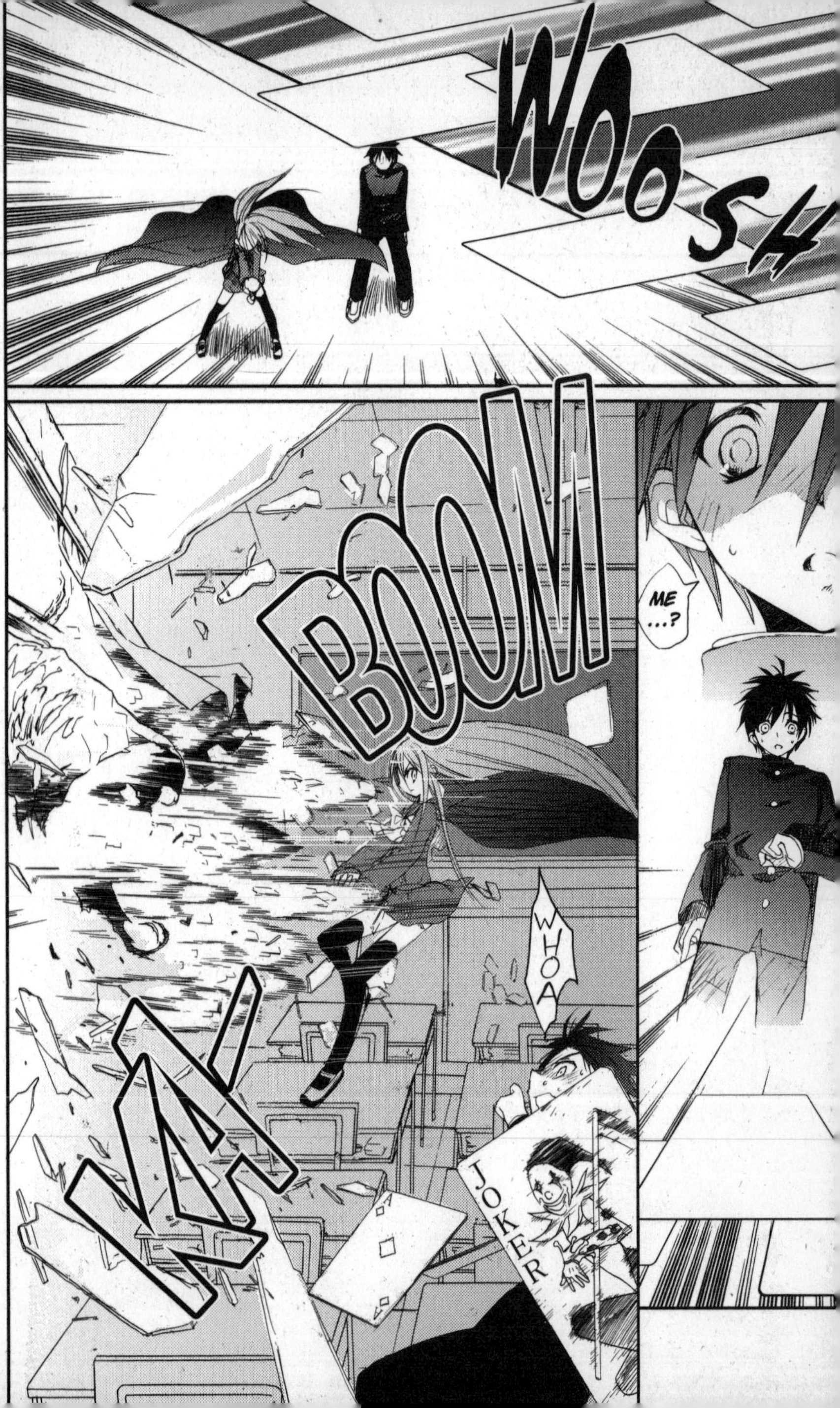
WOOSH
ME ...?
BOOM
WHOA
JOKER

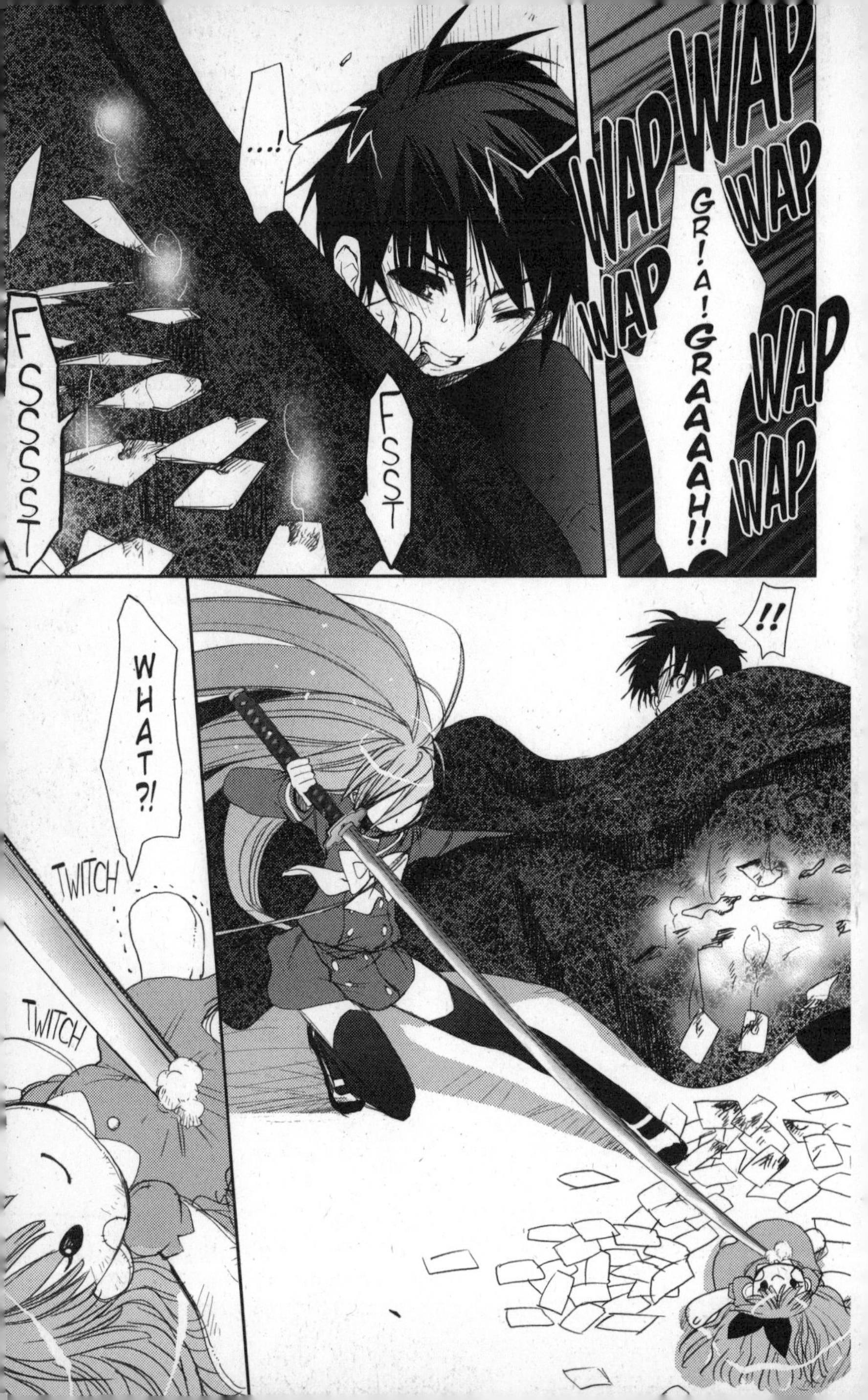

WAP WAP WAP WAP WAP WAP WAP WAP
GR!A!GRAAAAAH!!
...!
FSST
FSSSST
!!
WHAT?!
TWITCH
TWITCH

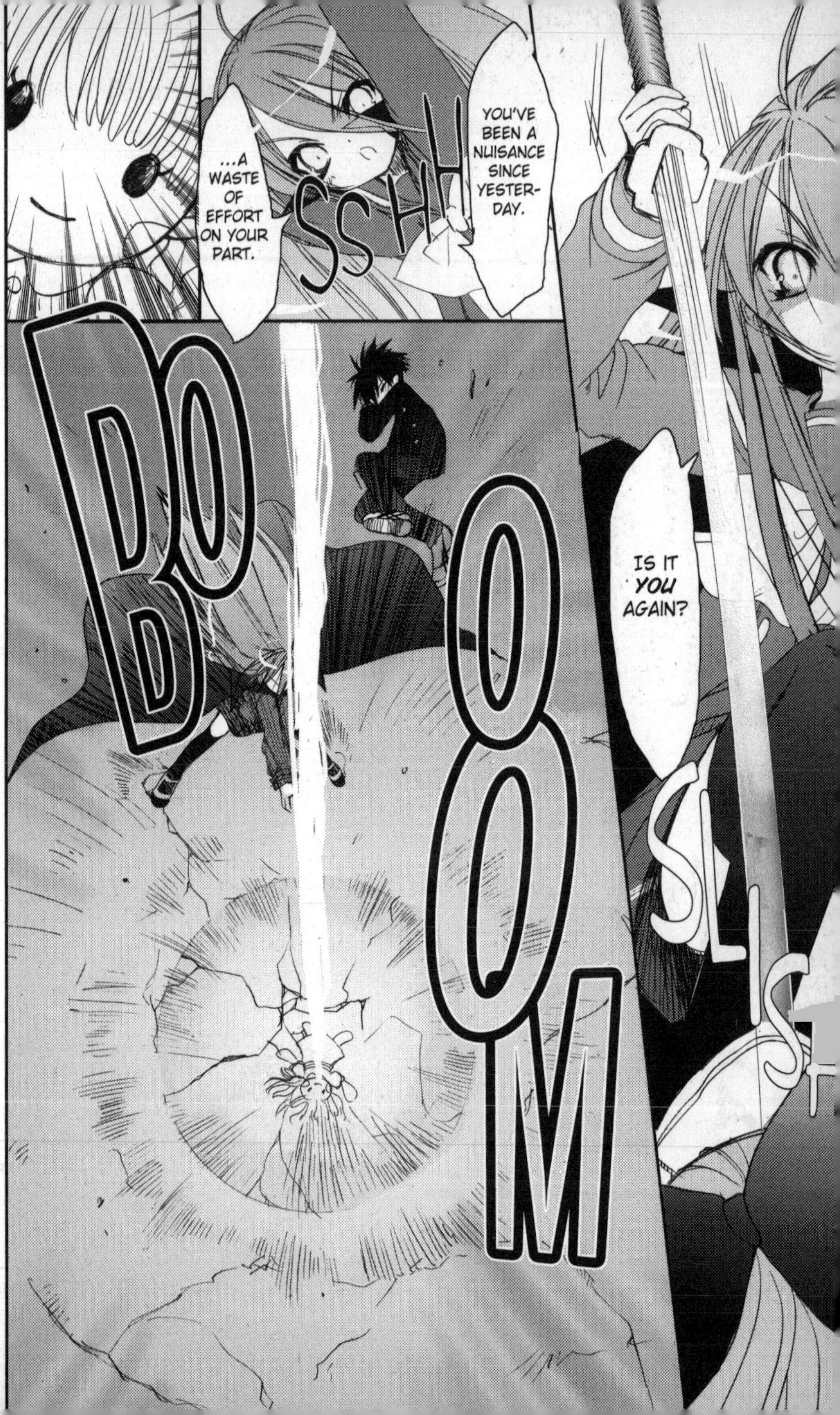
IS IT *YOU* AGAIN?
SLISH
YOU'VE BEEN A NUISANCE SINCE YESTER-DAY.
SSHH
...A WASTE OF EFFORT ON YOUR PART.
DOOOM

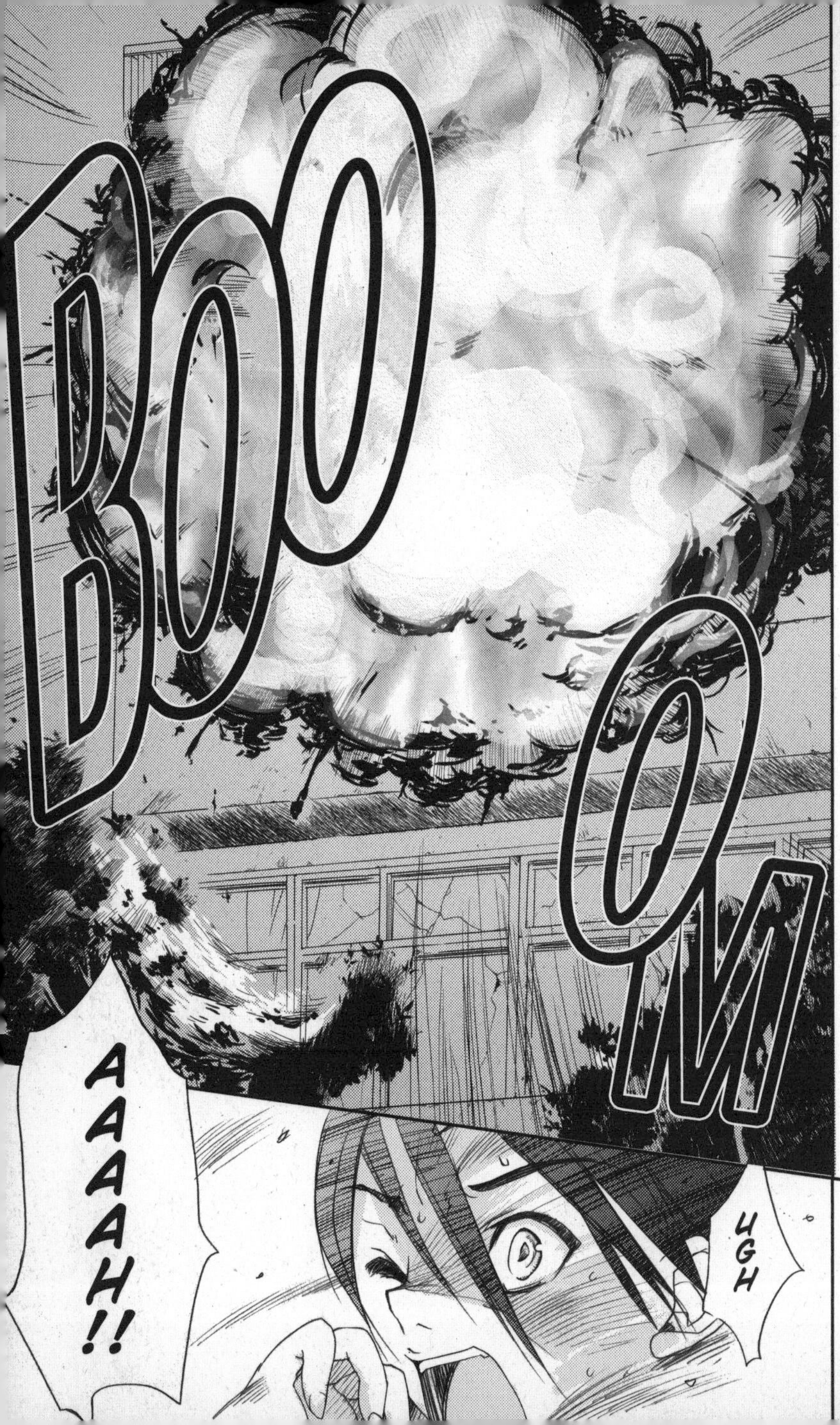
BOOOM
UGH
AAAAAH!!

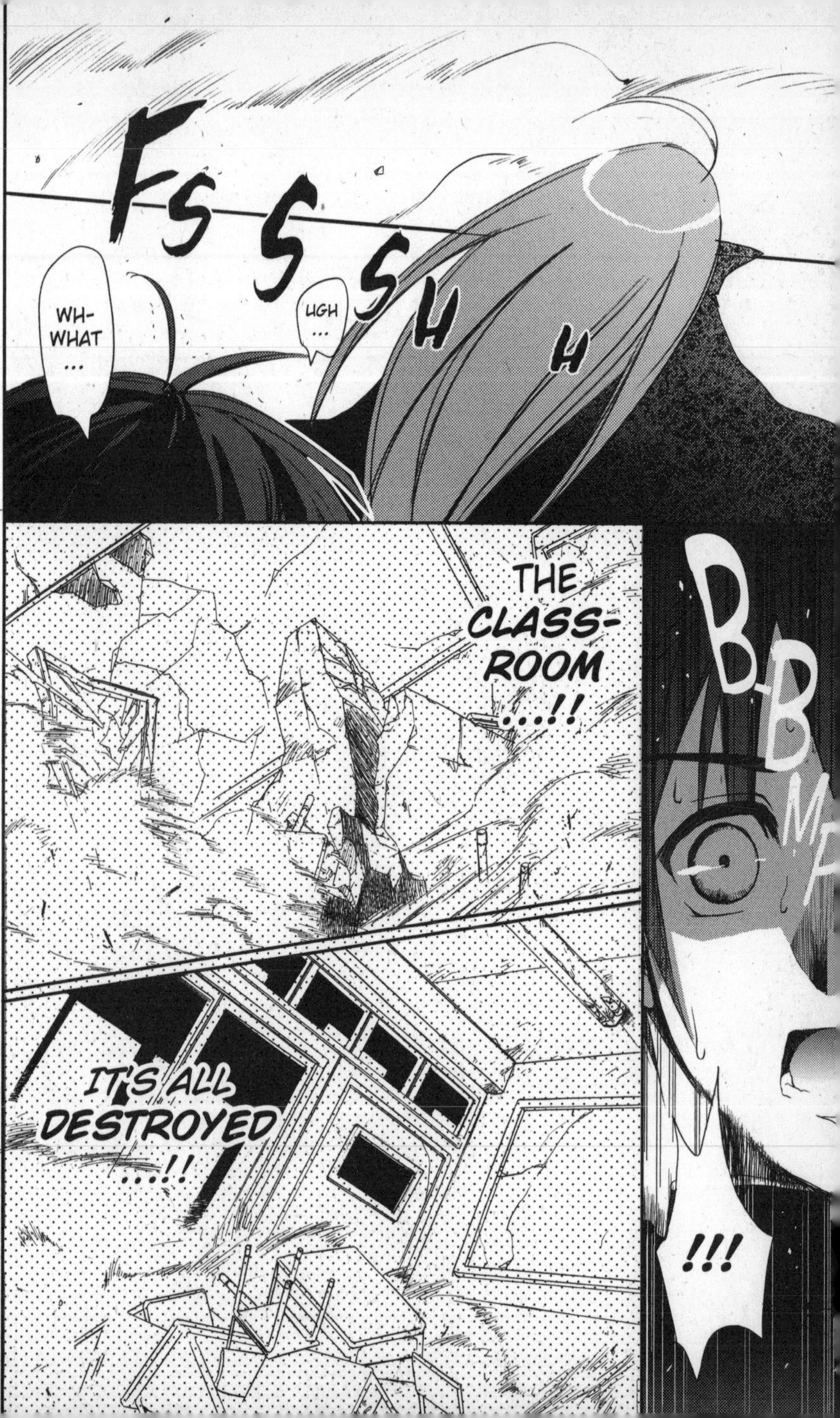
FSSSHH
UGH...
WH-WHAT...
B-BMP
!!!
THE CLASSROOM...!!
IT'S ALL DESTROYED...!!

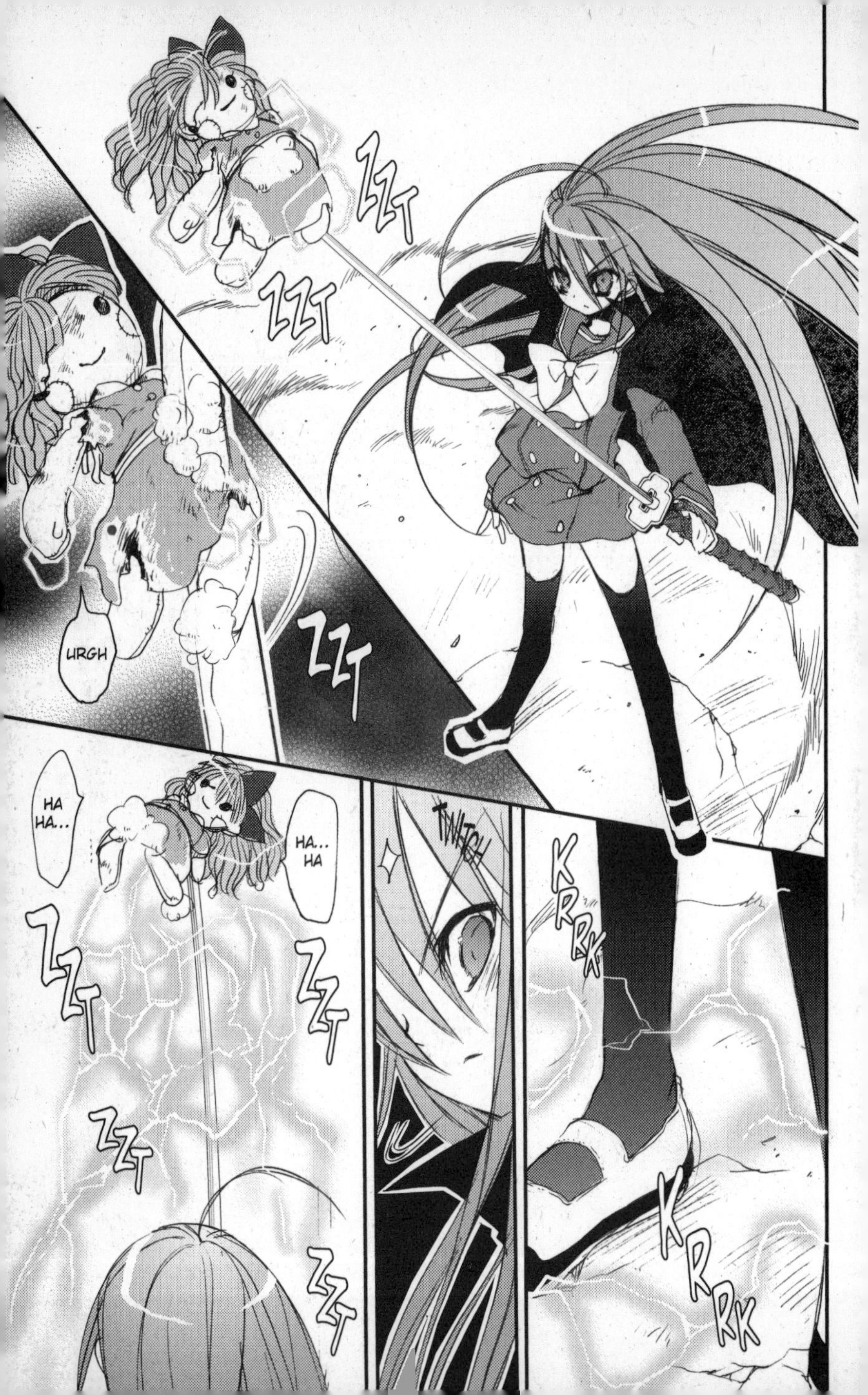
ZZT
ZZT
URGH
ZZT
KRRK
KRRK
TWITCH
HA... HA
HA HA...
ZZT
ZZT
ZZT
ZZT

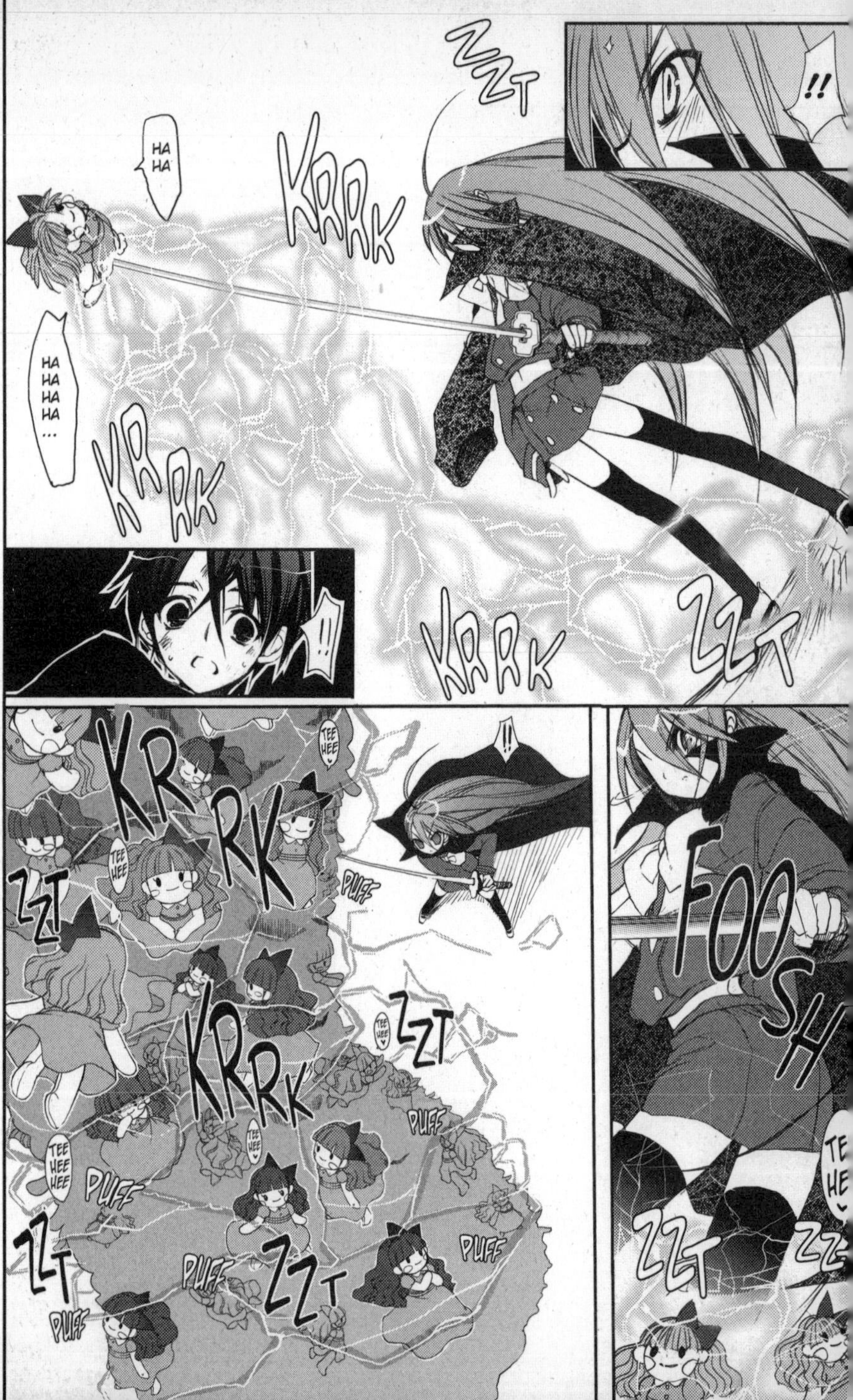
!!
ZZZT
KRAAK
HA HA
HA HA HA HA ...
KRAAK
ZZZT
KRAAK
!!
FOOSH
ZZZT
!!
TEE HEE
KR RK
TEE HEE
ZZT
PUFF
TEE HEE
ZZT
KRRK
TEE HEE
PUFF
TEE HEE HEE
PUFF
PUFF
PUFF
ZZT
PUFF
ZZT
PUFF

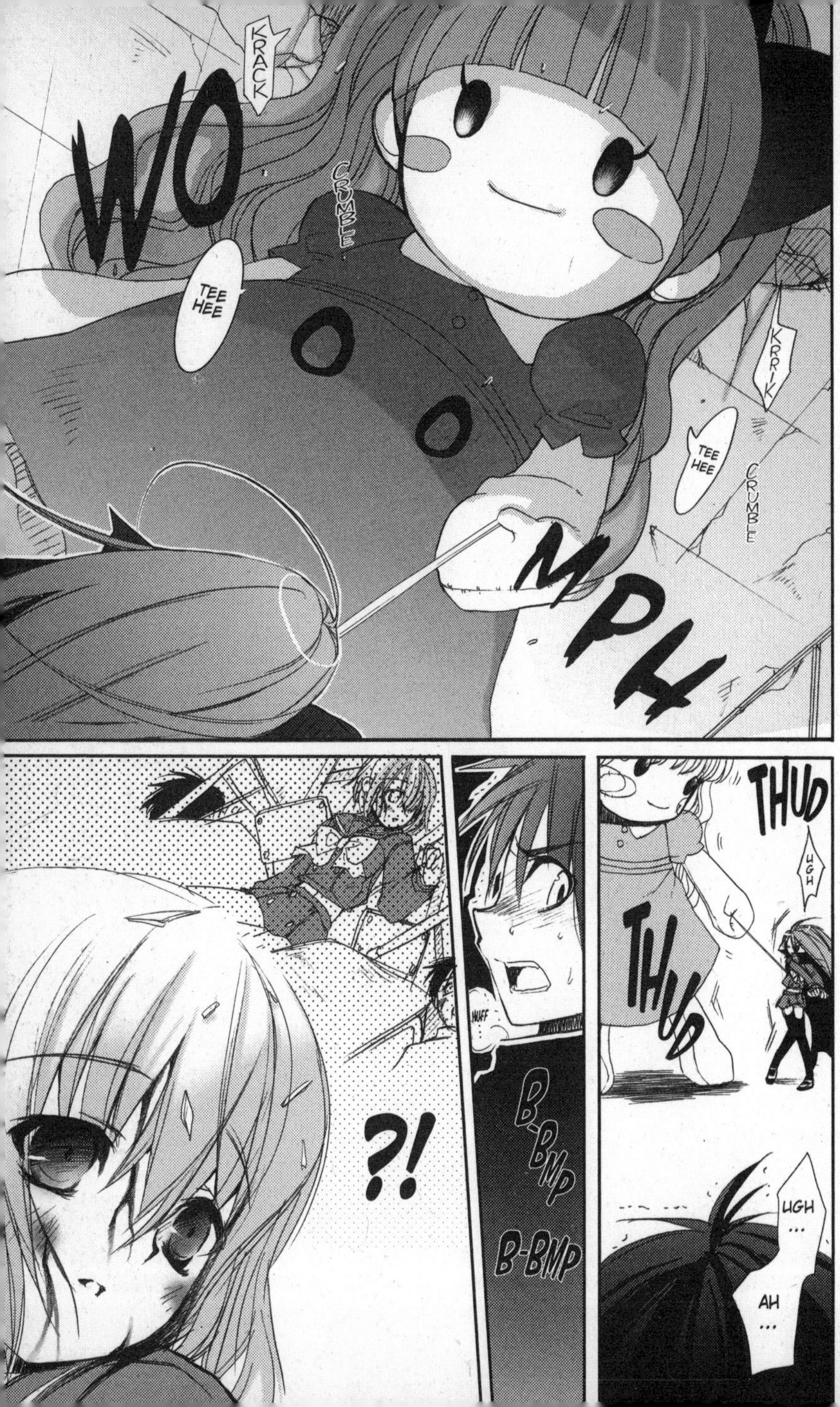
KRRIK
TEE HEE
CRUMBLE
KRACK
WO
CRUMBLE
TEE HEE
MPH
THUD
UGH
THUD
UGH
...
AH
...
HUFF
B-BMP
B-BMP
?!

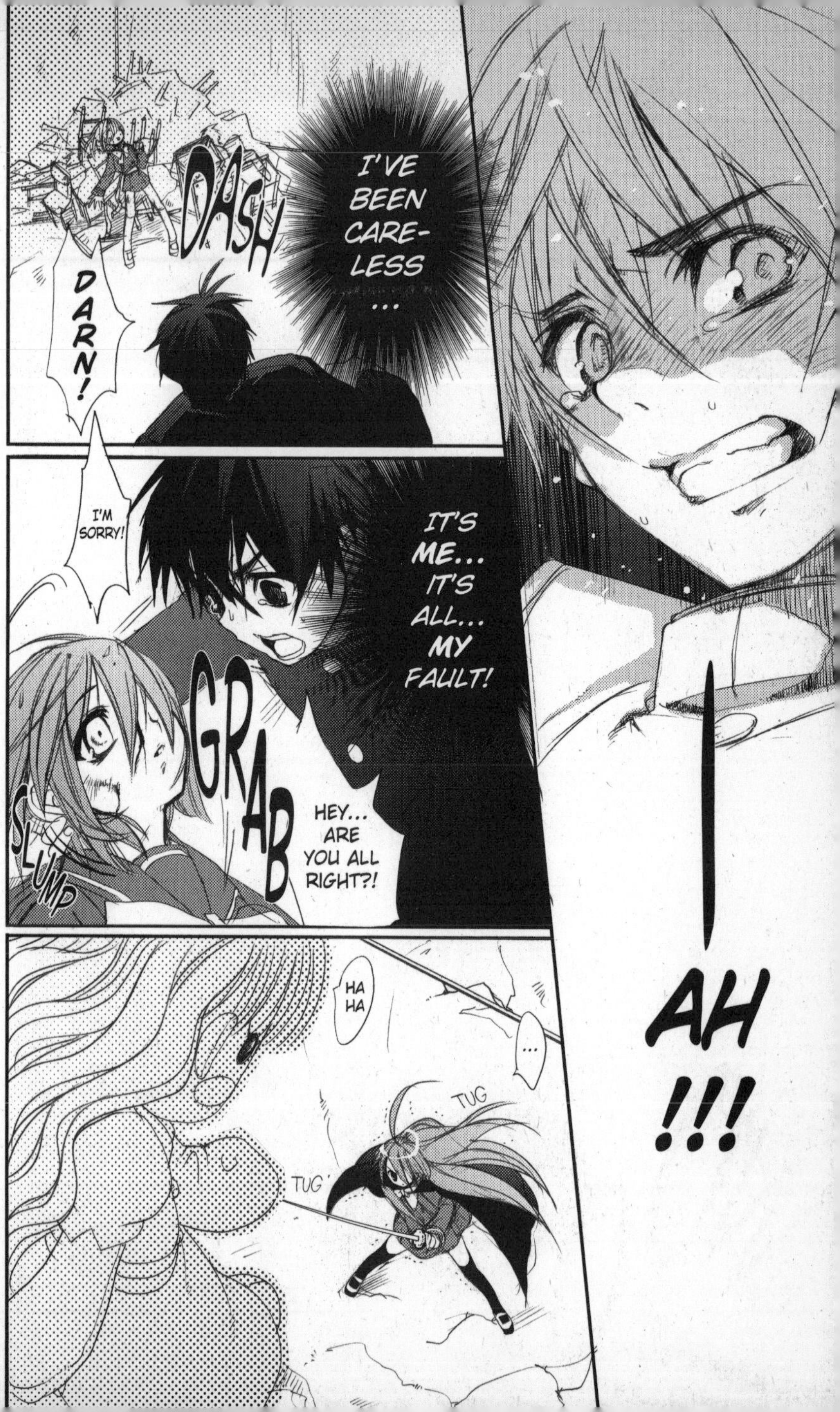
AH!!!
I'VE BEEN CARE-LESS...
DASH
DARN!
IT'S ME... IT'S ALL... MY FAULT!
I'M SORRY!
GRAB
HEY... ARE YOU ALL RIGHT?!
SLUMP
...
HA HA
TUG
TUG

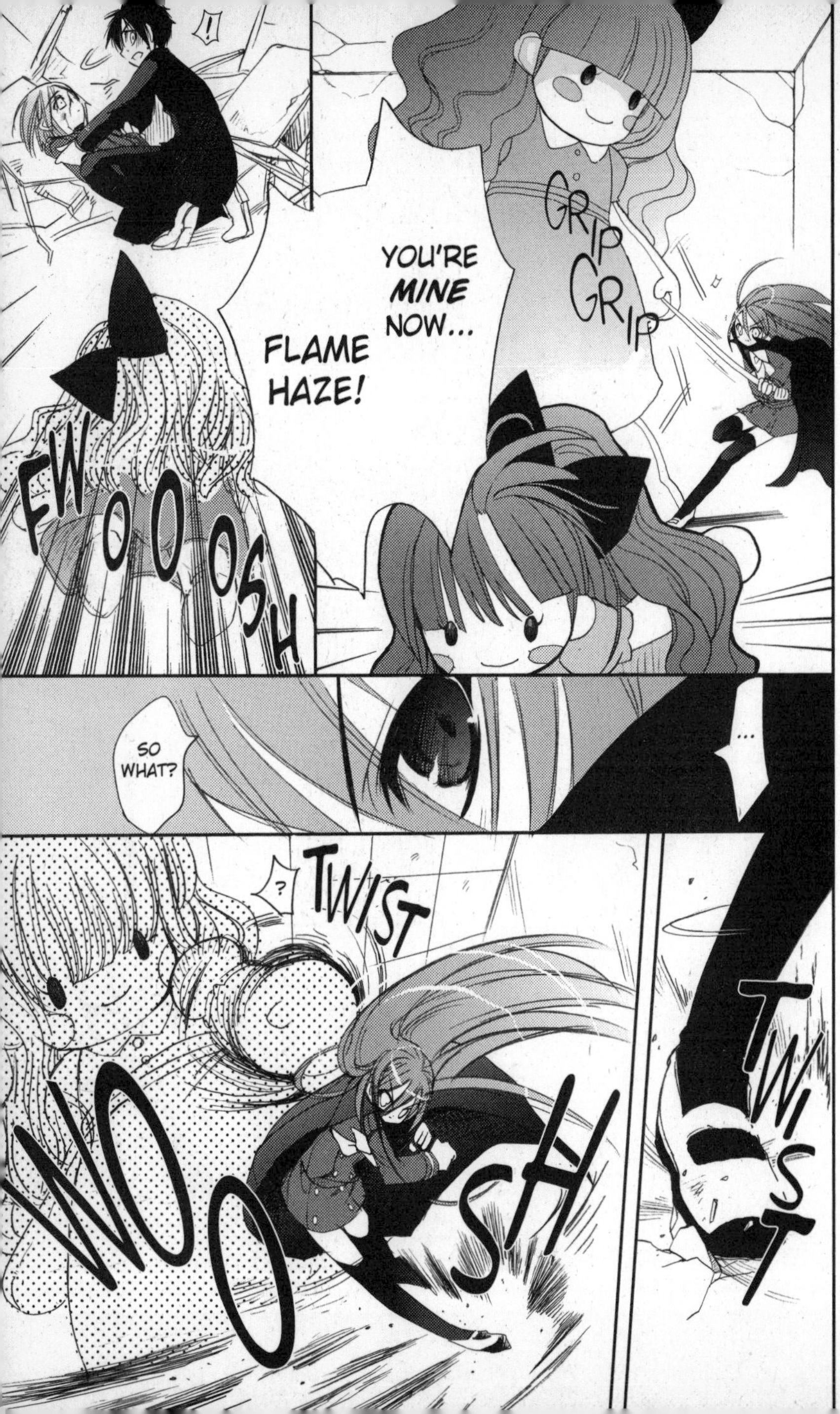
GRIP GRIP
YOU'RE *MINE* NOW...
FLAME HAZE!
!
FWOOOSH
...
SO WHAT?
TWIST
?
TWIST
WOOOSH

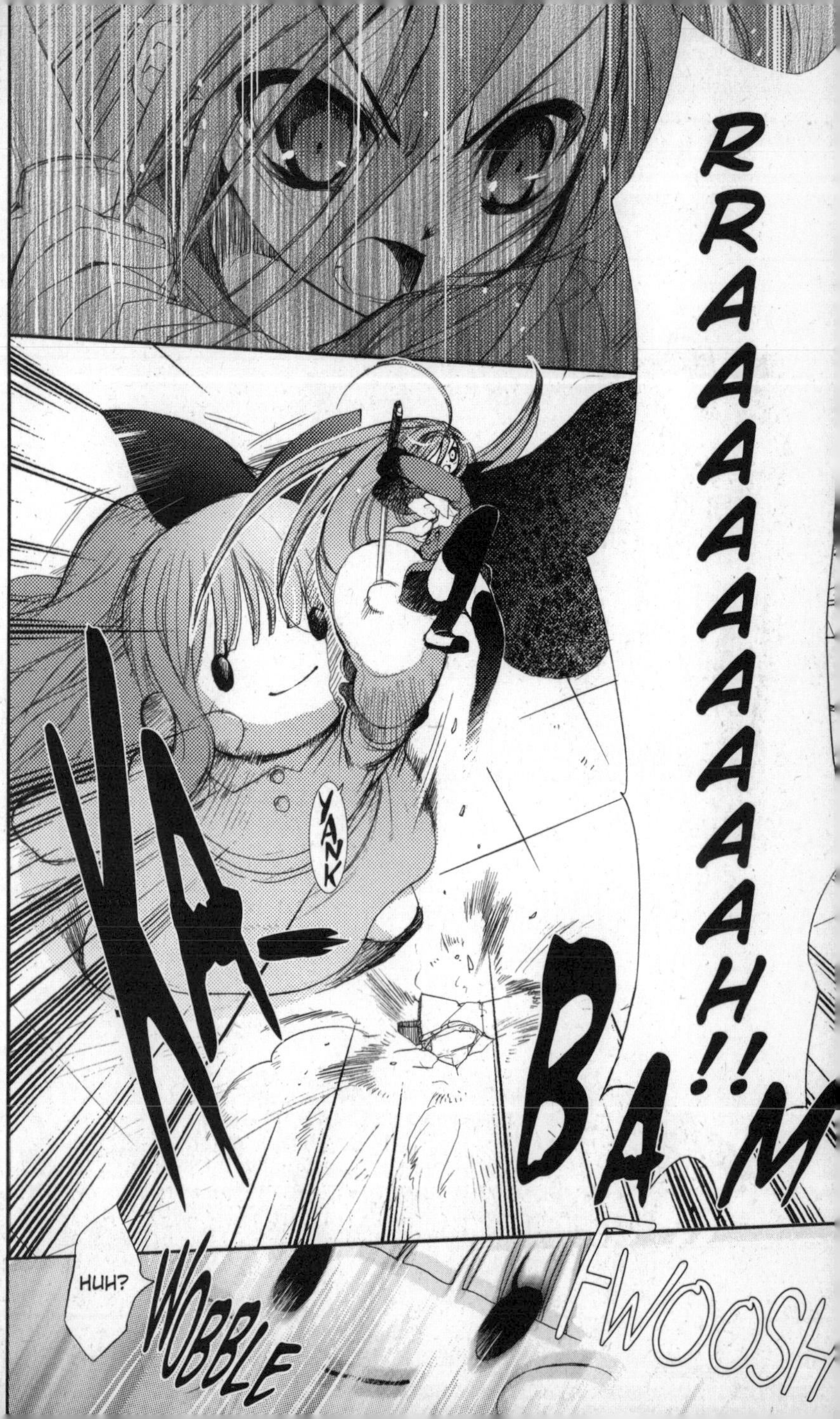
RRAAAAAAAAAAAH!!
YANK
KA-
BAM
FWOOSH
WOBBLE
HUH?

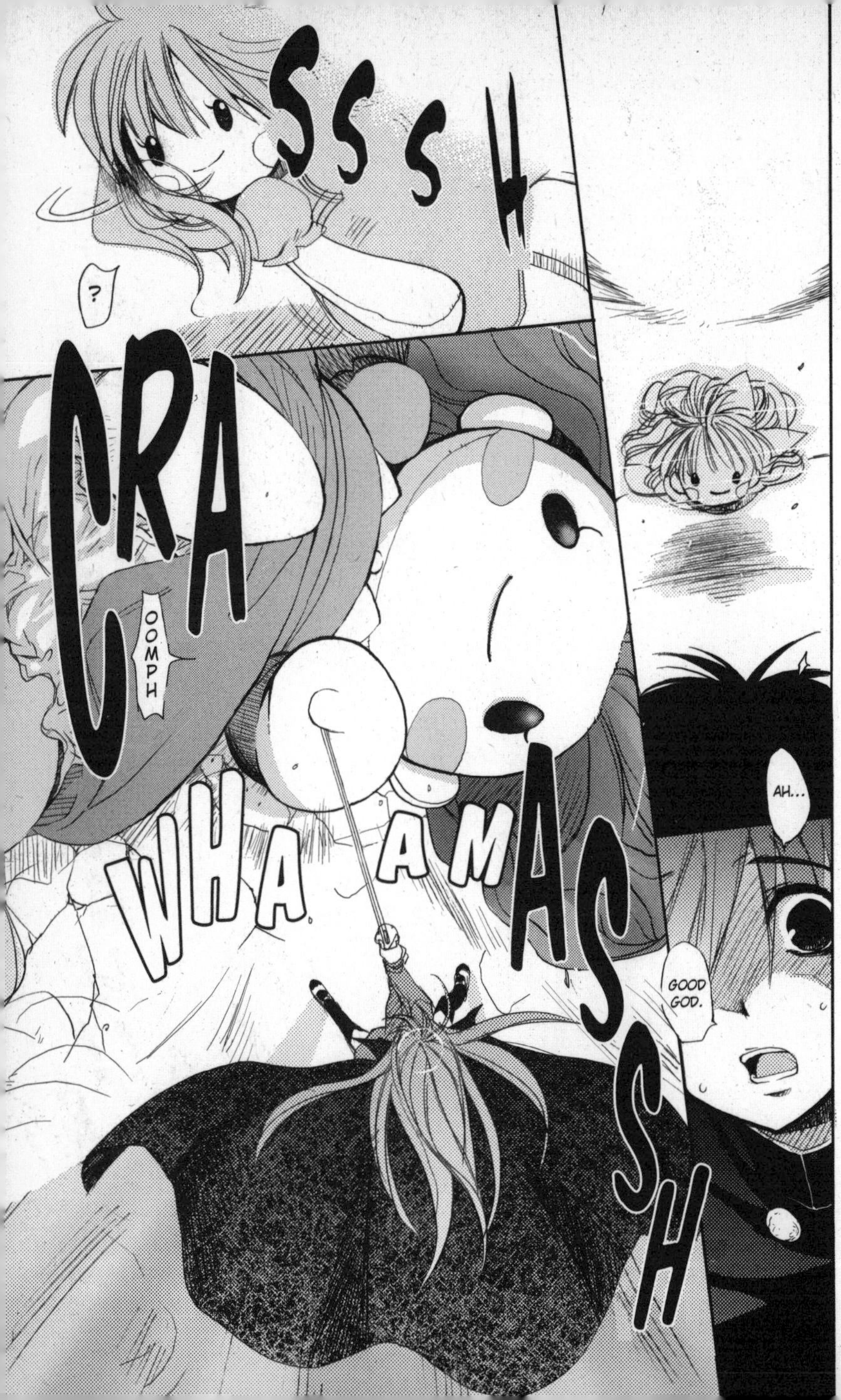
SSSSH
?
CRA
OOMPH
AH...
WHAAM
AMASSH
GOOD GOD.

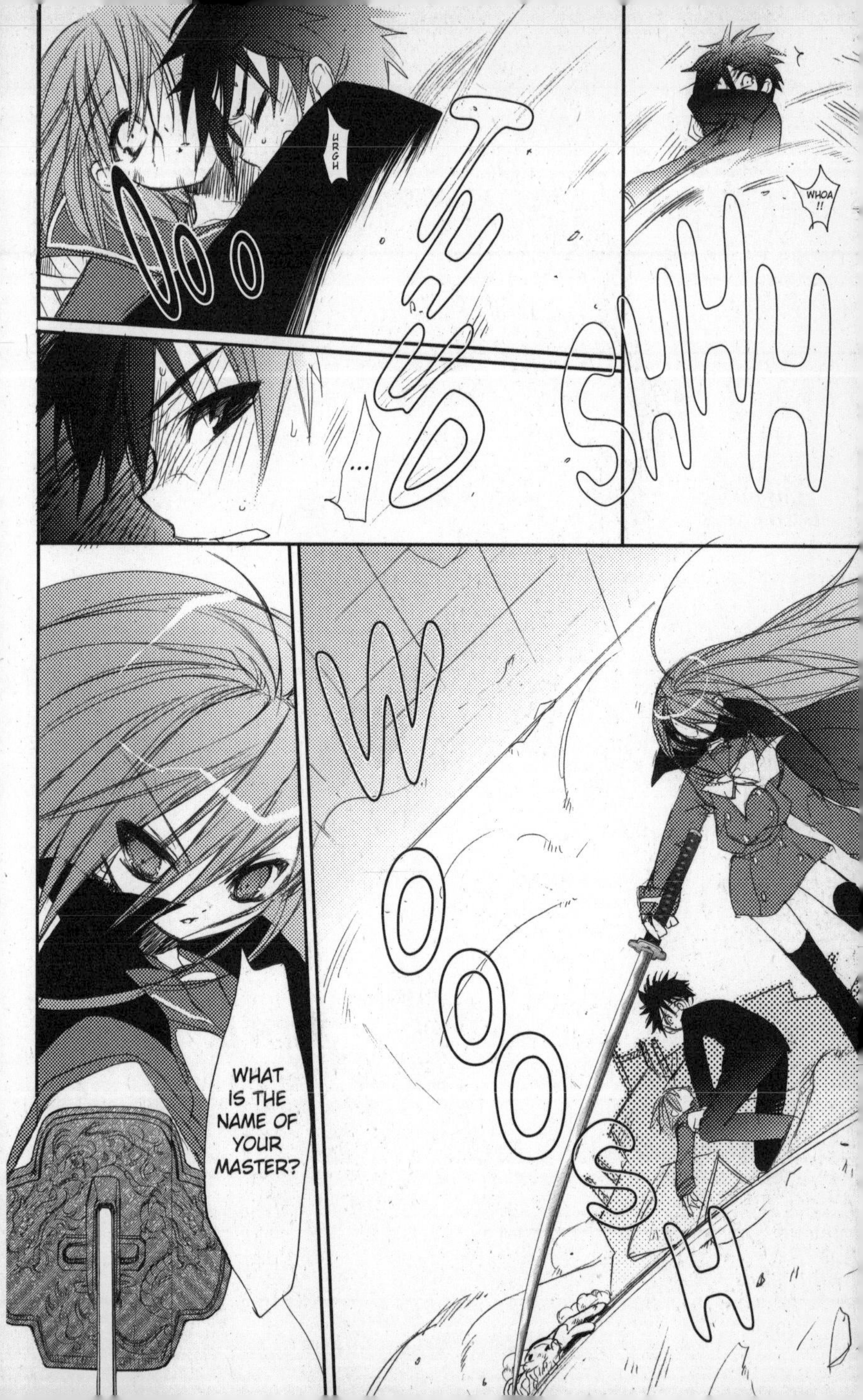
WHOA!!
SHHH
URGH
THUD
...
WOOOOSH
WHAT IS THE NAME OF YOUR MASTER?

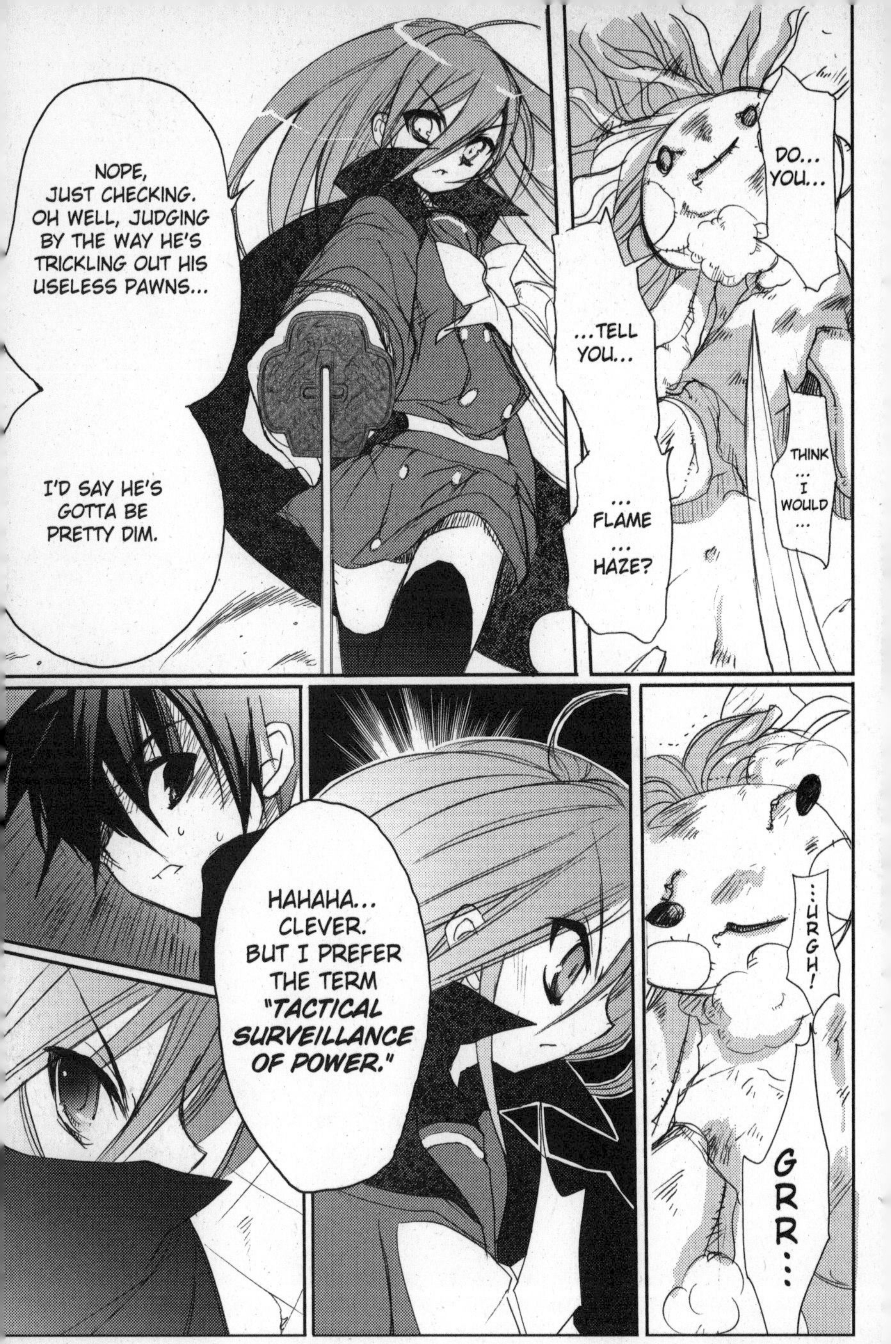
DO... YOU...
THINK ... I WOULD ...
...TELL YOU...
... FLAME ... HAZE?
NOPE, JUST CHECKING. OH WELL, JUDGING BY THE WAY HE'S TRICKLING OUT HIS USELESS PAWNS...
I'D SAY HE'S GOTTA BE PRETTY DIM.
...URGH!
GRR...
HAHAHA... CLEVER. BUT I PREFER THE TERM "TACTICAL SURVEILLANCE OF POWER."

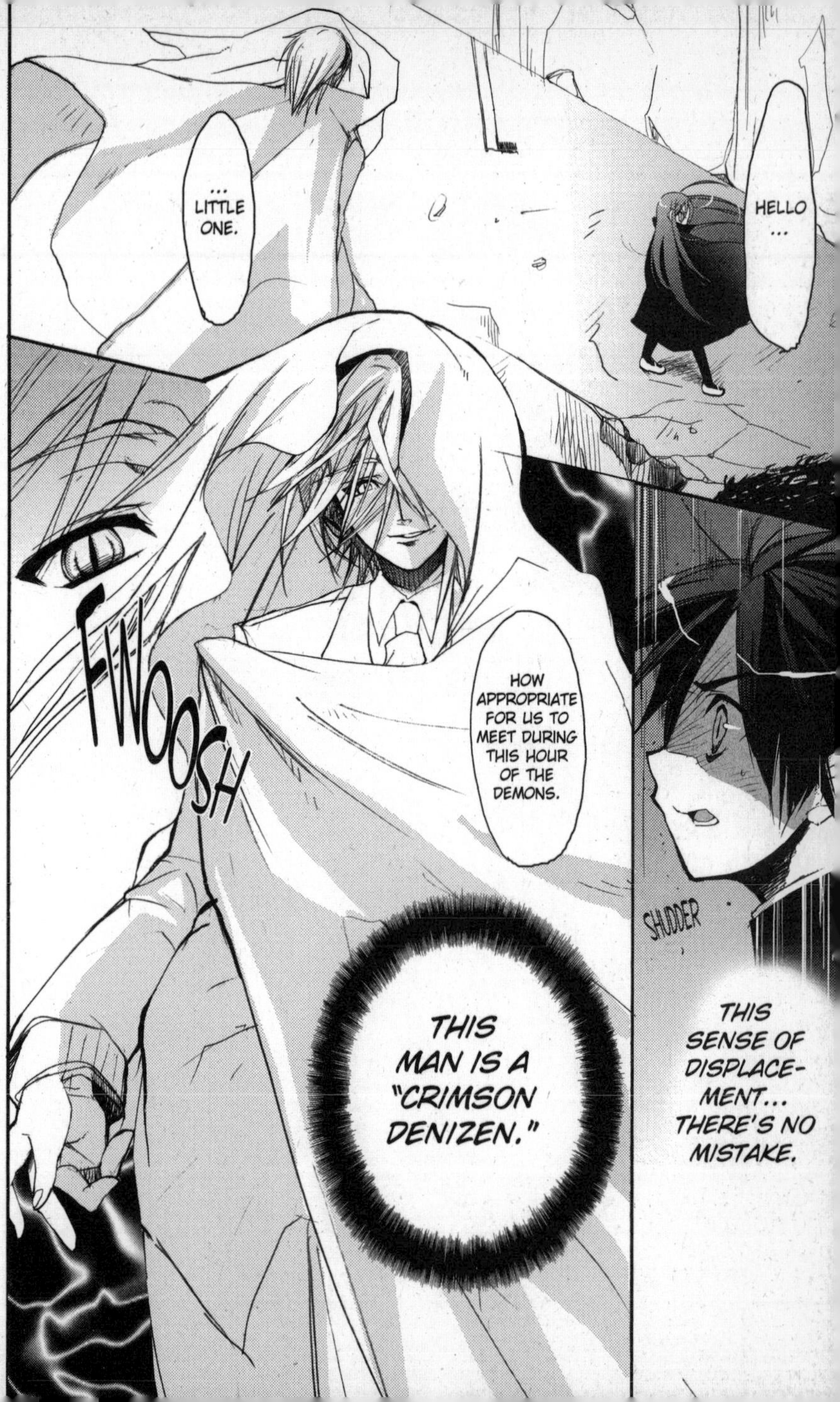
HELLO ...
... LITTLE ONE.
SHUDDER
THIS SENSE OF DISPLACE- MENT... THERE'S NO MISTAKE.
FWOOSH
HOW APPROPRIATE FOR US TO MEET DURING THIS HOUR OF THE DEMONS.
THIS MAN IS A "CRIMSON DENIZEN."

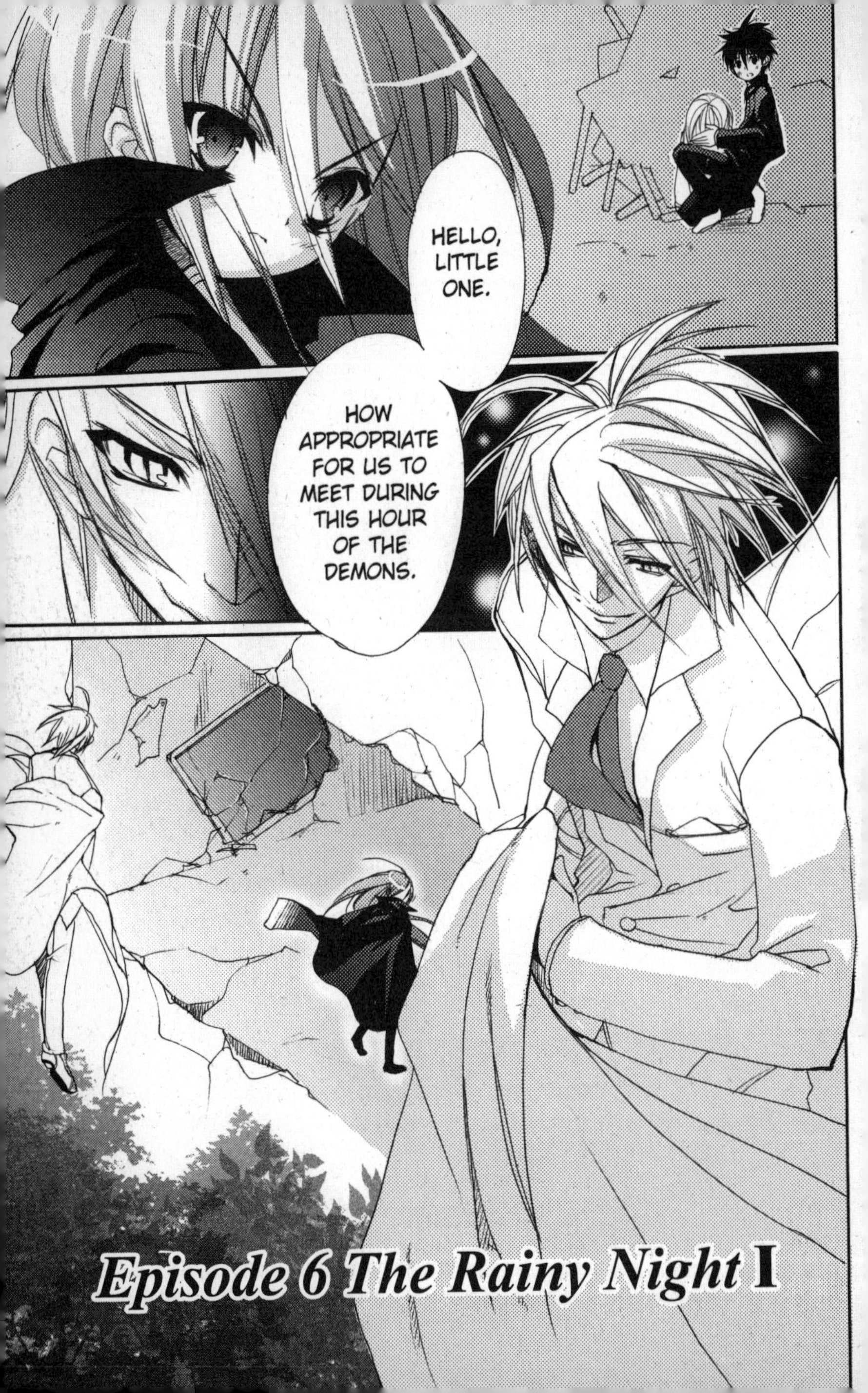
HELLO, LITTLE ONE.
HOW APPROPRIATE FOR US TO MEET DURING THIS HOUR OF THE DEMONS.
Episode 6 The Rainy Night I

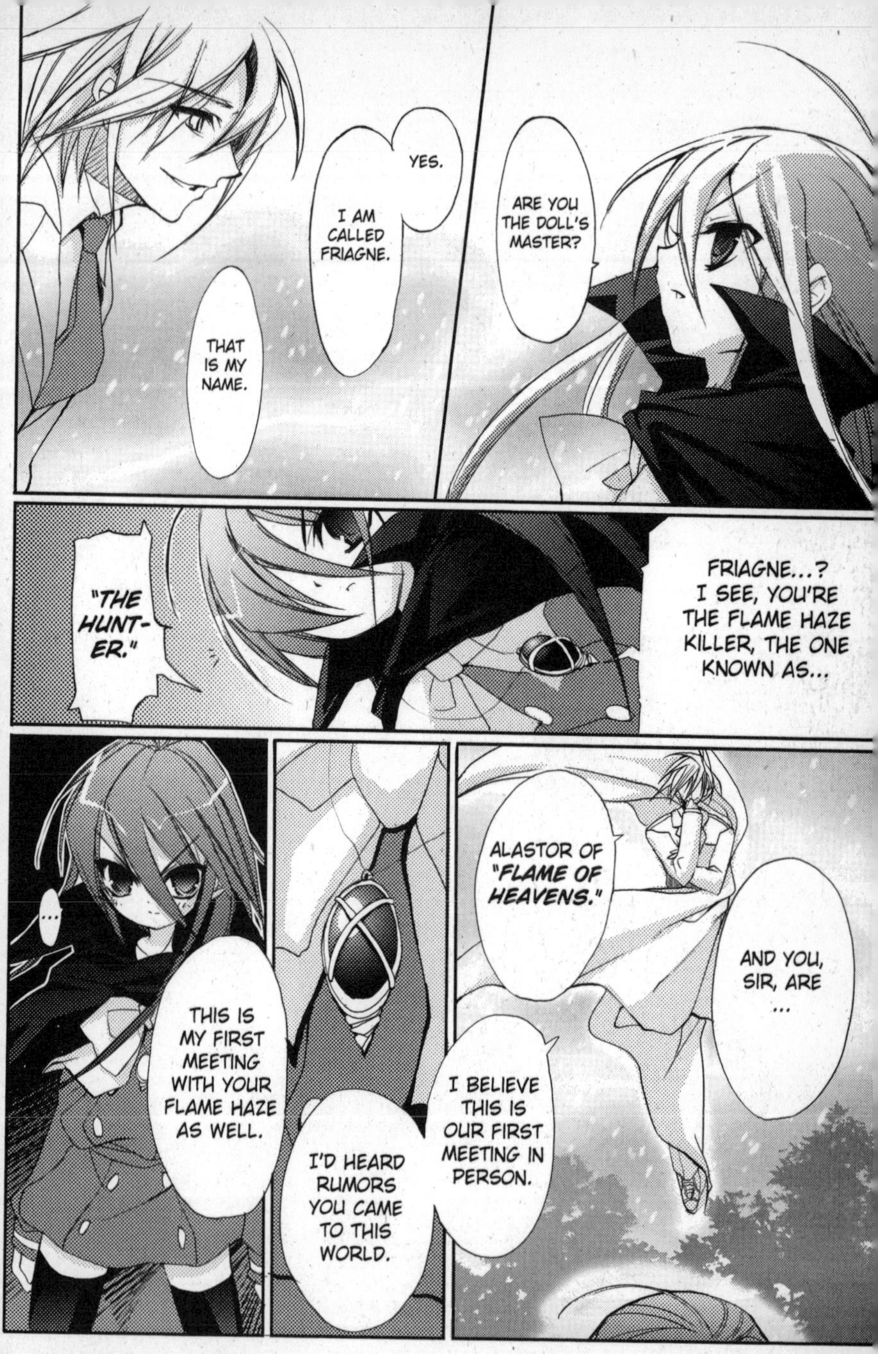
ARE YOU THE DOLL'S MASTER?
YES.
I AM CALLED FRIAGNE.
THAT IS MY NAME.
FRIAGNE...? I SEE, YOU'RE THE FLAME HAZE KILLER, THE ONE KNOWN AS...
"THE HUNTER."
AND YOU, SIR, ARE ...
ALASTOR OF "FLAME OF HEAVENS."
I BELIEVE THIS IS OUR FIRST MEETING IN PERSON.
I'D HEARD RUMORS YOU CAME TO THIS WORLD.
...
THIS IS MY FIRST MEETING WITH YOUR FLAME HAZE AS WELL.

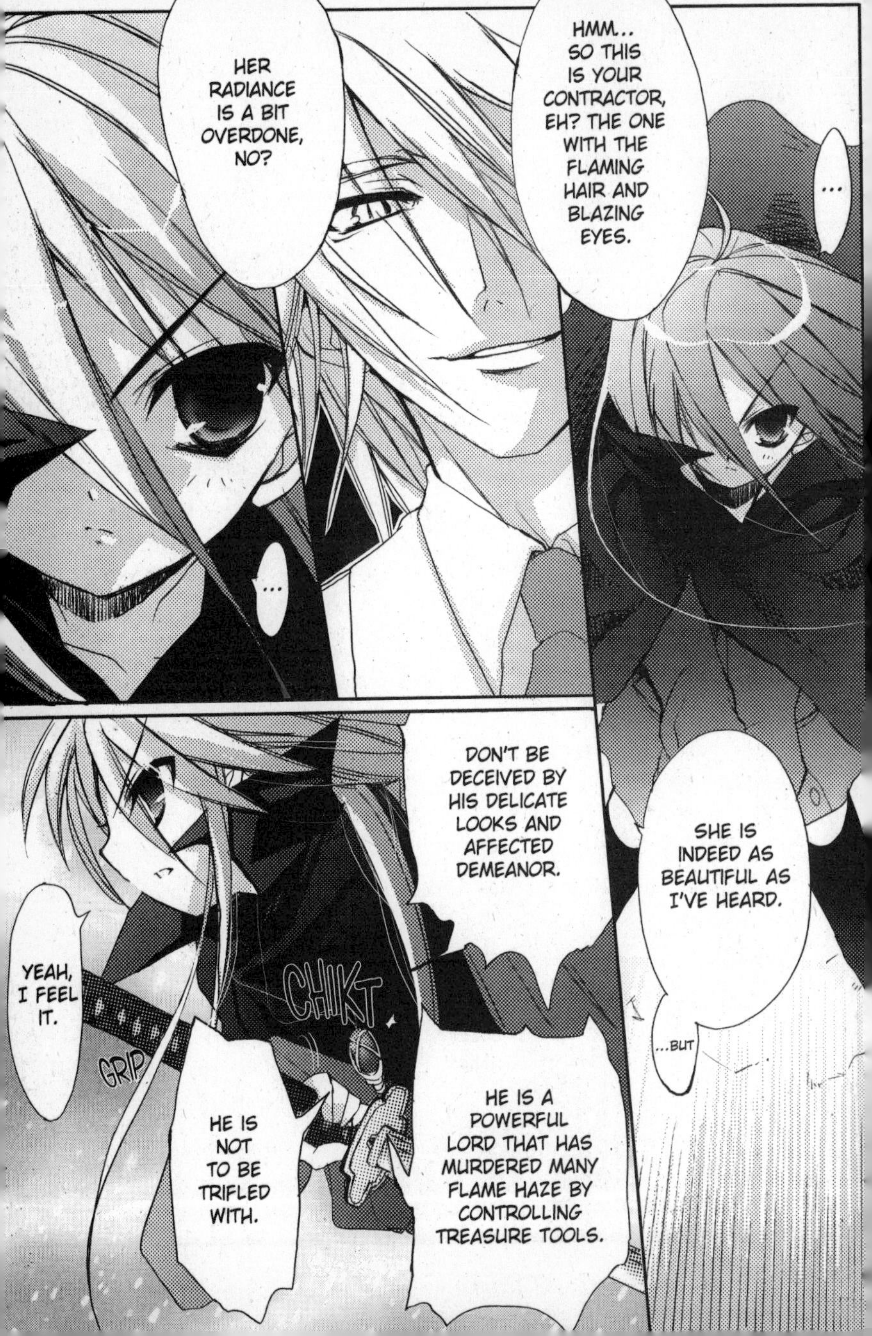
HMM... SO THIS IS YOUR CONTRACTOR, EH? THE ONE WITH THE FLAMING HAIR AND BLAZING EYES.
HER RADIANCE IS A BIT OVERDONE, NO?
...
...
SHE IS INDEED AS BEAUTIFUL AS I'VE HEARD.
...BUT
DON'T BE DECEIVED BY HIS DELICATE LOOKS AND AFFECTED DEMEANOR.
HE IS A POWERFUL LORD THAT HAS MURDERED MANY FLAME HAZE BY CONTROLLING TREASURE TOOLS.
HE IS NOT TO BE TRIFLED WITH.
YEAH, I FEEL IT.
CHIKT
GRIP

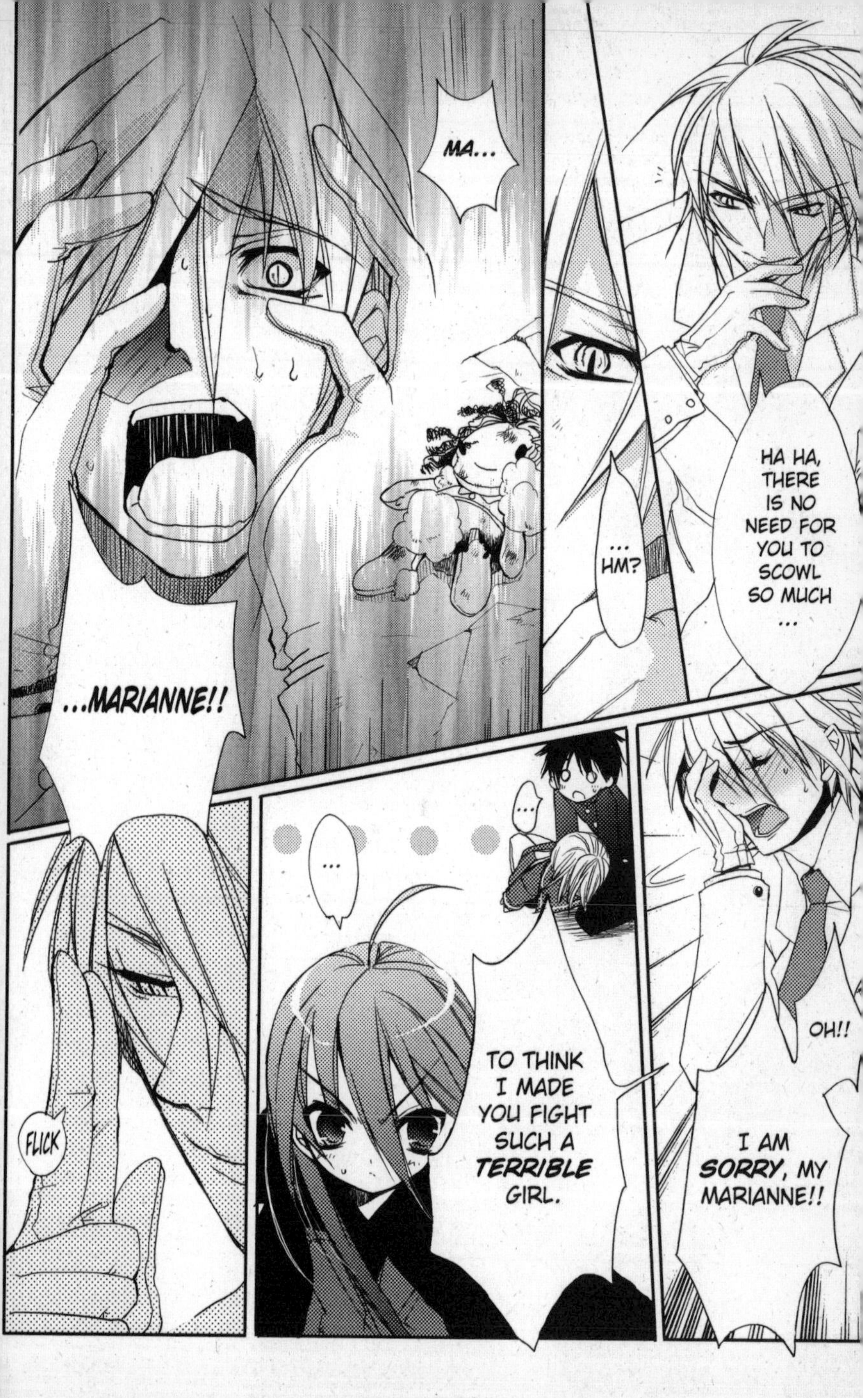
HA HA, THERE IS NO NEED FOR YOU TO SCOWL SO MUCH ...
... HM?
MA...
...MARIANNE!!
OH!!
I AM SORRY, MY MARIANNE!!
...
...
TO THINK I MADE YOU FIGHT SUCH A TERRIBLE GIRL.
FLICK

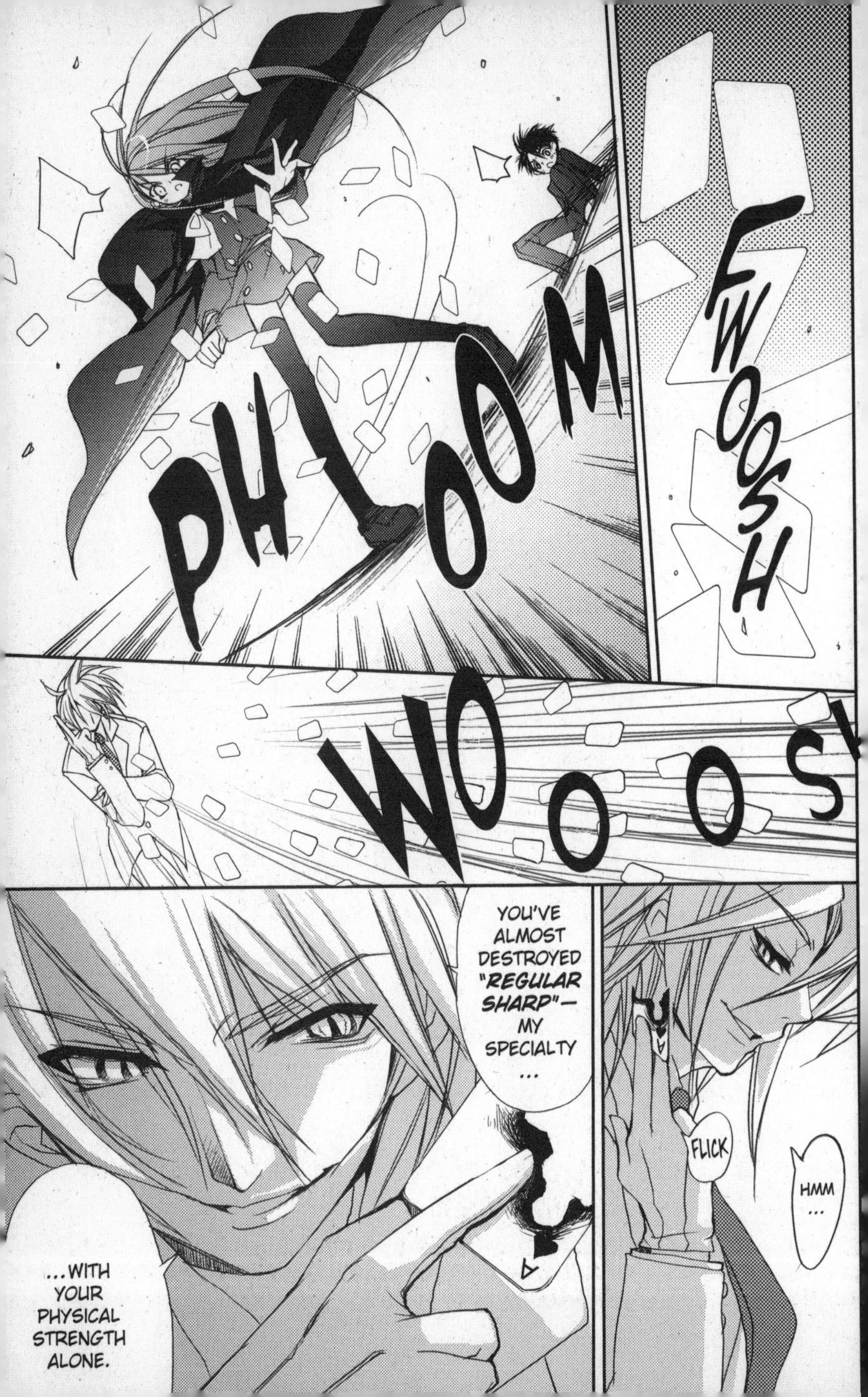
FWOOSH
PHWOOM
WOOOOS
FLICK
HMM...
YOU'VE ALMOST DESTROYED "REGULAR SHARP"—MY SPECIALTY...
...WITH YOUR PHYSICAL STRENGTH ALONE.

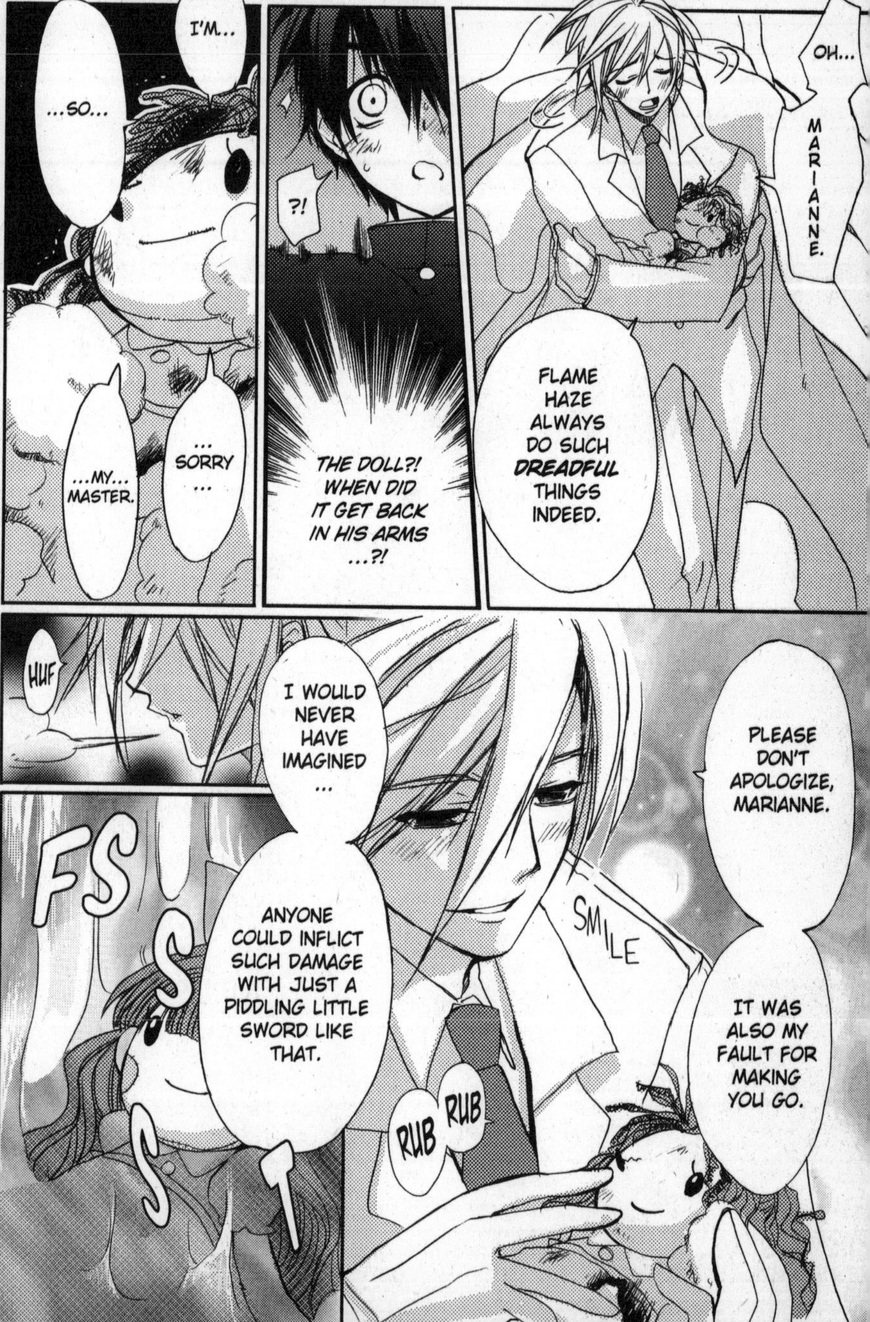
OH... MARIANNE.
FLAME HAZE ALWAYS DO SUCH **DREADFUL** THINGS INDEED.
?!
THE DOLL?! WHEN DID IT GET BACK IN HIS ARMS ...?!
I'M...
...SO...
... SORRY ...
...MY... MASTER.
PLEASE DON'T APOLOGIZE, MARIANNE.
IT WAS ALSO MY FAULT FOR MAKING YOU GO.
SMILE
I WOULD NEVER HAVE IMAGINED ...
ANYONE COULD INFLICT SUCH DAMAGE WITH JUST A PIDDLING LITTLE SWORD LIKE THAT.
RUB RUB
HUF
FSSST

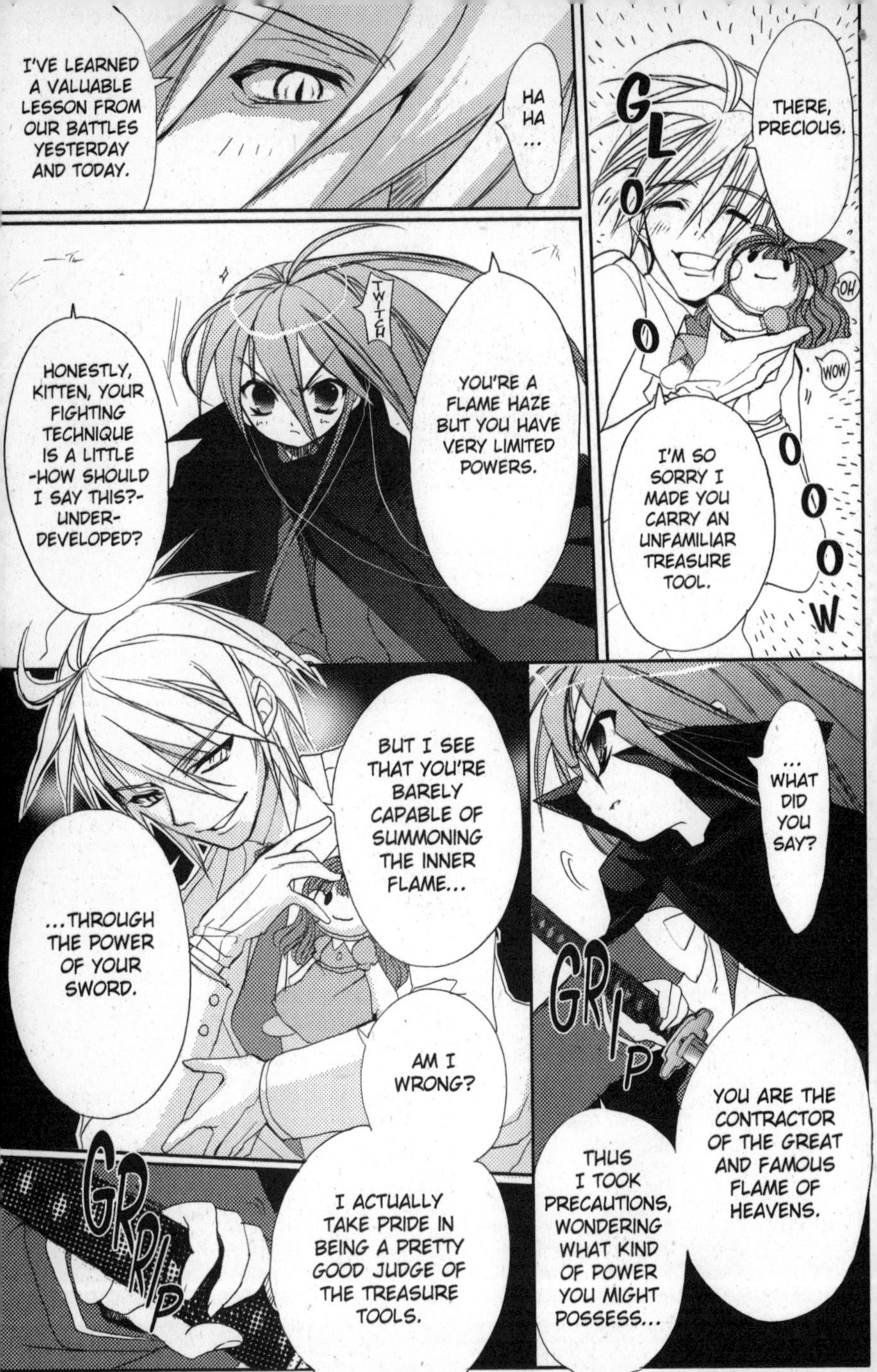
THERE, PRECIOUS.
GLOOOOOOW
OH
WOW
I'M SO SORRY I MADE YOU CARRY AN UNFAMILIAR TREASURE TOOL.
HA HA ...
I'VE LEARNED A VALUABLE LESSON FROM OUR BATTLES YESTERDAY AND TODAY.
TWITCH
YOU'RE A FLAME HAZE BUT YOU HAVE VERY LIMITED POWERS.
HONESTLY, KITTEN, YOUR FIGHTING TECHNIQUE IS A LITTLE -HOW SHOULD I SAY THIS?- UNDER-DEVELOPED?
... WHAT DID YOU SAY?
GRIP
YOU ARE THE CONTRACTOR OF THE GREAT AND FAMOUS FLAME OF HEAVENS.
THUS I TOOK PRECAUTIONS, WONDERING WHAT KIND OF POWER YOU MIGHT POSSESS...
BUT I SEE THAT YOU'RE BARELY CAPABLE OF SUMMONING THE INNER FLAME...
...THROUGH THE POWER OF YOUR SWORD.
AM I WRONG?
I ACTUALLY TAKE PRIDE IN BEING A PRETTY GOOD JUDGE OF THE TREASURE TOOLS.
GRRIP

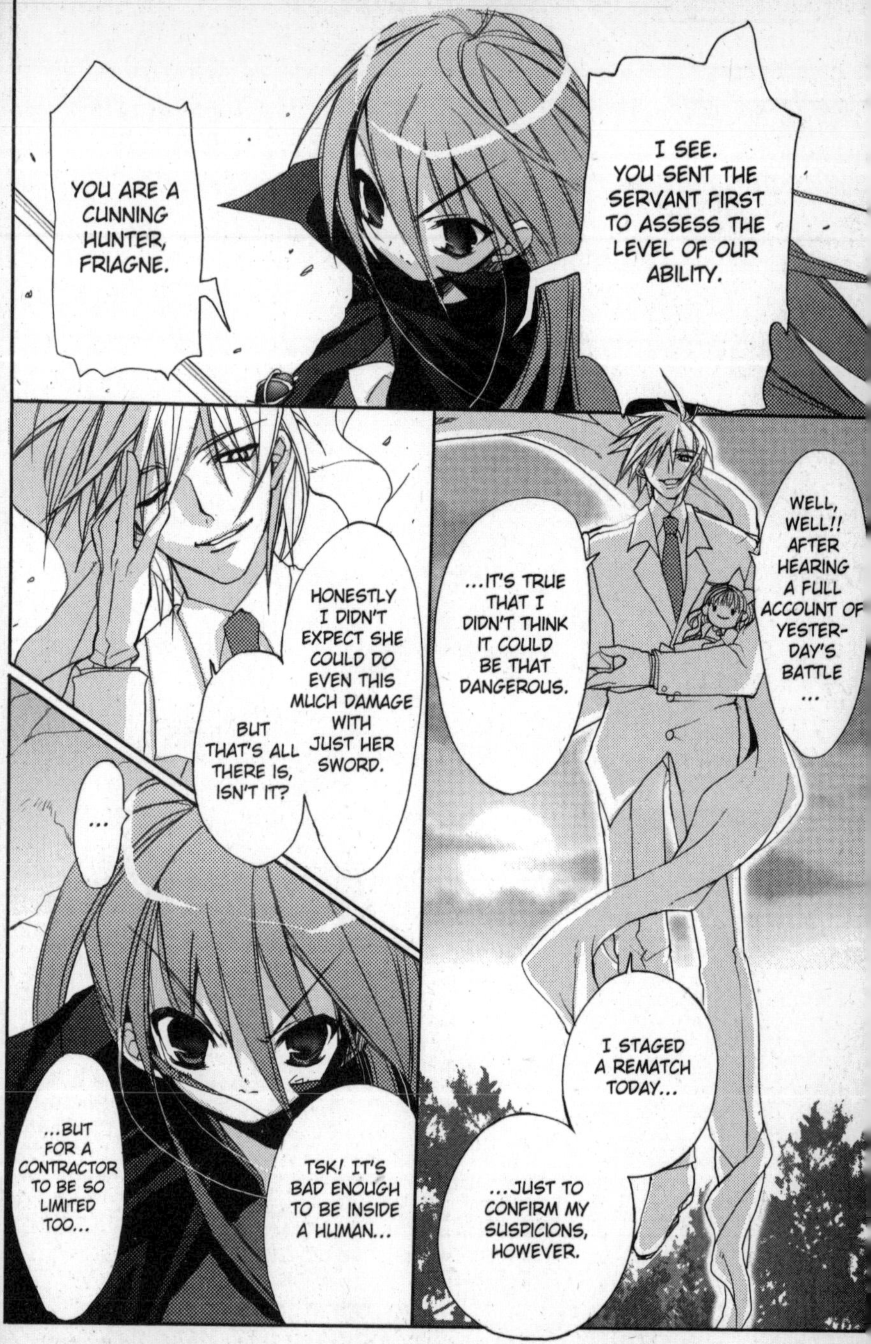
I SEE. YOU SENT THE SERVANT FIRST TO ASSESS THE LEVEL OF OUR ABILITY.
YOU ARE A CUNNING HUNTER, FRIAGNE.
WELL, WELL!! AFTER HEARING A FULL ACCOUNT OF YESTER-DAY'S BATTLE...
...IT'S TRUE THAT I DIDN'T THINK IT COULD BE THAT DANGEROUS.
I STAGED A REMATCH TODAY...
...JUST TO CONFIRM MY SUSPICIONS, HOWEVER.
HONESTLY I DIDN'T EXPECT SHE COULD DO EVEN THIS MUCH DAMAGE WITH JUST HER SWORD.
BUT THAT'S ALL THERE IS, ISN'T IT?
...
TSK! IT'S BAD ENOUGH TO BE INSIDE A HUMAN...
...BUT FOR A CONTRACTOR TO BE SO LIMITED TOO...

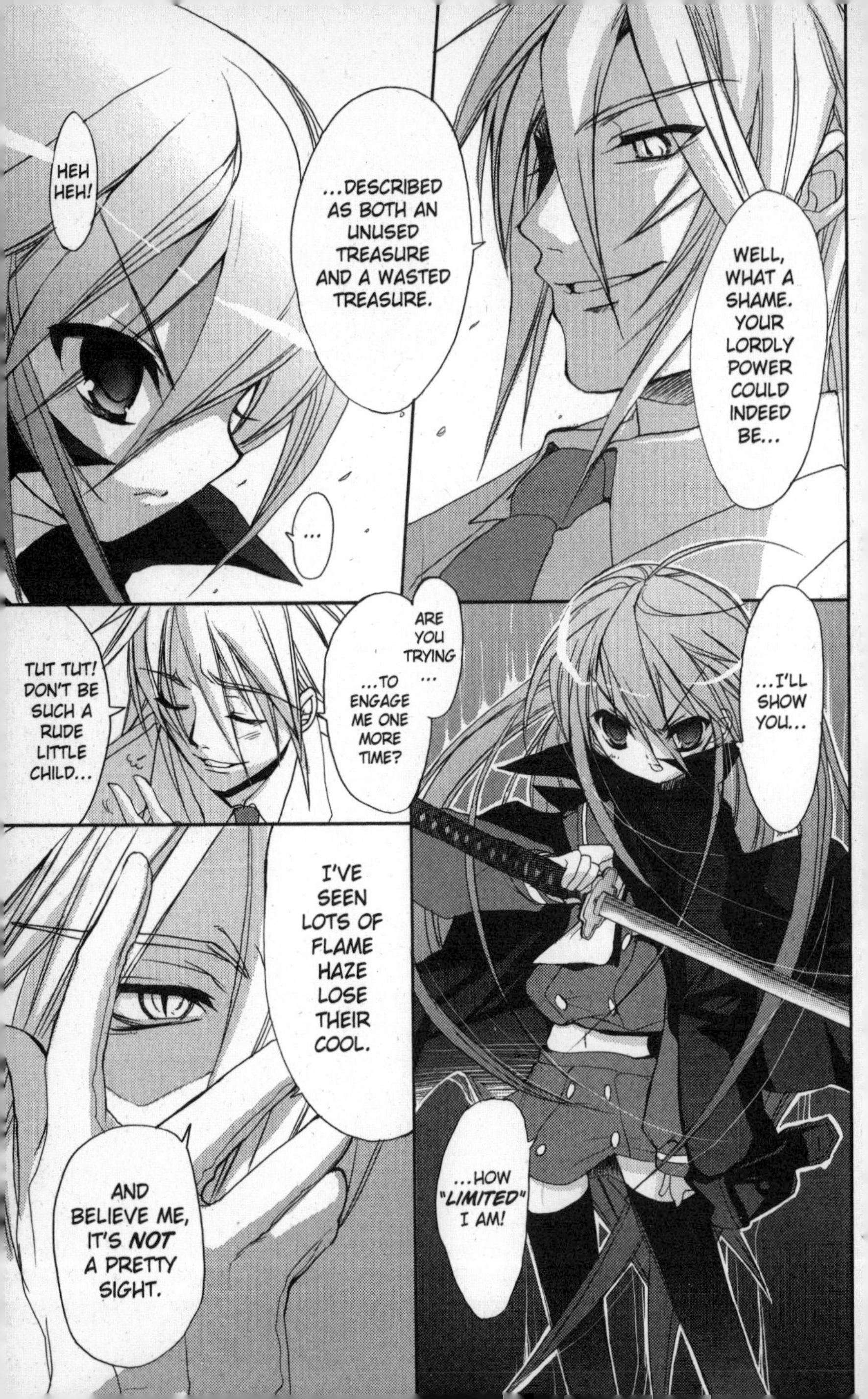
WELL, WHAT A SHAME. YOUR LORDLY POWER COULD INDEED BE...
...DESCRIBED AS BOTH AN UNUSED TREASURE AND A WASTED TREASURE.
HEH HEH!
...
...I'LL SHOW YOU...
...HOW "*LIMITED*" I AM!
ARE YOU TRYING...
...TO ENGAGE ME ONE MORE TIME?
TUT TUT! DON'T BE SUCH A RUDE LITTLE CHILD...
I'VE SEEN LOTS OF FLAME HAZE LOSE THEIR COOL.
AND BELIEVE ME, IT'S ***NOT*** A PRETTY SIGHT.

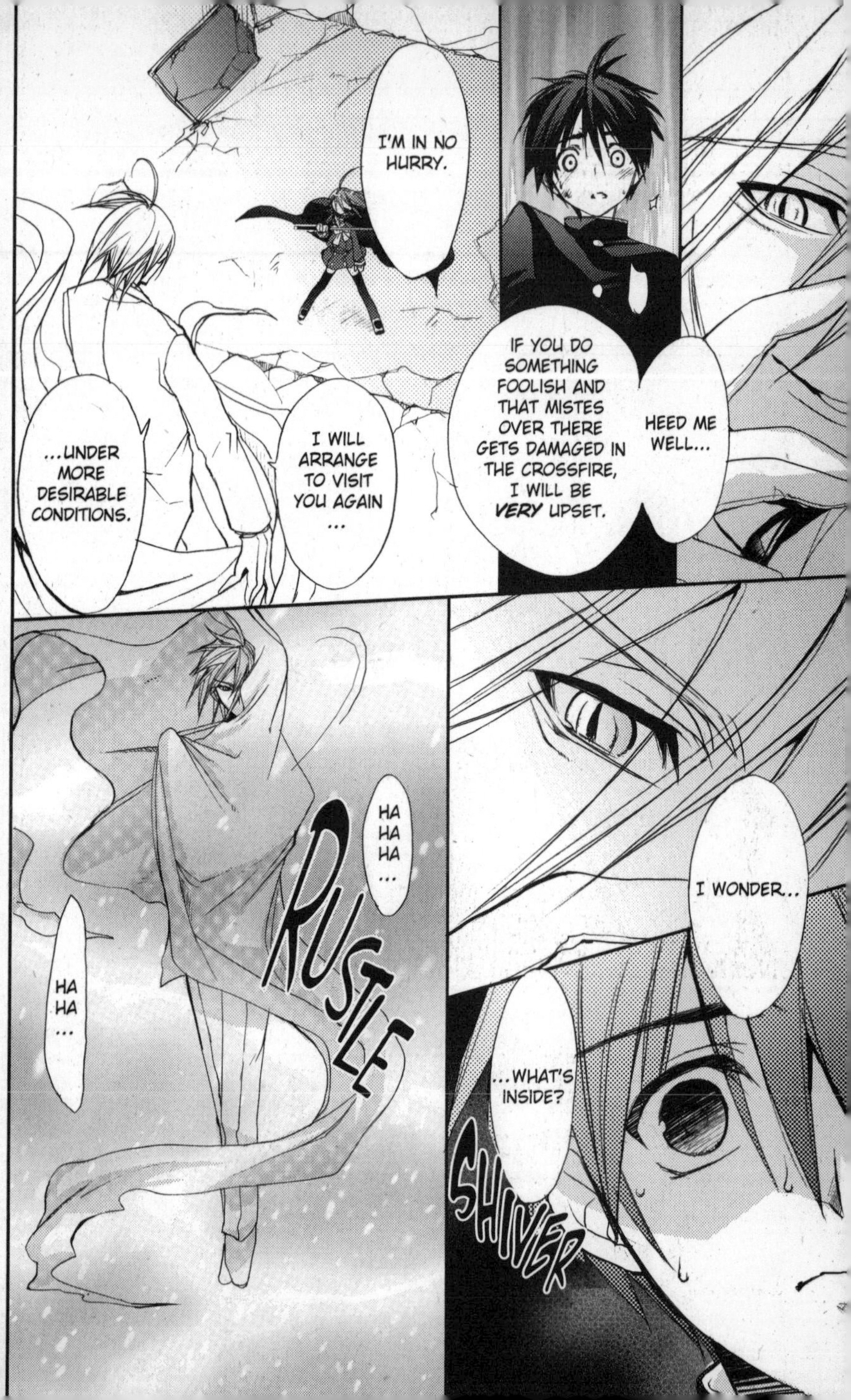
HEED ME WELL...
IF YOU DO SOMETHING FOOLISH AND THAT MISTES OVER THERE GETS DAMAGED IN THE CROSSFIRE, I WILL BE *VERY* UPSET.
I'M IN NO HURRY.
I WILL ARRANGE TO VISIT YOU AGAIN...
...UNDER MORE DESIRABLE CONDITIONS.
I WONDER...
...WHAT'S INSIDE?
SHIVER
HA HA HA...
RUSTLE
HA HA...

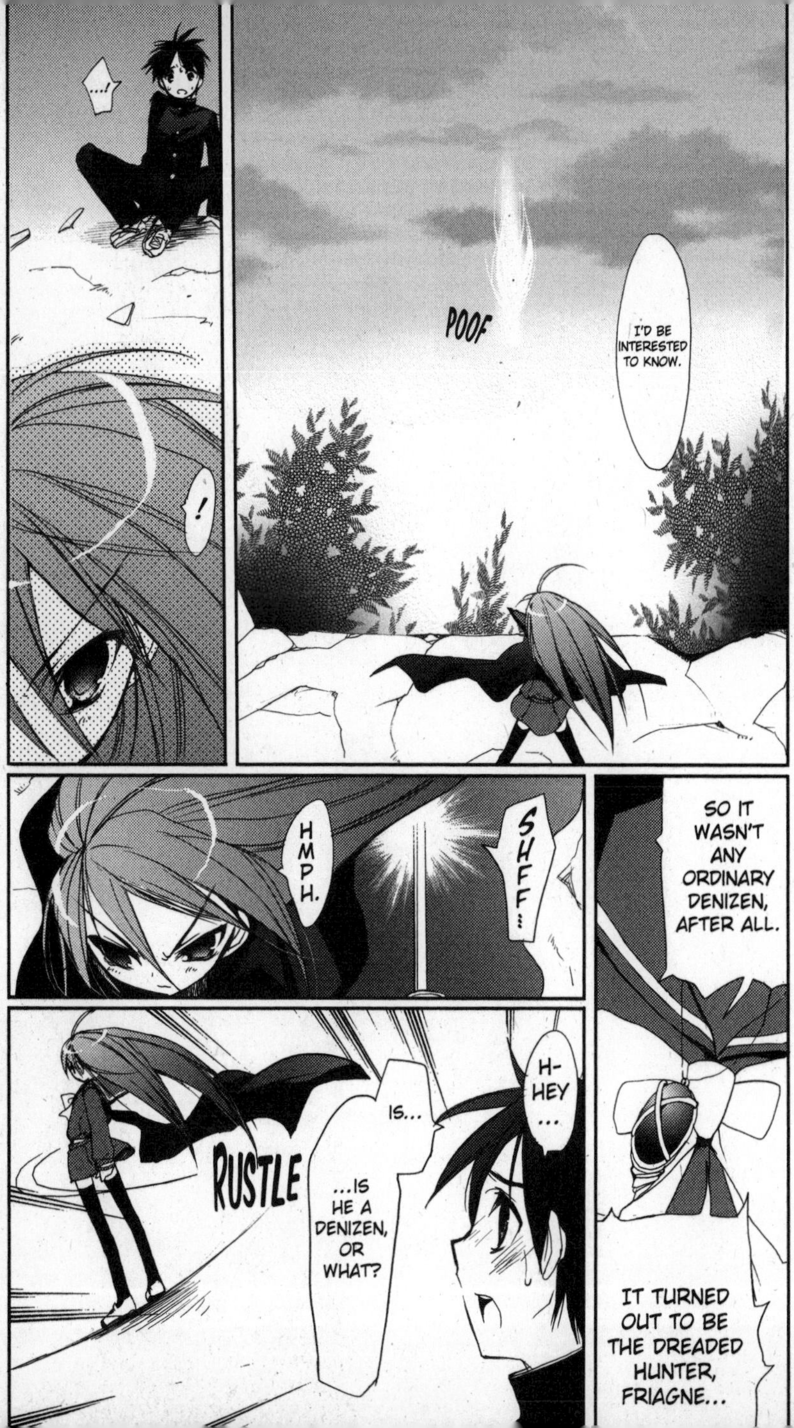
I'D BE INTERESTED TO KNOW.
POOF
...!
!
SO IT WASN'T ANY ORDINARY DENIZEN, AFTER ALL.
IT TURNED OUT TO BE THE DREADED HUNTER, FRIAGNE...
SHFF..
HMPH.
H-HEY...
IS...
...IS HE A DENIZEN, OR WHAT?
RUSTLE

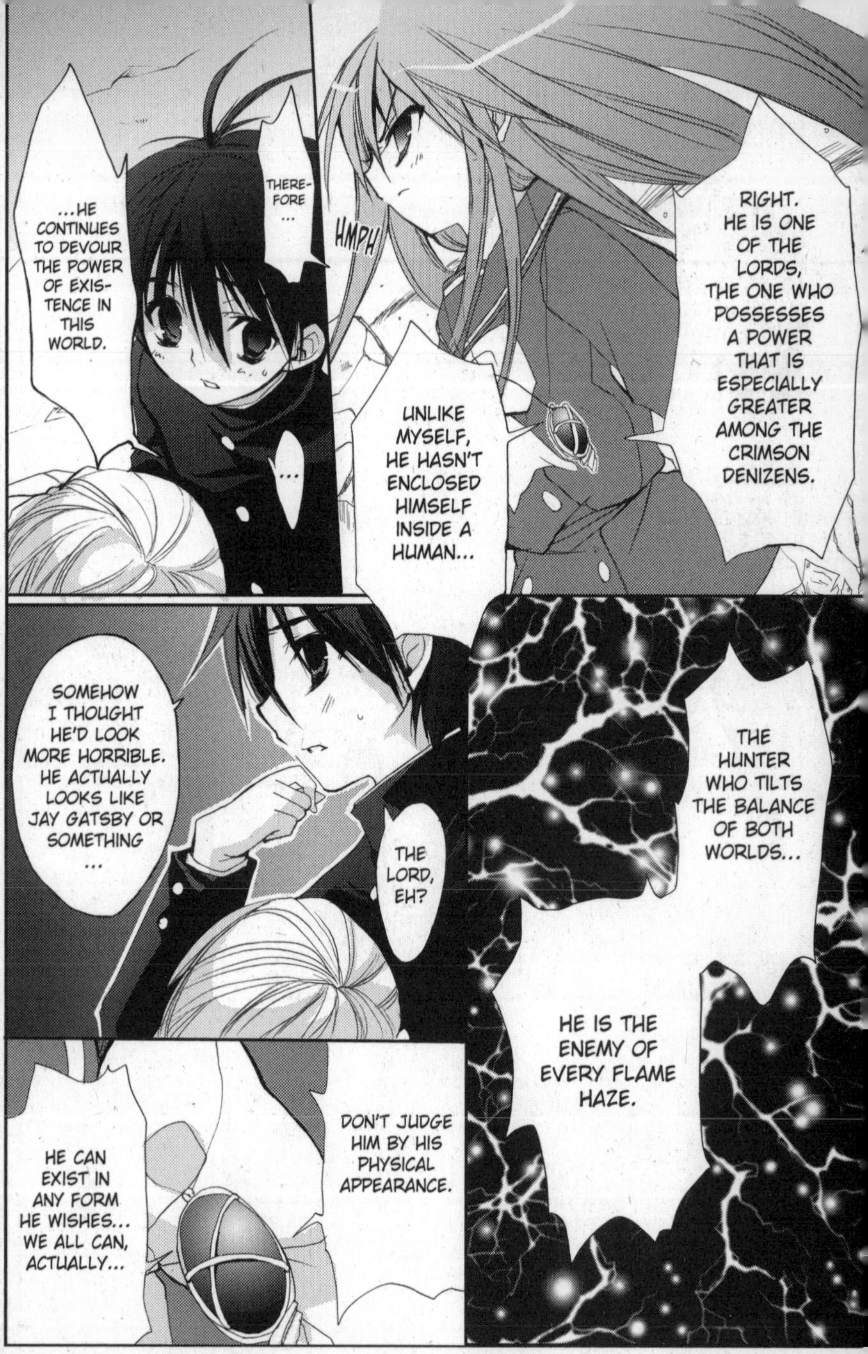
RIGHT. HE IS ONE OF THE LORDS, THE ONE WHO POSSESSES A POWER THAT IS ESPECIALLY GREATER AMONG THE CRIMSON DENIZENS.
HMPH
UNLIKE MYSELF, HE HASN'T ENCLOSED HIMSELF INSIDE A HUMAN...
THERE-FORE ...
...HE CONTINUES TO DEVOUR THE POWER OF EXIS-TENCE IN THIS WORLD.
...
THE HUNTER WHO TILTS THE BALANCE OF BOTH WORLDS...
HE IS THE ENEMY OF EVERY FLAME HAZE.
THE LORD, EH?
SOMEHOW I THOUGHT HE'D LOOK MORE HORRIBLE. HE ACTUALLY LOOKS LIKE JAY GATSBY OR SOMETHING ...
DON'T JUDGE HIM BY HIS PHYSICAL APPEARANCE.
HE CAN EXIST IN ANY FORM HE WISHES... WE ALL CAN, ACTUALLY...

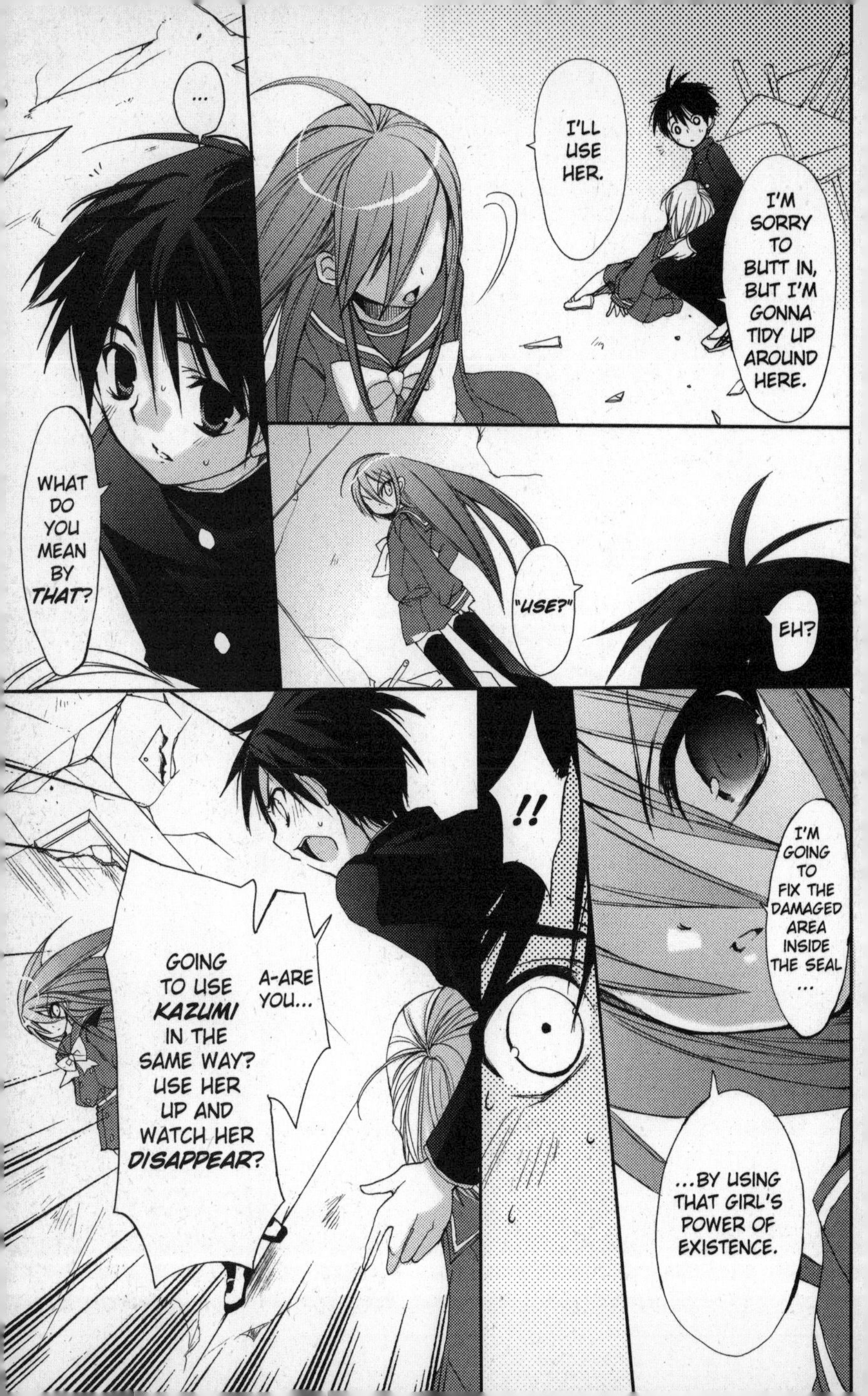
I'M SORRY TO BUTT IN, BUT I'M GONNA TIDY UP AROUND HERE.
I'LL USE HER.
EH?
"USE?"
...
WHAT DO YOU MEAN BY THAT?
I'M GOING TO FIX THE DAMAGED AREA INSIDE THE SEAL...
...BY USING THAT GIRL'S POWER OF EXISTENCE.
!!
A-ARE YOU...
GOING TO USE KAZUMI IN THE SAME WAY? USE HER UP AND WATCH HER DISAPPEAR?

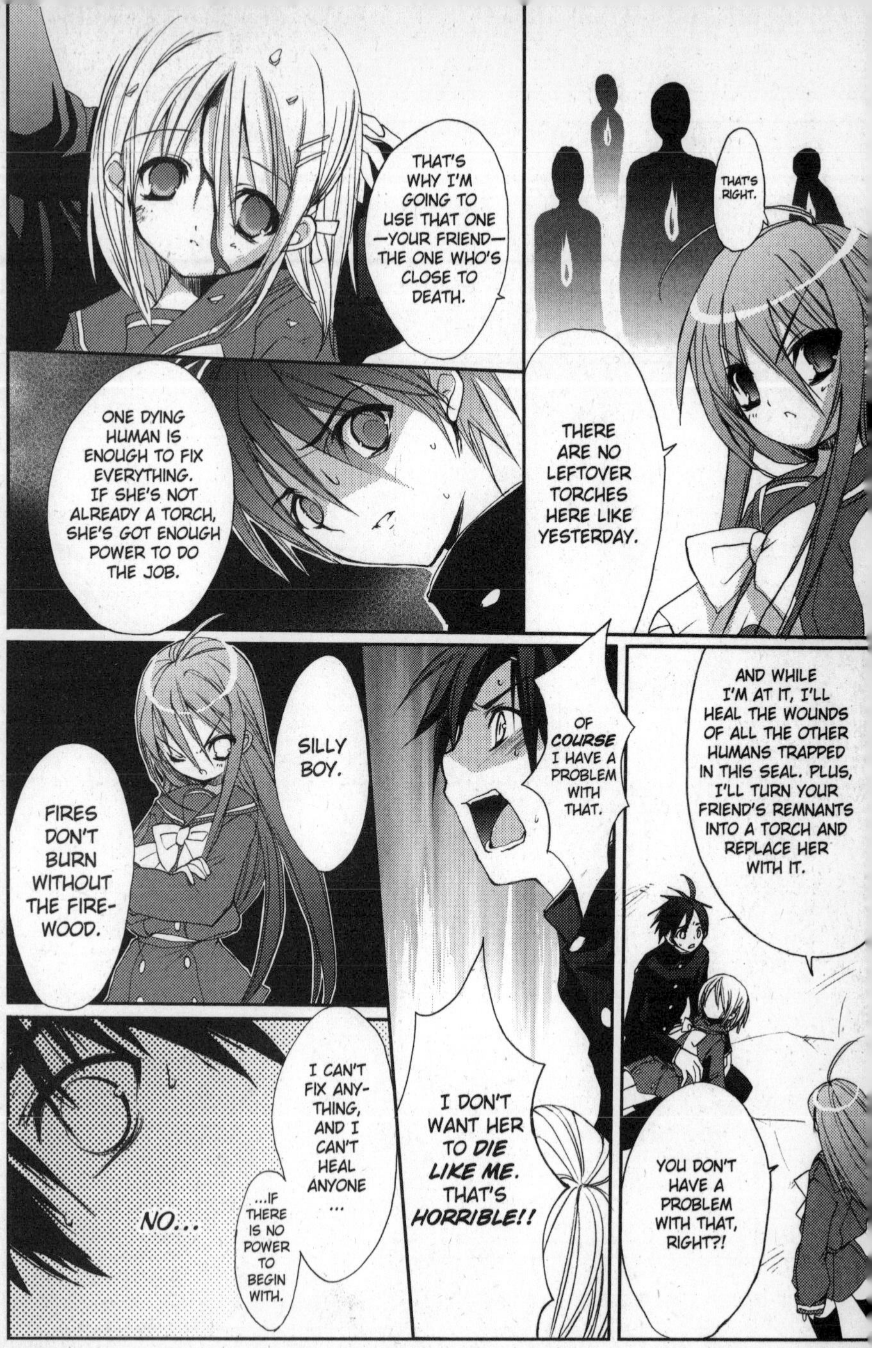
THAT'S RIGHT.
THERE ARE NO LEFTOVER TORCHES HERE LIKE YESTERDAY.
THAT'S WHY I'M GOING TO USE THAT ONE —YOUR FRIEND— THE ONE WHO'S CLOSE TO DEATH.
ONE DYING HUMAN IS ENOUGH TO FIX EVERYTHING. IF SHE'S NOT ALREADY A TORCH, SHE'S GOT ENOUGH POWER TO DO THE JOB.
AND WHILE I'M AT IT, I'LL HEAL THE WOUNDS OF ALL THE OTHER HUMANS TRAPPED IN THIS SEAL. PLUS, I'LL TURN YOUR FRIEND'S REMNANTS INTO A TORCH AND REPLACE HER WITH IT.
YOU DON'T HAVE A PROBLEM WITH THAT, RIGHT?!
OF *COURSE* I HAVE A PROBLEM WITH THAT.
I DON'T WANT HER TO ***DIE LIKE ME***. THAT'S ***HORRIBLE!!***
SILLY BOY.
FIRES DON'T BURN WITHOUT THE FIRE-WOOD.
I CAN'T FIX ANY-THING, AND I CAN'T HEAL ANYONE ...
...IF THERE IS NO POWER TO BEGIN WITH.
NO...

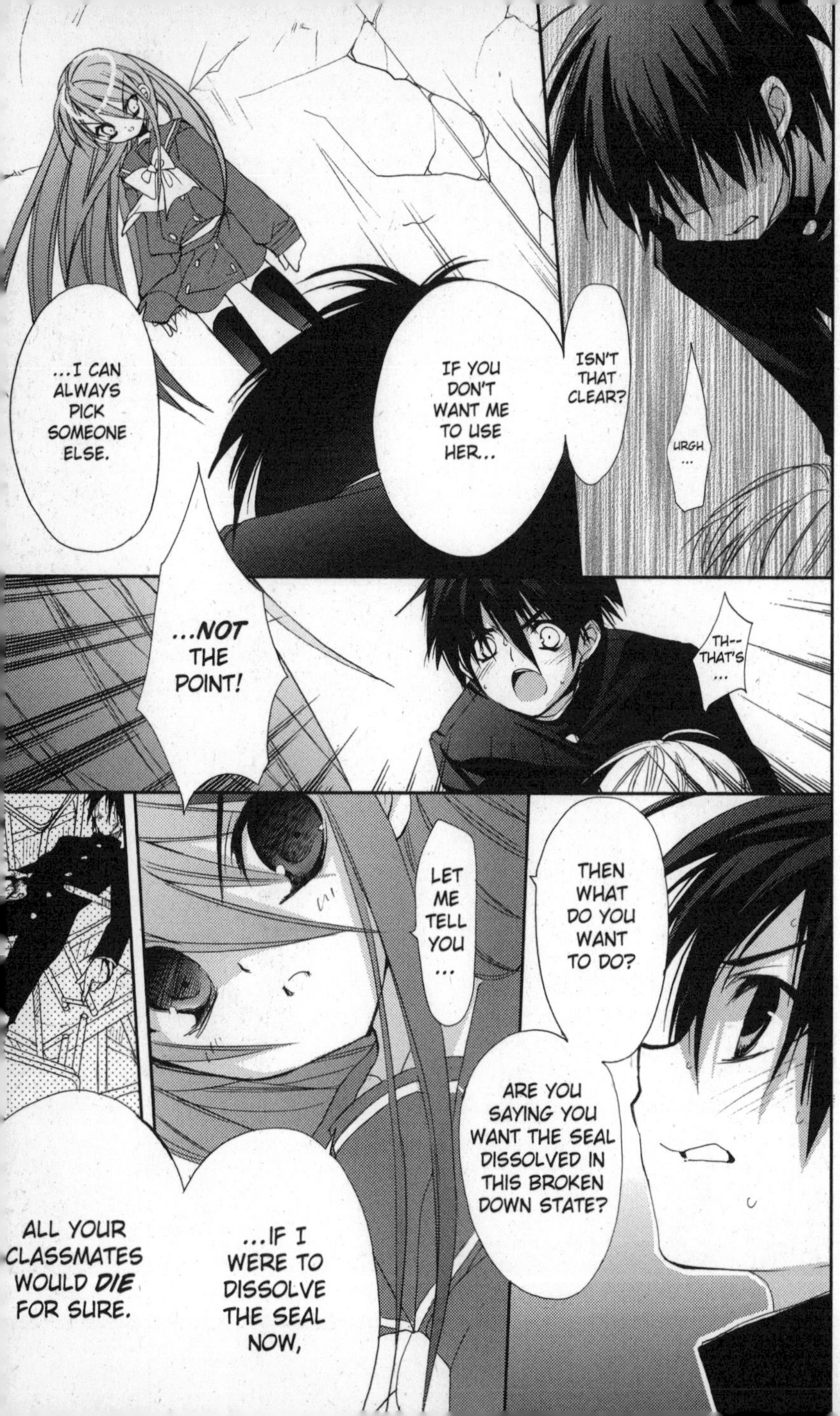
ISN'T THAT CLEAR?
URGH...
IF YOU DON'T WANT ME TO USE HER...
...I CAN ALWAYS PICK SOMEONE ELSE.
TH--THAT'S...
...*NOT* THE POINT!
THEN WHAT DO YOU WANT TO DO?
ARE YOU SAYING YOU WANT THE SEAL DISSOLVED IN THIS BROKEN DOWN STATE?
LET ME TELL YOU...
...IF I WERE TO DISSOLVE THE SEAL NOW,
ALL YOUR CLASSMATES WOULD *DIE* FOR SURE.

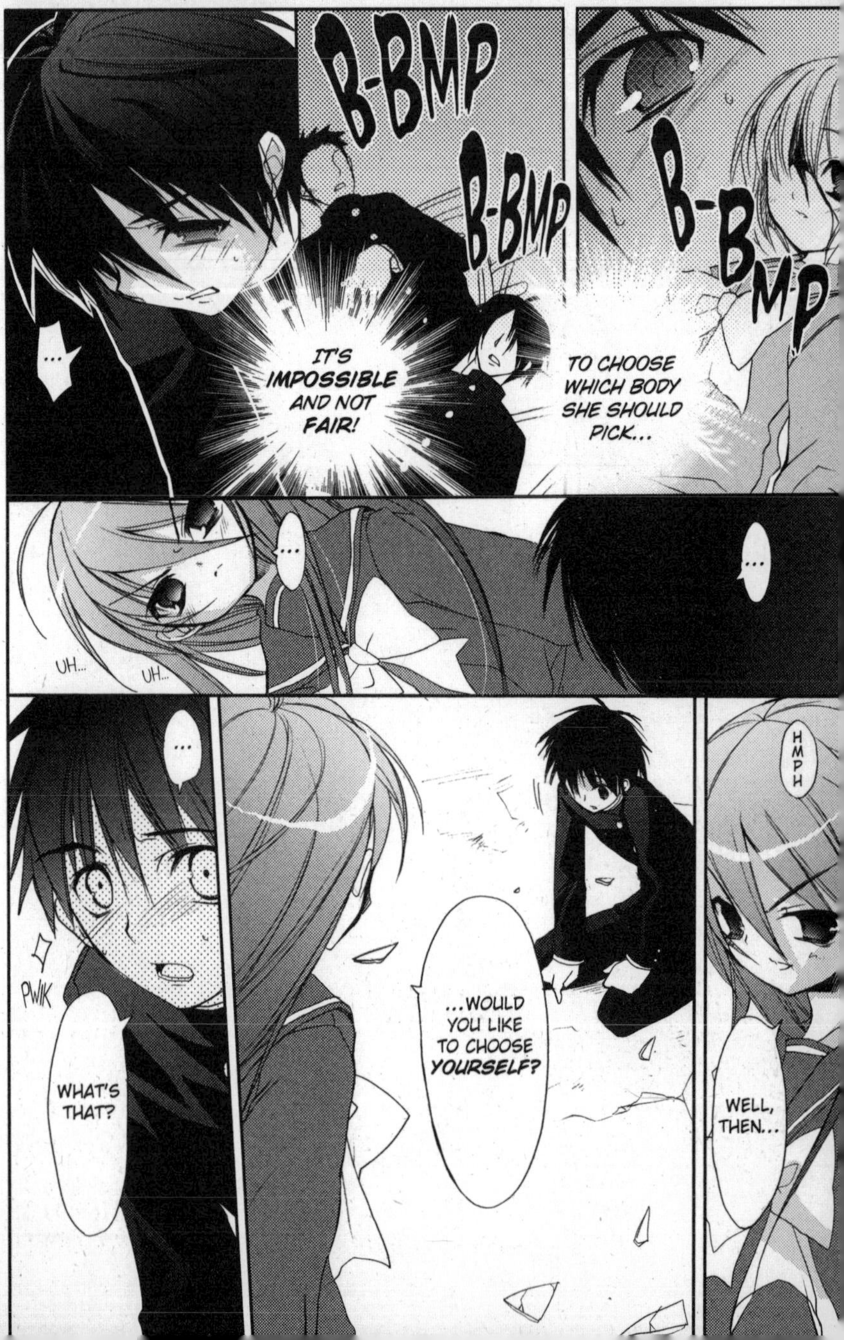
B-BMP
TO CHOOSE WHICH BODY SHE SHOULD PICK...
B-BMP
B-BMP
IT'S IMPOSSIBLE AND NOT FAIR!
...
...
...
UH...
UH...
HMPH
WELL, THEN...
...WOULD YOU LIKE TO CHOOSE YOURSELF?
...
PWIK
WHAT'S THAT?

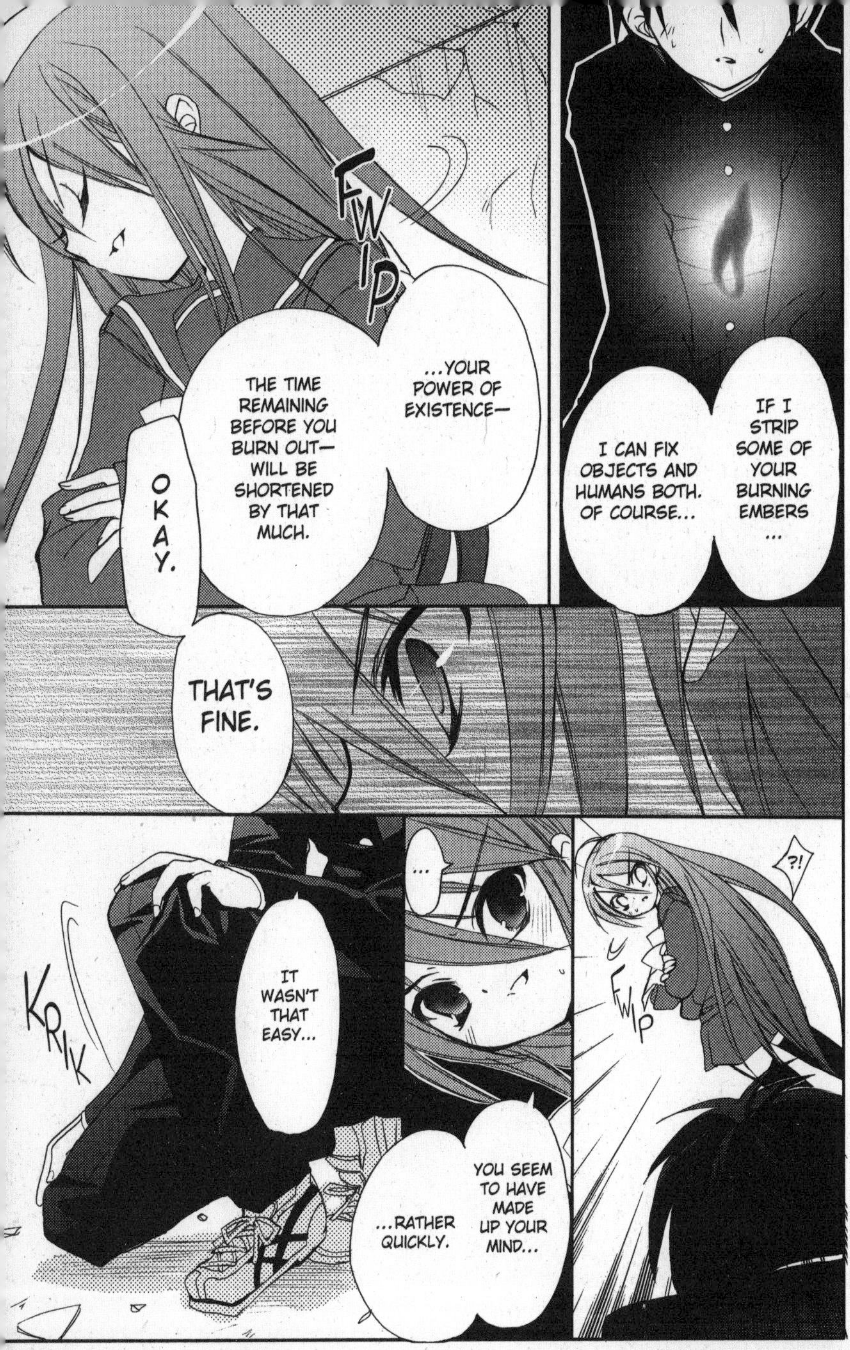
IF I STRIP SOME OF YOUR BURNING EMBERS...
I CAN FIX OBJECTS AND HUMANS BOTH. OF COURSE...
...YOUR POWER OF EXISTENCE—
THE TIME REMAINING BEFORE YOU BURN OUT— WILL BE SHORTENED BY THAT MUCH.
FWIP
OKAY.
THAT'S FINE.
?!
FWIP
...
YOU SEEM TO HAVE MADE UP YOUR MIND...
...RATHER QUICKLY.
IT WASN'T THAT EASY...
KRIK

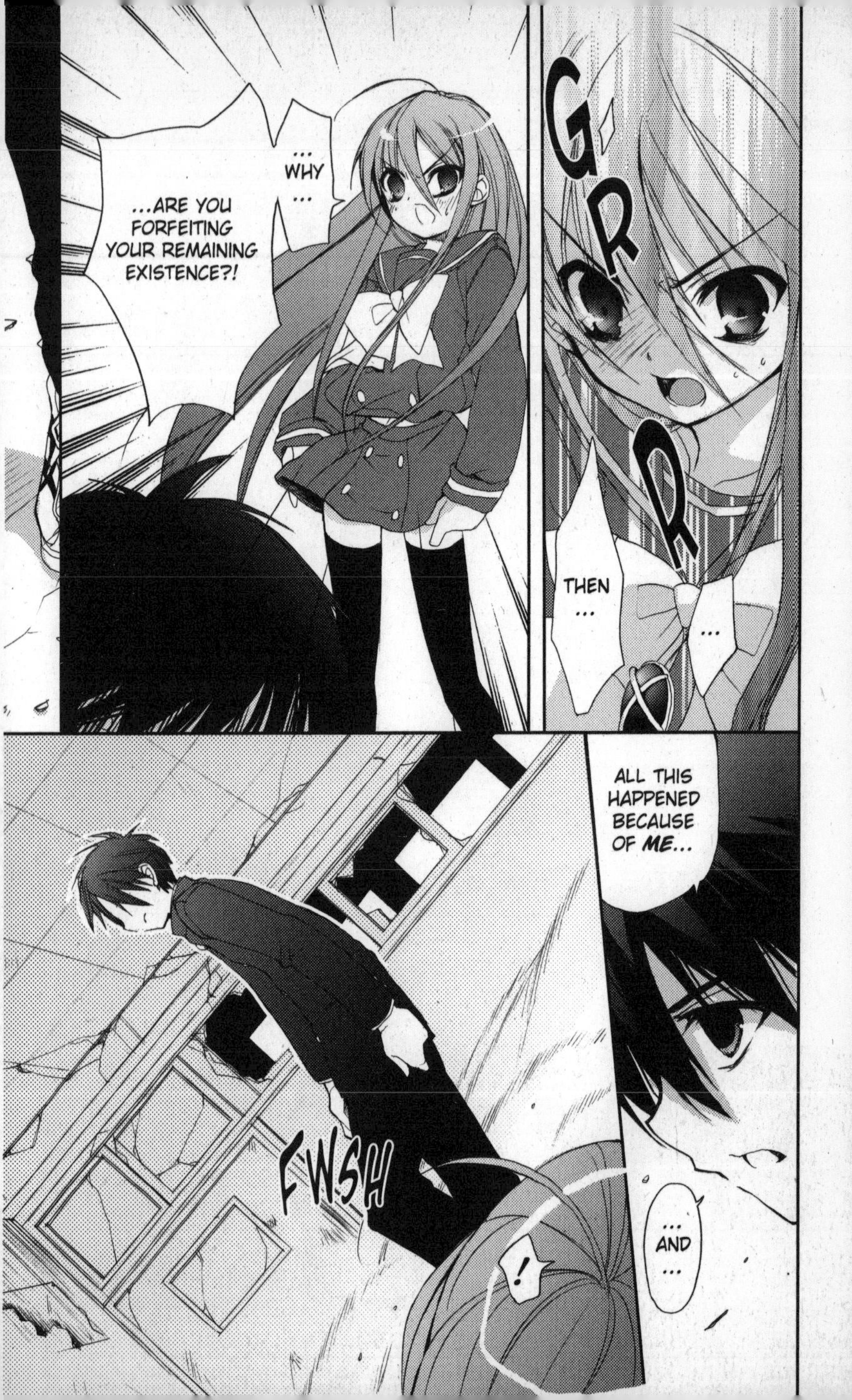
GRR
THEN ...
...
... WHY ...
...ARE YOU FORFEITING YOUR REMAINING EXISTENCE?!
ALL THIS HAPPENED BECAUSE OF ME...
... AND ...
!
FWSH

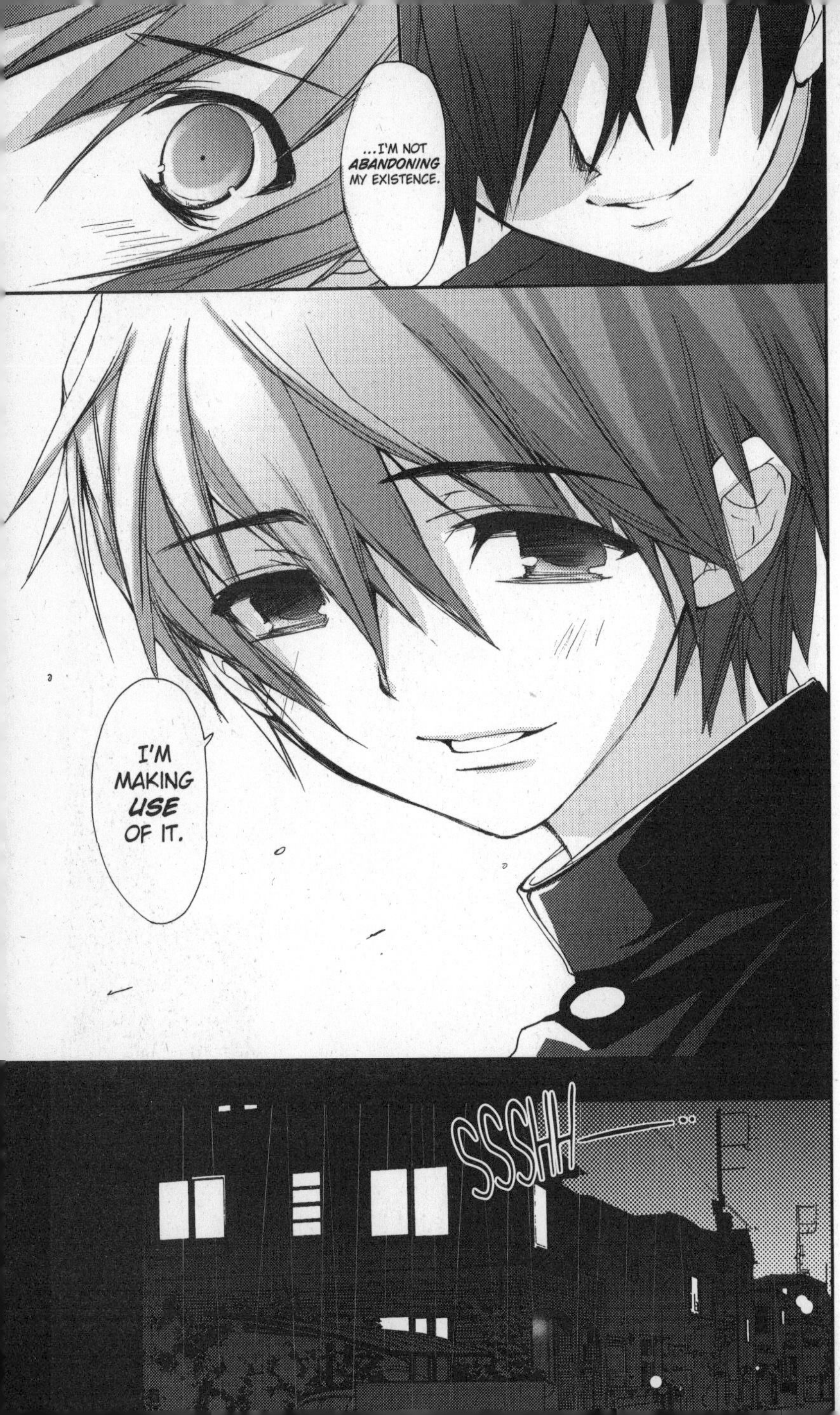
...I'M NOT ABANDONING MY EXISTENCE.
I'M MAKING USE OF IT.
SSSHH

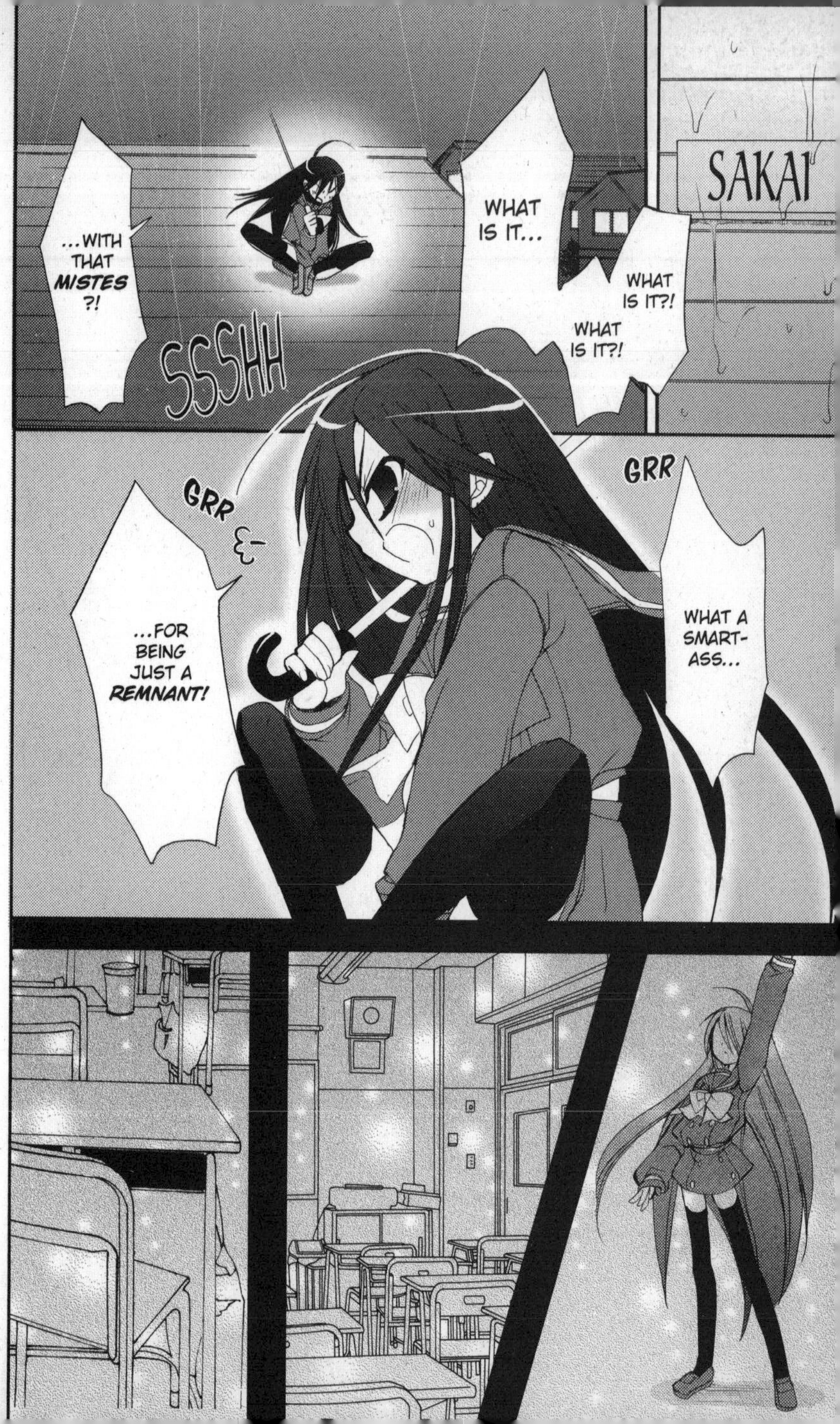
SAKAI
WHAT IS IT...
WHAT IS IT?!
WHAT IS IT?!
...WITH THAT *MISTES* ?!
SSSHH
GRR
WHAT A SMART-ASS...
GRR
...FOR BEING JUST A *REMNANT!*

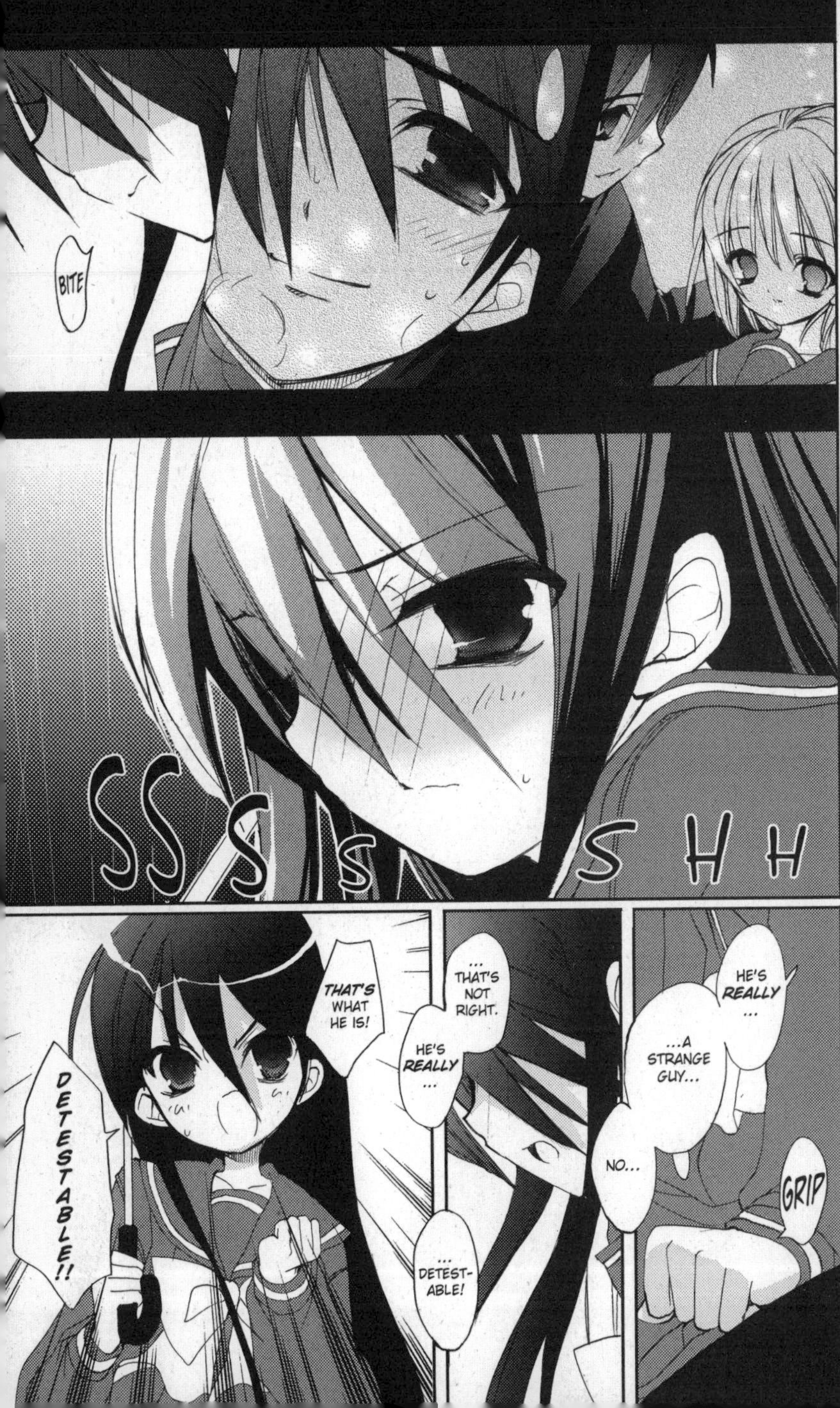
BITE
SSSSSHH
HE'S REALLY ...
...A STRANGE GUY...
NO...
GRIP
... THAT'S NOT RIGHT.
HE'S REALLY ...
... DETEST-ABLE!
THAT'S WHAT HE IS!
DETESTABLE!!

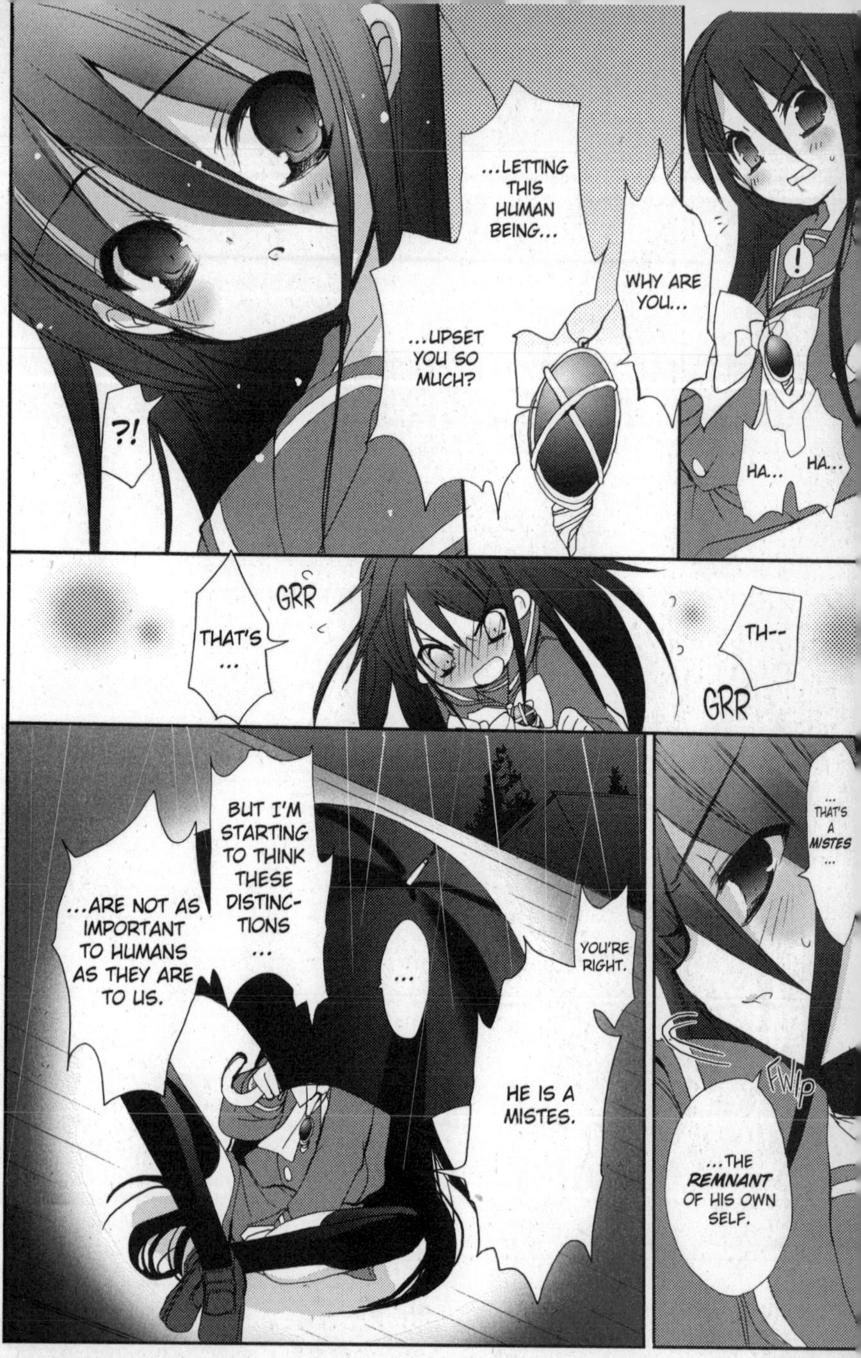
!
HA... HA...
WHY ARE YOU...
...LETTING THIS HUMAN BEING...
...UPSET YOU SO MUCH?
?!
TH--
GRR
GRR
THAT'S ...
...THAT'S A *MISTES*...
FWIP
...THE *REMNANT* OF HIS OWN SELF.
YOU'RE RIGHT.
HE IS A MISTES.
...
BUT I'M STARTING TO THINK THESE DISTINCTIONS ...
...ARE NOT AS IMPORTANT TO HUMANS AS THEY ARE TO US.

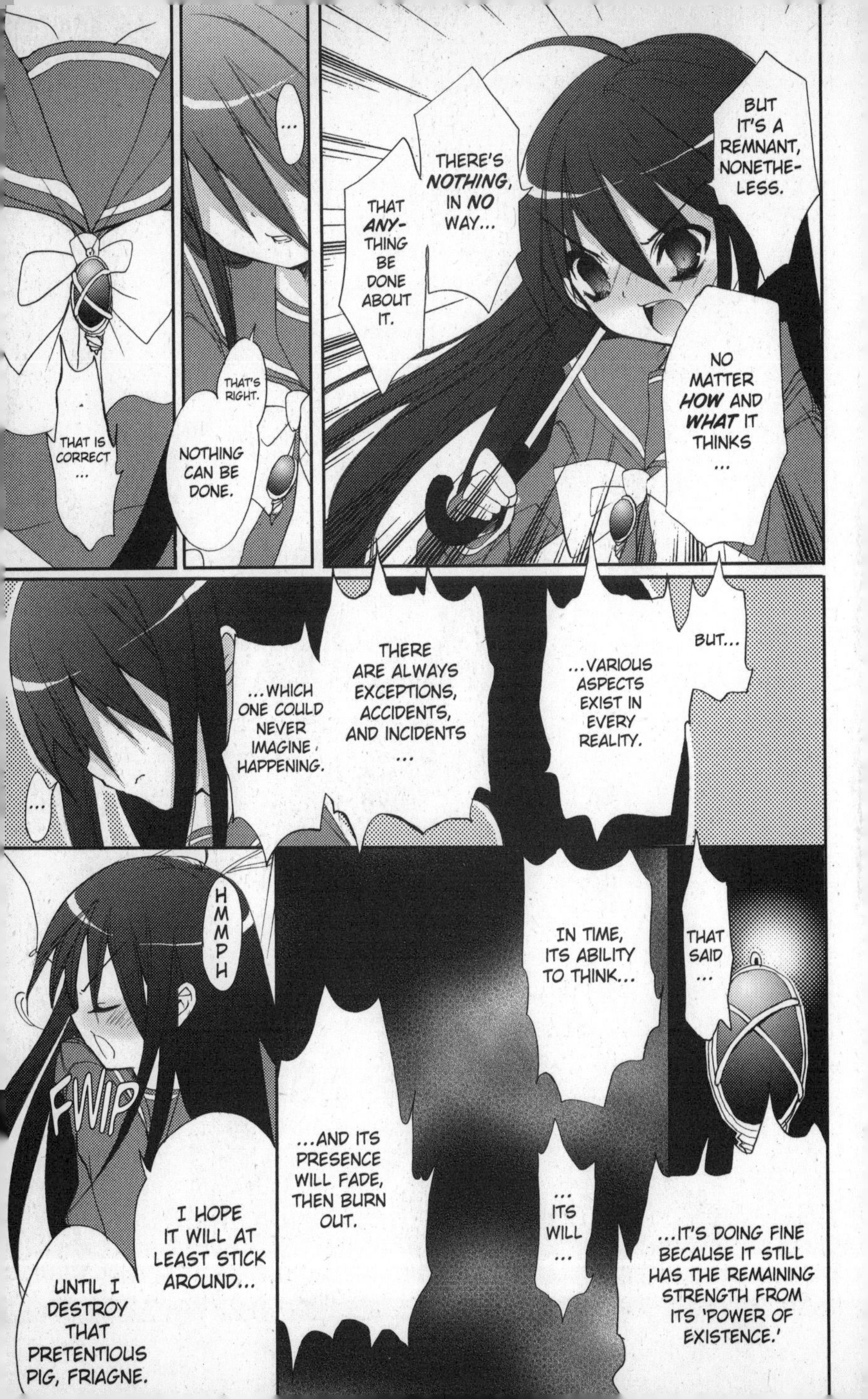
BUT IT'S A REMNANT, NONETHE-LESS.
NO MATTER *HOW* AND *WHAT* IT THINKS ...
THERE'S *NOTHING*, IN *NO* WAY...
THAT *ANY*-THING BE DONE ABOUT IT.
...
THAT'S RIGHT.
NOTHING CAN BE DONE.
THAT IS CORRECT ...
BUT...
...VARIOUS ASPECTS EXIST IN EVERY REALITY.
THERE ARE ALWAYS EXCEPTIONS, ACCIDENTS, AND INCIDENTS ...
...WHICH ONE COULD NEVER IMAGINE HAPPENING.
...
THAT SAID ...
...IT'S DOING FINE BECAUSE IT STILL HAS THE REMAINING STRENGTH FROM ITS 'POWER OF EXISTENCE.'
IN TIME, ITS ABILITY TO THINK...
... ITS WILL ...
...AND ITS PRESENCE WILL FADE, THEN BURN OUT.
HMMPH
FWIP
I HOPE IT WILL AT LEAST STICK AROUND...
UNTIL I DESTROY THAT PRETENTIOUS PIG, FRIAGNE.

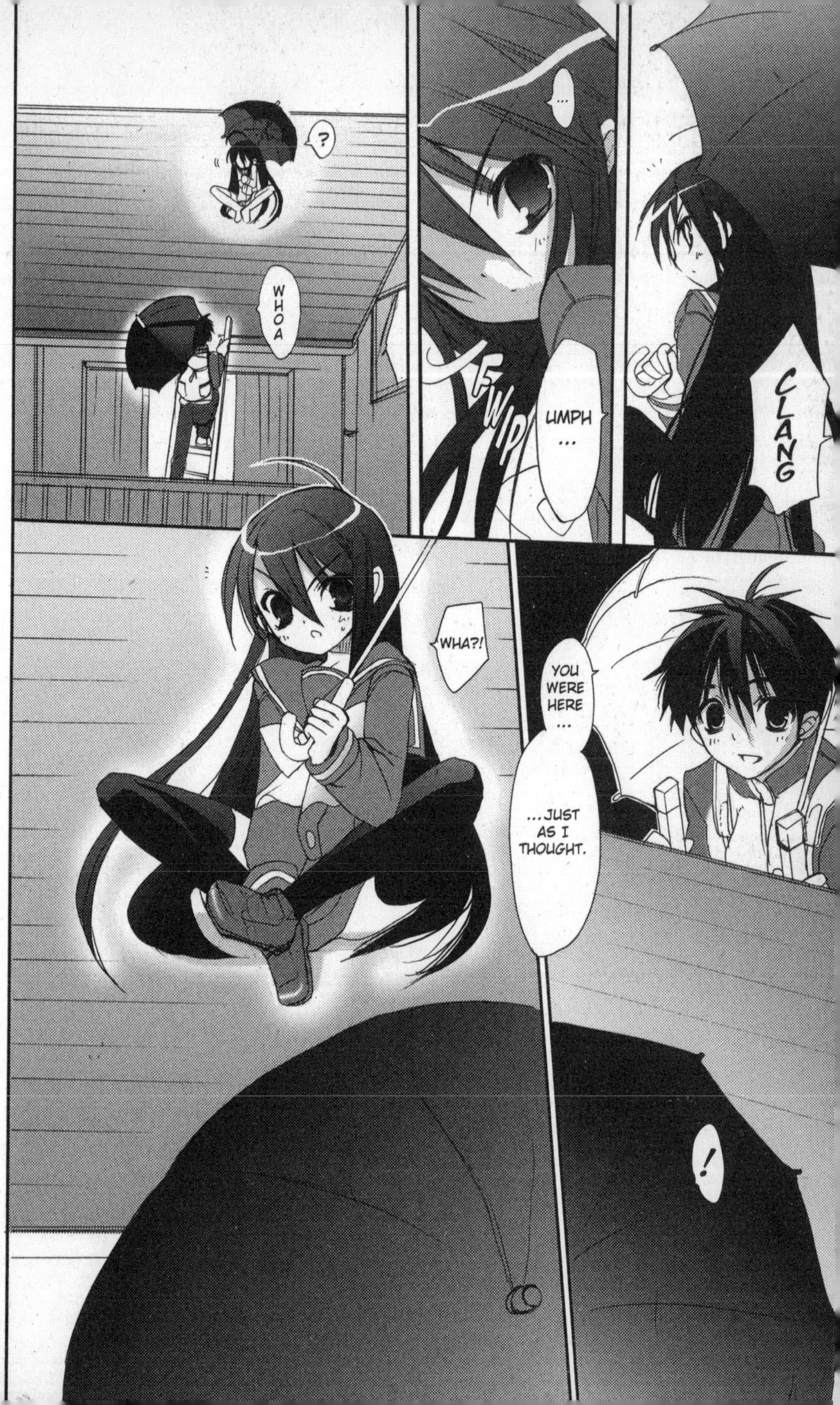

CLANG
...
FWIP
UMPH ...
?
WHOA
YOU WERE HERE ...
...JUST AS I THOUGHT.
WHA?!
!

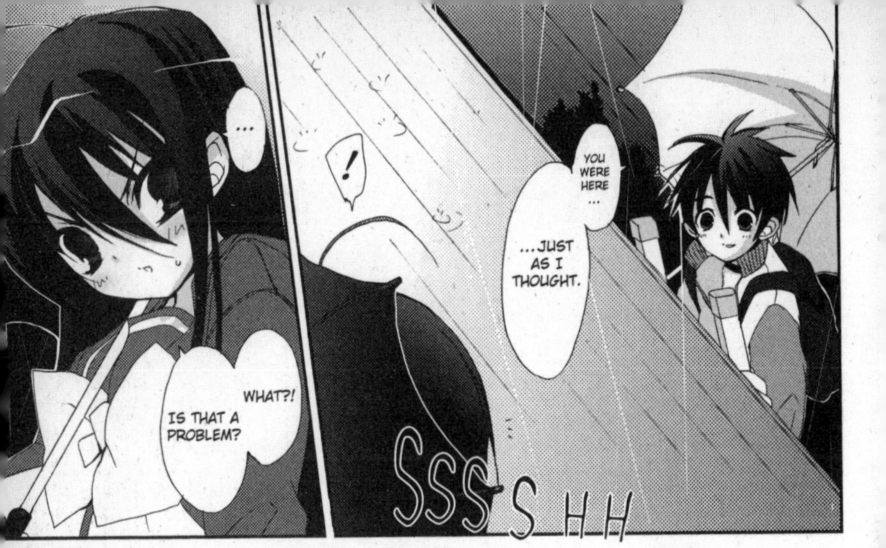
YOU WERE HERE ...
...JUST AS I THOUGHT.
!
SSSSHH
...
WHAT?! IS THAT A PROBLEM?

灼眼のシャナ SHAKUGAN NO SHANA

Episode 7 The Rainy Night II

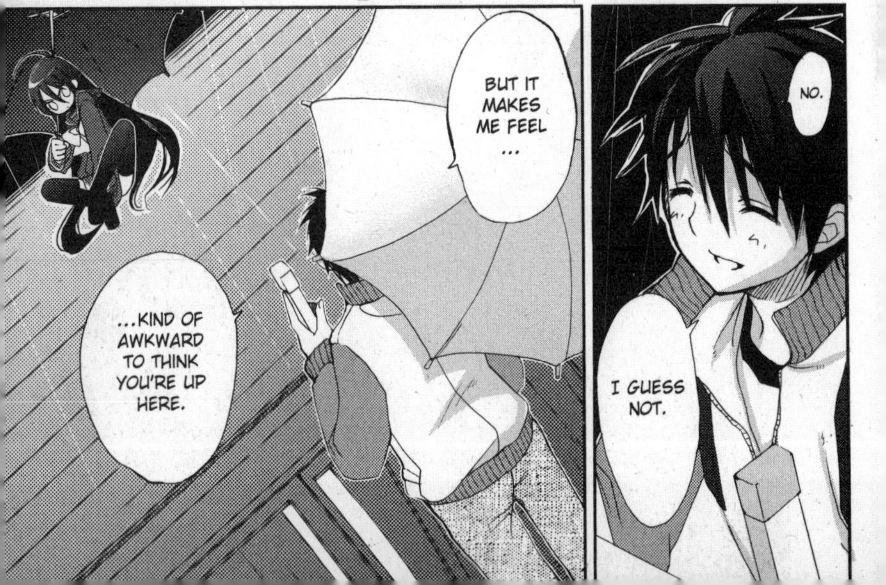
NO.
I GUESS NOT.
BUT IT MAKES ME FEEL ...
...KIND OF AWKWARD TO THINK YOU'RE UP HERE.

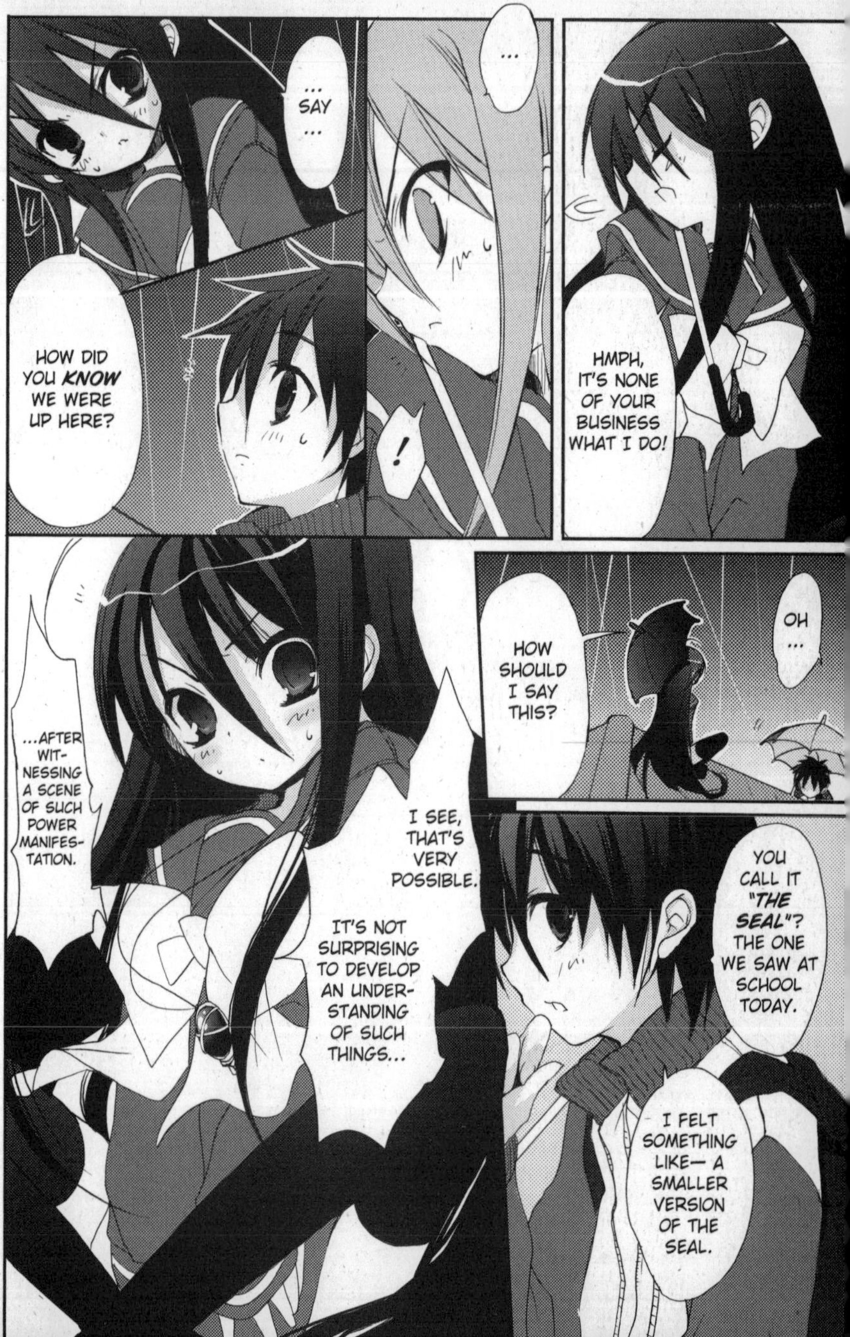
HMPH, IT'S NONE OF YOUR BUSINESS WHAT I DO!
...
!
... SAY ...
HOW DID YOU *KNOW* WE WERE UP HERE?
OH ...
HOW SHOULD I SAY THIS?
YOU CALL IT "*THE SEAL*"? THE ONE WE SAW AT SCHOOL TODAY.
I FELT SOMETHING LIKE— A SMALLER VERSION OF THE SEAL.
I SEE, THAT'S VERY POSSIBLE.
IT'S NOT SURPRISING TO DEVELOP AN UNDER-STANDING OF SUCH THINGS...
...AFTER WIT-NESSING A SCENE OF SUCH POWER MANIFES-TATION.

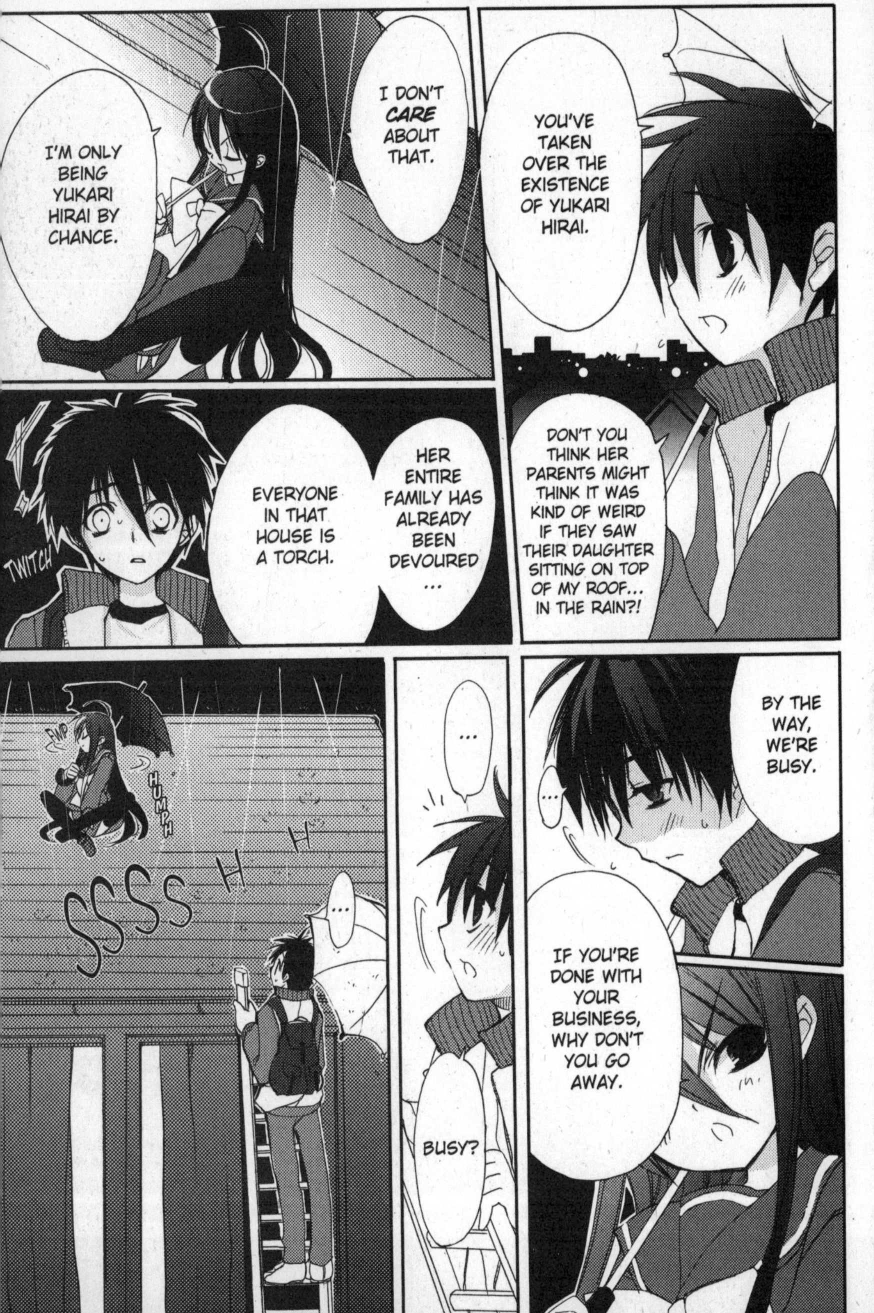
YOU'VE TAKEN OVER THE EXISTENCE OF YUKARI HIRAI.
I DON'T CARE ABOUT THAT.
I'M ONLY BEING YUKARI HIRAI BY CHANCE.
DON'T YOU THINK HER PARENTS MIGHT THINK IT WAS KIND OF WEIRD IF THEY SAW THEIR DAUGHTER SITTING ON TOP OF MY ROOF... IN THE RAIN?!
HER ENTIRE FAMILY HAS ALREADY BEEN DEVOURED...
EVERYONE IN THAT HOUSE IS A TORCH.
TWITCH
BY THE WAY, WE'RE BUSY.
...
IF YOU'RE DONE WITH YOUR BUSINESS, WHY DON'T YOU GO AWAY.
...
BUSY?
HUMPH
SSSS H H
...

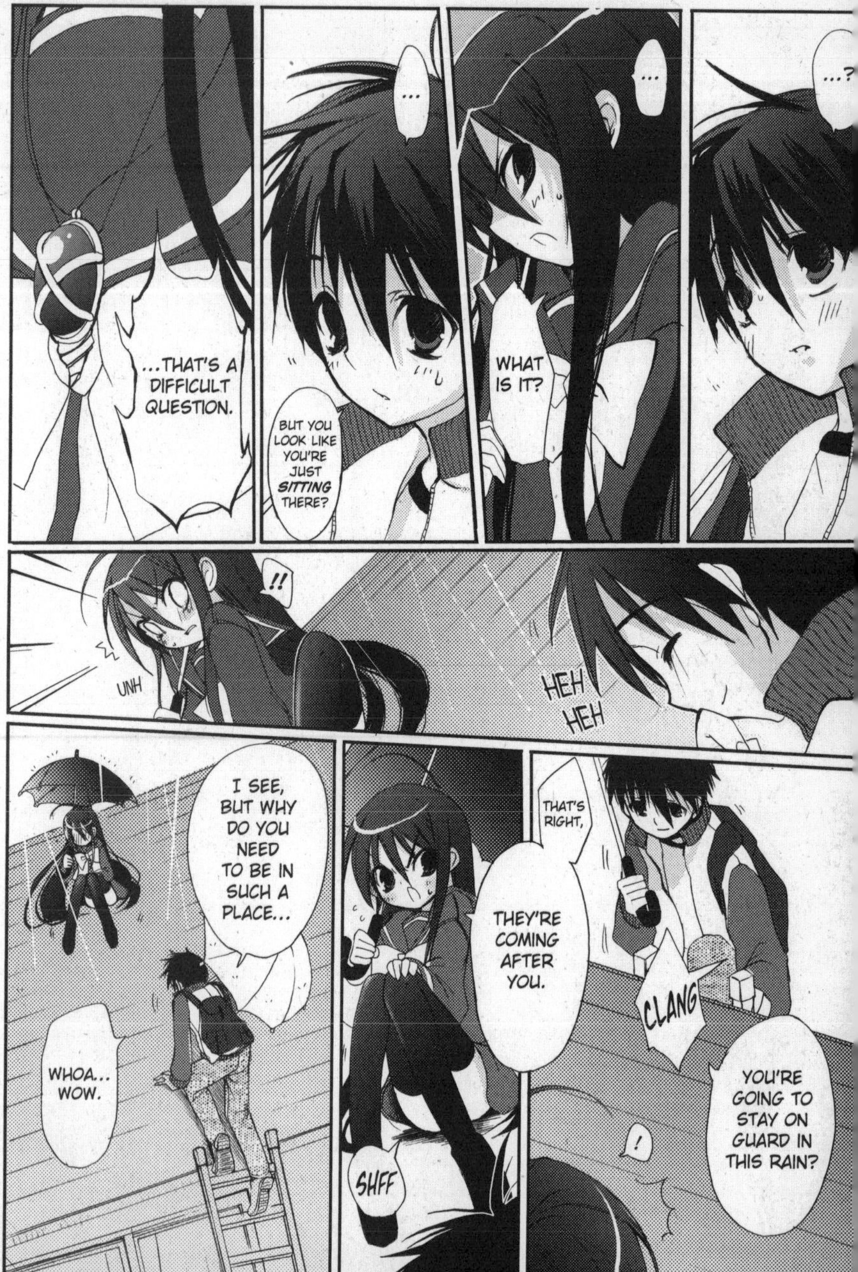
...?
...
WHAT IS IT?
...
BUT YOU LOOK LIKE YOU'RE JUST *SITTING* THERE?
...THAT'S A DIFFICULT QUESTION.
HEH HEH
!!
UNH
THAT'S RIGHT,
THEY'RE COMING AFTER YOU.
CLANG
YOU'RE GOING TO STAY ON GUARD IN THIS RAIN?
!
SHFF
I SEE, BUT WHY DO YOU NEED TO BE IN SUCH A PLACE...
WHOA... WOW.

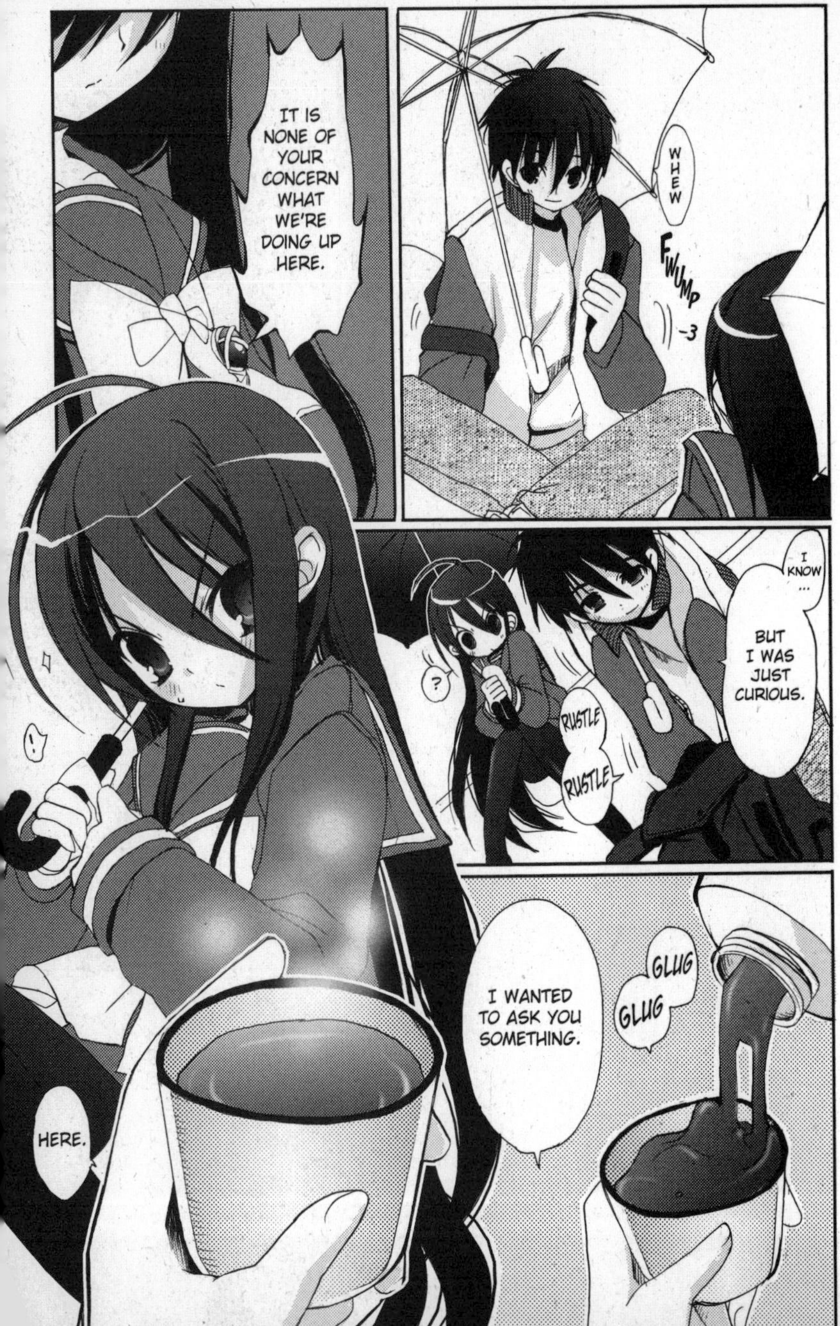
WHEW
FWUMP
-3
IT IS NONE OF YOUR CONCERN WHAT WE'RE DOING UP HERE.
I KNOW...
BUT I WAS JUST CURIOUS.
?
RUSTLE
RUSTLE
GLUG
GLUG
I WANTED TO ASK YOU SOMETHING.
!
HERE.

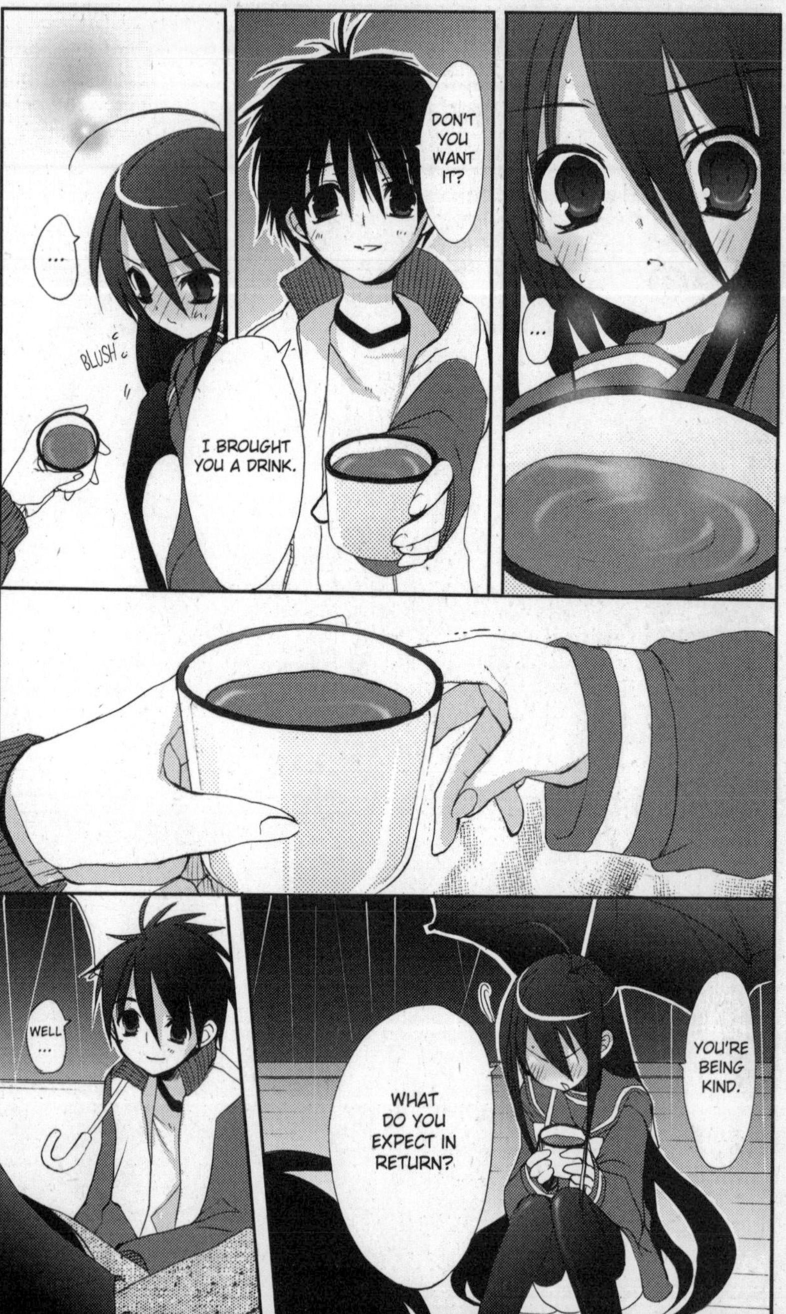
...
DON'T YOU WANT IT?
I BROUGHT YOU A DRINK.
...
BLUSH
YOU'RE BEING KIND.
WHAT DO YOU EXPECT IN RETURN?
WELL ...

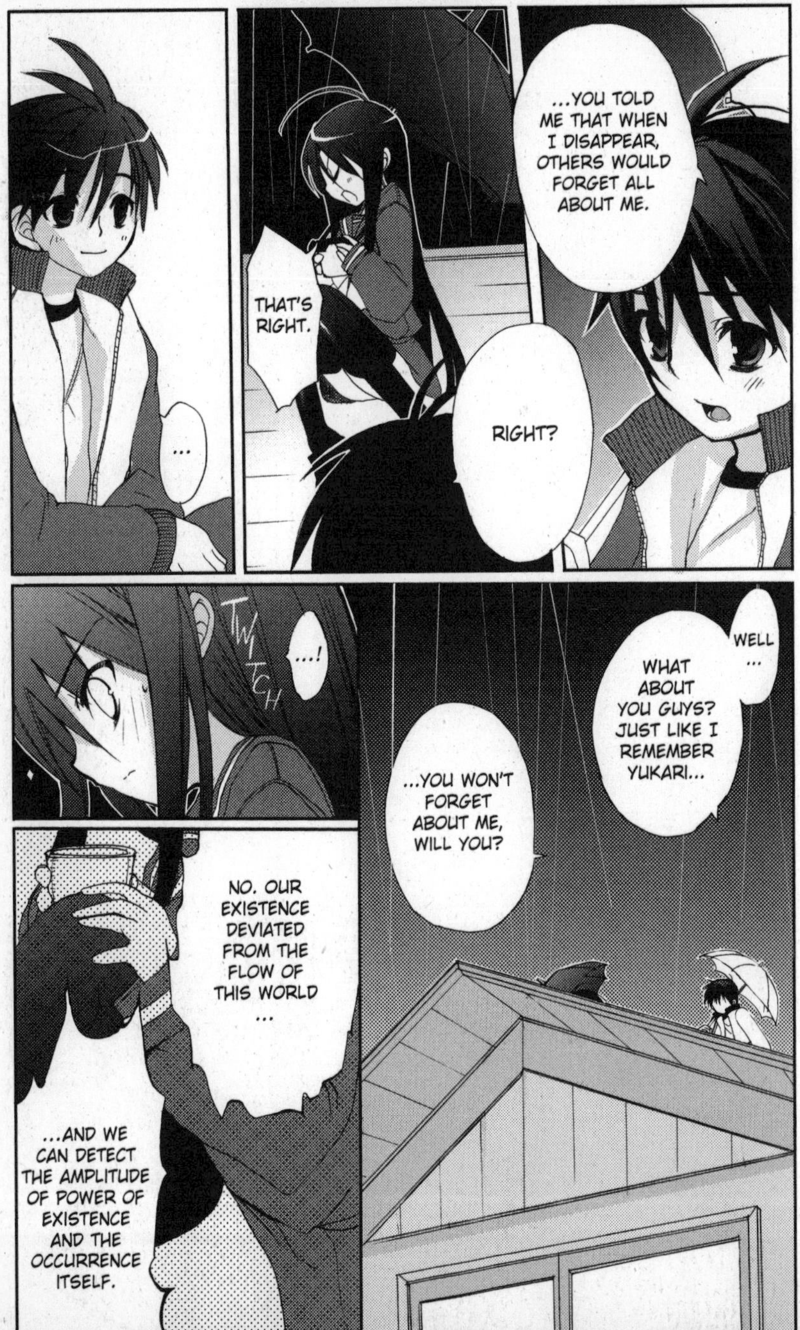
...YOU TOLD ME THAT WHEN I DISAPPEAR, OTHERS WOULD FORGET ALL ABOUT ME.
RIGHT?
THAT'S RIGHT.
...
WELL...
WHAT ABOUT YOU GUYS? JUST LIKE I REMEMBER YUKARI...
...YOU WON'T FORGET ABOUT ME, WILL YOU?
TWITCH
...!
NO. OUR EXISTENCE DEVIATED FROM THE FLOW OF THIS WORLD...
...AND WE CAN DETECT THE AMPLITUDE OF POWER OF EXISTENCE AND THE OCCURRENCE ITSELF.

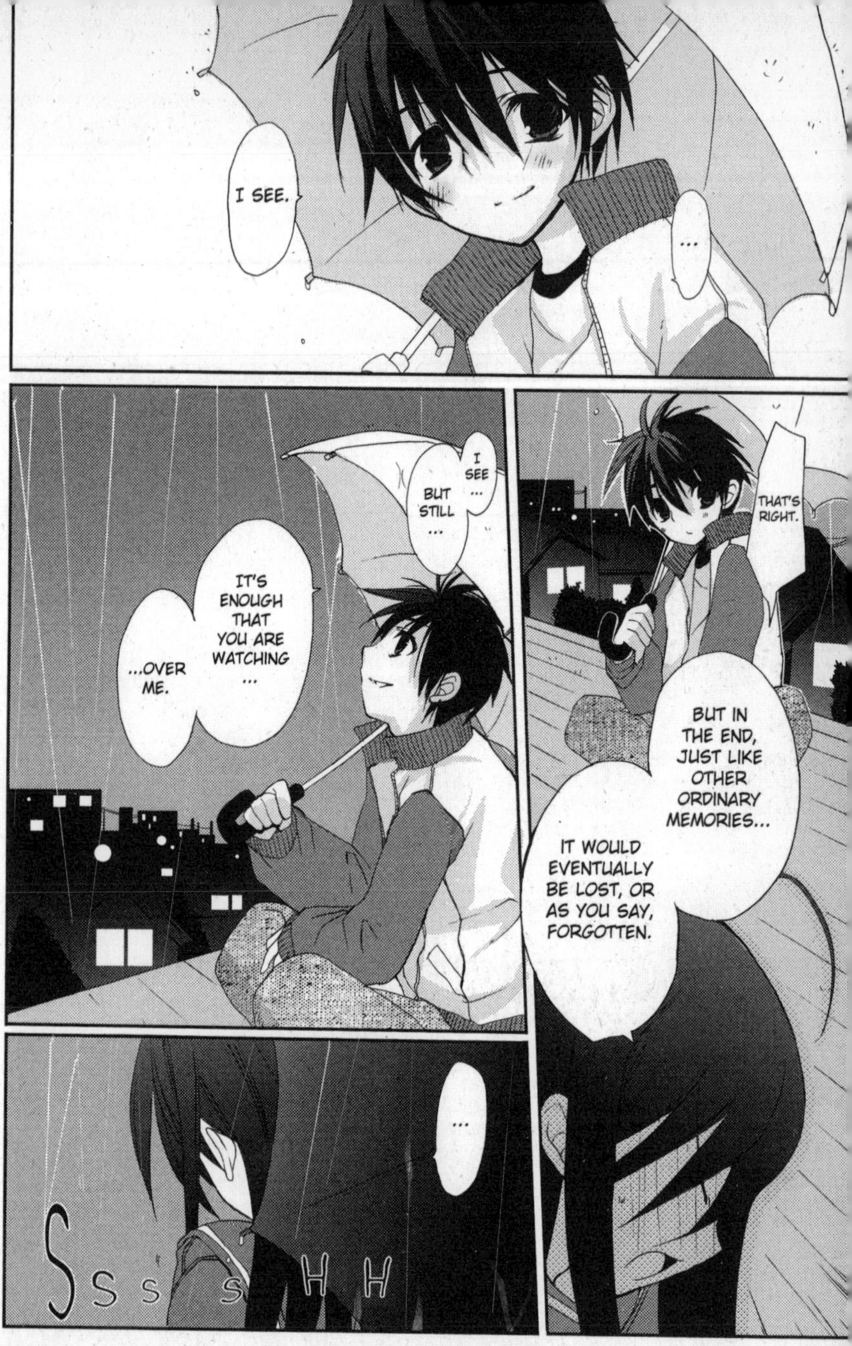
...
I SEE.
THAT'S RIGHT.
BUT IN THE END, JUST LIKE OTHER ORDINARY MEMORIES...
IT WOULD EVENTUALLY BE LOST, OR AS YOU SAY, FORGOTTEN.
I SEE ...
BUT STILL ...
IT'S ENOUGH THAT YOU ARE WATCHING ...
...OVER ME.
...
SsssHH

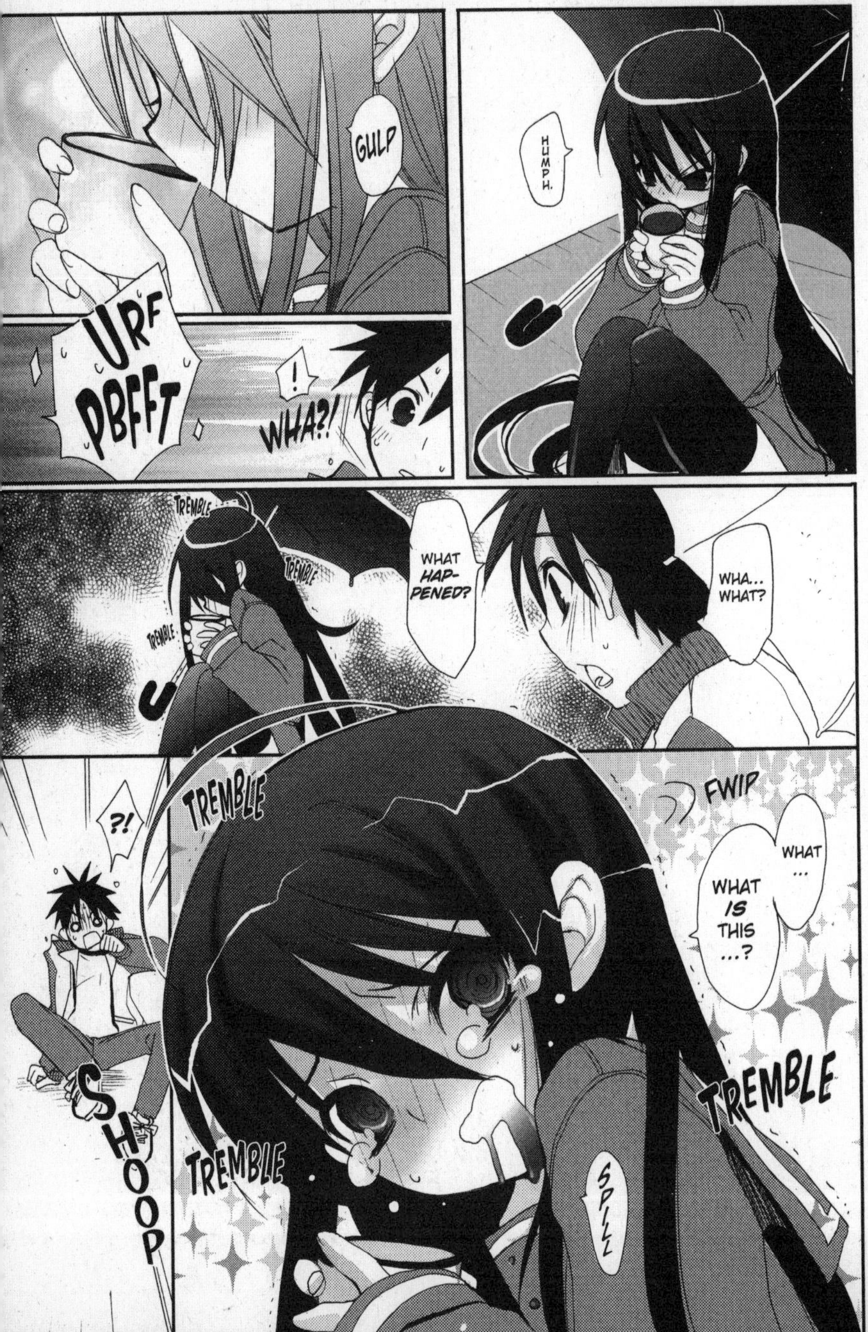
HUMPH.
GULP
!
WHA?!
URF PBFFT
WHA... WHAT?
WHAT HAP-PENED?
TREMBLE
TREMBLE
TREMBLE
FWIP
WHAT...
WHAT IS THIS...?
TREMBLE
TREMBLE
SPILL
TREMBLE
?!
SHOOOP

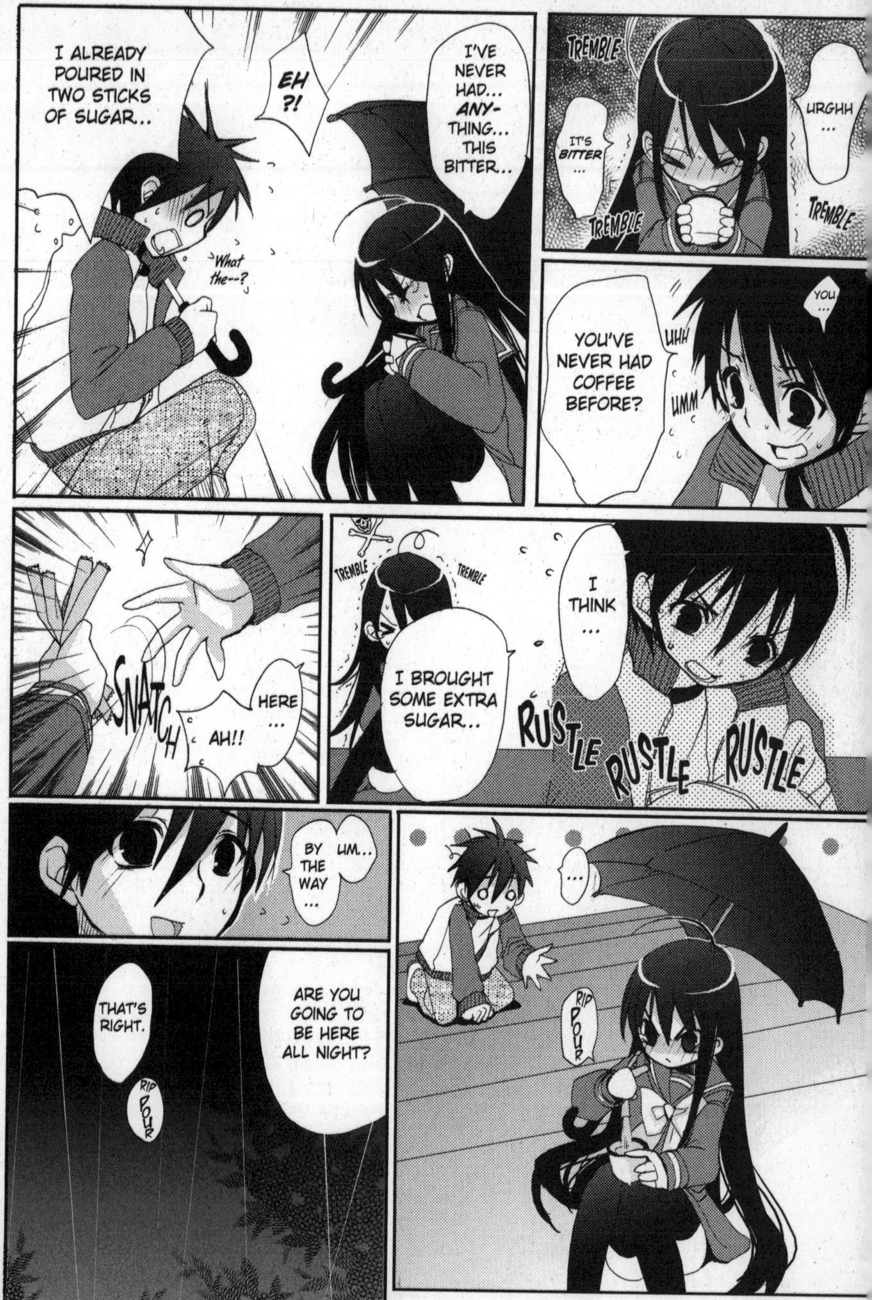
TREMBLE
URGHH...
IT'S BITTER...
TREMBLE
TREMBLE
YOU...
YOU'VE NEVER HAD COFFEE BEFORE?
UHH
UMM
I'VE NEVER HAD... ANY-THING... THIS BITTER...
EH?!
I ALREADY POURED IN TWO STICKS OF SUGAR...
What the--?
I THINK...
TREMBLE
TREMBLE
I BROUGHT SOME EXTRA SUGAR...
RUSTLE
RUSTLE
RUSTLE
HERE...
AH!!
SNATCH
...
RIP
POUR
UM...
BY THE WAY...
ARE YOU GOING TO BE HERE ALL NIGHT?
THAT'S RIGHT.
RIP
POUR

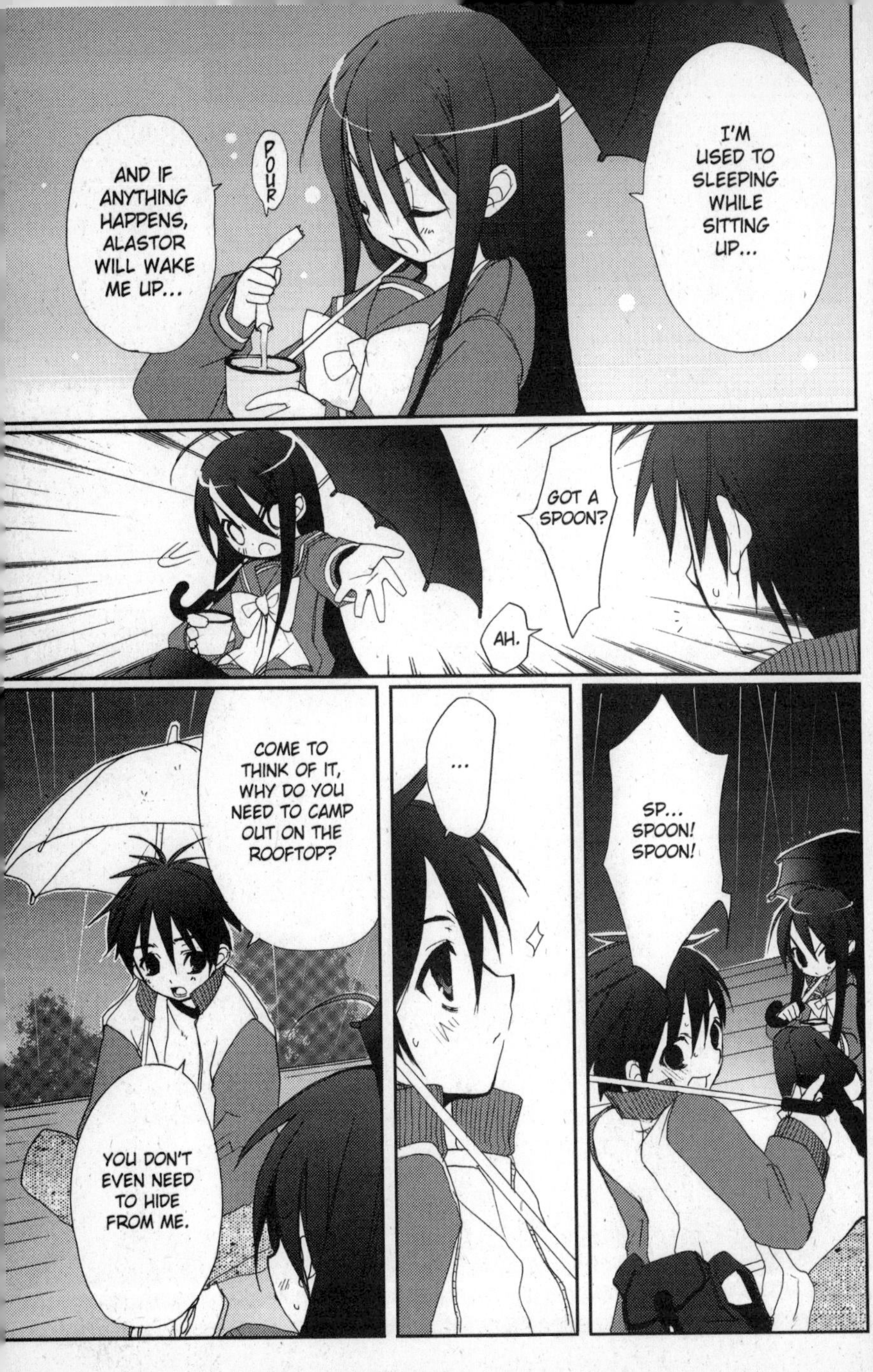
I'M USED TO SLEEPING WHILE SITTING UP...
POUR
AND IF ANYTHING HAPPENS, ALASTOR WILL WAKE ME UP...
GOT A SPOON?
AH.
SP... SPOON! SPOON!
...
COME TO THINK OF IT, WHY DO YOU NEED TO CAMP OUT ON THE ROOFTOP?
YOU DON'T EVEN NEED TO HIDE FROM ME.

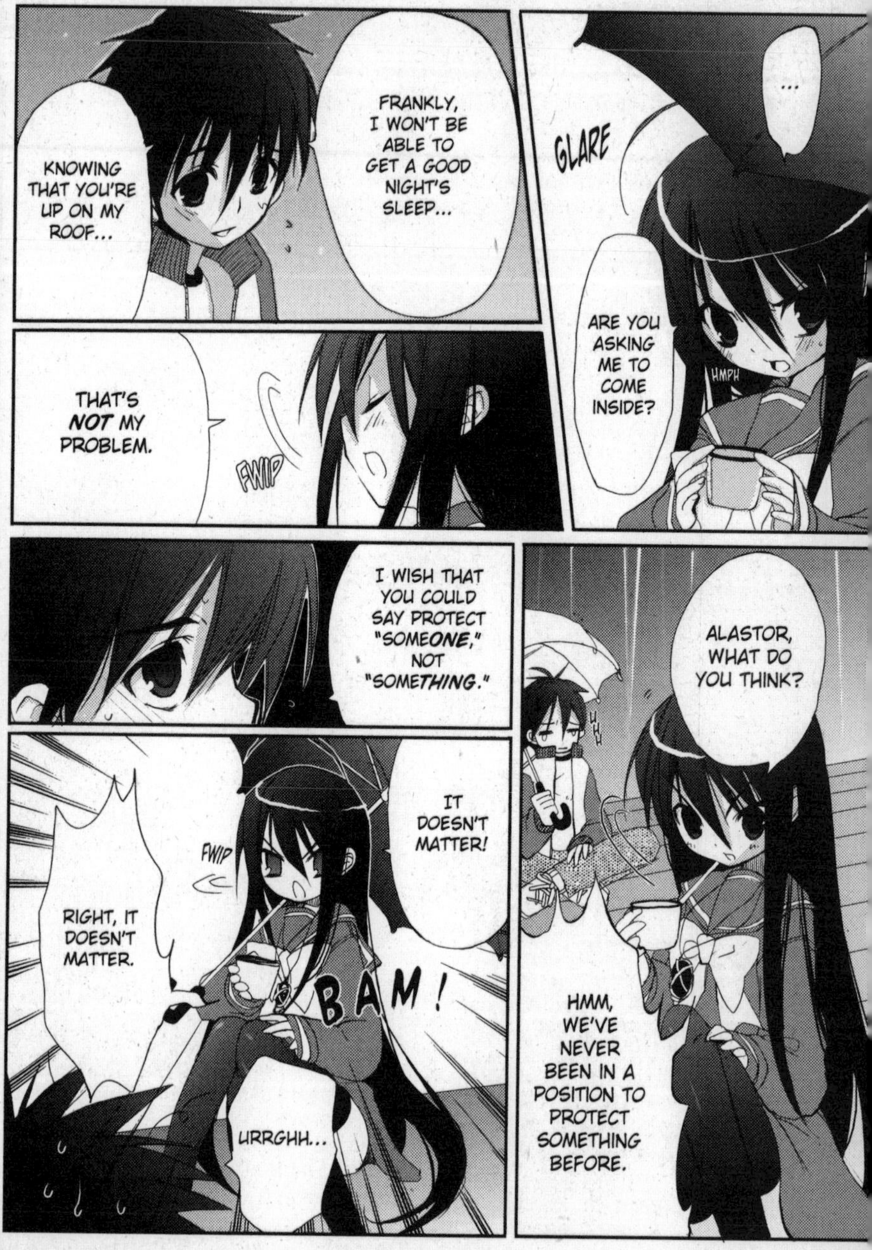
...
GLARE
ARE YOU ASKING ME TO COME INSIDE?
HMPH
FRANKLY, I WON'T BE ABLE TO GET A GOOD NIGHT'S SLEEP...
KNOWING THAT YOU'RE UP ON MY ROOF...
THAT'S *NOT* MY PROBLEM.
FWIP
ALASTOR, WHAT DO YOU THINK?
UHH
HMM, WE'VE NEVER BEEN IN A POSITION TO PROTECT SOMETHING BEFORE.
I WISH THAT YOU COULD SAY PROTECT "SOME*ONE*," NOT "SOME*THING*."
IT DOESN'T MATTER!
FWIP
BAM!
RIGHT, IT DOESN'T MATTER.
URRGHH...

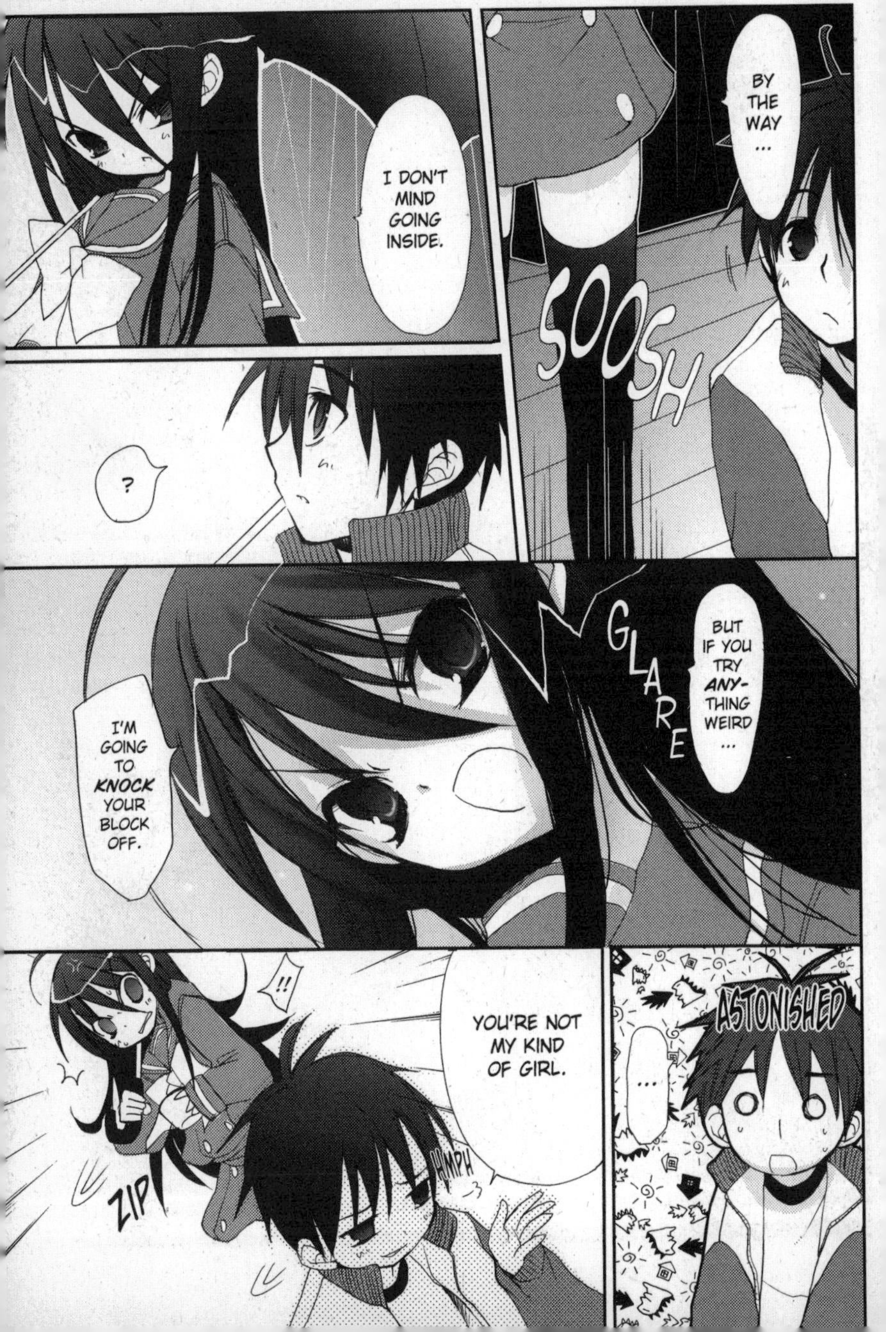
BY THE WAY ...
SOOSH
I DON'T MIND GOING INSIDE.
?
GLARE
BUT IF YOU TRY ANYTHING WEIRD ...
I'M GOING TO KNOCK YOUR BLOCK OFF.
ASTONISHED
...
YOU'RE NOT MY KIND OF GIRL.
HMPH
!!
ZIP

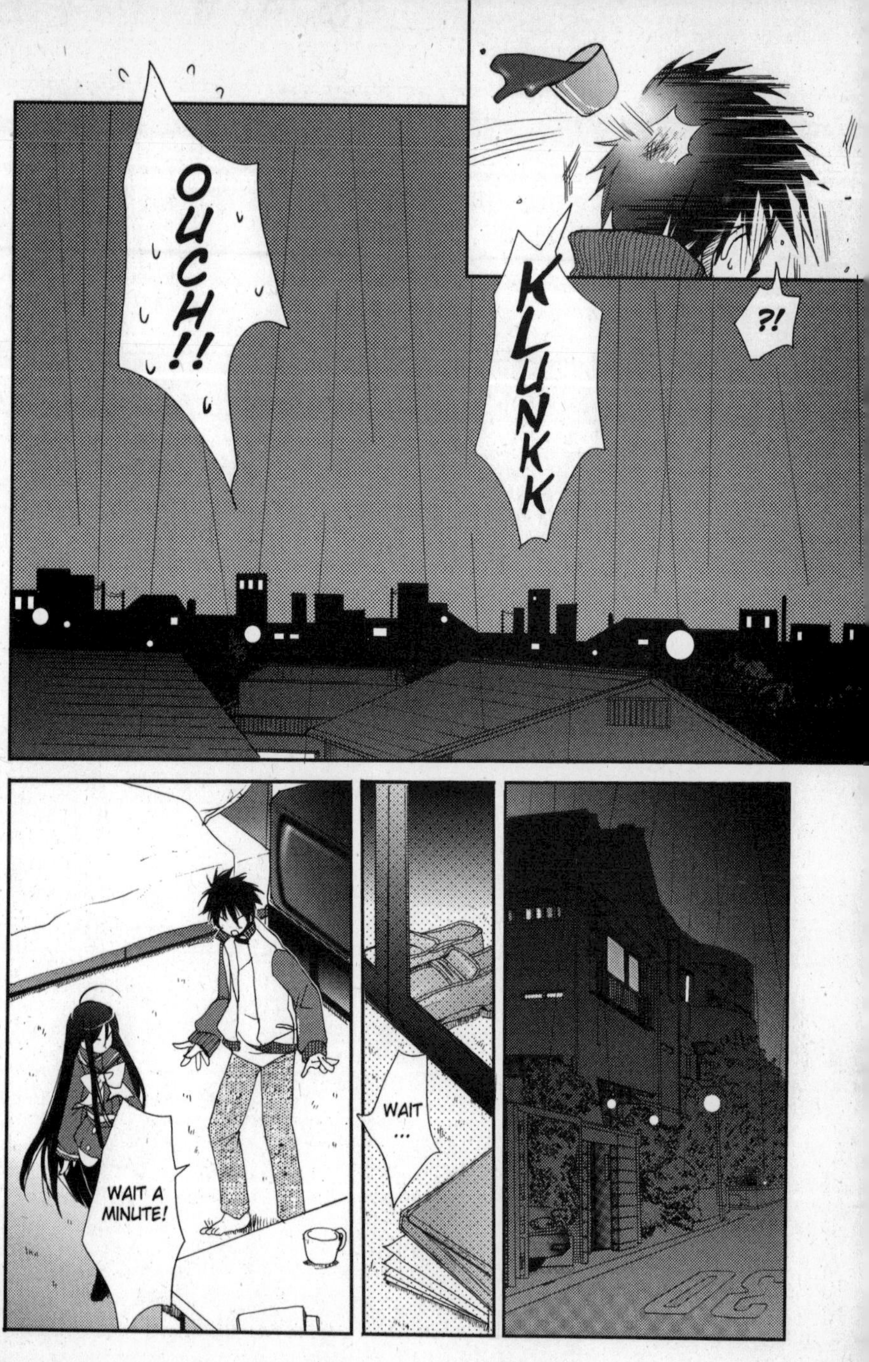
KLUNKK
?!
OUCH!!
WAIT ...
WAIT A MINUTE!

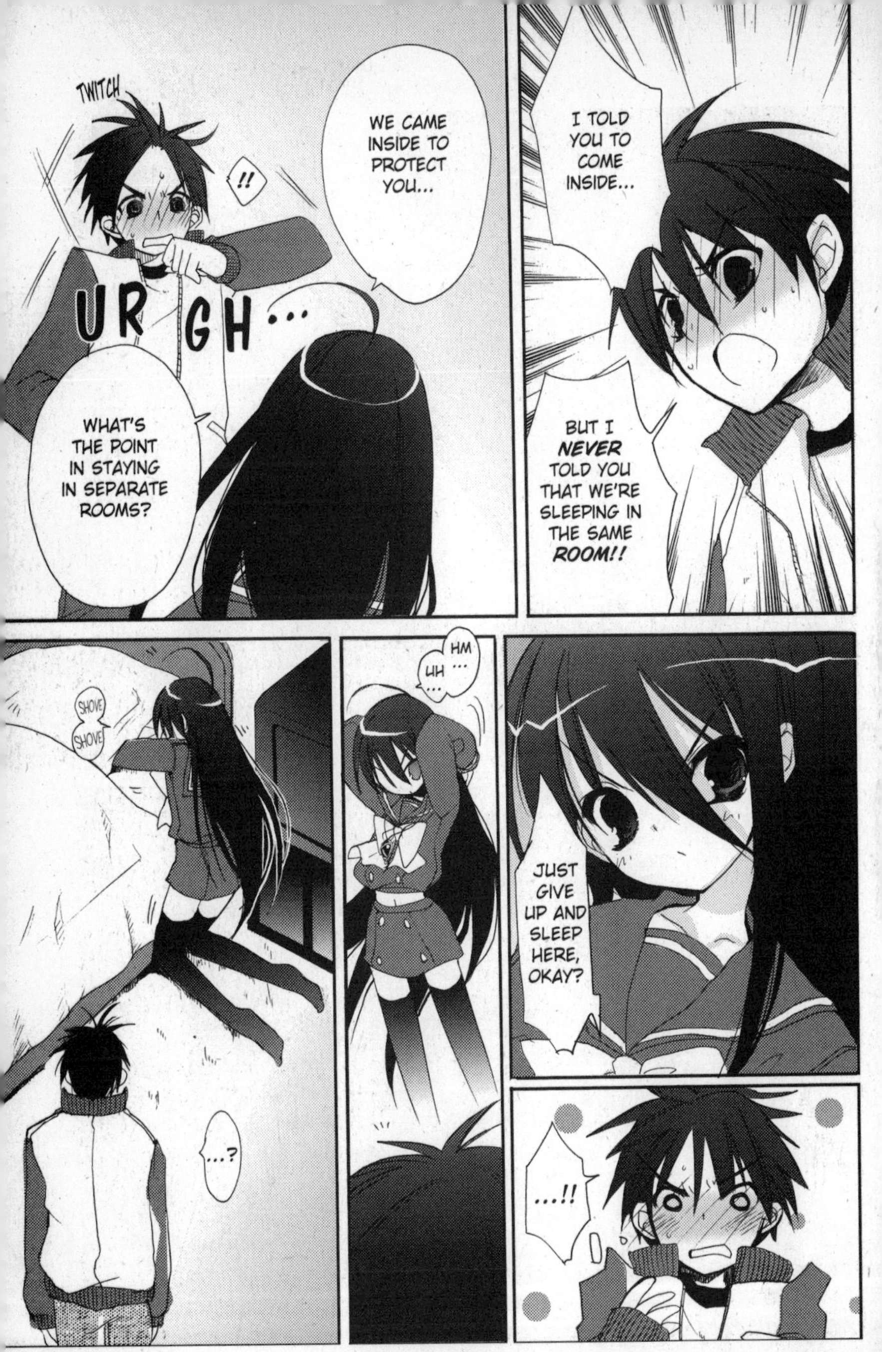
I TOLD YOU TO COME INSIDE...
BUT I ***NEVER*** TOLD YOU THAT WE'RE SLEEPING IN THE SAME ***ROOM!!***
WE CAME INSIDE TO PROTECT YOU...
TWITCH
!!
URGH...
WHAT'S THE POINT IN STAYING IN SEPARATE ROOMS?
JUST GIVE UP AND SLEEP HERE, OKAY?
...!!
HM...
UH...
SHOVE
SHOVE
...?

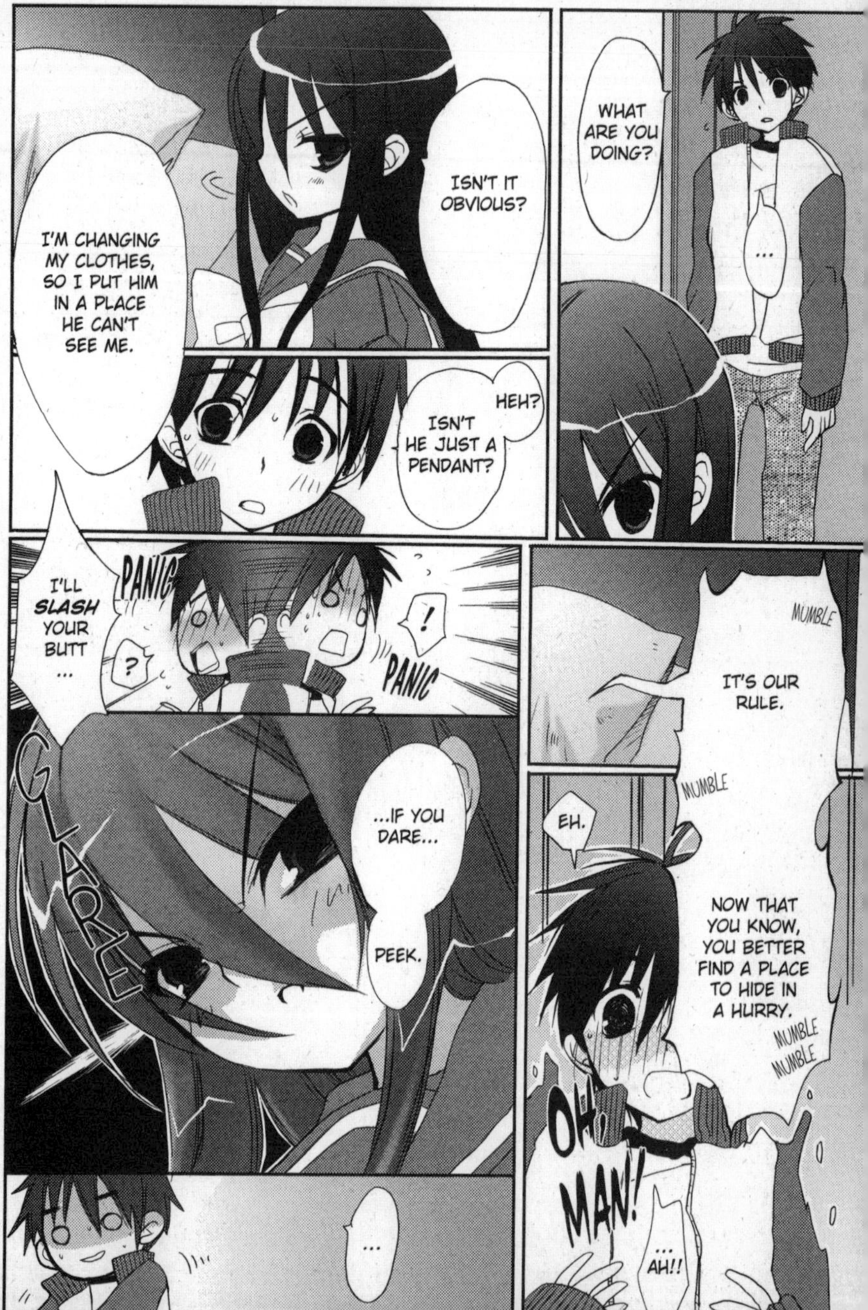
WHAT ARE YOU DOING?
...
ISN'T IT OBVIOUS?
I'M CHANGING MY CLOTHES, SO I PUT HIM IN A PLACE HE CAN'T SEE ME.
HEH? ISN'T HE JUST A PENDANT?
MUMBLE
IT'S OUR RULE.
PANIC
!
PANIC
?
I'LL SLASH YOUR BUTT ...
MUMBLE
EH.
NOW THAT YOU KNOW, YOU BETTER FIND A PLACE TO HIDE IN A HURRY.
MUMBLE MUMBLE
OH MAN!
... AH!!
GLARE
...IF YOU DARE...
PEEK.
...

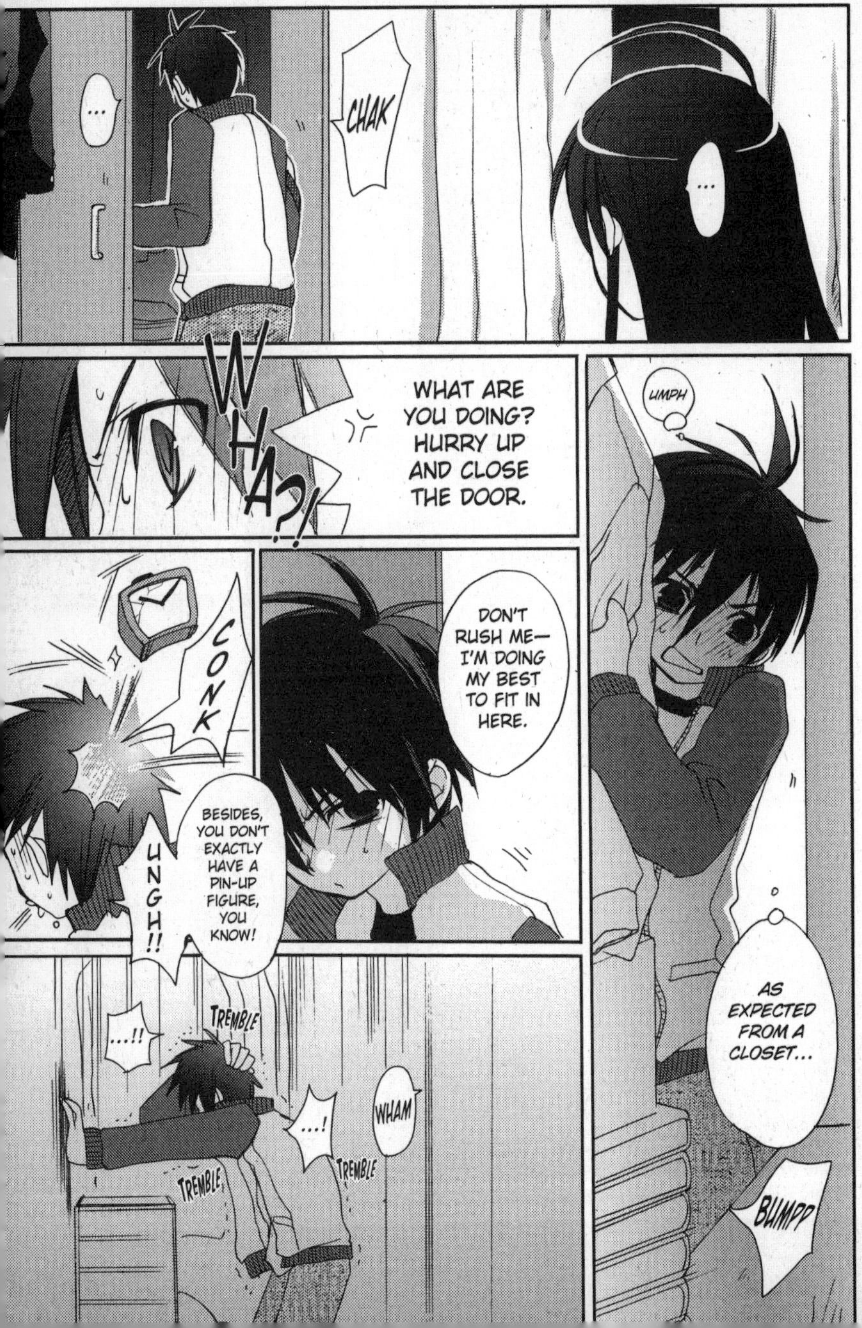
...
CHAK
...
UMPH
AS EXPECTED FROM A CLOSET...
BUMPP
WHAT ARE YOU DOING? HURRY UP AND CLOSE THE DOOR.
WHA?!
DON'T RUSH ME— I'M DOING MY BEST TO FIT IN HERE.
BESIDES, YOU DON'T EXACTLY HAVE A PIN-UP FIGURE, YOU KNOW!
CONK
UNGH!!
WHAM
...!
TREMBLE
...!!
TREMBLE
TREMBLE

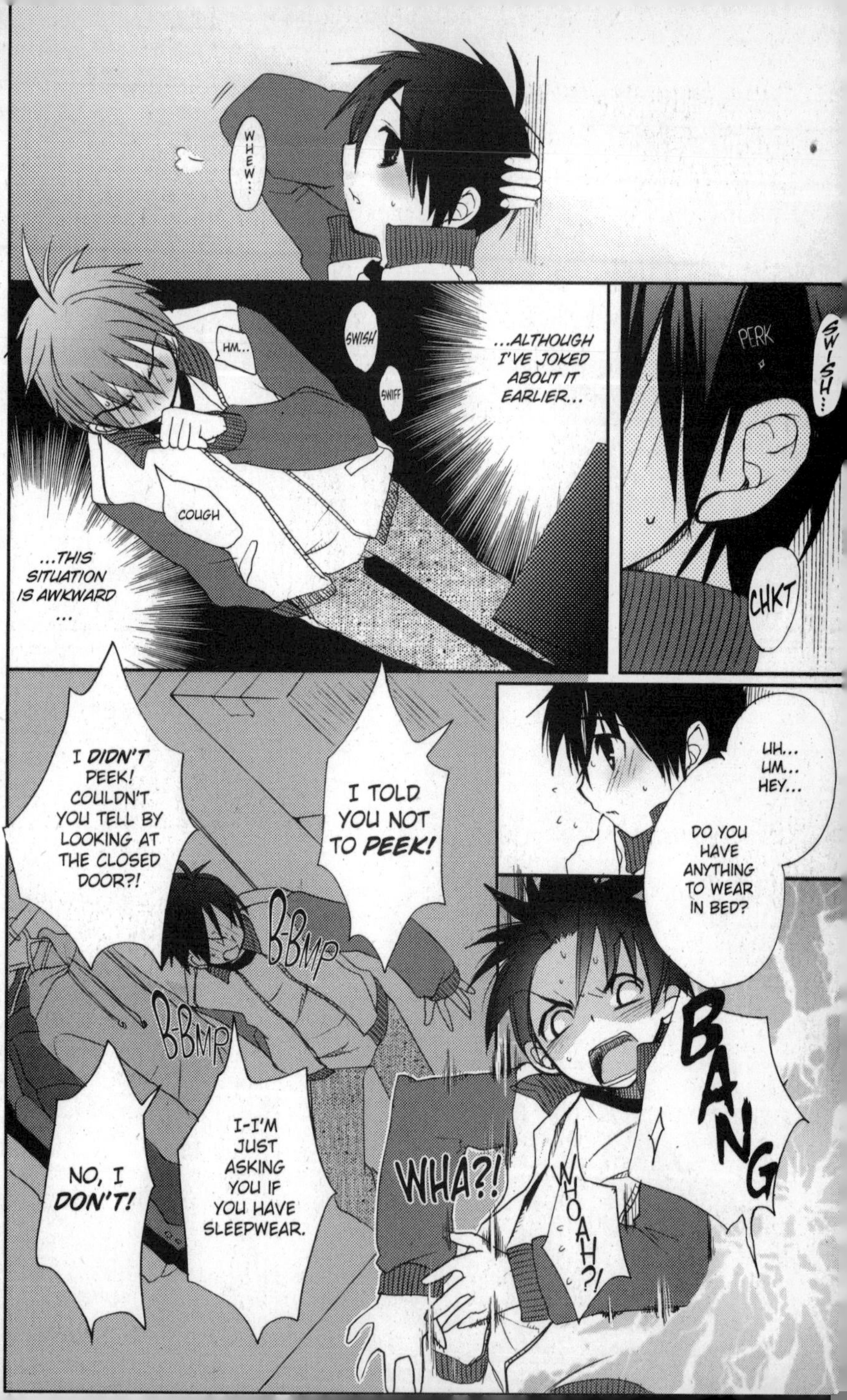
WHEW...
SWISH...
PERK
CHKT
...ALTHOUGH I'VE JOKED ABOUT IT EARLIER...
SWISH
SWIFF
HM...
COUGH
...THIS SITUATION IS AWKWARD...
UH... UM... HEY...
DO YOU HAVE ANYTHING TO WEAR IN BED?
BANG
WHOAH?!
WHA?!
I TOLD YOU NOT TO PEEK!
I DIDN'T PEEK! COULDN'T YOU TELL BY LOOKING AT THE CLOSED DOOR?!
B-BMP
B-BMP
I-I'M JUST ASKING YOU IF YOU HAVE SLEEPWEAR.
NO, I DON'T!

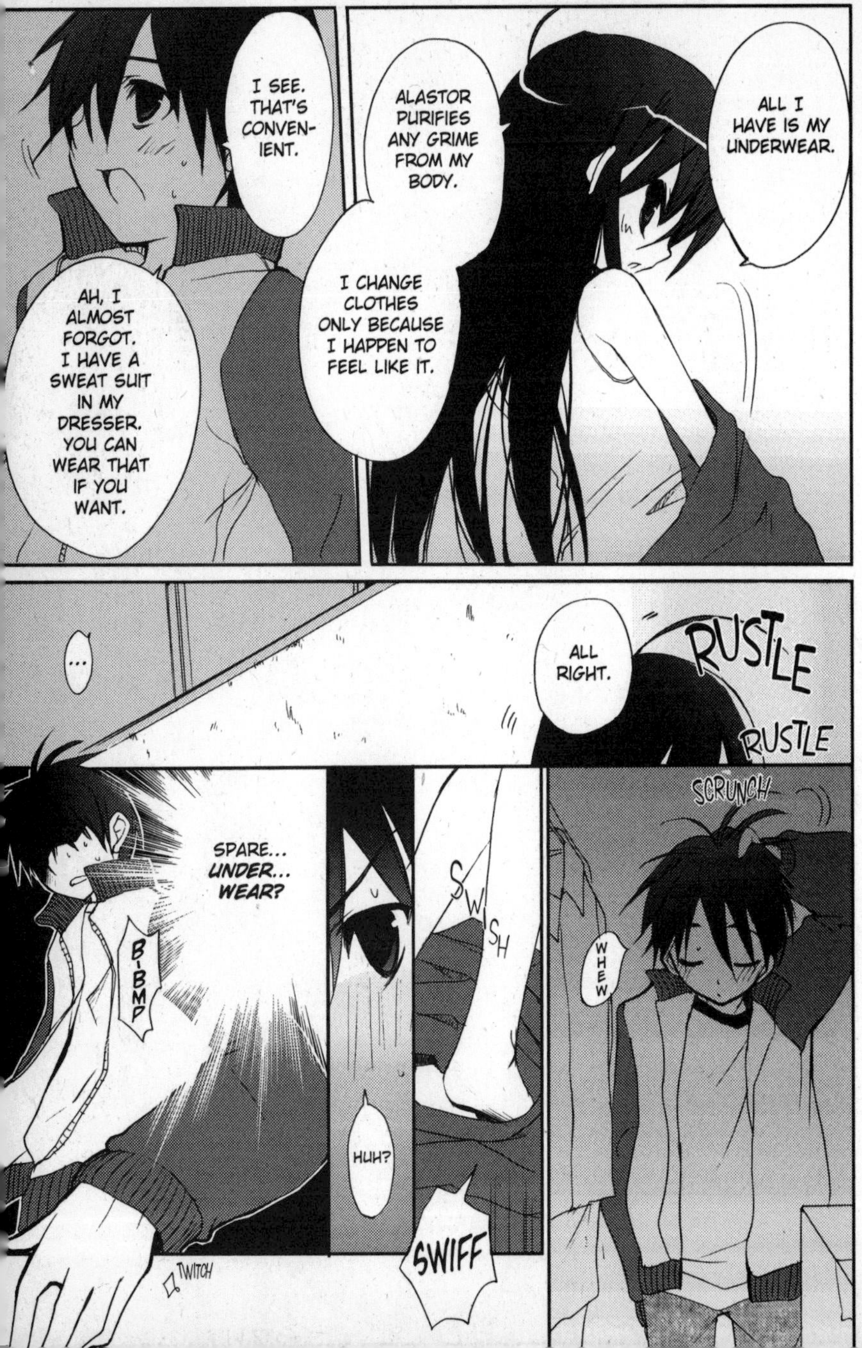
ALL I HAVE IS MY UNDERWEAR.
ALASTOR PURIFIES ANY GRIME FROM MY BODY.
I CHANGE CLOTHES ONLY BECAUSE I HAPPEN TO FEEL LIKE IT.
I SEE. THAT'S CONVEN-IENT.
AH, I ALMOST FORGOT. I HAVE A SWEAT SUIT IN MY DRESSER. YOU CAN WEAR THAT IF YOU WANT.
RUSTLE
ALL RIGHT.
RUSTLE
...
SCRUNCH
WHEW
SWISH
HUH?
SWIFF
SPARE... UNDER... WEAR?
BIBMP
TWITCH

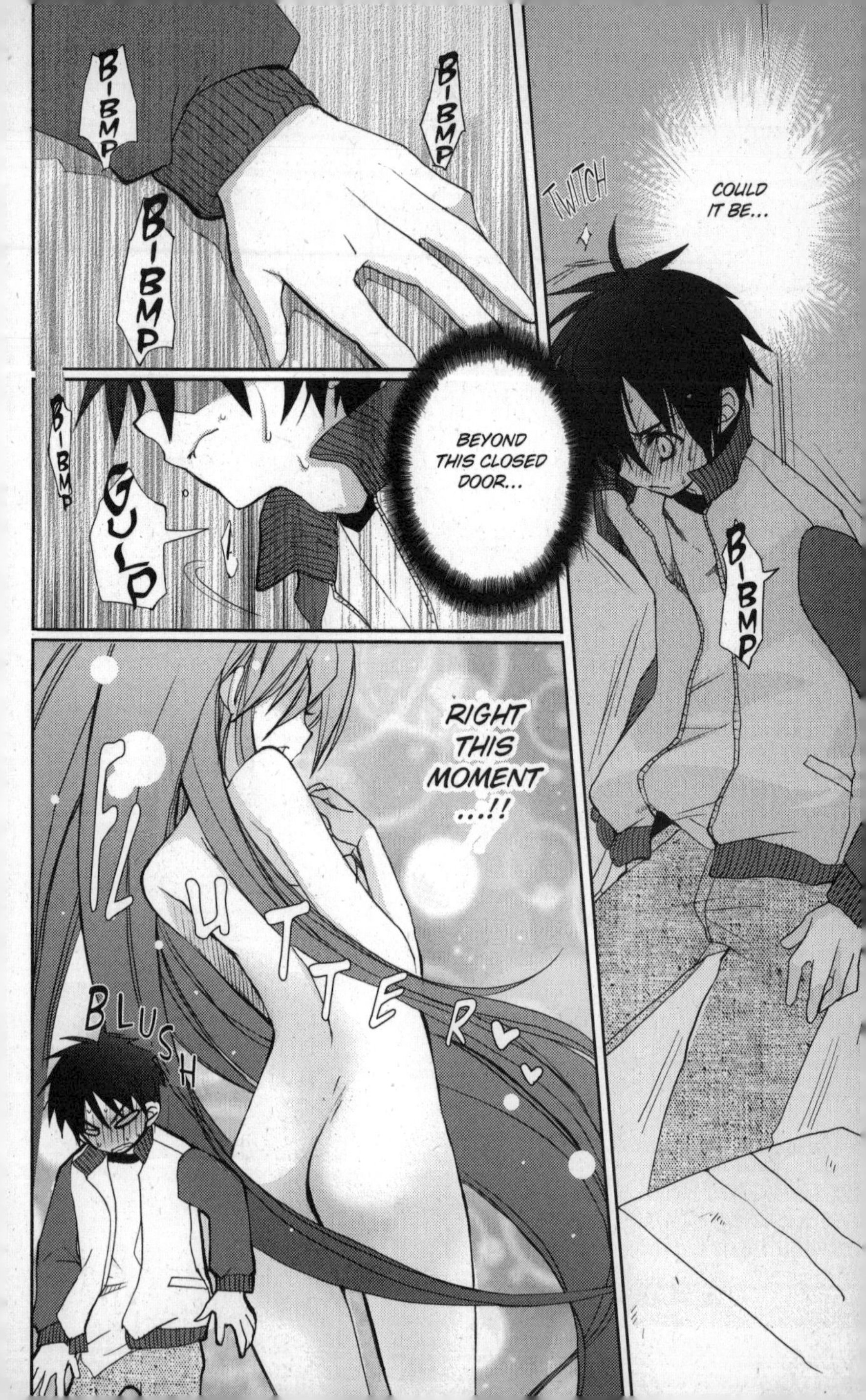
COULD IT BE...
TWITCH
BIBMP
BIBMP
BIBMP
BIBMP
BEYOND THIS CLOSED DOOR...
BIBMP
GULP
RIGHT THIS MOMENT ...!!
FLUTTER
BLUSH

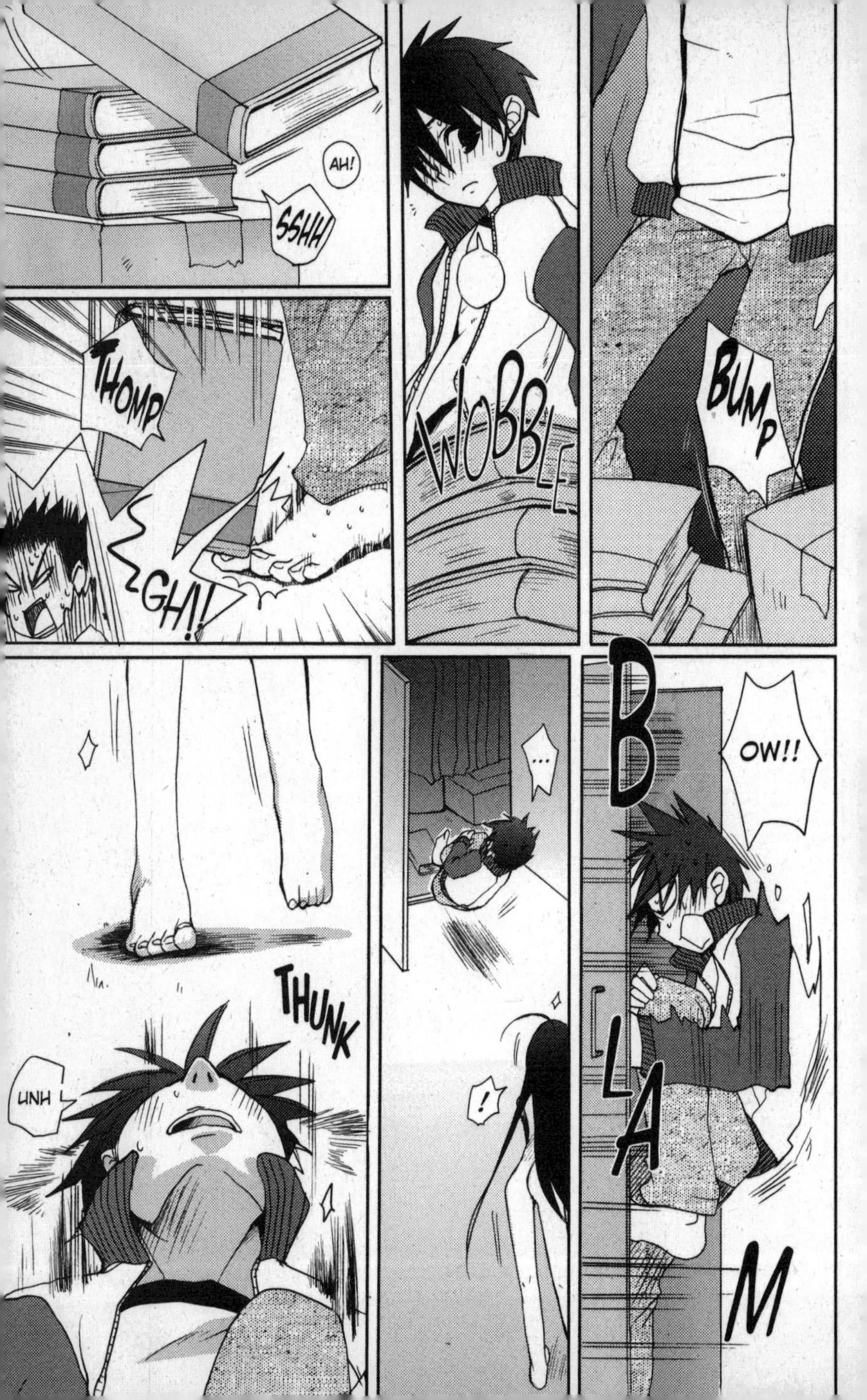
BUMP
WOBBLE
AH!
SSHH
THOMP
NGH!!
BLAM
OW!!
...
!
THUNK
UNH

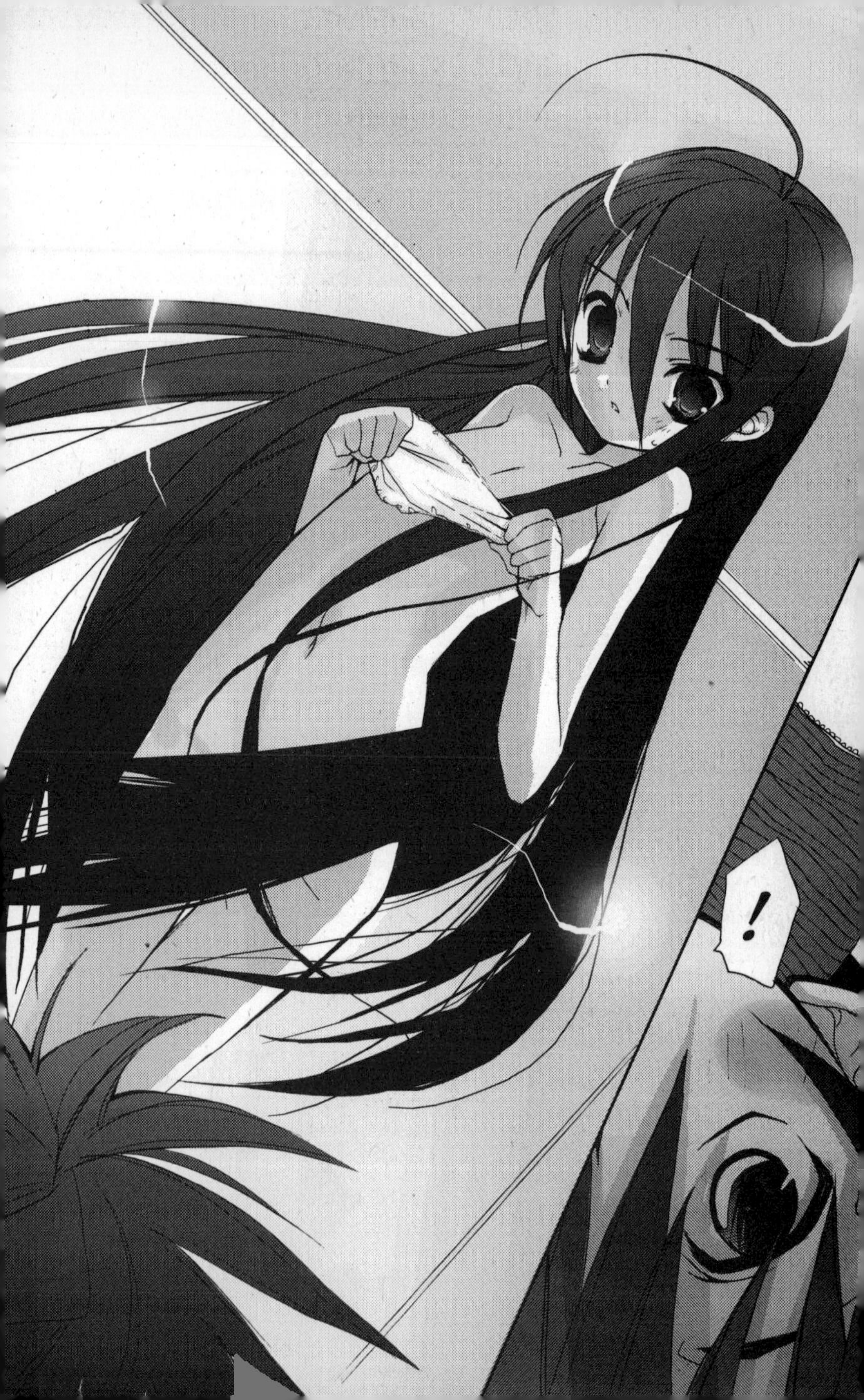
!

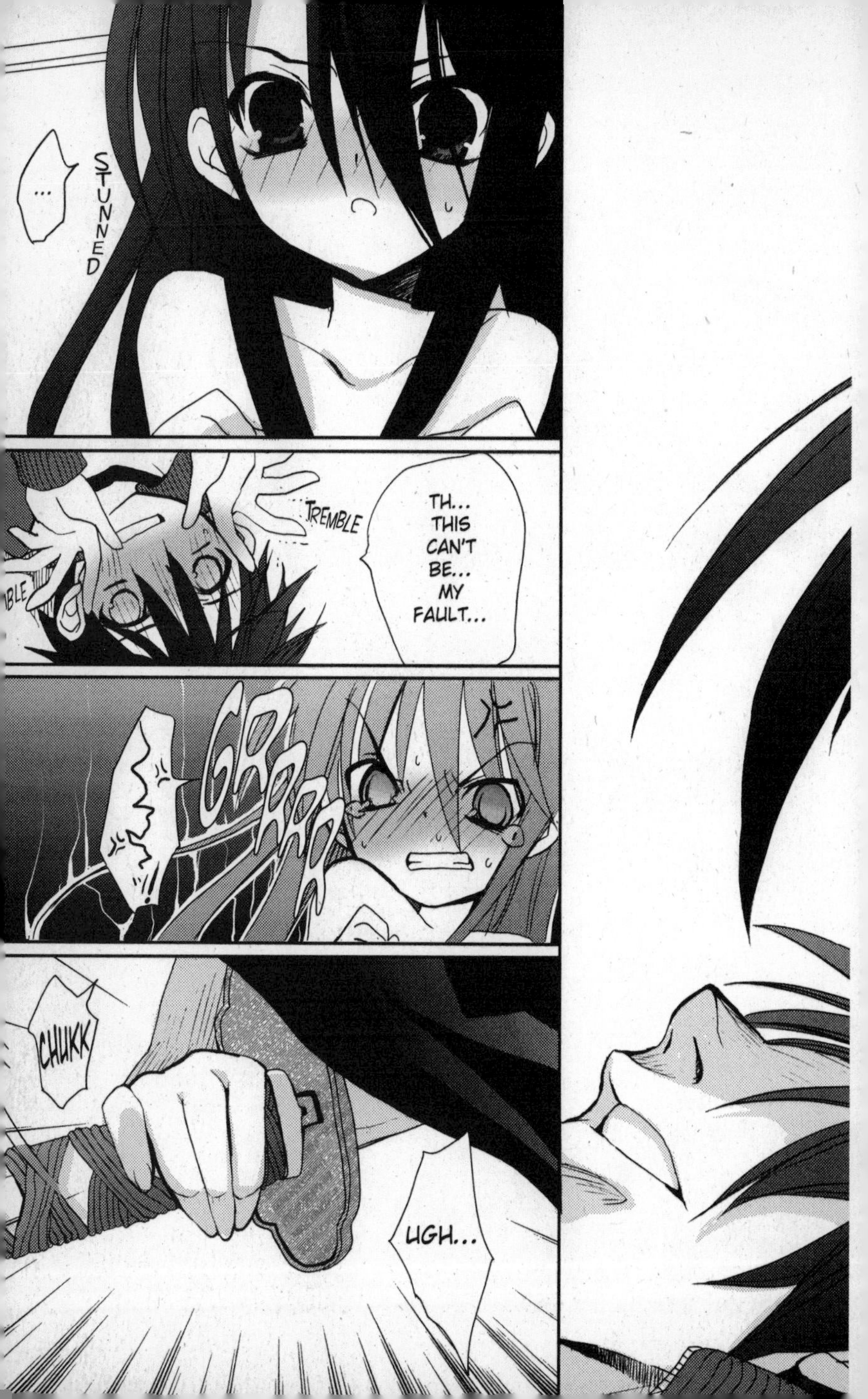
STUNNED
...
TH... THIS CAN'T BE... MY FAULT...
TREMBLE
GRRRR
CHUKK
UGH...

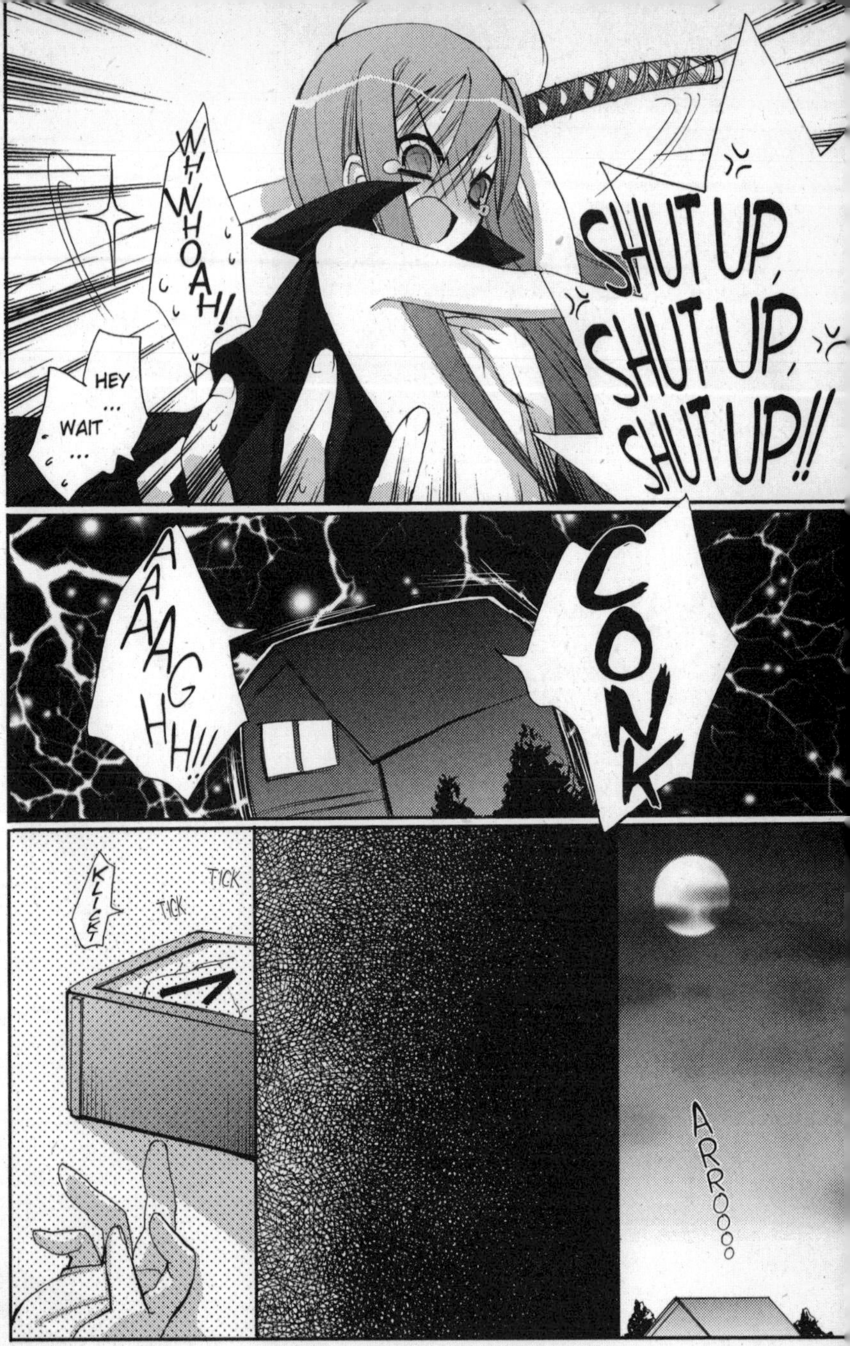
SHUT UP, SHUT UP, SHUT UP!!
WH-WHOAH!
HEY... WAIT...
CONK
AAAAGHH!!
ARROOOO
TICK
TICK
KLICK

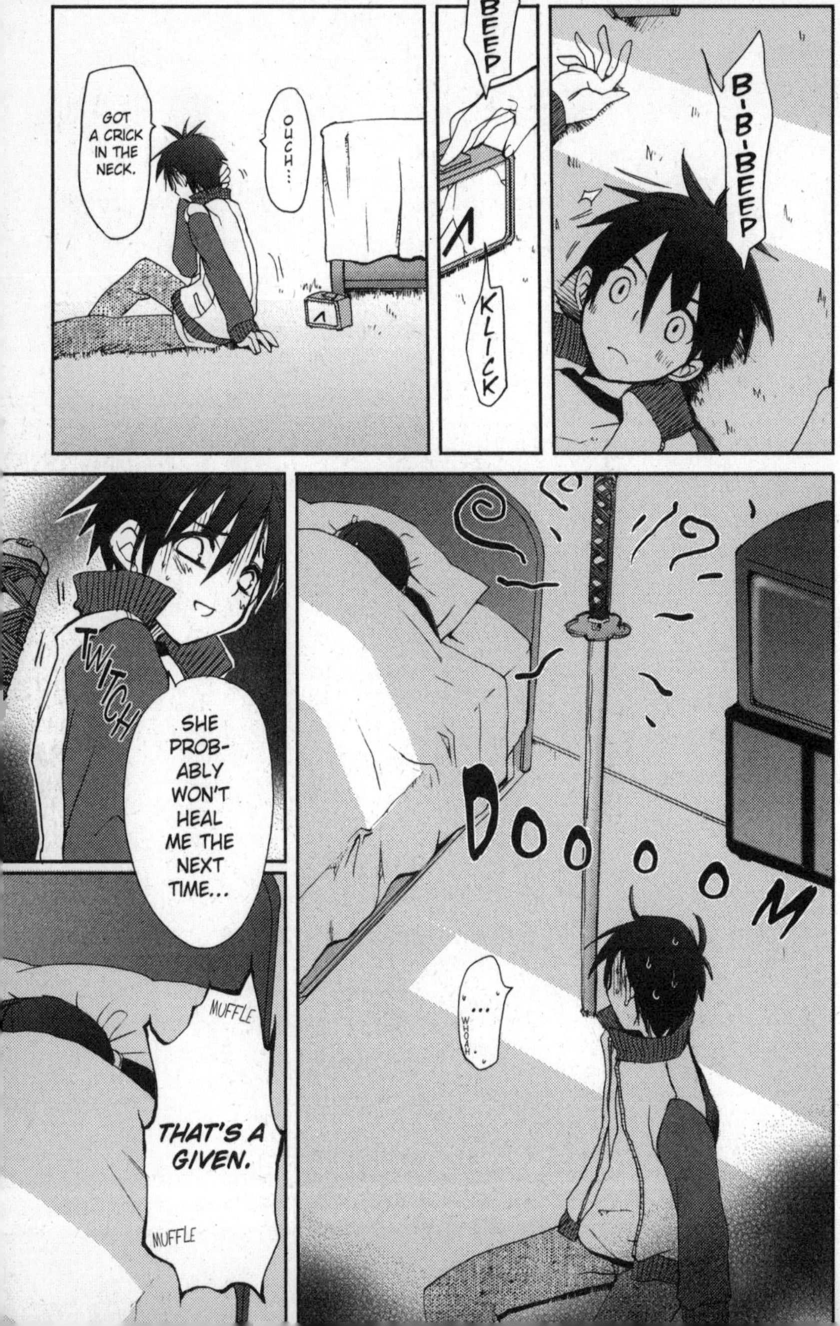
B-I-BEEP
B-I-BEEP
KLICK
OUCH...
GOT A CRICK IN THE NECK.
?!
DOOOOOM
...WHOAH.
TWITCH
SHE PROBABLY WON'T HEAL ME THE NEXT TIME...
MUFFLE
THAT'S A GIVEN.
MUFFLE

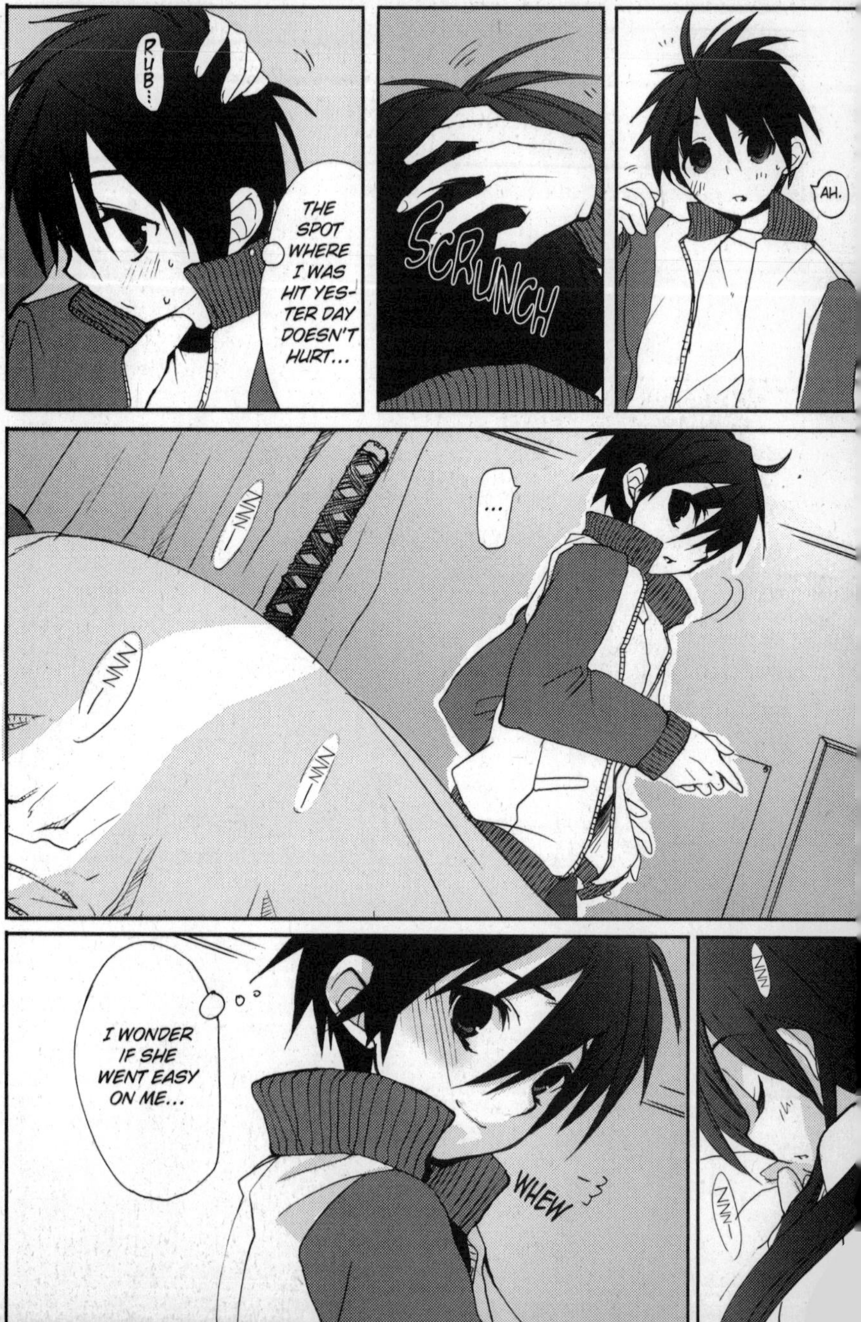
AH.
SCRUNCH
RUB...
THE SPOT WHERE I WAS HIT YES-TER DAY DOESN'T HURT...
...
NNN—
NNN—
NNN—
NNN
NNN—
I WONDER IF SHE WENT EASY ON ME...
WHEW

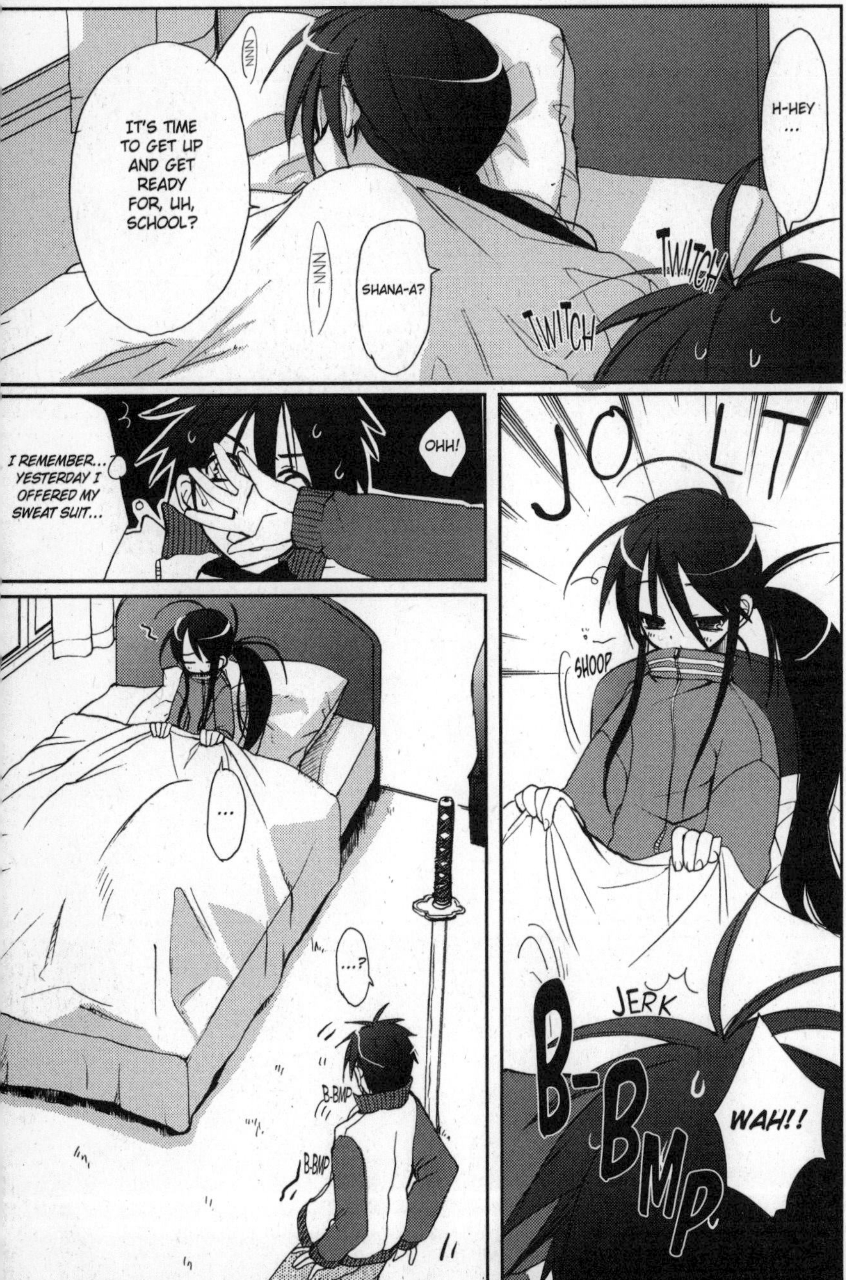
H-HEY ...
TWITCH
TWITCH
SHANA-A?
NNN—
IT'S TIME TO GET UP AND GET READY FOR, UH, SCHOOL?
NNN
JOLT
SHOOP
JERK
WAH!!
B-BMP
OHH!
I REMEMBER... YESTERDAY I OFFERED MY SWEAT SUIT...
...
...?
B-BMP
B-BMP

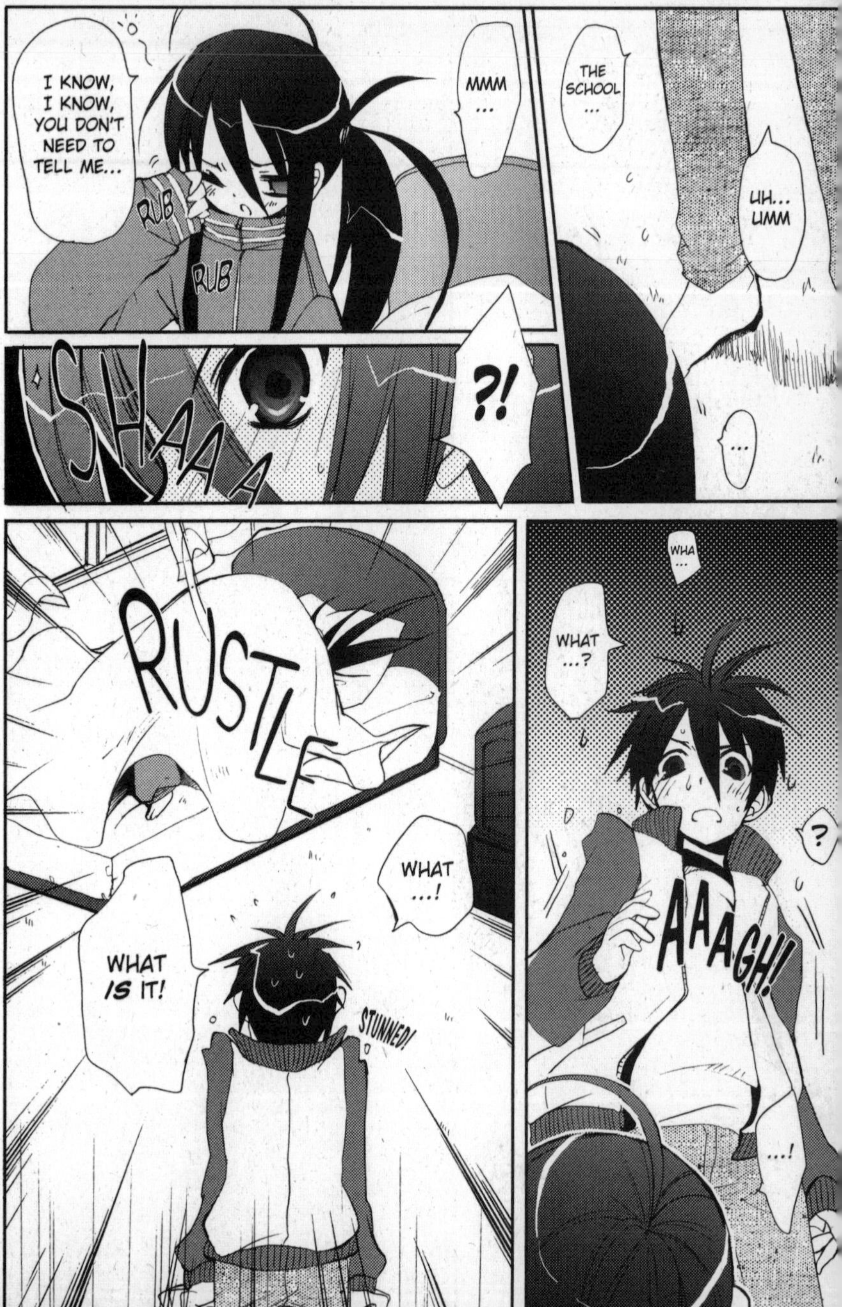
THE SCHOOL ...
UH... UMM
...
MMM ...
I KNOW, I KNOW, YOU DON'T NEED TO TELL ME...
RUB
RUB
?!
SHAAAA
WHA ...
WHAT ...?
?
AAAGH!
...!
RUSTLE
WHAT ...!
WHAT *IS* IT!
STUNNED!

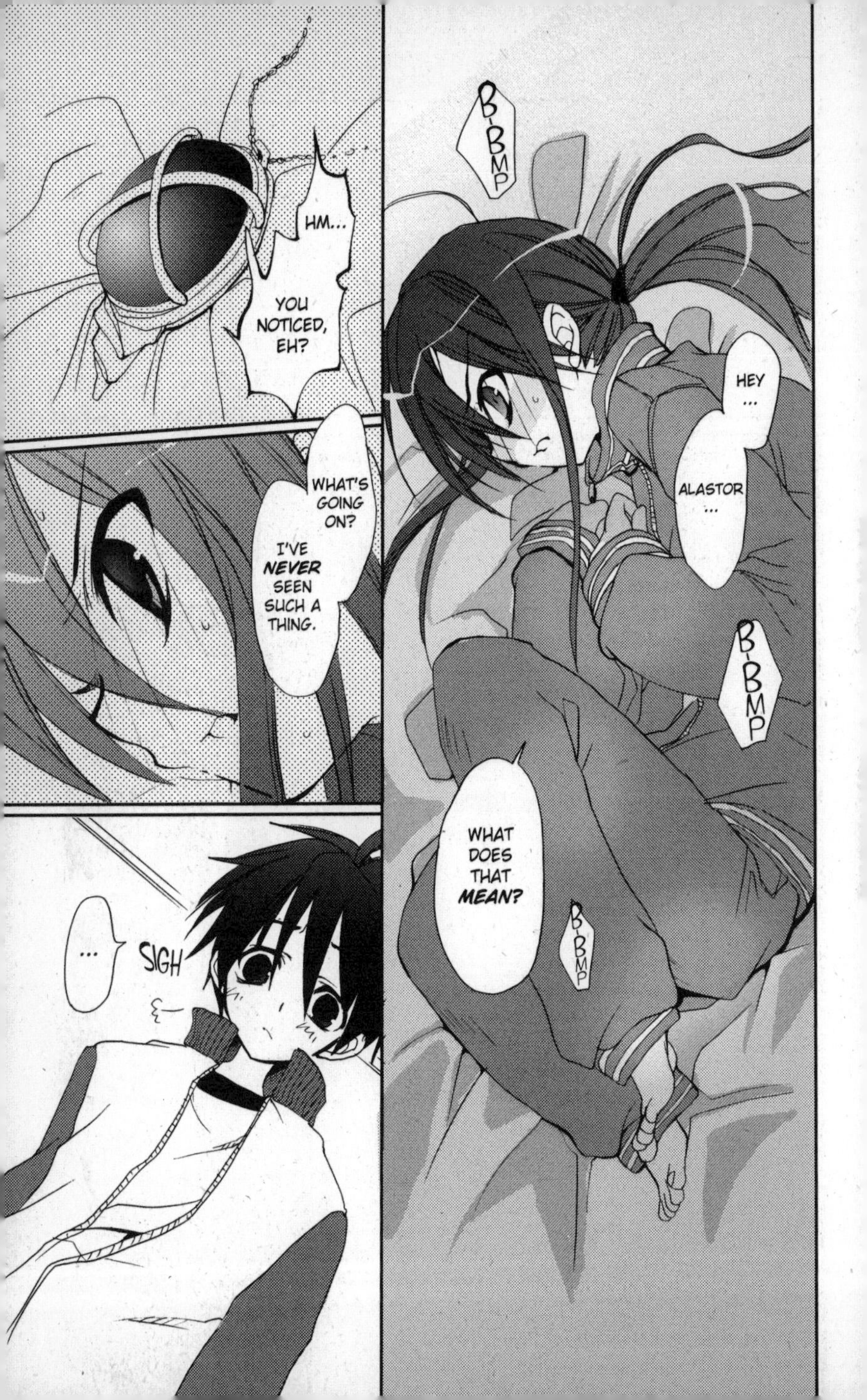
B-BMP
HEY...
ALASTOR...
B-BMP
WHAT DOES THAT **MEAN?**
B-BMP
HM...
YOU NOTICED, EH?
WHAT'S GOING ON?
I'VE **NEVER** SEEN SUCH A THING.
...
SIGH

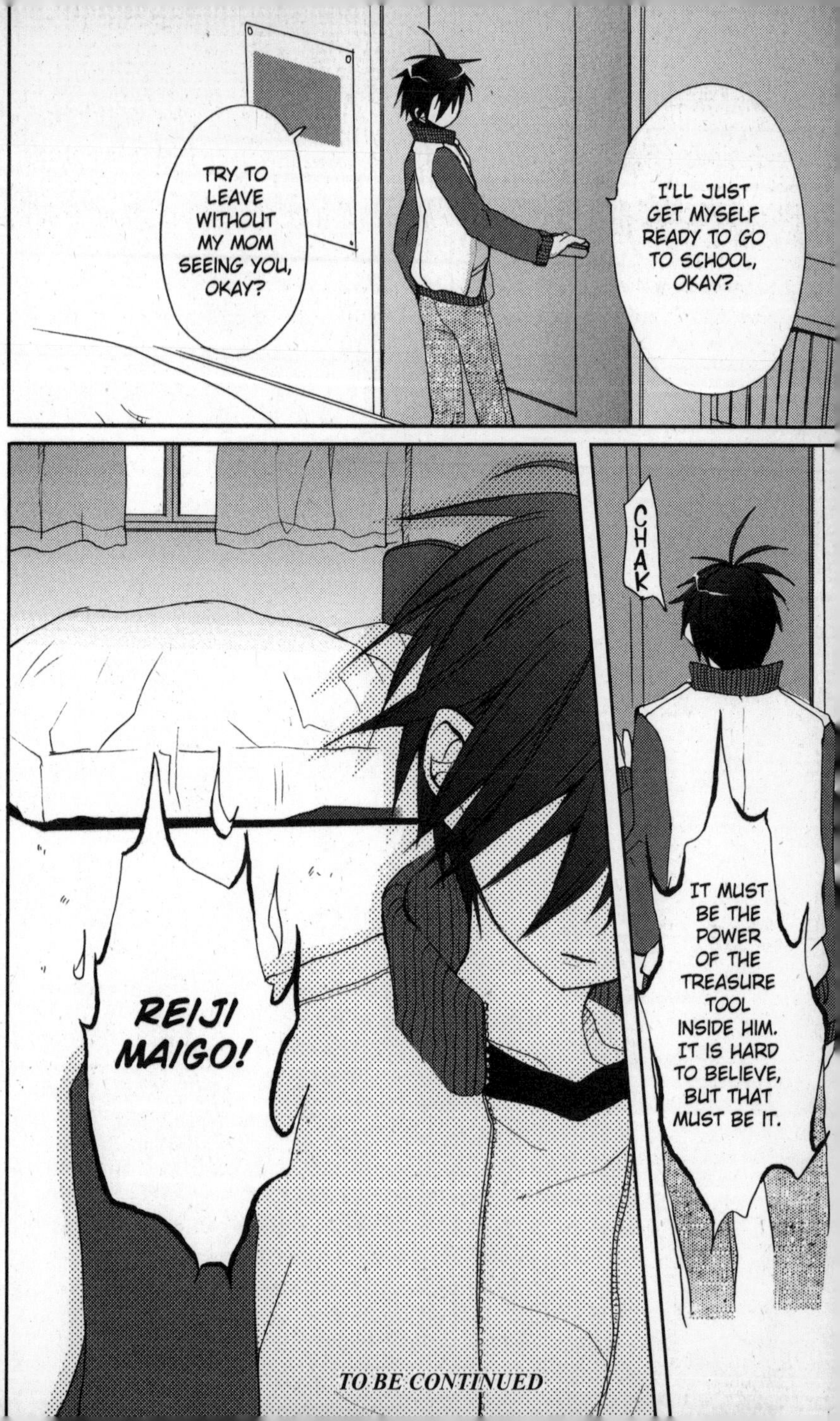
I'LL JUST GET MYSELF READY TO GO TO SCHOOL, OKAY?
TRY TO LEAVE WITHOUT MY MOM SEEING YOU, OKAY?
CHAK
IT MUST BE THE POWER OF THE TREASURE TOOL INSIDE HIM. IT IS HARD TO BELIEVE, BUT THAT MUST BE IT.
REIJI MAIGO!
TO BE CONTINUED

The *Shakugan no Shana* manga team would like to thank you for your support in buying vol. 1 of this manga!

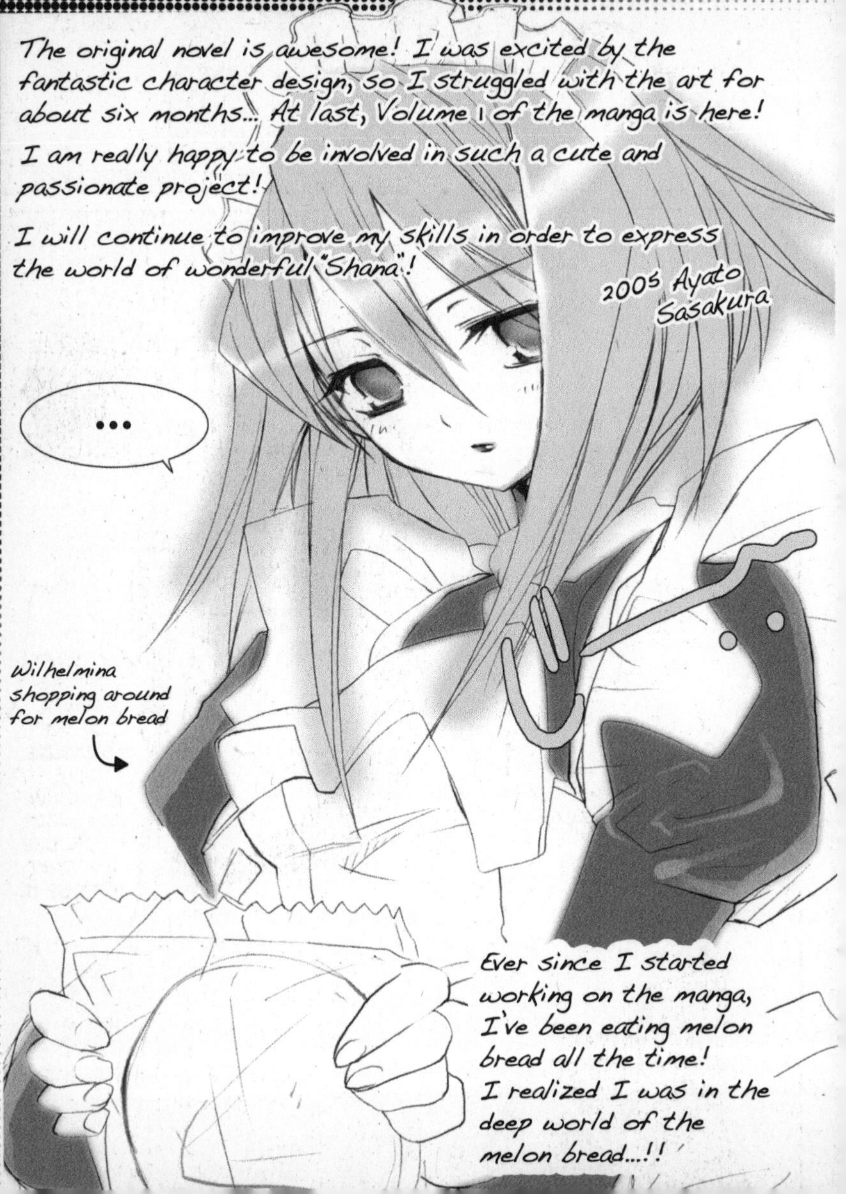
The original novel is awesome! I was excited by the fantastic character design, so I struggled with the art for about six months... At last, Volume 1 of the manga is here!
I am really happy to be involved in such a cute and passionate project!
I will continue to improve my skills in order to express the world of wonderful "Shana"!
2005 Ayato Sasakura
...
Wilhelmina shopping around for melon bread
Ever since I started working on the manga, I've been eating melon bread all the time!
I realized I was in the deep world of the melon bread...!!

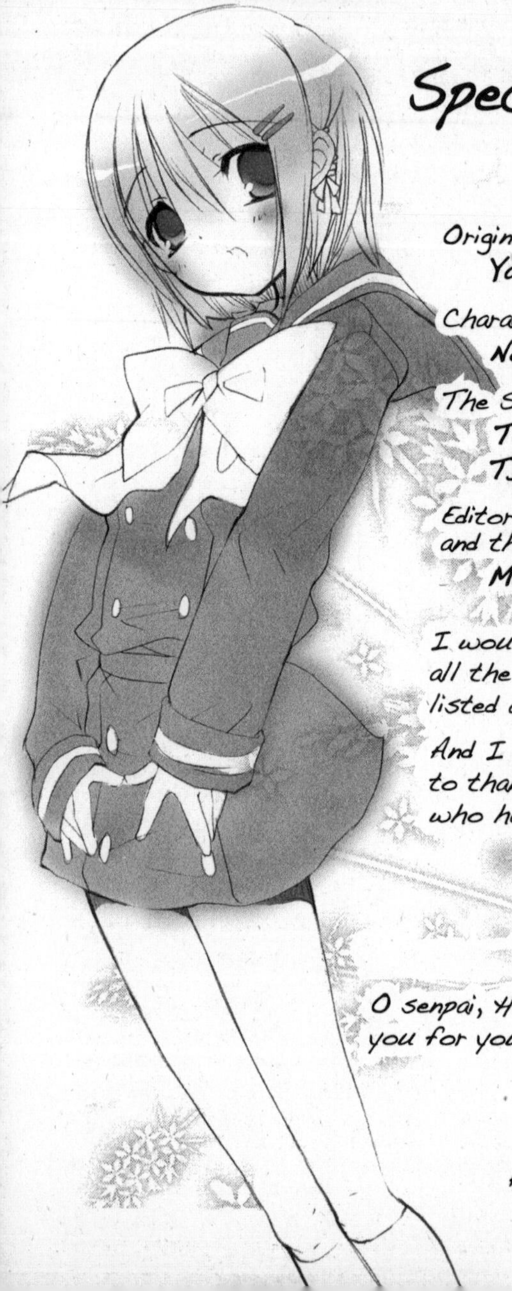

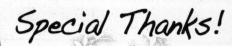

Special Thanks!

Original story:
Yashichiro Takahashi

Character Design:
Noizi Ito

The Seal Design:
Tsukasa Kiryu
TDK ROTTERDAM

Editor of the novel and the manga:
Miki and Ogino

I would like to thank all the skilled people I listed above.

And I also would like to thank all the readers who have read this far!

O senpai, H senpai, and Az, thank you for your help as always!

10-27-2005
Ayato Sasakura

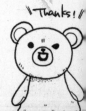

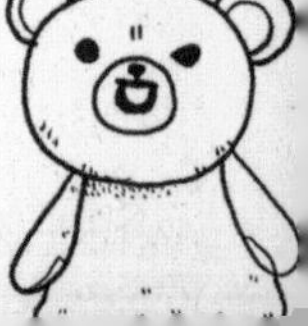
Thanks!

FROM THE AUTHOR AND CHARACTER DESIGNER

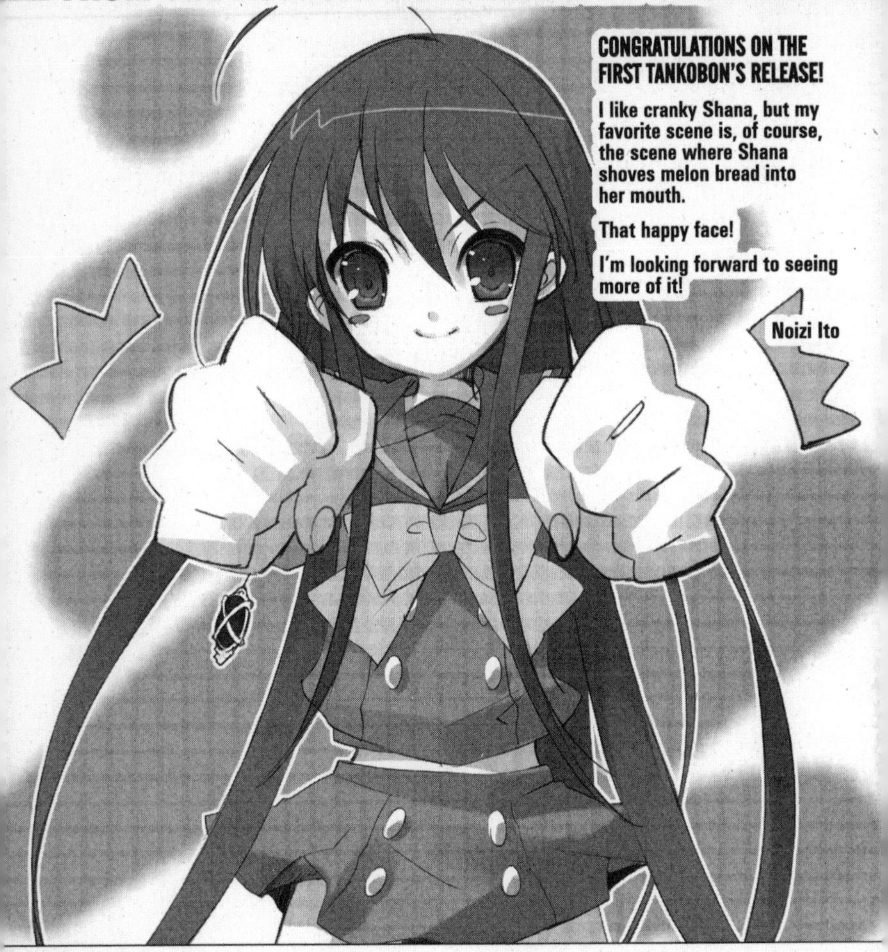

CONGRATULATIONS ON THE FIRST TANKOBON'S RELEASE!

I like cranky Shana, but my favorite scene is, of course, the scene where Shana shoves melon bread into her mouth.

That happy face!

I'm looking forward to seeing more of it!

Noizi Ito

Hello, I'm Takahashi, the one responsible for the original story.

Thanks very much for purchasing the manga version of *Shakugan no Shana*. This manga is a great example of detailed visualizing and "comicalizing" of the original novel.

After reading this, I think you can imagine how much expertise was required by Mr. Ayato Sasakura to maintain the unique characteristics of Noizi Ito's original illustrations from the novel.

Some of the strengths of the manga are the flowing visual scenes and casual gestures that are not in the novel or illustrations. Even as the creator of the original story, I've made fresh discoveries and learned something new.

I would like to ask you, the readers, to enjoy this manga, not as a "part of many Shanas," but as "one unique Shana."

I truly appreciate the great fortune of being able to work with this great artist.

September 2005
Yashichiro Takahashi

SHAKUGAN≡SHANA™

SHAKUGAN NO SHANA
Vol. 1
VIZ Media Edition

Story by
YASHICHIRO TAKAHASHI

Art by
AYATO SASAKURA

Character design by
NOIZI ITO

Translation/Yuki Yoshioka & Cindy Yamauchi
Touch-up Art & Lettering/James Gaubatz
Cover and Interior Design/Sam Elzway
Editor/Ian Robertson

Editor in Chief, Books/Alvin Lu
Editor in Chief, Magazines/Marc Weidenbaum
VP of Publishing Licensing/Rika Inouye
VP of Sales/Gonzalo Ferreyra
Sr. VP of Marketing/Liza Coppola
Publisher/Hyoe Narita

Published by VIZ Media, LLC
P.O. Box 77010
San Francisco, CA 94107

10 9 8 7 6 5 4 3 2
First printing, April 2007
Second printing, June 2007

store.viz.com

VIZ media
www.viz.com

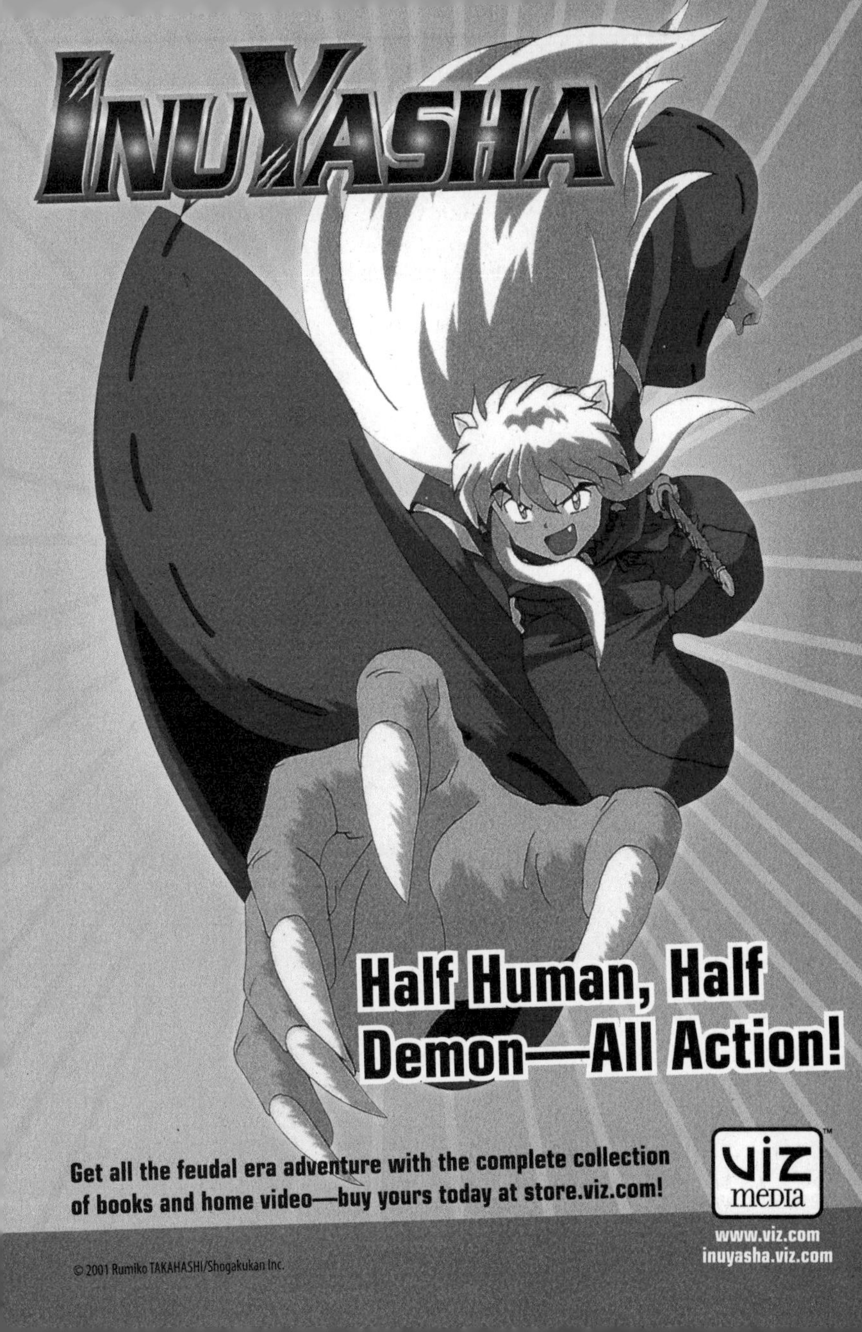

INUYASHA

Read the action from the start with the original manga series

Full color adaptation of the popular TV series

Art book with cel art, paintings, character profiles and more

TV SERIES & MOVIES ON DVD!

See more of the action in *Inuyasha* full-length movies

www.viz.com
inuyasha.viz.com

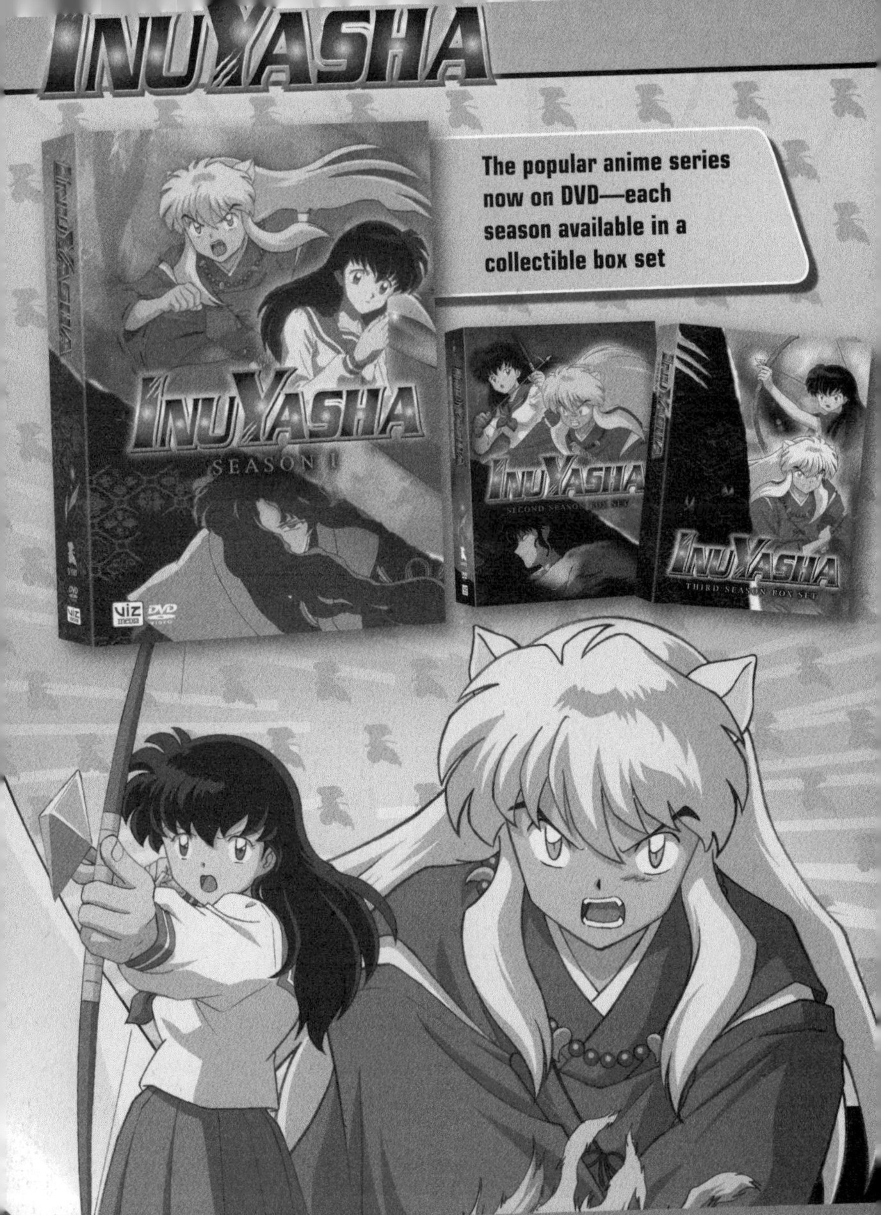
INUYASHA
The popular anime series now on DVD—each season available in a collectible box set
INUYASHA
SEASON I
viz media
DVD
INUYASHA
INUYASHA
THIRD SEASON BOX SET

HELP US MAKE THE MANGA
YOU LOVE BETTER!